THE COMPLETE IDIOT'S GUIDE

Starting Your Own Business

Fourth Edition

by Edward Paulson

ALPHA

A member of Penguin Group (USA) Inc.

This book is dedicated to my late father, John Paulson, who continues to get smarter as I get older.

International Standard Book Number: 1-59257-138-7
Library of Congress Catalog Card Number: 2003111796

05   04   8   7   6   5   4   3

Interpretation of the printing code: The rightmost number of the first series of numbers is the year of the book's printing; the rightmost number of the second series of numbers is the number of the book's printing. For example, a printing code of 03-1 shows that the first printing occurred in 2003.

Printed in the United States of America

Note: This publication contains the opinions and ideas of its author. It is intended to provide helpful and informative material on the subject matter covered. It is sold with the understanding that the author and publisher are not engaged in rendering professional services in the book. If the reader requires personal assistance or advice, a competent professional should be consulted.

The author and publisher specifically disclaim any responsibility for any liability, loss, or risk, personal or otherwise, which is incurred as a consequence, directly or indirectly, of the use and application of any of the contents of this book.

Most Alpha books are available at special quantity discounts for bulk purchases for sales promotions, premiums, fund-raising, or educational use. Special books, or book excerpts, can also be created to fit specific needs.

For details, write: Special Markets, Alpha Books, 375 Hudson Street, New York, NY 10014.

Publisher: *Marie Butler-Knight*
Product Manager: *Phil Kitchel*
Senior Managing Editor: *Jennifer Chisholm*
Acquisitions Editor: *Mikal E. Belicove*
Development Editor: *Nancy D. Lewis*
Senior Production Editor: *Christy Wagner*
Production Editor: *Megan Douglass*
Copy Editor: *Ross Patty*
Illustrator: *Chris Eliopoulos*
Cover/Book Designer: *Trina Wurst*
Indexer: *Angie Bess*
Layout/Proofreading: *Karen A. Gill, Becky Harmon, Donna Martin*

Contents at a Glance

Appendixes

Contents

Foreword

The *Complete Idiots Guide To Starting Your Own Business* is a handy practical guide that could have made my life a lot simpler when I started my business, "Mrs. Fields Cookies," over 25 years ago. I spent countless hours on the job learning these valuable lessons and tools. Here, they are presented in one place right before your eyes! For those of you who wish to take on the American Dream, Congratulations!

Mrs. Fields Recipe for Success:

¼ cup Passion

¼ cup Perfection

¼ cup Perseverance

¼ cup People

Passion—You need to absolutely, passionately love what you do! I love baking, eating, and sharing my cookies with friends and family. Never go into business with your first priority to make money. That is the by-product of doing something you love and doing it well.

Perfection—You must constantly strive for perfection because for your business to succeed and have staying power, you have to do it better than anyone else! In building Mrs. Fields, my Philosophy of Excellence and my motto "Good Enough Never Is" kept us focused on constantly improving, while stamping out mediocrity.

Perseverance—Stick with it! What you need is *guts*. Guts to start, guts to believe in yourself. Guts to take on the many challenges, guts to face failure, and guts to stick it out! Do not be afraid of failure! On the first day of my business, I had a counter full of cookies, no customers, no sales receipts, and a 21 percent interest rate on my loan. Desperately failing, I thought if I continue standing in my store that I definitely would fail and go out of business. As a result, I piled cookies high on a cookie sheet and took to the streets offering samples to passersby. That early failure turned into a great sales day. I learned not to fear failure but to simply stop what is not working and try something else until it works.

People—No business can succeed without its greatest asset, people; no matter how good its product. I always believed that my business was not just about selling cookies but selling a feel-good experience. I wanted a team that loved making, eating, and sharing my cookies as much as I did.

How? I would audition prospective cookie lovers! In the interview process, I would ask them to try my cookies. If they *loved* them at *first bite*, I knew I would never have to train them to sell. *Passion* sells!

When it comes to building a business, you need folks that will do whatever it takes to make the customers happy. The Mrs. Fields "purpose" in business is simple: "To build the best cookie in the world and to make our customers smile." If we did those two things without compromise, we would succeed.

Love what you do, set high standards, make family and friends a priority, surround yourself with people who believe in your purpose, and never give up pursuing your dream. This is my recipe. Without these ingredients, Mrs. Fields would never have existed. Could you imagine a life without soft 'n chewy cookies putting smiles on millions of faces?

Debbi Fields Rose, Chief Cookie Lover and Founder

Mrs. Fields Cookies

Introduction

Congratulations on taking your first step toward financial freedom—you opened this book and started reading. Many dream of owning their own business, but few take the concrete steps and do the work needed to make that dream a reality. You really can be one of those who makes it.

Hundreds of thousands of people have purchased the three earlier editions of this book. Many of those readers have kept me posted about their success, and their feedback was used to make this fourth edition a very different and much better book than ever before:

- The prior content was completely reorganized, updated, and revised.

- Several new important chapters were added.

- Special emphasis was placed on not only writing a great business plan but also on preparing you for its presentation to possible investors.

- Important sections are included to help those of you in the corporate world make the transition to business ownership.

- A fabulous CD was included with editable versions of most of the legal forms you will need. The CD alone is worth the price of the book.

- The CD also contains supplemental information to that already included in the book. This extra material makes valuable reading for those of you looking to find that extra edge.

This was all done with one special end goal in mind: to help you succeed!

To be successful, you need smart guidance along with the most accurate information available on the legal, financial, operational, and practical aspects of starting a business. Every attempt has been made to include all of the information that I and other business owners regretted not having when we started our own businesses. Tons of real-world lessons are presented in these chapters because the detailed reality of being a business owner is often much different from what we believe when first starting out.

I have been part of several startup companies, including a few of my own, and I know there is nothing more exciting than seeing your idea become a thriving reality—and there are few things more painful than seeing it die. I learned a lot of lessons along the way, which are passed on to you in this book. You don't have to go through a windshield to learn to wear a seat belt. I and my colleagues have already been through several business "windshields." Treat the thoughts and ideas in this book as your seat belt. Take them to heart and apply them where appropriate to avoid having an accident in the first place.

You are on the verge of a wonderful roller-coaster ride where you decide the direction of the track and the speed of the cart. Use this book to pick the optimal track layout, and then apply the presented tools to successfully steer the cart.

Letting uncertainty about the future stop you from moving forward with your dream may be doing yourself the biggest disservice of your life. Your business idea will unfold as you work your way through this book, and as that idea develops, you will feel more of yourself come to life. If you are *really* lucky, you will put your plan to work and never have to worry about financial freedom again. It will be yours in abundance, and well deserved. There is nothing idiotic about that, is there?

How to Use This Book

The book is divided into four parts. The sequence is designed to lead you through the business plan writing, business formation, and startup management process step-by-step:

Part 1, "Starting the Right Business," is designed to help you get off on the right foot in creating your plan and starting your business. Chapter 1 helps you evaluate the strengths that you bring to the company and to also know where you will likely need help in the future. In this way, you can be on the lookout for the right people from the start. Chapter 2 spells out the details related to the business plan writing process, which sets your expectations for what is involved in turning your idea into a credible business plan. Chapter 3 is the hub around which much of the rest of the book revolves. It presents the sections that your business plan must include and then points you to the particular chapters in Part 2 and Part 3 that are designed to help you write the sections of the plan. Chapter 4 is a special chapter that helps you determine your funding needs and determine ways of presenting your idea to potential investors in the least risky way.

Part 2, "Matching Your Plan to a Legal Structure," presents the legal aspects of business formation. Chapter 5 introduces various legal business structures, such as sole proprietorships, partnerships, and corporations. It's kind of dry but critically important. Chapter 6 goes into more detail about what is involved with setting up and running a corporation. Chapter 7 helps you decide whether you should set up to run out of your home or use an office. Take the time to read this part because it truly lays the foundation upon which everything else is built. The benefits you get from this section in conjunction with the companion CD files will pay for the price of the book.

Part 3, "Writing a Great Plan," adds the meat to the business plan sections presented in Chapter 3. The chapter sequence in Part 3 corresponds to the business plan section sequence designated in Chapter 3. Starting with Chapter 8 you can, chapter by chapter, write your way through your plan. By the time you get to Chapter 15, you will have defined your market opportunity, assessed your competition, set up your marketing and sales approach, laid out your production plan, learned how to handle employees and payroll taxes, and understood financial statements along with their usefulness. There is a lot of content in these chapters, and when you add the information from Chapter 15 to your plan, you should be just about done with the plan-writing process.

Part 4, "Running a Healthy Business," presents all that stuff that nobody ever tells you about running a successful business. This section assumes that you will be successful in not only writing your plan but also in getting it funded and started. It teaches you how to manage your cash flow, set up for credit card sales, make sure your customers pay on time, deal with your banker, use automation, and include Internet technology into your operation. Knowing the information in this section will help you make that transition from startup to survivor. Read this section when writing your plan to make sure that you include important forward-thinking thoughts into the proper sections. But also keep Part 4 next to your desk so that you can refer to it as your run your business. The lessons included in these chapters were costly for those who went through them. Reading this part will give you a fighting chance of dodging all that pain. A bonus chapter is included on the CD for those of you interested in moving overseas.

At the very back, I included several appendixes to give you further sources of insight and information. Appendix A contains a complete business plan that I wrote but never used because it didn't meet my personal objectives. It's a real plan that some of you might choose to try. Go ahead! It would be great to see it making someone money. Most important, it presents you with a concrete starting point for your plan.

Appendix B gives you resources that you can use if you want more information than is provided in this book. Appendix C gives you definitions for oodles of terms used not only in this book, but in the industry as well. Appendix D (located on the CD) gives you a listing of books and other printed matter you can use to further round out your background.

More About the Kwik Chek Business Plan

Almost anything is easier to do when you have a picture of how it's supposed to look when it's done. It's kind of like trying to assemble a model or toy without the picture of what it's supposed to look like all put together. It's one thing to read about how a business plan is created and something completely different to see or read an actual plan.

For this reason, I included an actual business plan in Appendix A. This plan is one I wrote for a used-car evaluation service business I called Kwik Chek. When I wrote this business plan many years ago, I did it so that I could find out whether the idea would fly or whether I should go back to the drawing board. My original intent was to franchise the business nationwide, and I created the plan to see if I could meet that goal.

The Kwik Chek business concept didn't work for me because I wanted to be an absentee owner and franchise the concept rather than be an owner-operator. Fortunately, by going through the process of writing the business plan, I could see that this business wasn't going to help me achieve my goals. The idea still seems sound, but it's just not right for me.

Should you decide to pursue the idea using this business plan, good luck! If you succeed with the idea, please let me know; send me a dozen free car inspection certificates, and buy me dinner some time when you're passing through the Chicagoland area. Or a new Porsche would be nice!

You might, early on, want to read through the Kwik Chek plan because I frequently refer to it throughout the book. Although the format I used in preparing the Kwik Chek plan is not the only one that works, it provides a starting place and a guide for you to follow when you start to write your own plan.

Extras

To guide you through the minefields of starting your own business, this book also provides additional tips and bits of information from those who have been there.

For starters, each chapter begins with a little story. Read these stories because they not only help you understand what the chapter talks about but also because every one of those stories is based on something that really happened. You can learn a lot from the stories alone.

You'll also find words of street wisdom, cautions, terminology, and helpful tips in these additional boxes:

 On the CD _____

This box lets you know that the companion CD has a legal form or additional chapter content on it that directly applies to the topic under discussion. Don't leave the CD in the sleeve. Pull it out and put it to work. This information is invaluable and can save you hours of frustration and potentially loads of money in professional fees.

> **Been There ... Done That**
>
> This box gives you perspectives from business people who have gone through the same decision-making process you're going through now. Use their advice to help you make the right decisions.

> **Smoke Signals**
>
> This box provides warnings to let you know about major, potentially business-threatening pitfalls along the way.

> **Listen Up**
>
> This box shows you street-smart information, shortcuts, and helpful advice.

> **Talking Business**
>
> This sidebar defines technical business terms for you.

Acknowledgments

There are numerous people to acknowledge and thank for their contributions to this fourth edition. Up front, let me thank all those who contributed to the earlier editions. The following people provided vision, comment, inspiration, talent, and information that made this book more than it would have been.

Thank you, Alpha Books and Penguin Group (USA) Inc. for your success with the *Complete Idiot's Guide* series and for your strong commitment to this fourth edition. Thank you to Marie Butler-Knight for keeping this book available as a valuable tool for our readers, to Mikal Belicove for moving this entire project to success, to Nancy Lewis for great and constructive development editing, and to the other members of the production staff for adding the final touches that make this product special. Thank you, Marcia Layton, for your input on the first and second editions. A huge thank you is included here to Steve Maple for his creation and providing of the incredibly valuable legal content included on the CD. Thank you, Oprah, for opening my eyes to the great potential of women as entrepreneurs and business owners. Thanks go to my literary agent Susan Barry, from the Barry-Swayne Agency, for doing what she does so well.

There is a lifetime of experience and thank yous that go out to everyone whom I have worked with over the years. It is very possible that one of your stories is included in these chapters. This is only a partial listing of the new contributors: Uday Om Pabrai, Mike Borch, Dan McManus, Mark Hallam for thinking like a banker, Kate Clevenger for credit card processing information, Bill Cartmill and Henry Wong for continual updates on life in Silicon Valley, Bill Hagara for business life updates in Austin, Texas, my students from DePaul University for detailed feedback, and my consulting clients who taught lessons but will remain nameless. War stories were provided by Dave Kalstrom, Jeff Kolling, Jim Herlinger, Ted Keane, Al Shugart, John Chambers, Michael Dell, and Dr. An Wang, among others. A very special thank you is offered here to my wife, Loree, who not only tolerated me but also scheduled around me during the writing phase and to my mother, Jean, who put her professional secretary skills to work keeping my sentences readable.

How-to-do, and not-do, insight was provided by various people from GenRad, Plantronics, Seagate, NuTech Testing Services, DAVID Systems (DSI ExpressNet), Telenova, IBM, Wang Laboratories, AT&T, and hundreds of clients and customers. If you are not mentioned here, please accept my apologies along with a thank you for the contribution you know that you made.

Special Thanks to the Technical Reviewer

The Complete Idiot's Guide to Starting Your Own Business, Fourth Edition was reviewed by an expert who double-checked the accuracy of what you'll learn here, to help us ensure that this book gives you everything you need to know about starting your own business.

Special thanks are extended to Theresa A. Pickner, Attorney at Law.

Theresa has operated her own law practice in Colorado since 1989. She practices primarily in the areas of business law, trusts and estates, and taxation. Her educational background includes a Bachelor's of business administration with a major in accounting, a law degree from the University of Denver, and a Master's of laws in taxation, also from the University of Denver.

Theresa has over 500 small business clients in the Boulder/Denver area. She has been teaching startup business classes through the Small Business Development Center since 1996. Currently, Theresa sits on the Board of Directors of the Boulder Chamber of Commerce. She was named the chamber's Volunteer of the Year in 1999.

Trademarks

Part 1

Starting the Right Business

Sure, you can be a successful entrepreneur. Oodles of people have done it before you—and many of them with worse skills and fewer resources than you. Yes, you read that right: I'm agreeing with you. You can be successful at becoming your own boss.

To give your new business a fighting chance, you need to perform some honest self-analysis to determine what you do best and then match your business to those skills and interests. Then you need to figure out whether you can make money in this business of yours. You also need to create a plan for starting and running it and then find the money to get it up and going.

Sounds like a lot of stuff to do, doesn't it? Well, don't worry; this first section helps with all of it and then acts as your roadmap to the rest of the book.

Your Business Starts with You

In This Chapter

◆ Understand the relationship between you and your company

◆ Do you have what it takes to start a business?

◆ A look at your personal goals

◆ A look at your financial goals

◆ Transitioning from corporate employee to business owner

"Aren't you supposed to go into the office today?" asked Judy's husband Mike, nudging her shoulder from his side of the bed.

"Just let me sleep a little while longer. It's Saturday and I've had a long week," grumbled Judy.

Mike sat for a moment waiting to see if she would say more. She didn't.

"Okay. What's up? You have a big contract proposal due on Monday and I think you said that it will take you all day to prepare it. So what's the deal?"

Judy rolled over to face him. He was right and she knew it. But she just wanted a day off, even if it was a Saturday. On the other hand, she stood a reasonable shot at winning this proposal and it would set her up for at least three months of work. Not a bad deal in a slow economy.

"I'm just missing being home with you and the kids," she said. "I get tired of working alone all the time and the thought of working all day on a weekend by myself while you guys are off playing bums me out."

Mike had seen her like this before and had a proposal for her.

"Tell you what. You get your butt out of bed and head into the office for the morning. Get as much done as you can by 1 o'clock and the kids and I will bring you in some sandwiches. We'll do a picnic at work on that little lawn area."

Judy looked resolute in her lethargy so Mike pulled out the big negotiation guns. He knew that once she started she would finish.

"Okay. I'll sweeten the pot a little. If you win this job, we'll plan a vacation to spend some of the money you will earn. How does a week in Paris sound?"

Judy brightened up with the thought of a vacation. It had been well over a year since they just took some time off and she would need it if she won this project.

"Throw in lunch today with Paris and you have a deal," she replied, feet already on the floor and heading toward the shower.

Every journey has its beginning, and your journey to becoming a successful small business owner starts with this chapter and you. Here we discuss your interests, your personality traits, and your goals as they relate to starting your own business. Simply stated, it is just silly for you to start a business that you will grow to resent or to create a lifestyle for yourself that you wouldn't wish on someone you didn't like. Your business must support your personal goals, including those that are financial, family, lifestyle, and intangible in nature.

Believe it or not, not everyone is meant to be an *entrepreneur*. There are plenty of people who prefer working for someone else. (In fact, some people are better off working for someone else.) Understanding your own motivations is critical to deciding whether starting your own business will bring you happiness or grief.

You'll quickly learn that it's really easy to start a business. All you have to do is sell something or fill out a few forms, and you're in business. However, starting a business that generates adequate and consistent income while providing personal reward is more difficult. This chapter provides the help you will need to make decisions that will be both fulfilling and profitable.

Talking Business

An **entrepreneur** is an individual who starts and runs his or her own business rather than remaining an employee of someone else's company. You can start an antique store and be an entrepreneur.

Understand That You Are the Company—at First Anyway

Perhaps the one characteristic that differentiates a startup business from all others is the dramatic impact that the founders/owners have on the operation of the company. There is simply no way to separate the owners from the company in the early stages. Customers write checks to the company name but they think of themselves as doing business with the founder/owner. After all, when a company is small, there is really only one major decision maker: the owner. Owners set the ethics, quality, and value standards of their company, and those who think otherwise are kidding themselves. You create the public reputation and operational standards by which your future, larger, company will function. Make them ones that not only make you money but are also those that you can personally live with.

Startups are usually cash poor and must make due with as few employees as possible to stretch out the initial funding as long as possible. Keeping the employee overhead low is best accomplished with the founders doing as much of the work as possible until the cash flow becomes predictable enough to justify adding employees along with their associated expenses.

Listen Up

The founders should have a clear handle on their respective personality strengths and weaknesses along with a comprehensive inventory of each founder's specific skills. In this way, they can use themselves to best advantage keeping employee expenses low. As the company grows, founders struggle with another difficult skill: letting go of all of those things they did when the company was small.

Do You Have What It Takes?

There is a lot of folklore out there about startups and their founders. It is often difficult to separate fact from fantasy when evaluating founders, their startups, and their successes or failures.

Here are a few things that I have learned from entrepreneurs, about entrepreneurs:

♦ Most have started multiple businesses with the first few not really doing very well. Many have gone bankrupt multiple times and keep coming back to try again.

♦ Most resent bureaucracy and tend to fall behind in maintaining the administrative sides of their businesses.

- Most get restless when things are going smoothly and are always looking for that next growth opportunity.

- They have a difficult time balancing the need for personal control with the need to trust employees to act on their behalf. Holding on too tightly to the reins often limits their business's growth opportunities in the process.

- Most treat the business like it is a child at first and later as a family member. Don't laugh. It will likely happen to you as well. Think about it: You will likely spend more time with your business than with your family, all the while knowing that this time is improving your family's financial security.

- Most will complain about the level of personal risk they live with and then risk it all again on what they believe is their next great idea.

- Most earn a decent income but very few earn the Bill Gates billions that make such great publicity.

- Most are normal people with a strong work ethic and commitment to providing the best quality to their customers.

- Most enjoy the freedom that comes with running their own show and paying their own bills, and are willing to accept the responsibilities that come with having that freedom.

- Many run their own businesses for a few years and then return to work as employees, no longer wanting to have the headaches associated with running their own shops. These people often make great employees as they have a more senior-level perspective of what is required to make a business run.

Do any of these points sound attractive to you? Do you have the intense desire to exercise your own judgment, take your own risks, and create something from nothing? Do you want the financial independence that provides you with the freedom to do things with your life that you couldn't do otherwise? Do you have an idea that nobody at work supports or thinks is a good idea? Do you believe strongly enough in the idea that you have to try it yourself, or you will always wonder how it would have turned out?

If this is the case, then you have the passion, the "right stuff," for becoming a successful entrepreneur. Now it is time to see if you have the personality traits and skills needed to turn your business passion and idea into a profitable reality.

What Makes a Great Entrepreneur?

Whether an entrepreneur is born or made is a topic for scholars and philosophers. Suffice it to say that entrepreneurs come in all shapes, sizes, races, genders, and nationalities. Also suffice it to say that they have a few common characteristics that tend to differentiate the entrepreneur from those folks who work as an employee. These differences are not themselves a criteria for success. They are required to deal with the typical demands of the entrepreneurial life.

Here are a few "truths" about the typical entrepreneurial situations:

♦ Money is usually in short supply.

♦ Ideas are not fully developed and indeed are often developed while simultaneously introducing the product.

♦ There is never enough time to fully research or plan an idea or strategy.

♦ Things rarely turn out as you expected, which is really related to the prior point. The less research done, the more uncertainty there is with respect to future occurrences.

♦ Entrepreneurs must move forward in the face of uncertainty or ambiguity.

In summary, dealing with these typical startup situations, entrepreneurs must …

♦ Have the ability to move forward in the face of large uncertainty.

♦ Be willing to start—to get going when others might wait.

♦ Be highly self-motivated.

♦ Be willing to adapt along the way as things change from the expected.

♦ Believe in their ability to do what must be done to fulfill their customer commitments and business obligations.

♦ Make the image of success secondary to functioning on a shoestring.

♦ Have faith in their idea when others are not sure, while also not holding on too long to a bad idea to the extent that the financial health of the company comes into jeopardy.

Listen Up

I have entrepreneurs come in to speak to my university classes. The students regularly tell me that they acquire a higher level of respect for entrepreneurs after learning the daily realities that come with starting your own business. Some feel that entrepreneurship is not for them after better understanding the realities that come with opportunities and return more happily to their normal "day job."

◆ Be able to sell their products or services to prospective customers—be perceptive enough to determine how to create a fit between the customer needs and their company's offering. Creating this fit might involve a complete redesign of their offering, but it may be worth it to secure the business.

◆ Be able to quickly understand the important aspects of a situation and then act appropriately to those important aspects. This is particularly important in the early selling phase of the company, when reputation is limited and customer-perceived risk is at an all-time high.

What Are Your Strengths and Abilities?

Before you start your business, you'll want to be sure that you have a solid foundation in the major aspects of business management, or make friends with good people who do. You also want to know where your personal strengths lie and where you will need help.

Answer the following questions as honestly as possible by placing a number between 1 and 10 in the blank. Use a 1 when you feel that the statement least applies to you and a 10 when it very strongly applies to you.

This is important: Don't look at the paragraphs following this table before completing the personal assessment. Make it as honest as you can.

Personal Assessment Procedure

Assessment (1 = LOW 10 = HIGH)	Statement
_____	I am comfortable with moving forward and making decisions when I don't have all the answers to important questions.
_____	I am typically the one initiating things for my family, friends, or at work.
_____	I can keep myself on track even when nobody else is watching or monitoring my performance or activities.
_____	I can adapt my thinking and focus along the way as events change.
_____	I trust my current capability level and also believe that I can learn what is needed to meet future demands.
_____	I care more about getting the job done than how good I look doing that job. Performance is more important than image.
_____	I trust my business judgement and am willing to move forward on what I believe to be a good business idea even if others are not supportive of that idea.

Assessment (1 = LOW 10 = HIGH)	Statement
_____	I trust my sales ability and know that I can sell my business along with its products and/or services as well as anyone.
_____	I tend to see the truth of a situation before others and can take the most effective actions for a given situation.
_____	I have enough money in savings, or access to enough money, to pay my personal and business bills for at least 6 months.
_____	Sum Total of All Rows (Between 10 and 100)

Make sure that you add up the total of all the table rows and write that total in the space allocated.

No doubt you will be higher in some areas and lower in others. That is normal for all people, including entrepreneurs. This process gives you a general guideline as to where you fit on the overall successful entrepreneurship scale and also tells you something about your areas of strength and areas where you could use some improvement.

If you scored less than 50, you may not be cut out for starting your own business. You may be better suited as an employee instead of being the personal responsible for all of the pressure and uncertainty of running your own show. You might want to keep your "day job" and spend more time talking in depth with entrepreneurs to get a better sense of what their day really looks like. You may have shortchanged yourself on your initial answers, but if your initial answers were accurate, then you need to surround yourself with people who will help you in your lower-rated assessment traits.

If you scored between 51 and 70, you show some entrepreneurship tendencies but might be better served working for a small business for a while first to get a better idea of what is involved. I would call this group a transition group.

If you scored over 71, you are likely champing at the bit to get started on your own business. You are probably beyond thinking about whether you "should or shouldn't" and are on to when, how, how many, and for how much. This will be particularly true for those of you who score higher and have fairly routine jobs with little excitement or uncertainty. This group should beware jumping on the first idea that comes along and should spend the time preparing the plan outlined in Chapter 3 and its supporting chapters.

No simple test like this can possibly evaluate all of the skill and personality aspects that make you who you are. And no generalization could possibly tell you *with absolute certainty* whether you will or won't make it starting your own business. Ultimately, the decision is yours.

If you are interested in a more detailed assessment procedure, stop by my website (www.edpaulson.com) and take the Detailed Entrepreneur Assessment Questionnaire.

Do yourself a favor. Don't skimp or delude yourself on this portion of your evaluation process. All small business entrepreneurs quickly learn that they are their companies' most important assets. They also learn that they will spend an immense amount of time doing what is required to make their businesses succeed. Doing what you want improves your chances of success. Doing what you like improves the quality of life as you work toward that success. Not ensuring a match in both of these important areas plants the seeds of failure before you even start. Before you commit money, energy, and time to your venture, make sure that it is something you really want to do.

> **Been There ... Done That**
>
> All business owners fantasize about giving up the administrative hassles of running a business from time to time. I'll even admit to fantasizing about taking a job counting screws in a hardware store every once in a while!
>
> A few years ago, when things were on a downturn with my business, I was talking with a fellow entrepreneur. When she asked how things were going, I said, "They are pretty bad right now, and I think some radical changes are due." She asked, "Are you think-ing of getting a job?" I smiled and said, "No," to which she replied, "Then things aren't that bad."

What Are Your Needs?

When determining the viability of a startup business idea, you must consider the compliment between the business you plan to start and how well it fits with your financial, family, and personal (spiritual) requirements. Otherwise, a few years down the road, you may find yourself resenting the company right at the point where it is poised to become the financial success you intended it to be. If your company does not make any money, it is a hobby. It helps to know how much you need to make ends meet.

This section prompts you to evaluate your own needs so that you can later map them against the requirements of your intended business. The overall intention is to best ensure that what your intended business will ask of you will be just what you are will-ing to give. Now that is business success if I ever heard it.

Financial Needs and Goals

How much money do you *want* to make, and how much money do you *need* to make? Understand that these two amounts are not the same. I've never met anyone who made as much money as they wanted, but most people make as much money as they need. It all comes down to how well they manage the money they make.

Wealth is a relative term. If you make $100,000 per year and spend $110,000, you are living beyond your means. Most people would consider you poor. However, if you make $65,000 and spend $50,000, then you're saving or investing $15,000 a year. Over the course of just a few years, you would be considered wealthy.

Talking Business

Wealth means consistently having money left over after you pay all of your bills.

In short, don't just calculate how much money you want to bring in; look also at what it costs to live your current lifestyle. Calculate how much money you need to cover all your living expenses. You'll also have to account for the expenses associated with your business—federal taxes, state taxes, health insurance, life insurance, tuition assistance programs, vacation time, and so on. Don't guess at these amounts. Find out what you spent in each area over the last 12 months and use that as your baseline measurement for monthly financial survival. Let's face this issue head on—if you do not have a reasonable chance of making this amount of money in a short period of time, you should likely not start the business you intend. You simply cannot support yourself for a long period of time if the business cannot pay you enough salary to cover your monthly living expenses.

The total of your minimum living costs and fixed business expenses is the amount you need to earn to live as comfortably as you are living now. You have to make at least this amount of money, or one of the following three things must happen:

1. You decrease your expenses.

2. You figure out a way to make more money from your venture.

3. You stay with your current job until your finances are in order.

Look at your finances both on a short-term (12 months) and long-term (2 to 5 years) basis. First, you need to get through the short term to make it to the long term. If you do not have the money to support yourself for at least 12 months (some say 18 to 24 months), then you should hold off starting your venture until you have the needed savings. Or you can look for outside sources to provide the money you need, such as family members, friends, or banks and government agencies. (See Chapter 4 for more details.) You need to be able to support yourself during those initial lean months when your business probably will not be making enough to pay your rent or your mortgage. So start saving those pennies now.

You should also consider how much money you're willing to invest before you pull the plug on a business that is a cash drain. You may go to Las Vegas determined to stop gambling after you lose $500. Likewise, you should set a limit on how much you're willing to invest in a new business before it must pay for itself. Your odds of success at entrepreneurship are much better than at the gambling tables, but it is still a risk and must be treated as such.

Setting your limit in writing up front can help you make the decision to shut your business down if and when the time comes. That is one reason for writing a business plan. It's hard to set limits, but doing it up front can save you a lot of time and money. The "Funding Needs" section of your business plan should detail these up-front needs with a high degree of confidence, or you have done yourself a disservice.

Listen Up

Most people dream of running their own businesses because they believe that it's the only way they'll become wealthy. For some, this is true. Most of the extremely wealthy members of our society obtained their money by owning a business, either one they started or one that they were given. In many cases, they saw an opportunity to introduce a new product or service to the market and jumped in quickly. Some have succeeded and made millions—even billions. How about Larry Ellison of Oracle, Debbie Fields of Mrs. Fields' cookies, or even Henry Ford?

In their book *The Millionaire Next Door,* authors Thomas Stanley and William Danko suggest that owning a business is one strategy for becoming wealthy. Only 20 percent of American workers are self-employed, but they comprise two-thirds of American millionaires.

Not everyone who starts a business becomes wealthy. Statistics suggest that only 20 percent of all new businesses will be around in five years. When a business fails, the owner rarely makes a lot of money on the deal. The average 1998 self-employed household makes around $65,000, and the 1998 average business owner/manager household income is around $124,000 according to a 2001 Small Business Administration report.

That may not sound bad to some of you, but just keep in mind the number of hours entrepreneurs have to put in to make that money. It's hard work! If you are already making that amount of money at a job you like, why would you take the chance? Many won't.

Also look at the total amount of money you will need to invest in order to get the business up and running. That total investment includes not only the amount of *cumulative cash requirement* of the business, but also the high likelihood that you may have to work for a significant length of time without taking a personal salary. If you reach the point where your projected cash supply is spent and you still can't afford to pay yourself a reasonable wage, it's time to decide whether this particular business is right for you. Your enthusiasm might be pointed in the wrong direction. Shifting your focus to a new business may be the key that opens the door to your financial success!

Talking Business

Cumulative cash requirement is the sum of all cash put into a company from the initial investment, including the total of all monthly cash provided to cover monthly net income shortfalls. The largest projected value represents the total amount of cash needed to fund the startup phase of your business.

Family Motivations and Goals

If you are the type of person who cannot leave your family alone for the evening or weekend without having intense feelings of guilt, then you should examine your startup intentions and your family's needs before you begin a new business venture. Without your family's support, it will be difficult for you to succeed. There will be times when you will need to work at night, on weekends, and on holidays. At these times, you will have to choose between family involvement and business commitments. Your family needs to accept your commitment to your business without being hurt or angry.

Communicate openly with your spouse, children, parents, and friends about what you want to do and what kind of a time and energy commitment it will take. It's a good idea to prepare them in advance for some of the sacrifices that you and they may have to make. And make sure they're willing to make those sacrifices!

Been There ... Done That

People often don't understand that your startup business is like your boss. You might have to work after hours in a "normal" job. Why should you not have to do the same for your own business? You should have to, and your family must understand that this is true. Working for yourself doesn't mean that you take off whenever you, or they, like.

If you sense from initial discussions that your family may resent your directing attention away from them and toward a business, think about ways that you can involve them in the company. Instead of thinking that you have to choose between business and family, talk with them about what you can all do together to run a business.

Putting your children on the payroll may be a savvy tax strategy to consider. In addition, making your spouse an employee may enable you to pay for your family's health insurance through the company. It's definitely something to look into. The more they have invested in the success of the business, the more they will support you to do the work needed to make it succeed.

Many divorces have resulted from the feeling that the business is more important than everything else in the business owner's life. Be sure your family knows that this is not the case. Typically, just telling them won't do it; you have to show them by setting aside time to be with them.

Spend the time to get your family involved from the beginning. Set their expectations properly to best avoid having recurring ugly scenes later. Your family can become a source of strength if they understand the importance of their support in your and the business's success. Nobody is an island, and you may end up alone snuggling your checkbook if you don't handle your family situation with respect.

What Are Your Spiritual Goals?

Spirituality has more to do with what makes us feel good as human beings than with formal religion. For some of us, a business helps us achieve spiritual goals through the belief that by providing a valued service to our clients, we are improving their lives. Spiritual goals can also be reached by creating an organization to perform social service work, such as a food kitchen or a halfway house. Some entrepreneurs want to create an organization where their employees can realize their full potential. In a world of compromised corporate ethics, some people start their own business to ensure that they can always work in an ethical environment of their own creation. This is motivation enough for them.

One of my clients is determined to start her own business, but not for any of the personal financial reasons we've discussed so far. She has enough money to support herself and has started businesses before. But she now wants to start one to bring new attention to the plight of people in recovery for alcohol or substance abuse. Her belief is that by creating products to better meet the needs of this group, she can draw attention to and help support them, donating the bulk of the profits to related charities and human service agencies. Like many other entrepreneurs, she is dedicated to her business idea; she just happens to be doing it for spiritual reasons.

In essence, don't neglect the nonbusiness side of your soul when deciding to start your own business. In fact, there are many people who believe that you should look here first.

Escaping the Big House—Leaving Corporate America

This section is for those of you who are now working for someone else and are interested in branching off into your own business. It may be that you have seen many of your fellow employees be "right-sized," and you are wondering when your turn will come. It may be that you now don't trust corporate life as the secure lifetime investment you previously assumed it to be and want to have more control over your employment destiny.

I contend that employees are really contract workers in today's work environment. I don't mean that from a legal perspective but more from a practical perspective. Very few people I talk to today believe that they will still be working for their current employer when they retire.

Employees work for their employer by choice. If a better job offer comes along, many will likely take it. Most publicly held companies have now shown themselves prone to laying people off if needed, even if the cash reserves to suffer a downturn is on-hand. This is the essence of a contracting relationship: The contractor chooses the client and the client selects the contractor, both knowing that the relationship will end at some future date. They negotiate the financial and responsibility details that apply during the contracting period, but both know that the relationship is temporary and not one for life.

Once you realize that you are essentially a contractor, your approach to work changes. You start to manage your time differently, always looking over your shoulder for your next engagement, knowing that the steady paycheck will at some point come to an end. You start to increase your savings, knowing that you might have a period of no income between engagements. You start to set up your medical and other personal benefits so that you, and not the client, has primary control over them.

I speak quite often on this topic and provide the following advice to those aspiring entrepreneurs who are currently employed:

◆ Start building your savings so that you have the financial resources to weather an unexpected job termination. This should be a minimum of 6 months of living expenses (12 months preferred), but don't stop there—keep saving. It will always pay off.

◆ Start the personal evaluation and business planning process while you are still employed. This way, you already have a running start should you be terminated.

◆ Knowing that you have someplace else to go (your own business) may make you more effective in your current job. You lose nothing by planning out your personal business while still employed.

♦ You may come to appreciate your current job more as you realize what is involved in going it alone. It will likely give you a more mature look at what happens at your employer, letting you treat work as a "lab" of sorts. Consider going to night school to take business-oriented classes. They will make you a better manager for your employer and for your own business, and your employer may pay the tuition to boot!

♦ Keep it to yourself that you are planning to go off on your own. You may never take the entrepreneurship plunge, and nothing is gained in letting others know about your aspirations early in the planning process.

♦ Keep your entrepreneur's eye open at work for opportunities that could make your employer your first startup customer. But don't bring it up at work until you really are ready to go it alone since they may fire you on the spot if they know you are planning to leave. You just never know. Have a lot of your plan finished, and proven viable, before talking about it in public.

♦ Don't set yourself up to resent your current job if it is one that allows you to do what you enjoy, to do what you are good at, to make a good income with solid benefits, and provides a sense of personal satisfaction. If you are already happy with what you are doing, there may be little motivation to change jobs; but it is always a good idea to have a contingency plan in place should your job suddenly disappear.

Listen Up

Just as you might occasionally envy the entrepreneurial lifestyle, the entrepreneur occasionally envies those of you who have a job you love working for someone else. More than one entrepreneur has returned to corporate life after selling their own business simply to not have the headaches that come with that "enviable" entrepreneurial lifestyle.

If you already have a job, great! If it is a job you love, even better! There is little in professional life more satisfying than working within a group of dedicated people doing what they love while making a positive difference in the world. Larger companies can provide this opportunity where, by contrast, starting your own business is usually a very solitary experience, especially in the early days. Just know that a shifting of the economic times at your company could cost you your job through no fault of your own. At that point, you want to have taken the steps outlined in this section to make sure that you are ready for the change, perhaps using it as a starting point for becoming a successful entrepreneur.

What Is Your Personal Bottom Line?

Ultimately, it all comes down to you. What do you want, and why do you want it? Do you think that running your own business will give you the fulfillment that's been missing in your current job? Are you willing to earn less money for a while as you try to establish your company? How far are you willing to go to make your business work? Are you willing to get up and go to work even when nobody is going to yell at you if you stay home and watch soap operas?

If you like the stability of working 9 to 5, wake up! Owning your own business means that you don't have set hours because you'll be working long hours in the early stages. If this paragraph alone is enough to talk you out of pursuing your own business, then send me a thank you card. You are not ready yet to make that kind of commitment. It doesn't mean that you never will, just that right now is not your time.

On the other hand, if after reading this chapter you not only feel that starting your own business is the right thing to do but also have a better idea of what you bring to its success, then congratulations! You have just crossed a first major hurdle toward not only thinking and acting like an entrepreneur but also trusting that you are the right person to start your business. Some feel that these may be the most important decisions you will ever make in creating a successful business.

 On the CD

> When you start your own business, you *are* the business. People may think that they are working with a "company," but underneath it all, they know that they are working with a person: you. Your word and your integrity are all you have in the early days since you really don't have a track record. Take a few minutes to read the special bonus section I put on the CD entitled "Your Ethics and Your Business" (CD01-1). Make sure you keep this very important issue in the front of your thinking. You can usually recover from a mistake, but it is really difficult to recover from a breach of integrity.

The Least You Need to Know

◆ Understanding your personal needs, goals, skills, and personality before you start your own business is critical to later success.

◆ Setting a limit on your losses and time investment is a valuable step before you start your own business and one important reason for writing a business plan.

◆ Make sure you have enough money saved to support yourself for at least 12 months in addition to the money needed to fund and establish your new business.

◆ Getting your family's support and acceptance for starting a business is a necessary step, or you might find yourself choosing between the two, which is a no-win for everyone.

◆ Planning to start your own business while still employed is a good move that protects you and your family from an unexpected job termination.

Chapter 2

Business Planning Basics

In This Chapter

♦ Why you should create a business plan

♦ Understanding where your plan is generally headed

♦ Matching your plan to your business stage

♦ Turning your planning into action

"You look about as glum as I have ever seen you," remarked Peter as he looked across the table at his friend Bill.

"No doubt," said Bill shaking his head. "I've gotten myself and my company into a huge mess, and I'm not sure what to do to get out of it."

"What happened?"

"Remember when I decided to take on the large distribution contract for South America earlier this year? Well, I just found out that our major customer in Argentina is going under and taking a chunk of my receivables with them. They fell behind on their payments and we kept shipping believing—perhaps more accurately, hoping—that they were good for it. Now, I'm not sure that I can make payroll since those receivables were used to secure my line of credit with the bank."

"Ouch! That really hurts."

"Not as bad as knowing that I could have avoided the whole thing by staying with my original business plan instead of being seduced by the prospect of making 'big money' in a short period of time. We never planned to go to South America in the first place and had no initial interest in carrying those products. I just got greedy and now have put the entire company and a year's worth of work in serious jeopardy. When will I learn to listen to my own advice?"

There are so many little decisions that need to be made and so many factors to consider on your way to becoming a business owner that you may become overwhelmed before you even start. But if you take it step by step, you can carefully weigh all your options—and there are a lot of them. A business plan helps you to make sure that you take all of the right steps that lead to the same successful conclusion—your successful business.

Chapter 3 presents all of the details you need to know about creating the plan itself. This chapter presents the big-picture approach that will help you in creating that plan. Any major project has a higher likelihood of success if you appreciate the magnitude of the undertaking and are clear about where you are starting and where you want to end up.

Taking a few minutes to read and absorb the information presented in this chapter will keep you from having to rewrite portions of your plan. The time spent here will save you time later on.

Why Prepare a Business Plan?

Although you might have heard that you only need a *business plan* if you are trying to get financing to start a company, this is not true. In addition to using a business plan to secure funding from others, there are several other reasons to write one:

Talking Business

A **business plan** is a document that can be as small as 10 pages or long enough to fill a book, with a reasonably detailed plan usually running 30 to 50 pages. It includes sections on the product or service you intend to sell, your industry and marketing strategy, your staff, your business operations and equipment, your competition, and your financial resources and estimates.

- Putting your goals and ideas down on paper helps to organize your thinking.

- Writing down your plans and goals demonstrates your commitment to your business, which impresses potential investors, suppliers, and employees.

- Once you have your plan down on paper, you have a guide to achieving your goals that you can refer to regularly to measure your progress.

- Not only do you have a guide that helps keep you on track, it also ensures that all your employees understand where you plan to take the business.

♦ Your plan helps focus your organization on its mission, reducing the chance that the business becomes sidetracked by other less important activities.

♦ As your own ultimate investor, you deserve to prove to yourself that your business idea is a good one.

Let's face it: Others do not believe in your idea nearly as much as you do. Part of the reason is that they probably don't know as much about your business, your product, and your plans as you do. For everyone else to believe in your idea, they need to see what you intend to do. In this way, the plan is also a sales document; those who read it will be sold on your idea, vision, and approach. There will probably be many different people who want to see your business plan, each for different reasons, including some of the following:

♦ Banks and other funding sources will use your plan to determine whether you are truly capable of starting and running the business.

♦ The Small Business Administration (SBA) will review your plan to make sure it will be profitable so that you won't have any problem repaying their guaranteed loan (if you opt to apply for one).

♦ Your board of directors or management team will want to review your plan to understand the future direction of the company.

♦ Employees will want to see sections of the business plan to understand whether the company has long-term career opportunities for them and to understand what is expected of them.

♦ Strategic partners or joint venture participants will want to read your plan to determine whether your overall direction is in alignment with their plans and mission.

As a result of the planning process, you will learn more about your business idea than you ever thought possible. Treat it as a learning experience, and watch where it takes you. The plan will start quickly to take on a life of its own.

Think of It as a Simulation

A business plan is just a simulation. It is a way of predicting the future success of a business idea. Will the plan be correct? Perhaps, but the only way you will know if you were right with your predictions is after you have already taken the plunge and implemented the plan. Large companies spend much money preparing a business plan because the levels of money involved with introducing a product on a national, or even international, scale is very large and can run into the hundreds of millions of dollars. Whenever the money investment levels are large, it is worthwhile to invest more money in creating the plan so that as much uncertainty as possible is removed from the future projections. Small business people rarely have this large planning and funding luxury; as a result, they produce less comprehensive plans. These smaller companies then have to adapt quickly to unexpected future events since there is a higher level of uncertainty resulting from the streamlined planning process. (See Chapter 4 for more information on venture capital and other types of funding.)

My point here is that the business-planning process produces more than simply a written document. It produces a simulation of how you expect your business startup plan to function. It produces a way for you to determine, as best you can without actually doing it, whether the business idea stands a reasonable chance of success. It produces a way of thinking about and acting on your business idea. It increases your likelihood of being successful. You are much better served spending a few extra days up front adding "meat" to the business simulation (a.k.a. plan) than spending weeks or years and hundreds of thousands of dollars "experimenting" in the real world. Experiment on paper and then use your scarce time and money to make your planned idea a reality.

The Overall Plan-Writing Process

Many people plan more extensively for a vacation than they do for a new business. "Oh, I have been in business for a long time. I can wing it." Big mistake! Don't quit your day job until you research the type of business you want to start and feel confident that you can succeed. Unless you are pretty sure that over time you can earn a better salary with your own business than you can if you stay at your current job, why risk what you have? However, if you take the time to plan all the steps involved in starting and running your new business, you are on your way to success.

The plan is a representation of your level of professionalism, so make sure that it is (1) easily understood and without spelling or basic grammar errors, (2) printed on white paper using laser jet or comparable print quality, (3) laid out to be easily read, using page numbers and minimum 1-inch margins so readers can make notes as they go through it, (4) double-spaced using a standard 12-point typeface such as Times, Helvetica, or Courier, (5) nicely bound in such as way that the sheets don't fall on the floor when being read, and (6) written with the intent of creating reader understanding as its primary goal instead of assuming that the reader knows as much about your company and its offering as you do. Don't laugh. This is a common mistake for novice and experienced business people alike.

Some sections of the plan can remain confidential (such as financial information, new technology overviews, or client data); you won't typically share them with outsiders until they have earned that right. However, you should assume that many sections of the plan will become public because you'll be sharing it with many different audiences. Those less-sensitive sections might include information about your personnel, existing products and services, industry analyses, and any other company background information that normally appears in marketing literature. Taking a modular approach to your plan writing lets you mix and match the sections as appropriate to the intended reader.

Being Honest

If you want to show your business plan to potential investors, include the assumptions you made when writing the plan, potential risks and rewards, and any important milestones to ensure that the investors understand the whole picture. Making your situation appear too "rosy" will make investors skeptical, but making it appear too risky might scare them off. By simply being honest about what you see as the strengths and weaknesses of your situation, you allow investors to make up their own minds based on as much information as you have.

Being up front with potential investors helps you avoid problems down the road if things don't go as well as you planned. Given the right opportunity, you can lead professional investors into a minefield, as long as you first tell them that there is a minefield. Investors bring resources to the table that can keep you from getting into big trouble if and when it arises. However, if they feel you misrepresented your company and the potential rewards they can expect, you will seriously damage your working relationship.

Listen Up

Don't worry about hitting your business projections exactly; experienced investors know that things can go "off plan" as a project unfolds and that these figures are your best guess. Investors simply want to minimize the likelihood of losing their investment due to mistakes or poor management on your part. The business plan provides a framework for working out the details of your relationship with investors. Use it as such. If you can't work together on the plan, you will likely not work well together when actually starting the business.

You want to be honest with yourself as well even if you do not intend to show the plan to a third party. Favorably skewing your sales and expense projections so that your plan shows, on paper, you making the income level you want does you no good at all if reality is substantially less cooperative, which is usually the case, and you cannot support yourself. Remember, you are investing your time and money in this venture, and you want your simulation to represent as accurately as possible your likelihood of making money on that investment.

Getting Help

You are not alone when you prepare your plan, even though it might feel that way. Organizations out there have a vested interest in helping you succeed at starting your own business. These include the local Chamber of Commerce, entrepreneurial associations, and the Federal government. Here are a few resources that can help:

- ◆ The Small Business Administration (SBA at www.sba.gov) works with a group of retired executives called SCORE (Service Corps of Retired Executives at www.score.org) to help you create a business plan and acquire funding. These are people who have already been where you plan to go; they can help you assemble the plan. Better yet, their services are free! Simply contact your local SBA office and ask for the phone number of the local SCORE office.

- ◆ Small Business Development Centers (SBDCs), which are collaborative programs developed by the SBA and local colleges and universities, also provide free counseling help to people starting a business. There are more than 750 SBDC locations across the country to assist you. You can find a local office by calling 202-205-6766.

- ◆ Women- and minority-owned companies can also turn to Minority Business Development Centers (MBDCs) for low-cost assistance at rates typically under $20/hour. Centers across the U.S. help minority and women-owned companies write a business plan, develop a marketing campaign, and pursue government contracts.

See Appendix B for contact information for these and other resources.

You'll Never Have All the Information You Need

Of one thing you can be sure: You will never have all of the information you need to take all of the risk out of your venture. Even the large companies, who spend millions of dollars on research, cannot take all of the risk out of a new product launch.

At some point, you are going to have to say "enough is enough." Assume that the information you have is solid enough and the analysis comprehensive enough to present a "reasonable" level of certainty regarding the viability of the idea.

This is a scary time because you always know more about a plan's flaws after you have been working on it for a while. You know what the assumptions are and where the hidden traps are located. Don't beat yourself up about that. Nobody is perfect, and neither is your plan. You can only get it as close to ready as possible and then decide to move forward with implementation or drop the idea and move on to your next startup opportunity.

Experience tells many entrepreneurs when that time is right and the analysis is as reasonably complete as it is going to be. If you do not have that level of experience, then I suggest that you hire someone who does have it so that your plan can be evaluated in an objective way but with a seasoned eye. If you don't have the experience and cannot afford a seasoned veteran to review your plan, then I suggest that you follow your gut instinct. If you have excitement butterflies, then don't let them keep you from moving forward. But if you have a queasy, uncertain feeling that something is wrong, then likely there *is* something wrong. It might be something that you forgot. Or something of a critical nature that requires more detailed research. Or simply that the pieces of the plan don't tie together as neatly as you would like.

In any of these cases, I suggest that you look to the source of this *analysis paralysis* and determine its origin. You may look at the source of the fear that is causing the uneasiness and dismiss it as simply paranoia. Or you may realize that this fear is well founded and more work is required. Just be honest with yourself, and you will find the source of the concern, address it, and then make the right decisions.

Talking Business

Analysis paralysis is a point where the analysis process takes precedence over the ultimate goal of starting a business. The need for more detailed information, of which there is never enough, keeps the entrepreneur from moving forward with starting the business. The analysis process becomes an end in itself, which is counterproductive.

The Minimum That Your Plan Must Cover

Few people who read your plan will remember everything that it contains. They will walk away from the reading remembering only a few basic points—usually those that are of the most importance to their particular interests.

Here are a few basic points that your plan must cover to adequately serve you as the writer/manager/owner and other likely readers:

◆ A detailed definition of the proposed business idea and why this idea is a good one in light of the market conditions

- How much money is required to get the business up and running on a solid financial footing

- When the business will not only recover the initial investment but also to show a reasonable profit (return on investment) for investors

- Why this business, run by you, stands a reasonable chance of succeeding

- A listing of the major challenges that this business faces in becoming successful and how they will be addressed

- Details of how revenue is going to be generated through marketing, sales, and promotion activities

Your plan will include tons of information that you are responsible for researching, analyzing, and presenting. The ultimate goal of the presentation (the plan) is to answer the preceding points. Remember that you are simply trying, through your simulation, to remove as much perceived risk as possible from the prospect of investing in your company. If your plan accomplishes that goal with integrity, then it is a success.

Listen Up _____

Busy people, which includes most investors, won't take the time to read a plan that is too long. They also won't figure out what you're talking about if you haven't been crystal clear. A small plan that clearly and concisely addresses all the major points of interest will be better received than a lengthy one that drones on about irrelevant information for pages and pages. You need to do the work for them; spell out your information in plain English. Lead your readers through the plan, step-by-step, explaining your idea and how you intend to make money doing it. Present the information succinctly and professionally.

Dealing With a Bad Business Idea

What a drag! You perform the entire analysis to discover the idea does not hold financial water. Now what? Be thankful! You have just saved yourself from a nasty experience.

If you find that the business just won't work, then your original assumptions were not valid. If you had pursued the venture based on those assumptions, you would be either personally bankrupt after investing all your hard-earned savings or apologizing to your angry investors. Take heart! A negative outcome on this round does not negate the entire venture. You can now consider a different, potentially more successful approach.

Take a look at your approach to the business to see if modifying it can provide a better, and more profitable, strategy:

◆ Is the problem with the idea itself or simply how it is presented?

◆ Are you the right person to shepherd the idea to success, or should you be looking for others to round out other critical positions? Should you look at merging your talents with another, more established firm?

◆ Do you need more money to buy you additional time to achieve the needed market recognition?

◆ Should you initially offer a product or service that is more readily acceptable and then convert your customers over to your new product or service line once they are already familiar with you and your company?

◆ Are your sales estimates too low? What could you do to increase the sales faster, and what would be the additional cost?

◆ Are there things you can do to minimize the level of perceived risk?

Keep your chin up and remember: Creating a successful business plan is a lot like solving a mystery. You have many stray facts that need to fit together properly before the venture makes sense on all levels. Take the time to learn the facts.

Stages of Company Growth

Just as people go through many stages in their lives, companies evolve and change over their years of operation. It is important for you to remember that you are writing a plan for a company in its early stages of development.

This is of particular importance if you are leaving a larger company to start your own business. It is difficult for mid-level managers of larger corporations of say a few billion dollars in sales annually to realize that their small company will be just them. Instead of having departmental chats at the company water cooler, you *own* the water cooler. Instead of completing your expense report for accounting, you *are* accounting. It will likely surprise you at the number of things that you take for granted working for a larger organization that will simply not be there with your startup. At first, anyway. As your company grows, many of those realities will reappear since they are required for any larger organization, but keep in mind that the early days will probably be only you and, possibly, a few others.

The following sections present the natural evolutionary stages that your company will go through as it becomes successful. Make sure that your plan is focused on the earlier stages, from "Idea" to "Rampup," and possibly even into the early phases of "Evolution." Once you get your company through these earlier stages, you will naturally begin planning and implementing the "Sustaining" activities that ensure your longer-term success. This type of mature business planning is beyond the scope of this book but important nonetheless.

Idea Stage

You are likely already here, or you would not be reading this book. This is the stage where you have an idea for a product or service that you think has potential. You may not know what to do with the idea at this stage, or even if it is a good idea, but you have an idea that has captured your attention and imagination and just doesn't seem to want to let go. Congratulations! You have taken your first step toward entrepreneurship.

Planning Stage

This book takes you through the Planning Stage. It is in this stage that you evaluate your idea in light of business and market realities. Here you determine many of the details associated with turning your idea into a viable business that not only supports itself but you and your family as well. A major goal of this stage is to create a plan that convinces you and others that your idea is a good one and worthy of time and money investment. This stage may take a minimum of 30 days of dedicated effort, or it may take years depending on your particular circumstances.

Funding Stage

This stage is where you acquire the money needed to start your business. If you are self-funded, then this might be a very short stage for you. If you need other people's money, then you now become salesperson and evangelist with respect to your business idea. At the conclusion of this stage, you should have the money needed to get your business started or know what needs to be modified with your idea and plan to secure the needed funding. If you spend a lot of time at this stage and cannot secure the needed money and cannot, or will not, fund it yourself, then you may have to go back to the Idea Stage and start all over again. If you did your work honestly and accurately in the Planning Stage, it is much more likely that you will get the funding you

need since the idea and plan will financially speak for itself. (See Chapter 4 for
details related to the various stages of
funding, such as "Seed" and "Mezzanine,"
and their various risk and reward characteristics.)

This stage takes as long as it takes, but if you
find that you have presented your idea to
dozens of funding prospects who all have
turned you down, take their feedback to heart.
They may see something that you don't. On
the other hand, if you still feel that you have
a great idea, then persevere.

Listen Up

Silicon Valley folklore is full of
stories about people like Steve
Jobs of Apple Computer and
Sandy Lerner of Cisco Systems
getting turned down dozens of
times by venture capital firms who
simply did not think that they had
the right stuff. I'll bet those venture
capital guys have kicked themselves more than once thinking
about that decision!

Startup Stage

"Start Your Engines!" This is where you start putting your plan into action. In this
stage, you start spending the money received from the Funding Stage. You start product development, create marketing and sales materials, start calling on customers, and
work to create your first set of success stories. A major goal for this stage is to get your
first set of dedicated customers who become the basis for referral to other prospects.
This is a critical stage of development; you must ensure that customers are happy at
this stage, or you may never make it past this stage. The marketing and sales sections
of your plan are very important. Expect this stage to last up to six months with faster
customer adoption being good news.

Rampup Stage

At some point, you will find customers that you did not directly contact asking about
your offering. They likely heard about you from other satisfied customers. You are
now headed into the Rampup Stage. It is in this stage that you will experience faster
and larger growth rates than you have seen to date, which is normal for a business
that is doing things correctly in a solid marketplace. Beware this stage because it can
put you out of business if you cannot handle the rapid growth while also maintaining
the levels of product and service quality that got you here in the first place. The way
your company uses automation and implements employee management activities,
which should be included in your plan, are very important to your not only weathering
but excelling from this stage. Expect the Rampup Stage to start around six months
after active marketing begins and continue indefinitely, with annual revenue percentage growth rates exceeding 100 percent not uncommon.

Listen Up _____

The Rampup Stage of a startup's development is arguably one of the most exhilarating times of a business's life. What you have worked for so long to see happen is finally happening. Customers are coming to you in droves, and the supply of customers wanting your offering seems endless. Don't kid yourself. The customer demand will eventually taper off, and you will want to ensure that you have kept all of your customers happy while also controlling your ego as the money and attention starts pouring in. Enjoy this stage and revel in the rewards, but never lose sight of the business ball—to keep your business viable and healthy through this stage so that you can remain and thrive through the Evolution and eventually into the Sustaining Stage.

Evolution Stage

When you get to this stage, you find yourself asking, "What will we be doing next year?" instead of "Will we be around next year?" Your future survival is no longer a major point of uncertainty, and your questions start to revolve around how you will look as you continue to survive. Your company and its offerings evolve at this stage, possibly past whatever you expected when you initially wrote your plan. This is a tricky stage in that you will have to balance the need to build on what made you successful to date while not limiting your future growth by what you did in the past. You know more about your business, customers, and marketplace at this stage than you did when you started.

Renewed planning, perhaps with the help of outside consultants, is a good idea at this stage and beyond the scope of your initial startup business plan and this book. You may make some guesses about your evolutionary future while writing your startup business plan, but know that these early predictions are really only guesses. The timeframe within which this stage kicks in is dependent on your industry, products, and services, but a rule of thumb is that you will have to address these types of evolutionary issues around the 18 to 24 month point after you started active marketing.

Sustaining Stage

This is where you will be when you grow up. When you reach this stage, you are an accepted, regular player in your marketplace. People now refer to your company as one of the guys to beat when starting a new company and as one of the companies that defines how business should be done. This stage is well beyond the scope of your initial startup plan and should be given minimal attention other than to define what you would like your Sustaining Stage company to look like and stand for from an ethical perspective. Trying to define the details of this stage when writing a startup business plan is like designating one of your children to be a doctor before the child has even been conceived. Wishful thinking on the part of the parent? Sure. Bankable reality? Not likely.

Short- and Long-Term Planning

Nothing happens in the long term without *short-term* actions that move you toward your desired outcome. Short-term actions cannot help achieve any particular goal if no goals have been set or no plan has been developed. You have to know where you're going before you can figure out a route to get there, right?

Taking the time to determine your own goals and your company's *long-term* mission and objectives will guide your daily actions. Without this framework, you and your employees may be busy, but the business will not move forward because everyone is pulling in separate directions. Making sure everyone knows and understands the goals and objectives of the company will make life a lot easier—for you as well as your employees. Defining the company's goals will minimize employee frustration because they will know what they're working toward. You can minimize confusion by identifying and eliminating activities that don't directly support the goals of the company.

Talking Business

Short-term goals refer to those goals you set for up to one year. **Long-term goals** refer to goals you hope to meet within the next two to five years.

It all starts with you. Take the time to learn more about yourself, your personal motivations, and your long-term goals to ensure that you take the company in the proper direction for you and your investors. For example, if you like the idea of working alone from a home office, make sure that you're not setting your business up to grow to a point where you have to hire employees or get an office outside your home. If your business starts to grow in a direction or at a speed that makes you uncomfortable, you may start to resent the business and eventually unravel what is otherwise a good thing. You can avoid this by simply deciding up front what kind of business you want to have, both short term and long term. Once you decide, you can move ahead to make it happen.

The Least You Need to Know

◆ Setting your goals helps you to define the actions needed today to get you "there."

◆ A plan analysis that shows an idea as not viable saves you time, money, and headaches. Review the plan from a new perspective to see if it is salvageable when approached differently.

◆ Your business plan isn't only for other people to read. It is for you to read and use as well.

◆ Your initial startup plan will only cover the early stages of your company's development. Future plans will address the Evolution and Sustaining Stages.

◆ Honesty is the best policy. Keep your plan accurate, and don't make claims you cannot back up without stating them as your best guess.

Preparing Your Business Plan

In This Chapter

◆ Defining your mission statement

◆ Describing your business idea

◆ Understanding the plan sections and their contents

◆ Using the plan to sell investors on your business

"Why the special staff meeting?" asked Jake, the sales manager. "Not sure," was the reply from his colleague, who was responsible for production.

The company started out as a small beverage manufacturer; it now sold millions of dollars a year in fruit-drink products. It recently introduced two new lines of frozen fast foods. The response to the new products was tepid at first, but it was slowly improving.

The company's real moneymaker, the main beverage product line, was doing well and supporting the new ventures, but Jake had reservations about how long it could last without the new frozen food lines carrying their respective part of the profits (which was just starting to happen). It seemed a good time to maintain the status quo, but the company president (who was also the founder) liked new projects.

Jake didn't think the company could stand another product introduction so soon after the frozen food lines' near-fiasco.

"Thanks for coming," said the president. "Now that I have more free time, I have been experimenting with new methods of food preparation. I think the American people will pay for fresh, vegetable-based foods that taste good and are easy to prepare. As a result, I want to introduce three new, fresh vegetable side-dish lines that will open up new markets for the company and take us into new retail outlets. I expect the full support of management in taking these products to market."

Jake mustered his courage and asked, "Sir, don't you think we should wait a little while before moving into new markets? Our frozen foods line is just now being accepted, and I have a concern that diffusing our efforts with fresh vegetable lines may be too much for us now. Why don't you take some time and perfect the recipes and give our distribution channel a chance to settle down?"

As the president and founder, what would you do? Would you make Jake sell rice noodles for not supporting your plan? Would you listen to him and take his advice? Would you thank him for his input and do what you want anyway? How you respond to questions like these will determine how your company grows, and whether it grows in the right direction. How do you determine what the proper response should be?

Many managers use the business plan as their touchstone when making major impact decisions like the one presented in the opening scenario. It is the business plan that presents an approach, which, at the time of the plan writing, was considered the best possible option. Deviating substantially from that plan may indeed be a solid idea, but there should also be some type of justification as to why the new approach is better than the one presented in the plan. The carefully reasoned approach of the original plan contains a rationale that I believe requires an alternate set of reasoning if it is to be substantially changed. In short, the plan is the play book for your startup business's success. Staying with the play book at all costs may not be a great idea, but neither is disregarding the play book without valid reason. It confuses management, employees, customers and, in particular, investors, who invested with a set of plan-created expectations and have every reason for concern if future actions do not lead to fulfilling those expectations.

This chapter presents the details associated with writing the business plan and is designed to be used in conjunction with later chapters that deal with specific sections of the plan.

Briefly Describing Your Business Idea

This sounds like a simple thing to do but is often quite difficult as it requires you to simplify the various complexities of your business idea into just a few sentences. Once you can present your idea in a few sentences, you are well on your road to understanding the essential aspects of your business. This description should be no longer than two paragraphs of around four sentences each, and once someone has read these two paragraphs he or she should know this about your business: (1) what your business does, (2) why it does these things, (3) what makes it unique when compared to other similar businesses, and (4) why the reader should care about your business in the first place. Getting all of this into a few sentences is a great exercise, and you will likely find yourself rewriting these few sentences many times as you work your way through the business plan writing process, so don't get discouraged.

Your Mission: Why Does Your Company Exist?

This simple statement covers, in just a few sentences, the reason for your company's existence. It provides the overall umbrella under which all other goals and actions fall. It says what your company does and who it does it for.

A typical *mission statement* for a clothing retailer, for example, might be the following:

> To provide trendy, natural-fiber clothing to health-conscious women between 18 and 35 years old, at reasonable prices in an environment where buying is fun or to be the number one or number two market share provider in every market in which we participate within 18 months of market entry.

Notice that the mission statement is brief and to the point, determining the overall direction of the company. It also sets limits. If a vendor tempts you with a hot men's clothing line, you can see that men's clothing would clearly be in violation of the mission statement. Either the company's prescribed mission statement needs to be changed, or the idea to add men's clothing needs to be dropped so that the company can stay focused on its core mission.

Notice that the second mission statement, dealing with market share, requires that the company only pursue offerings that have tremendous sales potential, which virtually eliminates the consideration of niche market products or services.

Talking Business

A **mission statement** is a written description that explains why you're in business. Usually only two paragraphs long at most, it explains to employees and customers what values the company has, such as excellent customer service, the lowest prices, and a fun work environment.

When you create your company's mission statement, consider the following:

◆ What do you plan to do? For example, "We will sell second-hand office equipment."

◆ Who do you plan to do it for? For example, "We will focus on price-sensitive customers in the local geographic area."

◆ What best ensures success? For example, "We will target sale prices of products to be at 60 percent of new retail price for comparable products."

You can embellish these simple objectives with more specific points that add more details to the mission statement frame. Additional items might include the following:

◆ The time frame within which it will be done, such as within the next 18 months or the next 5 years.

◆ How your company will deal with changes in the marketplace (such as technology advancement or new competition), for example, by investing in new equipment or hiring more staff.

◆ The *benefits* (not the *features*) of your product or service, which will persuade customers to buy from you (such as a high customer-convenience purchasing approach). By focusing on benefits, rather than features, you will concentrate on the true value of your offering to the customer.

◆ How following the mission statement will contribute to the company's short- and long-term success, such as by keeping the company focused on a high-growth market or keeping expenses down.

Talking Business

Features are the different characteristics of a product or service. For example, the features of a drill bit may include its size, length, and the type of material it is made of.

Benefits are what the customer gains by using your product or service. One benefit of the drill bit is that it makes holes of a specific size. Customers buy something to obtain the benefits associated with using it. The features get them the benefits.

It may take you days to write these simple sentences. But these sentences define everything else that occurs within the plan and ultimately within the company, so defining them clearly is time well spent.

After defining your company's mission statement, you can define the company's over-all *objectives*, or *goals*. These are projects that comply with the mission statement and have specific time frames and measurable results. A typical objective may be to "add three new products to the line over the next 12 months."

You can then break these goals down into individual *tasks* that you assign to individuals, to be completed within specified time frames. All these tasks contribute to the fulfill-ment of a particular objective. A task in our scenario may be "review the new product lines for 15 potential vendors within the next six months with the intention of select-ing three as our primary vendors."

Tasks give rise to *action plans* that literally define who is doing what on which day. For example, "Visit XYZ Dress Company on Tuesday from 1 to 3 P.M.," would be a typical action item that helps complete a particular task. Completing the task moves the com-pany closer to achieving its objectives and continues to support its mission.

Talking Business

Action plans are the specific detailed activities you do to help the company achieve its goals. These include meetings, proposals, visits, or creations. **Tasks** are indi-vidual assignments given to people to help the company reach its objective. Each task is broken down into action plans.

Objectives or **goals** are large projects that affect your company and involve several people. Objectives help the company grow and become more successful. They are usu-ally rather involved and may take several months to reach.

Action plans, tasks, and objectives are related to each other. Actions lead to larger task completion, which leads to the achievement of major objectives. The following figure shows how they all stack up.

Once you've got your business up and running, you should periodically take a look at the specific actions you are performing (say, within the last week) and then read your mission statement. Do your actions support that mission statement and further its over-all intent? If so, congratulate yourself on your focus. If not, then you should evaluate how you spend your time. Have you gotten yourself into areas that do not correspond with your initial intentions? Does your initial mission statement need modification, or does how you spend your day need modification?

All actions ultimately support the mission statement by achieving short-term (one year or less) and long-term (two to five years) goals.

The Pieces of Your Plan

Effective business planning is a lot like assembling a jigsaw puzzle. All these stray pieces need to be put together in a logical order for the puzzle to work. As you become more familiar with the pieces, the proper fit reveals itself, and there is only one way to assemble the puzzle that makes any sense.

> **Been There ... Done That**
>
> Always keep these important investor-related points in mind as you prepare your plan: Investors are primarily interested in making as much money as possible, as quickly as possible, with as little risk as possible. They may have a passion for a particular industry, technology, or entrepreneur but ultimately their investment decision will be based on business realities.

I tend to look at a startup business plan as initially a sales document and secondarily, and very importantly, an operational document. The particular flow of the plan presented here is designed to enhance the sales document aspect of the plan, assuming that the reader has minimal background in your particular industry or with your particular idea. The operational component is intrinsic to the plan and will generally require that only particular sections be shared as opposed to sharing the entire plan at once as is done with investors.

The business plan is a document that is broken into sections. Each section deals with an important aspect of your business idea and its investment prospects. Your business plan should contain the following basic elements:

I. Cover Sheet

II. Table of Contents

III. Executive Summary

IV. Business Description

V. Market and Industry

VI. The Competition

VII. Marketing Strategy

VIII. Operations Plan

IX. The Management Team

X. Financial Overview and Funding Needs

XI. Summary and Conclusions Analysis

XII. Appendixes or Supplementary Materials

The next few sections of this chapter take a more detailed look at each of these business plan sections. Refer to the Kwik Chek business plan included in Appendix A for a sample of how these sections were implemented in an actual business plan.

Hot Tip

One of my early sales managers described an effective sales presentation in this way: First, tell them what you are going to tell them (Executive Summary), next tell them what you want to tell them (the detail sections), and then tell them what you told them (Summary and Conclusions). A business plan is ultimately a sales document that explains your business idea in a similar way.

Cover Sheet

This is your plan's first impression, so make it a good one. The layout of the cover sheet should be uncluttered, professional looking, and easy to read. At a minimum, it should contain your company's name, the type of company it is (e.g., corporation, sole proprietorship), home state of operation (e.g., Illinois), address and phone/fax information, URL, primary contact person name, and date of the plan. It is also a good idea to include a statement that this plan is for investment analysis purposes only, is a confidential document, and that it may not be copied or shared without your written permission. Adding a copyright statement and symbol is not a bad idea. Some people also number their plans and keep track of who the plans were given to as some way of maintaining a level of confidentiality control. In these cases, a special "Number" and "Presented To" section is included on the cover sheet. Some people recommend sending a copy of the plan to yourself using registered mail and then not opening it. In this way, they have an envelope date-stamped by the post office that verifies when the contents were mailed. Make sure you attach a copy of the plan to the outside of the envelope so that you don't forget what is inside. Don't laugh. It happens.

Table of Contents

The Table of Contents is not a major content element of your business plan, but it helps show the reader what information can be found in the coming pages while also helping the reader more easily refer to information that is contained in the plan. Because tables of contents are generally found in well-organized documents, you will make a good impression by including one at the front of your plan. It can't hurt you as long as you make sure that the section titles and page numbers shown in the Table of Contents match those actually in the plan. If you use the headings designated by your word processing software package when writing your plan, you may find that the Table of Contents creation is a painless and automatic operation.

Executive Summary

It is hard to over emphasize the importance of the Executive Summary. Although this section is the first in the business plan, it is better that you write the final version of it after you write all the other sections. Write one paragraph (at most) to describe each section of the plan. Finish the Executive Summary by listing the amount of money required, the projected return on investment, the major advantages your company will have over the competition, and why this is an excellent investment opportunity.

The Executive Summary should be one or two pages long (at most) and is often the only section a potential investor will read. Based on these few paragraphs, the investor will decide whether to read the rest of the plan. If the investor doesn't proceed to read the rest of your plan after reading this summary, you've just lost a potential investor. For this reason, your summary needs to catch and hold the reader's attention. Some people take a shot at writing the Executive Summary before writing the rest of the plan as a way of helping them frame the rest of the plan writing. They then come back and rewrite the Executive Summary after the plan is completed. You will learn things along the way as you write the plan, and that wisdom should be included in the final version of the Executive Summary.

Business Description

The Business Description part of the plan explains your product or service idea and how it meets the needs of your market. Describe exactly what it is you will be selling and why people, or businesses, will buy it. How is it different from similar items already on the market? If it is a revolutionary concept, explain why the world needs this new breakthrough.

Don't get sidetracked into talking about all of the great things that you believe about your company in this section. This is, to an investor, like hearing proud parents talk about how their child rolled over by himself last night. Make sure that the way you present your company to the reader is focused on what he or she must know to understand the benefits of your presented investment opportunity. You can include all of those other details as an appendix if you still feel the need.

Start by describing your product or service. For instance, is it a new kind of vehicle, a tasty new type of cookie, or a better housecleaning service? Explain what the product or service does for the user—what the benefits are and why customers will buy it. If there are similar products or services already on the market, briefly compare them to what you are offering and explain how yours is better. If your new product or service is unlike anything currently available, convince the reader that it is needed. Remember that there is a plan section dedicated to competitors, so only provide the competitive highlights here.

You may also want to include a History subsection here where you'll briefly touch on how your company has been organized, such as whether it has been structured as a corporation, partnership, or sole proprietorship, whether any stock has been issued, and who invested any money to start it and how much. (See Chapter 5 and Chapter 6 for help on determining the legal structure that is right for your business.) If you intend to use your plan for financing, these questions will come up immediately as you start to talk with investors, so you may as well take care of some of the questions right away. If your company is already in operation and looking for money to fund expansion, make sure to include a company success history as well, as that definitely helps minimize the perceived risk on the part of the investor.

Market and Industry Analysis

The Market and Industry Analysis section presents information describing the market need for your product or service. This is where you detail all the information you gathered regarding the size of your market, the number of potential customers for your product or service, and the growth rate for your market or for the industry as a whole (which usually means worldwide). This section not only relies heavily on the results of your research, but also on your ability to compile the information into a simple, concise, and easy-to-read format. (See Chapter 8 and Chapter 10 for details regarding creating market estimates.)

The Competition

Who are the established companies already selling products and services similar to yours? How will they react to your company? Depending upon your idea and how long your product or service has been available, your competition might consist of other new and aggressive companies just like yours or established companies from whom you intend to take business. We all think our business idea is unique, but the customer might think it's like dozens of others. Rely more on the market data you've collected rather than your opinion about whether there is a similar idea already in existence.

There is no reason to be afraid of competition. In fact, if you pretend that you have none or suggest that that's the case to others, no one will take you seriously. Accept that you have competitors and take every opportunity to learn from them. What are they doing right, and what can you do better? It is okay to mimic things your competition does well and to learn from their mistakes as long as you don't infringe on any trademarks or copyrights they may have in place. Generally, this means that you can copy certain ways of doing business, such as offering free delivery with your service or guaranteeing your work, but not their advertising or designs. I tell you more about dealing with the competition in Chapter 9.

> **Smoke Signals**
>
> Anyone who believes that they have no competition is in for a rude awakening, even if he or she has a totally revolutionary product. There is always someone out there willing and anxious to challenge companies with new and profitable ideas.

At this point, it's a good idea to provide a list of the other major players in the market-place to show that you know exactly who your competition is. You should also indicate your impression of their strengths, weaknesses, and overall success in the market. By learning about your competition, the reader of your plan can better understand how you will succeed: either by going after a market opportunity that no existing competi-tor is addressing or by doing what everyone else is doing, but with a different twist.

Marketing Strategy

If nobody buys your product or service, you're out of business. Period! Nothing ends a business faster than no customers. In this section of your business plan, you need to explain to the reader what you intend to do to get customers.

> **Listen Up**
>
> Don't make the mistake of think-ing that your product is so won-derful that customers can't help but buy from you. This assump-tion will almost certainly cost you the investor who reads your plan and will eventually cost you your company as well.

As part of your marketing strategy, you should describe how you intend to let the public know that you're in business, such as through a number of marketing methods that I cover. You should also explain your sales approach, such as selling by direct sales repre-sentatives, with a mail-order catalog, or through a retail storefront. You'll find a detailed discussion of all the different ways you can market your business in Chapter 10, but start to think now about how you'll describe your plans to the reader of your business plan.

Notice that the Marketing Strategy section is included after you have already pre-sented your business idea, the market conditions have been detailed, and competitive information has been presented. This section flow makes a lot of sense if you realize that the whole point of a marketing strategy is to obtain sales. Sales successes are dependent on market economic conditions, industry purchasing norms, and competitive offerings. Customers who must buy will do so either from your company or from one of your competitors, so you have to consider competitive pressures when developing your marketing strategy.

Operations Plan

This section describes operational procedures, manufacturing equipment, the level of production required, locations, international arrangements, licensing arrangements, and any other aspects related to providing the product or service defined in the idea section. (See Chapter 12 for a detailed manufacturing and production discussion.)

For those of you who are starting service businesses, this section might be short because service providers (such as management consultants, accountants, and attorneys) sell their time and experience. They don't use big machines to crank out words of wisdom, so production capacity is less of an issue. Assumptions should still explain how many hours per month you expect to spend on client-related work that you'll be paid for.

The Management Team

One of the most important elements of your business plan is the section telling the reader why you and your partners are the most qualified group to start and run this business. Investors give their money to people, not companies or product ideas. Investors want to feel confident that you have experience in the type of business you're starting and that other members of your management team complement your skills.

The management team is incredibly important to any new business and should take center stage in your thinking, explanations, and analyses. Your company has no historical track record. Investors cannot look to past company performance as a gauge of future performance, so they must assess the future based on the management team leading the company into that future: you and the other managers. When times are uncertain and risk is involved, you always want to be involved with people of high caliber. So do the investors. A great idea with the wrong team will not get funded. A great management team with a solid idea almost always will.

In this section, you need to briefly describe the backgrounds and experience of your management team to show the reader that you know what you're doing. If you have an associate with 25 years of experience in the business who's going to be working with you, be sure to mention it; it makes your company much more credible.

If you have advisers or consultants who have been working with you and giving you advice, mention them if they are fairly well-known or if they have a lot of experience.

If you've set up a board of directors, briefly mention the members of your board. The point of mentioning other people here is to show the reader that you're not trying to do everything yourself and that you recognize you don't know everything and rely on professionals in those instances. Many business owners think they know everything and don't need advice from other people. These are usually the ones who don't last very long. (See Chapter 6 for more information about setting up a board of directors.)

Financial Overview and Funding Needs

Now it's down to the bottom line. Everything else up to this point was presented as the foundation for the financial analysis. This section spells out the actual investment required and when and how the business will make enough money to pay it back. You define the amount of initial investment and how much you will need in the future based on certain sales and operations projections. The investors really want to know how much money will be invested, how much they can expect to make, and the time frame in which they'll make it. Everything else is simply a teaser to whet their appetite for the financial feast that follows. You should also include a *break-even analysis* that covers the volume required to push the company from a deficit to a profitable operation.

You should include an *income statement*, *balance sheet*, and *cash flow analysis* that projects the first three years of operations. These reports are usually called pro-forma financial statements. Pro-forma just means that the numbers are projections, or estimates, of future sales and expenses. (You'll learn more about preparing these forms in Chapter 15.)

Talking Business _____

A **break-even analysis** determines the production level (**break-even point**) at which you are paying your overhead expenses but still not making a net income. You are living at a subsistence level, with just enough money to pay the rent and put food on the table, but nothing extra for movies and popcorn. The **income statement** reflects all income and expenses for a particular period of time (usually a year). The **balance sheet** shows your total assets and liabilities. The **cash flow analysis** shows exactly how much you received and how much you spent on a monthly basis.

The initial capital required to start the business, cumulative cash flow, the funding sources, and how it will be spent is summarized in the "Funds Needed and Their Uses" portion of this section. (See Chapter 16 for a detailed discussion about projecting and managing cash flow, a critical talent that you will definitely have to master at some point if your business will survive.)

Summary and Conclusions

Some people don't include this section in their plans, but I think it is a good idea to summarize the many details presented throughout the plan in this special, final section. It reiterates much of what was presented in the Executive Summary but now adds additional insight based on the reader being far more informed on the idea, the market, the competition, and the financial requirements. In this section, you can tie up the plan in a neat package and ensure that readers understand your view of the overall opportunity instead of letting them drift off on their own. They may not agree with what you present in this section, but they at least will have a concise summary of what the plan was about and the conclusions you would like them to draw from the plan.

 Listen Up

I sometimes include a special section titled Risks and Opportunities before the Summary and Conclusions section. The purpose of the Risks and Opportunities section is to spell out for the reader what I believe to be the major risks to the success of this venture and also the special opportunities associated with giving this venture a try. More than likely, readers will see many of these for themselves, but I want to make sure that they know that I really do know about the risks while also ensuring that they completely understand the special attractive nature of the opportunities presented.

Appendixes or Supplementary Materials

The appendixes and supplementary materials are often referred to throughout the plan but appear as detailed references at the end. Included are the charts, graphs, extrapolations, resumés, and pieces of literature needed to convince the investor that you have done your homework. Including this information at the end instead of in the plan keeps the plan flowing along without getting bogged down with too much detail. As long as you let the detail-oriented reader know that there are more details in the appendixes and where he or she can find them, you have a plan that moves the big-picture reader along while still fulfilling the information cravings of the analytical investor.

Ethics and Your Plan

Nobody ever gives money to people they don't trust; people determine whether they trust someone based on how truthful they feel that person is. If you take liberties with your facts in preparing your plan, you run a very real chance of having a cumulative effect of the exaggeration being interpreted as lying. This is a problem if you intend to have people give you money.

Tempting as it is to present your idea with the brightest of projections, you must steer clear of stating conjecture as fact. If the reader finds out you have done this (which is likely when he or she checks out your plan in detail), you may not be able to recover the required level of trust needed between an investor and the startup management.

If your idea is a good one, then it will get funded. Trust that to be true and prepare the best possible business plan you can.

The Least You Need to Know

◆ The clearer you are about your business idea's benefits to investors, the more clearly you can convey those benefits in your plan.

◆ Your business plan is first a sales document to investors and then an operational plan that you use to keep your business on track.

◆ All of the plan sections need some level of attention since investors will likely have questions regarding all of these various topics.

◆ It is your responsibility to make the plan easy for the reader to understand. It is not the reader's job to decode your plan in the hope of discovering the investment opportunity.

Chapter 4

Methods of Funding

In This Chapter

- ◆ Understand the relationship between risk and reward
- ◆ Match funding risk with company stage
- ◆ Understand different funding methods
- ◆ Differentiate debt and equity funding
- ◆ Determine how much money you will need

Frank slammed the door on his car and tossed his presentation materials on the front seat. Taking a deep breath, he let back the seat and closed his eyes. A moment later his phone rang. Caller ID showed that it was his friend, Milton, a stock broker.

"So how did the presentation go?" asked Milton.

"Not well. They were polite, but I could tell that they really didn't get the idea and I'll be stunned if they buy in."

"Sorry. Did they give you any feedback on what they did or did not like about the plan? I, for one, like the second generation build-on idea a lot. What did they say about that?"

"Nothing," replied Frank with a slight pause. "I didn't tell them about it." He waited.

"Hmm. That was a good idea," sighed Milton with sarcasm in his voice. "Isn't that where you really expect your sales to increase and ramp you up enough to be a viable acquisition target?"

"Sure. It is. But is also the most unique part of the plan, and I am afraid someone will steal it if I am not careful. Until I know that they are interested, I am not going to tell them about it."

Frank could imagine Milton shaking his head on the other end of the phone. "Look, Frank. Your plan just isn't very attractive without revealing that second development stage. No credible investor will give you money if they don't see that part. Sorry to be the one to break the bad news."

"So what you are telling me is that I won't get the money if I don't reveal the second stage details. And my fear of revealing it may keep us from getting funded at all. Is that right?"

"Exactamundo," replied Milton enthusiastically. "If they can't see a way to make money off of their investment, why would they invest?"

It is hard for you to believe that people aren't lining up to give this great idea of yours money, isn't it? Be honest. Why are they all being so negative about your company's prospects? This idea will work. You can feel it in your bones, and all you need is a few hundred thousand dollars to turn it into reality. Sound familiar, or am I the only person who has ever had the experience of asking people for money to fund my business only to walk away confused and a little disheartened by their response?

It might not be them. Sorry. Perhaps you have unrealistic expectations about how they should react given the specific situation of you and your company. Perhaps they are reacting more objectively to the risk present in your venture than you are. Perhaps they are telling you something that is worth knowing about where your idea or plan falls short. Or, perhaps, they simply didn't understand the real financial, and possibly personal, benefit to them of getting involved.

This chapter helps you to sort through these points before you make those important investor presentations. It helps you anticipate the concerns that your investors may have so that you are better prepared to address them. The more credibly you can address their concerns, while infusing them with a strong dose of your own belief in the idea, the more likely you are to get the funding you are looking for.

Risk and Reward Relationship

There is an unbreakable link between the level of *risk* that an investor sees in an investment and the amount of *reward* that this investor will expect from his investment. Understanding the investor mindset is critical to making the right pitch that will get you your funding.

Talking Business

> **Risk** is the possibility that something, like an investment, will not turn out as good a reward as expected. The higher the risk associated with an investment, the higher the expected return on investment. **Reward** is what an investor expects to receive for having made the investment. This is usually some form of payment to the investor within a specified time frame.

Investors Give Money to Get Something Back

If you want a gift, go to your wealthy Aunt Sally. Oh, don't have a wealthy aunt or uncle? Hmm. That is a little bit of a problem. Now we have to deal with people who have no personal interest in us at all and who will get involved as an investor only if the investment makes financial sense. Let's take a look at what "financial sense" means to a realistic investor.

If you have money, you are always looking for ways for it to make you more money while best ensuring that you don't lose the money along the way. Anyone who has lost money in the recent stock market decline (which is probably all of us) knows that there is no such thing as "a sure bet." Even the incredible stock market run up of the 1990s could not predict the devastating decline we would see over these past few years.

So why put your money in the stock market? Simple. Assume that your bank savings account is now offering an annual interest rate of just under 1 percent. Assume also that you can tie up your money in a Certificate of Deposit (CD) for several years and perhaps get around 2.5 percent. Finally, assume that the stock market, on average over the past few decades, has shown annual returns of around 10 percent or so. Let's look at what this means: No-risk (savings) provides 1 percent. The CD is essentially risk free, but it ties up your money for a few years, which involves the risk that you might unexpectedly need it and have to pay a penalty to pull it out of the CD. For just a little more risk, the CD pays 2.5 percent, which is 1.5 percent more than the savings account. The stock market, which we all know is highly volatile and may require tying up your money for years to get a decent return and might or might not happen, is estimated to pay 10 percent on a prospective average basis.

Are you starting to see a pattern here? Why would you put money into something that is riskier than a savings account if you get the same percentage rate of return, 1 percent for the example here? You can get 1 percent without taking any risk at all, so if you are taking the risk of losing part or all of your money, then you are going to want to be compensated for taking that risk. How much more compensation? Therein lies the art of financial negotiations.

The Greater the Perceived Risk, the Greater the Required Return

These next two bullet points will explain the basic friction that exists in the investor/borrower conversation:

- ◆ Investors are ideally looking for huge returns on their investment, within a short period of time and with no risk.

- ◆ Borrowers ideally want to borrow as much money as possible for as long as they need it, to pay nothing to the lender for the use of that money, and have no obligation to repay it if the money is lost.

Disconnect! Notice that investors and borrowers come at the transaction from completely different points of view. The more seasoned you get at lending or borrowing, the better you get at resolving the friction points. There are also industry "norms" that help provide some ballpark within which typical financial transaction terms should fall. But, realize that there is a huge gap between how investors and borrowers look at the lending/borrowing transaction.

Every investor has some level of risk tolerance. This means there is an investment risk level above which the investor will not provide money. Some have a higher level of risk tolerance (venture capitalists) and others a low risk tolerance (bankers). To go to a banker with a high-risk investment, like your new startup company, is asking a low risk tolerance investor to invest outside of his or her comfort zone. It is likely not going to happen, and if it does, she will constantly be uncomfortable with having taken the risk and, likely, make you uncomfortable along with her. Plus, banks have legal constraints within which they must work to maintain their insurance and other protections that define the circumstances under which they can lend money.

You should now start to see that there is a fuzzy balancing act that you must perform between assessing an investment's level of perceived risk, the risk tolerance of the lender or investor, and the rate of investment return that this investor will require. Keep reading, and you will learn methods for assessing and presenting the risk level while also making sure that you are talking to the right type of investor for your particular situation.

It's Not Personal with Investors ... Well, It Kinda Is

Try to address investment discussions on a business, not a personal, basis. Investments can become sticky when they become personally based. Most experienced investors will avoid these situations since they are no longer ruled by financial risk and reward but become entangled with personal issues. If you try to make an investment personal, you are likely going to lose the investor.

Remember that investors are always looking for all those hidden or obvious risks to their investment—where they could lose all or part of their money or simply not make on the investment what they could have made if they had put the money elsewhere.

Remember also that your new company has no track record of its own on which to stand. Its only track record is your track record and that of the other founder/owners.

For these two reasons, you must also know that at this early stage, investors are going to be checking you out, personally, as well as your business idea. Actually, they may be checking you out more than your business idea. The idea won't be using their money— you will be.

Listen Up

Once you make an investment decision personal for either you or the investor, you run the very high risk of turning a business relationship into a battle of personalities and egos. Keep it business all the way when talking money with investors, and it will work out better for both you and them. You may sometimes need to play the "personal" card, but know that it has risks, and you can only play it so often before it not only gets "old" but starts to work against you.

Keep your personal finances as clean as possible and try not to commit them if you don't have to. Just be aware that the early round of investors may want a piece of your personal wealth as protection for their investment. Notice that the more you guarantee, the lower the risk becomes to the investor, which should also lower their return on investment requirements. If someone wants high returns and a 100 percent guarantee of their funds within the agreed upon timeframe, then they also have unrealistic expectations. Explain this in a business-like manner, without making it personal, and you might be able to educate them along the way. You can't blame them for asking for the sky, can you?

Comparing Debt and Equity Funding

Investors come in two flavors: those who provide *debt funding* and those who provide *equity funding*. Debt funding is funding that must be repaid and is usually a loan of some type. Equity funding means that an investor gave you money in exchange for stock (equity) in your company. Equity funding is usually paid back when the investor sells his stock either to the company, on public market, or to another investor.

Notice that debt funding has risk associated with it in that the loan may not be paid back. But debt funding usually has required payments along the way that reduce the level of risk to the debt investor every month. Plus, it is reasonable to assume that you might have had to personally guarantee the debt to get it in the first place. As a result of your personal commitment, the interest rate on the debt is likely reasonable for the current lending market since the risk associated with your not repaying the loan is small.

Talking Business

Debt funding is funding that must be repaid and is usually a loan of some type. **Equity funding** means that an investor gave you money in exchange for stock (equity) in your company. A **personal guarantee** is often required by lenders or all types as a way for them to go after you personally for debt repayment should the business cease to exist and default on a debt payment.

Equity, on the other hand, is a completely different story. An investor gives you his or her money today in exchange for a percentage of the outstanding shares of stock in your company. More than likely, the investor will not see a dime on that money until the stock is sold, unless your company pays a dividend, which is unusual for a small startup company since cash is always at a premium. If your company is an S corporation, it is even possible that the investor may have to pay tax on income passed to him or her through the Schedule K-1 but not actually receive any cash. By the way, if the company goes under, the equity investment is lost, and the investor gets nothing in return for the initial risk. Now that is a sweet deal for an investor, isn't it? See Chapter 5 for a detailed discussion about the various business legal forms and their benefits.

For these reasons, equity investors will likely only give you money if they can see (and believe) that a relatively large return on their investment will come their way within a few years. This "relatively large" return is usually anywhere from between 5 and 50 times their investment per share. For example, if she pays you $1 per share of stock today, she will likely want to have a reasonable (not risk free) chance of receiving $5 or more in a few years or so. Venture capitalists will generally want to see a chance of 30 times or more from their investment within three to five years before they will take the plunge.

Equity investors will generally only invest money in a startup that they can afford to lose since they know the risk level is just that much higher. It is not quite like gambling, but it is close. If you have someone close to you who intends to invest his or her total savings as an equity investment, make sure that person completely understands the risk associated with the investment.

Company Stages and Funding

The *perceived risk* level associated with you and your company will change over time. In the early stages, the risk level is high since there is not a lot defined, which creates uncertainty, and your company has no performance track record. As that track record gets established, the perceived level of risk decreases, assuming that you create a good track record. This is why companies like IBM are perceived as less risky than your startup. This section tracks the various stages that your company will go through and that stage's relationship to funding requirements and risk.

Talking Business

Perceived risk is the risk assessment as seen through the eyes of the investor. You always want to be working to minimize the level of perceived risk on the part of the investor.

Seed Stage

As the name of this stage implies, your company is a kernel of an idea waiting to sprout. You have an idea and might have scratched a few notes on the back of a cocktail napkin, but that is really it. You may now need some money to free you up from your "day job" so that you can write a great business plan using the recommended steps outlined in this book. Those of you looking to develop a product-based business will likely create some type of prototype of the product at this stage. This could mean a mock-up of a website or a plastic model, or bread board, of a more complicated electronic product.

The risk level here is high, but the funding needs are likely pretty low. Many people fund this out of their own pockets or treat it as a part-time job, without pay, while they keep their regular job. This approach is particularly applicable to those of you looking to eventually break out of the "big house" of corporate America.

Startup Stage

Plan and prototype in hand, you are now ready to start making your company a reality. You start to hire key people, set up an office, and create preproduction prototypes as opposed to the mockups from the seed stage. You have likely also beta tested your idea to see if actual customers are interested in what you have to offer. All of this information helps to convince investors that your idea and company is worth some more money. This is a time when some venture capital firms may be interested in getting involved. Know that funding at this stage is critical, and it may take quite some time to find.

The risk is still high, although not as high as with the seed stage, and the financing requirements are still relatively modest although much greater than the seed stage. Many unknowns still exist that can squash the entire deal, but you now have some management success that works in your favor. Keep the faith and keep asking for that money. If the idea and your team are as solid as you think, someone will buy into your idea. Make sure that you conserve money as much as possible at this stage since it is a waiting game in that you have to last, financially, until you get your startup funding.

First Stage

By this stage, you have a real company, with a real product and real customers. You have bumped your head a few times, had some wins, and learned a lot along the way. Your plan has been adjusted from what you initially thought in the seed stage, and you are rapidly moving forward.

> ### Been There ... Done That
>
> The personal dynamics of first and second stage success can be pretty intoxicating. You may be the darling company that everyone wants a piece of and the talk of the town. People all over are asking you for a job, and they actually know your name. Keep your ego and aspirations in check. All this attention can get you believing that things are better than they are or that customers will now start sending you money in buckets just because you are you. It may all be true and if so, great. If it is not true, and you believe it to be true, you and your company could be in for a rude, and sometimes catastrophic, wakeup call. It is the adrenaline rush of the first and second stage that keeps Silicon Valley startup people coming back for more.

Risk is substantially reduced when compared to the earlier stages, but the funding needs increase again since you must add manufacturing personnel, inventory, advertising, sales force, and any number of other expensive capabilities. This is when you can really make the case to the venture capital folks assuming you have an idea that shows that type of large-industry merit. This is also a time when people around you will be seeing that you have something going that is working and want to get involved. Selling shares is now easier, and less expensive, than at any other time.

Second Stage

Now you are really into needing big money, and your need for effective cash flow management has never been more important. Revenues are growing in the high double-digits or higher, and cash float management has become almost an obsession.

Sales activity is soaring, and production demand is growing like a weed. If your company has adequate operating margins and effective cash management (prompt account receivable collection and attractive vendor payment terms), then you might be able to internally fund this stage. More than likely, you will be short on cash and need to have some cash in reserve to cover the deficiencies that arise from having to pay vendors and employees before, sometimes months before, you have received customer payments.

There are firms that specialize in providing this second round of financing. These firms not only provide investment capital but also offer expertise on managing this perilous stage. Risk is again reduced from the first stage because you have not only a history but also a future with respect to forecastable orders and expenses. Accounts receivable can be used to fund this cash shortage as can other methods covered in Chapter 16.

It is not uncommon for a company at this stage to sell additional shares as a way of obtaining equity funding, which does not increase the cash drain on the company yet provides an important infusion of cash. This cash is really a safety net that protects the company from serious cash shortfalls, decreasing stress on management and improving the likelihood of making it to the third stage. Equity funding is not as expensive to the company to obtain since the level of overall perceived risk to the investor is much lower than seen at prior stages.

Third Stage (Mezzanine)

Your company is now a well-oiled machine. Your employees know their jobs, your operational systems are in place, you have an established name in the marketplace, and you are developing the next generation of products and services that will take you into the future. You are hiring managers specifically oriented toward management of a larger company, standardizing offerings, and maybe even broadening to international markets.

This level is often called Mezzanine financing in that it is a growth and financing stage "between" (or bridging) two other levels: third and harvest. Management is now actively working on ways to foster the right environment within which they can harvest their prior work. This stage involves refining the company operation so that it appears as financially viable and profitable as possible, and laying the groundwork for having the share selling price seen at harvest be as high as possible. Financing obtained at this stage is usually for a relatively short period of time, and everyone knows that the next step is the harvest.

Harvest Stage—Exit Strategy

This is the stage when employees, founders, and early shareholders reap the benefits of their earlier investment. This stage can be the sale of the company to another group of investors or to another company, or the offering of stock in an initial public offering (IPO). The prior shareholders offer their shares for sale and take the money, often making very large sums of money in the process. If a company does a public offering, it will likely sell shares over and above those already outstanding as a way of filling the company's cash coffers while providing a way for the prior shareholders to cash in on their investment. Now your startup is a real live, mature company that must carve a life for itself as an adult. It is a player in the marketplace. The shareholders who sell their shares "exit" the company and are no longer shareholders even though they may still be employees.

This is a time of management, employee, and focus change when leadership skills are incredibly important. Keeping now-wealthy shareholders focused on creating the next level of company success is not always an easy task. There is a big party on the day that the harvest transaction becomes final, but everyone still must come to work the next day to get on with it.

Know How Much Money You Will Need

Now that you have a solid idea about risk, reward, and company growth stages, you need to determine the amount of money you will need. In many ways, the business planning process is designed to help you determine a credible estimate of this cash requirement. The financials associated with your plan are discussed in Chapter 15. The following sections will help you frame the requirements that dictate much of your detailed financial planning.

Will You Make Money?

Before jumping in with both feet, wouldn't it be nice if you could get a better idea of whether your business will succeed? Yes, I've heard that fortunetellers can be helpful, but how about some basic financial analyses? Don't worry; you don't have to be an accountant to do this stuff.

Enthusiasm, skill, and guts will take you far, but combining these traits with cash will get you much closer to the brass ring. The reality is that *service businesses* (those that offer services such as accounting, consulting, or massage) generally cost less to start than *product businesses* (those that offer products, such as computers, clothes, or widgets). You could start a dog-walking company on little money as long as you keep your expenses on a short leash. (Sorry; the pun was too good to resist.) Seriously, though, leashes, collars, a phone line, and business cards are all you need to get into your own dog-walking business.

On the other hand, starting a product business often requires major machinery and equipment, office space, employees, and more. Maybe a lot more. Each of these items translates into more dollars and more delay before sales start rolling in.

Due to this fact of life, many companies start as service businesses and move on to include products as their cash and sales situation improves. For example, a computer programmer can start by offering software consulting (a service) and eventually develop and sell his or her own software programs (a product). Starting on a small budget doesn't mean you necessarily have to stay small, but it does help to keep expenses down when sales are lower.

Talking Business

A **product-based business** is a company that makes money by selling products that are either developed and manufactured by the company or purchased by the company for resale. Wal-Mart is an example of a product-based business. **Service-based businesses** are companies that make money by selling services, rather than products, provided by employees or contractors. Examples include doctors, consultants, and house cleaners.

How Much Can You Give Up and When Do You Make It Back?

You don't have to have millions of dollars to start a business—far from it. Many people start small, often on a part-time basis, spreading their money between living expenses and business startup costs. Other business owners get loans for thousands and thousands of dollars. For example, some fast-food franchises cost more than $100,000 just to open.

You have to decide for yourself how much money you are willing and able to set aside to start your business. It may be less than a thousand dollars, or it may be much more. Everyone's situation is different. Just be aware that the type or size of business you start may be somewhat limited by the amount of money you have available or can reasonably obtain from others. Don't expect to start a restaurant with just a couple thousand dollars, for example; it's highly unlikely that you could afford to pay for everything you need. Even if you were able to squeak by the first month, you may be jeopardizing your future by not having enough money to fall back on.

It All Comes Down to Numbers

Only by estimating how much money you can make and how much it will cost to run your business will you know whether you should continue to pursue your dream. If there is no money to be made by starting the business, then you should drop the idea. Although there are probably several reasons why you want to start your own business, the first and foremost must be that you expect to make money at it. Otherwise it is a hobby, not a business.

What's Your Potential?

Let's compare the long-term earning potential of product versus service businesses. Although a service business is less expensive to start, it is also harder to grow into a larger company. Why? Simple. Every night when your employees go home, your company stops earning money. The time your employees spend on customer work is how you make money. When they're sleeping, they're not billing your customers. Your company's growth is limited by the number of hours you and your employees can bill in a day.

A product business, on the other hand, can make money as long as it has products on hand. You can sell 20 products on Monday and 500 on Tuesday and work your equipment extra hard Tuesday night to manufacture more products to sell on Wednesday. While you sleep, your equipment is still churning out more products.

> **Smoke Signals**
>
> When calculating how much money you need to start your business, you must include the cost of your personal living expenses during the startup phase. You will start to resent the business if you find yourself lacking a decent meal several nights in a row. This can cloud your judgment and significantly dampen your enthusiasm. It happens.

Also, services are usually sold and provided by a set group of people (your employees). Products, on the other hand, can be sold through several different channels, such as retail stores, mail-order catalogs, and telemarketing.

Starting small, such as with a service orientation, can help to reduce your startup expenses. Later you can add products to your company's mix, when you have the money available to support it. But when you're first starting out, you need to be sure you have enough money to start up and sustain your company for at least a year.

To estimate the total startup costs of your company, determine how much money you need to start the business (cumulative cash flow) and how much money you need to pay yourself during that time to cover your basic living expenses. For example, if the business requires $50,000 in cumulative cash flow to start and you need $48,000 to cover your personal living expenses until the company is on its feet, then the initial investment required is $98,000, not $50,000.

Don't scale your living expenses to the bone when you estimate these costs because, if for some reason sales are slower to appear than anticipated, you don't want to be out of business just as things start to pick up. If no additional money is available, then the initial $98,000 could be lost just as the company is getting off the ground. Once you've already received one loan to get the company started, it is even tougher to go back to your investors and ask for just a little more to keep you going. Make sure you can cover your living expenses for several months, and give yourself some leeway.

It is either your money or your investors' money that funds the business. It will definitely be your time, and time is also worth money. Professional investors require a formal business plan before they will invest. Even if you don't need outside financing because you have the cash to invest yourself, be as serious about evaluating the opportunity as any investor would be. That is the reason you are reading this book and should work your way through all of the later chapters that deal with writing a credible business plan. Make sure that this is an investment you believe is going to pay off for you.

What else could you be doing with your money? How could it be spent if not working to start your business? All those other ways that you could have spent your money is what the financial pros call the *opportunity cost* of starting your business. Investors frequently look at situations in terms of opportunity cost: What other investment options are they giving up by investing their money here, rather than there? If the return from your business idea is lower than their next-best option, then they will not give you the money.

Talking Business

Cumulative cash flow is the total amount of cash needed to handle the sum of all month-to-month negative cash flow (loss) experienced until the company starts to make a monthly profit. **Opportunity cost** is the profit that you could have gained by pursuing another investment instead of the one you currently have.

Basic Types of Funding

Without funding, your business idea will go nowhere. You must find a way to support the business and you while it grows into a profitable, self-sustaining entity. Here is an overview of the various funding methods and how they may apply to your particular situation. Think of this as an a-la-carte menu from which you can select as needed to create the funding meal that is right for your situation.

Typical Funding Action Sequence

Here are few steps that will likely happen independent of your selected method of funding:

◆ Determine what you want to do and how much it will cost to do it.

◆ Prepare a business case of some kind that provides a prospective investor (even if it is you) with a justification for making the investment.

◆ Put the word out to the appropriate people that you are looking for funding.

◆ Meet with prospective investors and present your case and funding need request.

◆ Give them some time, along with a desired decision deadline, to verify what you have told them.

◆ Get your money or find out why this investment is not right for them at this time. Say "thank you" either way.

◆ Report to investors on a periodic basis (quarterly and annually is usually a minimum) about the performance of the company and the state of their investment.

◆ Always be on the lookout for people who can provide your next required level of funding.

As the top manager of your company, one primary responsibility is to ensure that the company has the money it needs to not only survive but also to capitalize on its next level of opportunity. This is an ongoing, never-stopping process, so just accept the fact that it is now part of your management landscape.

Funding Out of Your Own Pocket

Depending on the size of your new venture, you may be able to fund the early stages out of your own savings. If nothing else, you should plan to pay for your own living expenses for at least the first six months of business operation. If you can afford it, then you might consider funding the cumulative cash requirement as well since that way you don't have to go through a committee to make changes to the plan. You are the committee.

It all depends on how much you can afford to put into the venture and your living expenses before hitting your pain threshold or, even worse, your destruction threshold. Here are a few words of advice I hope you take to heart before using your own money:

◆ Don't cut your estimated need too close, or a cost overrun of some type or a slower sales rampup could put you in a cash crunch.

- Make sure that your significant other(s) all buy into your using the money for this purpose, or you could really feel pressure later on when it will be the least appreciated.

- If you are younger, you might be able to use a larger percentage of your nest egg, but those of you closer to retirement (50+) should be a little more conservative. After all, you don't have 25 years to make it back before retiring, do you?

- Ideally try to only use money that you can afford to lose. If the amount required will use all of your nest egg, then you might consider bringing in investors even if on the surface it doesn't look like you will need them. Sleepless nights over losing everything because a major client defaults on a receivable is a terrible way to live. Trust me on this one or check it out with someone who has already been through it.

Some people use the equity in their home to fund their business. This might also be a solid approach, as equity lines of credit are offered at very low interest rates and you can always sell your house to pay off the debt if the worst happens to your business. You don't get back the equity or money put into the business, but you at least aren't in debt if you end up closing your doors.

Been There ... Done That

Those of you starting a corporation might consider taking out an equity line of credit on your house at, say, 4 percent interest only and then lending that money to your corporation at some reasonable market rate of 7 percent or so, amortized over a 5 year period. (Check with a bank on this rate.) The company gets the cash, and you get to make 3 percent on your home equity while your house appreciates at housing market rates. Make sure that you execute a loan agreement just as you would if you were lending the money to a third-party company to keep the IRS happy.

Finally, there are people who start their companies using credit card financing. This is pretty expensive, even by today's credit card rate standards. Plus, once you run up your credit cards, where do you go to charge those daily items that will definitely be required? I have done this before and got myself in trouble in that I was making minimum payments instead of paying off the whole thing (Heck. The payment was just to me anyway, right?) I strongly recommend that you not take the credit card route unless the amount you need to start with is low enough that you could pay it off in a few months if things didn't go well. Otherwise, I fear that you might dig yourself into a credit charge hole that is difficult for some, and impossible for others, to dig out of.

Brother, Can You Spare a Dime?—Family Funding

Family and friend funding is a double-edged sword: (1) family may feel more inclined to help with your business idea because of a personal need to help you out, (2) they may have faith in you because they know you (or the opposite could be true for the same reason), and (3) they may hold it against you for years to come if the business fails, taking their investment with it. Can business be done with family members? Absolutely. It happens all the time. Should you be overly cautious when dealing with friends and family as potential investors? Absolutely, again. It is one thing to lose an investor. It is something altogether different to create a rift with a good friend or family member that causes serious strain to this important relationship.

> **Talking Business**
>
> **Angel investors** are people, or groups of people, who invest in ventures that nobody else wants to touch. They are willing to take the risk for any number of personal and professional reasons, such as helping the local community, working with women to get started, or helping recent high school graduates become financially independent.

I have a tendency to go overboard on disclosure when dealing with friends and family. My belief is that I can always find another investor, but it will be difficult to replace this personal relationship. If they still want to be involved after all the disclosure, which essentially tries to talk them out of it, then so be it. At least everyone's eyes were open. Also, make sure that you execute the same documents (such as loan agreements) with friends as you would with a third party. This is still a business arrangement and should be treated as such. Even (especially?) with family and friends.

Venture Capital—May Not Be for Everybody

Venture capital (VC) is a term that was bantered around a lot in the late 1990s as one Silicon Valley startup after another got funded, grew, almost became profitable (sometimes), and then went public. Who are these venture capital people, and how do you get some of their money?

First, the venture capital market today is much different from what it was in the booming 1990s. The tech-wreck of the past few years shook many of these firms to their core, and they are now far more conservative. Plus, your venture has to meet certain requirements before a VC firm will typically even look at it.

◆ Your initial investment amount should be at least $500,000, or it is not worth the time and money to investigate.

♦ You and your management team must be top-notch since the VC invests in you first and the idea second. These people know that large amounts of money behind a great team with a hot product in a growing market will strain the seams of the company and its management personnel. They want seasoned people at the helm who know how to responsibly manage this type of growth.

♦ The business plan must show that the VC can make at least 25 times their initial investment within a 5-year period or less, or they will not likely fund the company.

Listen Up

Run the numbers and see what has to happen to a company's value to meet the VC valuation increase requirement. Assume the $500K in VC funding buys 25 percent of the company. This puts the initial company value at $2 million (4 x $500k). Thirty times that value is $60 million in market valuation within 5 years. Possible? Sure. Easy to do? Not usually.

♦ Venture capital funds like to work with companies that have an existing marketplace, workable (or proven) product, and are credible so that the provided money enables rapid expansion. VC-funded companies are always racing the clock, so time is scarce and rapid sales growth essential.

Just on these points alone, particularly the required company valuation growth, most smaller businesses will not qualify for venture capital funding.

Agency Guaranteed Bank Funding

In today's tougher business climate, state and federal agencies have put together special guaranteed loan programs. The general theme is that the public agency guarantees the loan to the lender who evaluates and processes the loan for you, the entrepreneur and borrower. If you default, the agency pays the lender for the lost loan. The intent of these programs is some type of greater economic good to the community such as promoting small business growth as a way of stimulating the economy and increasing employment. Don't be afraid to talk to your banker about possible programs that would apply to your situation not only today but also as you grow and become more stable. Perhaps you can personally fund the company until it is large enough to qualify for one of these types of loans.

SBA and Governmental Program Realities

Without question, you should get to know the programs provided by the Small Business Administration (SBA). This is particularly true if you plan to purchase property as part of your business operation. SBA programs change, so I will not go into detail on any particular program here. Historically, SBA funding of nonproperty has been fairly restrictive, but there are rumors of the new and improved SBA being more accommodating to the realistic needs of the newer small business. The website is your best bet for initial information (www.sba.gov), but also look around your area for financial institutions that are SBA-approved to see if they can help you find and qualify for a loan that is right for your particular business.

Finally, don't overlook any leverage that you may have in qualifying for a special governmental program. This leverage may come from your being a woman, a member of a minority race, your geographic location, industry, age, education, income bracket, military background, or any number of other criteria. It never ceases to amaze me at the number of programs that the various governmental agencies offer. Someplace, somewhere, with patience and tons of paperwork, you might be able to find some funding for yourself.

Stock Sales (Not an IPO ... Sorry)

One reason to incorporate is to be able to sell stock for funding purposes. Notice that a stock sale makes the shareholders owners of the corporation, and you do not need to repay their stock investment. They are taking a risk with their investment and get a say in the company operation in exchange. Taking out a loan still keeps the company 100 percent under your ownership and control, but you have to repay the debt. These shareholders now own a portion of the company. This is called equity financing or equity funding.

Equity funding is obtained through three basic means: selling shares of stock to private investors, selling shares of stock to professional investors such as venture capitalists, and "going public," which involves selling shares to the general public on one of the stock exchanges. You will initially deal with the first two financing options and, if you are successful and lucky, eventually have the opportunity to go public, which is beyond the scope of this book.

Selling shares of stock looks pretty good on the surface: You sell a portion of the company in exchange for some cash. All you give up is a little ownership in the company to get the cash you need. What is the down side? As usual, it comes down to whom you choose as your investors.

The more sophisticated the investor, the better an ally he or she will make down the road. A professional investor knows the pitfalls associated with running a business and can guide you through potential minefields. However, professional investors also tend to be demanding and relatively heartless when you do not perform as expected. From their perspective, not living up to your plan indicates a lack of business control. A professional investor will take you to task if needed because he or she has a vested interest in your success.

Listen Up

Needing advice on how to take your successful company public with an IPO is what my brother would term a "high class problem." If you eventually get to that stage, make sure that you carefully pick your partners on that important journey and be thankful you have that opportunity.

Your Uncle Billy, on the other hand, might not need monthly reports from you on your progress and might purchase your company's stock on his faith in your ability alone. This makes getting your initial funding easier but might hurt you down the road. Suppose that the company has a rough quarter, for reasons that are out of your control, such as a flood or war. Billy might not understand why that dividend check you promised didn't arrive. He might not understand why you need more money due to unforeseen circumstances. In fact, Billy might not have deep enough pockets to fund the next round of investing.

In fact, the optimal investor might be another company with services or products that complement your offering. This other company might buy a certain percentage of your company's shares to provide a legal link between that organization and yours. This not only provides you with cash but also allows you to partner with them on a tighter basis when approaching the marketplace. (See my book, *The Complete Idiot's Guide to Buying and Selling a Business*, for additional detailed information on this important topic.)

Never knowingly involve someone in your business that you do not trust. You will be busy enough worrying about expanding your business; you do not need someone questioning your every move and undermining what you do. Stall, work harder, cut expenses, and play with cash float before getting involved with an investor who might be a potential headache.

Ultimately, it is your job to increase the value of the shareholders' investments. You can do this by improving the company's sales while decreasing the cost of making those sales. In short, your job is to make the company more profitable from one year to the next. If the profit that the investors see is not substantially greater than what they could get from other investments such as the stock market or bonds, then why should they invest in you? Your job is to give them a better return on their investment than they could receive with traditional methods.

Seller Financing

If you plan to purchase an existing company, you may find that the seller is willing to finance a portion of the purchase price. This is sort of like a house seller taking a second note on the purchase with the bank being in first position. In this case, the seller might be the primary lender and you make monthly payments to him instead of to the bank. There is something to be said for this approach since it keeps the seller interested in the business's success and gives him an incentive to work with you to make it successful. A successful business after purchase is a win for everyone.

Ethics and Funding

It is really hard to overemphasize the importance of keeping your ethics intact when looking for investors. People might take a chance on an idea that they feel is risky but has merit. Few people will give money to someone that they don't trust. If you find yourself wanting to shade the truth, take a deep breath and ponder the ramifications of what you are about to do. If you are found out, the impact on your business could be devastating, not to mention the impact on your relationship with this investor. Plus, it really is a pretty small world out there. The word will get out that you cannot be trusted, and it will take you forever to regain your good name.

In summary, fabricating information is not a very sound sales strategy when looking for funding. Plus, if you need to lie to get the money, perhaps you are trying to fund the wrong idea. The facts in your business plan should speak for themselves if presented professionally—the way you are taught in this book. Do your work up front and watch the investors convince themselves that your idea is one worth funding.

For Your Plan

Here are a few points that must be included in your business plan related to your need and request for funding:

♦ First, outline how you came up with the amounts that you are trying to fund. This will involve financial analysis and some explanation about the underlying assumptions associated with the analysis.

♦ Explain why you are structuring your funding requirements as you are with respect to the use of debt and equity funding.

♦ If you already have investors, provide that information in your plan to include their relative percentage ownership.

- Outline what the projected harvested return would be for an investor who gets in now. Make sure that everyone knows that these numbers are *not guaranteed* but are simply estimates. Explain how that harvesting is expected to happen, such as sale of company, merger, IPO, and so on, and in what time frame.

- Tell how the funds will be used and how the investors will be kept informed about fund usage and progress toward the achievement of outlined business goals.

The Least You Need to Know

- Debt funding must be paid back but is less expensive.

- Equity funding requires that you give up company ownership but also does not require that you make payments.

- Venture capital funding is usually only right for a small group of startup ventures.

- Banks don't typically lend to risky ventures.

- Funding requirements, and perceived investor risk, vary with the stage of company growth.

Part 2

Matching Your Plan to a Legal Structure

Now that you have an idea of what you want to accomplish with your business, you need to make some decisions about its legal structure. Some people start a business and never incorporate. Others incorporate first thing. Still others simply hang out a sign and start selling stuff.

I included an entire chapter that deals with the special issues related to corporations. The reason that people approach the process of incorporating very differently is that there are a lot of things to consider. From taxes, to liability, to taxes, to raising money, to taxes … there are many things to think about. In this section, you can figure out what kind of business structure might be best for you, as well as receive some tips on setting up a corporation, if that is what you choose to do. Did I mention anything about taxes?

Picking a Business Type

In This Chapter

- The difference between sole proprietorships, partnerships, and corporations
- The legal implications of each type of business structure
- How taxes affect each kind of business
- The type of business structure that is right for you

Bill shouted, "What do you mean I could lose everything I own? I didn't even know Ted bought that equipment for the company."

"The problem is that you never incorporated as you planned, and the law treats the two of you as a partnership," replied the attorney. "Under the law, you are responsible for the company obligations whether you agreed to them or not."

"No way," shouted Bill. "I'm not going to pay. Let them go after Ted first."

"The equipment company will first go after the business and then you and Ted at the same time. As far as the law is concerned, you and Ted are both equally liable for paying off the debt. Sorry, but you have no choice. Next time, pick your partners more carefully and consider incorporating to avoid this situation again."

Bill didn't like it, but he accepted what he heard as the truth. How could his life savings and a thriving company take a dive so quickly based on the irresponsible actions of one person? What could he have done differently? How could he have known?

Just as one house style does not meet the living requirements of all families, no single business structure meets everyone's business needs. Depending on your current situation and future business aspirations, one business structure might meet those needs better than another. Take the time to determine where you want the company to go not only in the next few months but over the next few years, at least. A long-term perspective helps you decide on the best structure for your specific situation. In this chapter, I review the different legal business structures and discuss the pros and cons of each one.

You should use this chapter as a general starting point. Understand the information presented and then apply it to your situation. This is your homework portion of the process. You should then run your assessment by the proper legal and accounting professionals to ensure that you are on the right track and to help set you up properly for your particular situation. Try to avoid the temptation to "go it alone" at this stage, because an error regarding your company's structure can have serious business, personal, and tax consequences later on.

An Overview of the Various Business Structures

The three basic business organizational structures are *sole proprietorships*, *partnerships*, and *corporations*. Under each category are subclasses that apply to specific situations.

A *sole proprietorship* is the most common and easiest type of business to create. Anyone who performs services of any kind, such as a gardener, caterer, or even baby-sitter, is by default a sole proprietor unless he or she takes specific action to set it up otherwise. A small company with only one employee is often kept as a sole proprietorship, but there are no restrictions on how big a sole proprietorship can become. It depends exclusively on the desires of the owner, or *proprietor*. The majority of small businesses in the United States are sole proprietorships.

A *general partnership* is formed whenever two or more people decide to enter a for-profit business venture. Typically, each partner owns a portion of the company's profits and debts, which can be set up in a written agreement among the partners. You do not need to file any special paperwork to form a partnership, but you should make sure you and your partners sign an agreement to minimize misunderstandings regarding each person's rights and liabilities. If you do not have an agreement signed by all parties, then any partnership-related disputes are handled under statutes based on the Uniform Partnership Act (UPA) used in most states. Most larger bookstores carry books that cover creating partnerships for your particular state. These books are inexpensive and helpful in making sure that you and your partners dot the right i's and cross the right t's. Once you have done the grunt work using both the book and the forms included on the companion CD, I suggest that you present it to an attorney to make sure all of the proper legal lingo is included and that everyone's interests are protected.

Corporations are often treated as an indicator of how serious you are about being in business since it is more involved and more expensive to set up a corporation than to set up a sole proprietorship or partnership.

When you form a *corporation*, you actually establish a separate organization—separate and distinct from you personally. Some of you may ask why that's such a big deal; what's the advantage? A primary advantage is that if the corporation is sued, you are not personally responsible for any damages that might be awarded (unless, of course, you are also named in the suit, which can always happen—corporation or not). This aspect of corporations provides you with limited liability. Paperwork and record-keeping is also more involved with a corporation, which is why some people decide it's not worth the hassles. You may also find it more advantageous from a tax perspective to be incorporated, which can completely separate your personal and business income. If you are not careful with how you handle the administrative aspects of your corporation, you can lose your limited liability protection, so do it right to avoid unwelcome surprises later.

Talking Business

A **corporation** is a separate legal entity created through the state where the business is incorporated. A corporation has owners who purchase shares in the corporation. A properly organized corporation bears all legal and fiscal liability, typically shielding shareholders (owners) from personal risk (unless they are also sued personally or they guarantee corporate obligations).

Corporations are legal entities created through the states where the business is incorporated. A corporation is created by owners who purchase shares in the corporation. The percentage of ownership of each shareholder is based on the number of shares owned by that shareholder compared to the total number of shares issued or outstanding.

Many corporations are formed in the state of Delaware because of its less restrictive incorporation laws. Delaware was one of the early states to allow you to incorporate while conducting business and keeping headquarters in another state. Most other states now allow the same procedure. Realize, however, that if you incorporate in Delaware and then operate in Illinois, for example, you will have to register your corporation with the state of Illinois, and now you have two states to deal with instead of one, which takes away from the Delaware incorporation benefits. Naturally, if you live in Delaware, that is where you would most likely incorporate.

It is important to understand that the various business structures have their own sets of tax-related problems and benefits, which are outlined throughout this chapter and in the next chapter that deals with detailed corporation considerations.

Just remember that the best business structure is the one that provides the required level of legal and tax protection along with enough flexibility to address future financial needs. This is a tricky balancing act that requires attention on your part.

Select the business structure that is right for you based on where you are today and where you want to wind up down the road. Consider the advantages and disadvantages of each business structure before making a decision.

Sole Proprietorship: Going It Alone

Judy woke up this morning and decided to begin selling those little wooden dolls she makes and gives away every Christmas. She just became the head of a sole proprietorship.

Once you begin providing and receiving money for products or services, you become a sole proprietor. Your business expenses are deductible, all income is taxable, and you assume the liabilities of the business. (More on the tax implications later.)

Notice that Judy did not have to create a separate name to start her business. She simply started her business and began selling her product, using her own name. This is why the sole proprietorship is such a popular business structure.

However, if Judy wants to call her business "Dolls and Such," she must file a Doing Business As (d/b/a) form with the local authorities, usually the county clerk's office in the area where she plans to do business. The d/b/a filing is sometimes called a *tradename*, a *fictitious name statement*, or an *also known as (a.k.a.)*. If no one else is using the name she chooses, after filing her d/b/a form, Judy can transact business as "Dolls and Such." Filing the d/b/a gives her legal rights to the name within the jurisdiction of the governing body, which is typically the county. If someone else later uses the name within the county, Judy can ask

the courts to order that person to cease operations under the name she legally owns. The
other business is then forced to rename itself.
Notice that this name registration is only for
the county and not for the state, which could
hurt Judy if she branches out to do business
in other parts of the state. A corporation's
name applies statewide.

On the CD

A sample Assumed Business Name
Certificate is included on the
companion CD as document 5-1.

A sole proprietorship is easy and inexpensive to create, and all profits go directly to
the owner. The major disadvantage is that all legal and financial obligations incurred
by the company are also passed directly to the owner. That means that if the company
is sued for any reason, such as if a child eats one of Judy's dolls and is hospitalized,
Judy is personally responsible for answering that lawsuit. Judy could lose everything
she personally owns if the business-related lawsuit is lost and the damages are high.
For this liability reason alone, many people choose to change their structure from a
sole proprietorship to a corporation.

Being a sole proprietorship does not limit whether you have employees, although
many sole proprietorships are one-person businesses. You can hire employees as a sole
proprietorship, but you, as the owner, become the target for any claims made against
the business as a result of any of the actions of your employees. You must apply for an

employer identification number (EIN) just as
a corporation does since this is the IRS's
tracking mechanism for employers. (See
Chapter 14 for details on obtaining an EIN.)
Oddly enough, you as the owner are not an
employee of the company even though you
draw a salary. Who said that IRS regulations
had to make sense! You file your sole proprietorship business taxes on Schedule C of
your personal Form 1040 tax return.

Talking Business

A fictitious name state-
ment, also known as a tradename, Doing Business As, or
d/b/a form, allows you to run a
business using a name other than
your own. The official name for
the filing form itself may vary from
one locality to another. You might
also use "a.k.a." (also known as)
when referring to a fictitious name.

The flexibility associated with being the only
owner is often attractive enough to keep people in business as a sole proprietorship, even
after the company grows large in revenues.

Partnership: A Business Marriage

Partnership is a wonderful term that evokes warm, comforting feelings. Who wouldn't
want a partner to share the good and bad times in a business? Well, if you have ever
been in a bad relationship, you know the damage it can do to your psychological and

On the CD _____

A sample Partnership Agreement (document 05-02) and sample Partnership Minutes (document 05-03) are included on the companion CD.

On the CD _____

A sample Limited Partnership Organizing Checklist (document 05-04), Limited Partnership Agreement (document 05-05), Limited Partnership Certificate (document 05-06), Limited Partnership Consent Resolution in Lieu of First Meeting of Partners (document 05-07), and Limited Partnership Minutes (document 05-08) are included on the companion CD.

financial well-being. You should treat business partnerships with the same amount of respect. Your personal partner may move the ketchup from the pantry to the refrigerator, but your business partner can bankrupt you, which is a way bigger problem than cold ketchup.

When two or more people form a partnership, they are essentially married, from a business standpoint. Either party can obligate the other via the business, and everything the business and the partners own individually is on the line. In essence, a partnership is like a sole proprietorship owned by several people. All liability is passed to the partners.

A special partnership type, called a _limited partnership_, provides certain partners with a maximum financial liability equal to their investment. To maintain this limited financial liability status, these partners, called _limited partners_, cannot participate in the daily operation of the business. The _general partner_ is responsible for the day-to-day management of the business. Limited partners invest in the company and rely on the general partner to run the business.

Talking Business _____

In a limited partnership, some partners (called **limited partners**) invest money but do not participate in the daily operation of the business. They are liable only for the amount of money that they each have invested. A **general partner** is responsible for the daily operations of the business.

A **limited liability partnership (LLP)** is a special type of partnership that is created by a special filing with the state where the partners operate. Partners other than the general partner who are part of an LLP protect their personal assets from being taken if the partnership gets into financial trouble. There is really no reason not to become an LLP.

Special laws govern the operation of a limited partnership, and if they are not precisely followed, the courts might hold that the partnership was general, not limited. The formerly limited partner might find himself as liable as a general partner for business-related debts. Be aware that you must complete and file special paperwork with the state to form a limited partnership.

Corporations: Share the Wealth

Creating a corporation is like creating a new business life. A corporation is a separate and distinct business entity that is responsible for itself. Upon formation, the corporation issues shares of stock to *shareholders*, the owners. The shareholders exchange money, goods, or services to receive their shares of stock. Shareholders are, in essence, transacting business with this fictitious legal entity called a corporation and not with "real" people, per se. If you plan to start a corporation, it is absolutely imperative that you keep the difference between you and the corporation straight. Beware, however, that stock obtained from contributing an item or cash is tax free but the IRS considers stock obtained from providing a service to the corporation as income and is subject to payroll taxes. You see, the IRS never sleeps.

 On the CD _____

A sample Limited Liability Partnership Organizing Checklist (document 05-09), Limited Liability Partnership Agreement (document 05-10), Limited Liability Partnership Registration (document 05-11), and Limited Liability Partnership Consent Resolution in Lieu of First Meeting of Partners (document 05-12) are included on the companion CD.

A *board of directors*, elected by the shareholders, manages the corporation. This board then appoints *officers* of the corporation to handle the day-to-day affairs of the company. In essence, the board members represent the interests of the shareholders in the company operations. Depending on the state in which the business is incorporated, the business owner in many small corporations may be the primary, or only, shareholder and only board member. This same person is listed as the president, secretary, and treasurer of the corporation.

The corporation pays taxes on its annual profits and passes the profits to the shareholders in the form of *dividends*. The board of directors determines the amount of the dividends.

Talking Business _____

In a corporation, **shareholders,** or stockholders, own a percentage of the business, expressed in terms of the number of shares of stock they own in relation to the total number of shares issued. The corporation is managed by employees who take their overall direction from a corporation's **board of directors.** Annual profits are passed on to shareholders in the form of dividends, although annual dividend payments are not mandatory. The amount of the dividends is determined by the board of directors. Corporation **officers** have the ability to legally commit the corporation, whereas standard employees have limited commitment ability, if any.

The major benefit associated with a corporate business form is that the corporation is liable for its own financial and civil liabilities. The shareholders risk only the amount of money they have invested in their respective shares of stock. This is referred to as limited liability.

Using the earlier "Dolls and Such" example, assume that the business is a corporation with $500,000 in its bank account. If someone were to win a judgment against "Dolls and Such" for $1 million, the company would probably go out of business, and only $500,000 would change hands. The person who won the legal judgment against the corporation would have no immediate legal basis for getting money from the shareholders personally.

Listen Up

Liability issues can also be addressed through insurance, so while limited liability is one reason to choose a corporate form of organization, check with knowledgeable advisors before making a final decision.

However, this is not the case with a partnership or sole proprietorship. As a partner or sole proprietor, your personal finances are put squarely at risk in this scenario, and you could lose a lifetime of work. You might end up owing an additional $500,000 to the judgment holder if that situation ever came to pass.

Another major corporate benefit involves raising money for the business by selling shares in the corporation. Once the buyer and seller agree to a price per share of stock, the buyer simply purchases the number of shares needed to equal the amount of money to be exchanged. For instance, assume you need to raise $100,000. If you find a buyer who is willing to pay you $4 per share, then you sell that person 25,000 shares of stock to receive the $100,000. Life is rarely this simple, but this example outlines the basic benefit associated with corporation finances.

On the CD

A sample Corporation Checklist for Offering Memorandum for Investors (document 05-13), Corporation Subscription Questionnaire (document 05-14), Corporation Investor Letter (document 05-15), and Promissory Note (document 05-16) are included on the companion CD.

To further illustrate the point, assume you still need $100,000 but don't know anyone with that kind of money on hand. Instead of selling 25,000 shares at $4 each to one person, you could sell 2,500 shares to 10 different investors for $4 each and still get the money you need. You now have 10 shareholders instead of 1, but you got the money you needed. This approach is often more attractive to investors in that they can share in your success but do not have to risk more money than they can afford to lose. Forming a corporation is the route to take if you eventually plan to sell a large amount of stock to a number of different people.

Public or Private?

There is a difference between a publicly held and privately held corporation. Publicly held corporations are traded on the various public stock exchanges, such as the New York Stock Exchange, American Stock Exchange, and NASDAQ. The shareholders are typically large numbers of people who never come in direct contact with each other. They trust the board of directors to manage their investments for them.

Privately held, or *close*, corporations are more common. The shares are held by a few people, often family members, who also sit on the board and participate as officers of the corporation. The shares are also not offered to the general public.

Talking Business

A **close corporation,** or privately held corporation, is owned by a small number of shareholders, often only one. In this case, the corporation may be viewed as an extension of the individual. You must still act as a corporation with separate checking accounts, loans, finances, and various corporate legal notifications and documents in proper order. I know it seems kind of silly to do all this if you are the only shareholder, but if you want to maintain the corporate benefits, then this is a necessary burden you just have to do.

Unless you are planning to create a very large business, you will probably create and continue to be a privately held corporation. It is generally easier to form a small or close corporation in the state where the principal shareholders reside and work. Because state tax laws vary, be sure to check with an accountant before making this decision.

If the number of shareholders exceeds 75, you must comply with the *Securities and Exchange Commission (SEC)* regulations for publicly offered companies. You will definitely need legal and accounting services if you plan to sell shares of stock to more than 75 people as part of your investment fundraising activities.

When a company "goes public," it offers to sell shares in the company to the general public. This is a common way for the founding members of a company to make (harvest) oodles of money from the large numbers of

Talking Business

The **Securities and Exchange Commission (SEC)** regulates public offerings of company securities. The SEC mandates strict guidelines for the dissemination and content of company financial information to help assure investors that the information they receive on public companies is reliable and reasonably comprehensive.

stock shares they received during the startup stages. The founders often buy or receive this stock at the outset for a nominal price, sometimes pennies per share. When the company goes public, the shares might sell for dollars per share. You don't need to be a CPA to figure out that several hundred thousand shares sold at a public offering can add up to a lot of money. This opportunity alone keeps many people actively working for startup companies, in spite of higher risks, instead of working for larger, more stable companies.

Subchapter S-Corporations: A Little Bit of Protection

Suppose you want the legal protection provided by a corporation but want the income to pass directly to you that you can declare it on your personal income tax statement. You can thank the IRS and Congress because they created the *subchapter S-corporation* for just this purpose.

On the CD _____

A sample Cover Letter to IRS for S-Corporation Election (form 2553) is included on the companion CD as document 05-17.

Talking Business _____

A *subchapter S* or *S-corporation* is a type of corporation with few shareholders. All profits are passed directly to the owners and taxed as income, which avoids double taxation. For this reason, the S-corporation is often called a "pass through entity." **Double taxation,** being taxed on income at both the corporate and personal levels, is avoided with the S-corporation.

In a subchapter S or "S-corporation," instead of the corporation paying taxes on its income, the business income is passed to the shareholders, who then declare the income on their personal income tax statements. Subchapter S-corporations retain all the legal protection provided by a standard C-corporation (any corporation that is not converted into an S-corporation).

Why opt for the S instead of C-corporation? If you are personally in a lower tax bracket than the corporation, then passing the business income to you decreases the overall taxes paid. In addition, if the corporation loses money, you can use that loss to offset personal income earned from other investments you may have up to certain limits. You can also avoid *double taxation* if you use an S-corporation, which can have a welcome tax-reduction effect around April 15 of each year. However, if you don't plan properly or if the company does better than you expected, you can find yourself with a huge personal tax bill at the end of the year because of the great performance of your S-corporation.

If you think the S-corporation is right for you, check with an accountant and an attorney before taking the plunge. A little prevention goes a long way to avoid unforeseen problems down the road. Notice that the decision is heavily based on how much revenue and net income that you anticipate the company will generate. This is why the strategic planning aspects of business are so critically important.

To form an S-corporation, you first incorporate as you would any corporation, and then file IRS Form 2553 to establish your S-corporation tax status.

Limited Liability Company (LLC)

How would you like the advantages of a corporation or partnership without some of the restrictions regarding shareholders? That's what a *limited liability company* (*LLC*) can provide.

Limited liability companies are now authorized in all 50 states. The reason for their new popularity is that LLCs provide business owners, called members, with personal liability protection, just as corporations do, and still provide tax profits at the individual level only, as subchapter S-corporations do. The LLC is also a pass-through entity.

What sets LLCs apart from the popular S-corporations is that LLCs do not have the traditional restrictions regarding the number of shareholders. S-corporations limit the number of shareholders to 75 and require that they be U.S. citizens; foreigners, domestic corporations, and co-owners of partnerships may not participate. LLCs, on the other hand, have no limits on the number of members and do not place restrictions on the makeup or citizenship of members. In addition, LLCs can have more than one *class* (*kind*) of stock and can own stock in another corporation. An LLC allows you to avoid the double taxation of a C-corporation but provides most of the legal options regarding liability protection and stock sales that a C-corporation has. For most small business owners, setting up an LLC may be overkill. Think of it conceptually as an S-corporation with much more flexibility with respect to shareholder types and numbers.

> **Talking Business**
>
> A **limited liability company** (**LLC**) is a new type of business structure available in almost every state that has many of the tax advantages of a partnership or subchapter S-corporation but fewer of the disadvantages. LLC shareholders are called **members** of the LLC.

> **Talking Business**
>
> Corporations can sell different **classes of stock**, such as preferred stock or common stock, at different prices. The various classes differ in when and under what circumstances dividends are paid.

Because of these advantages, some people expect that LLCs will exceed subchapter S-corporations, regular C-corporations, partnerships, and limited partnerships as the preferred organizational structure. Others feel that the added complexity associated with setting up an LLC will diminish their popularity. Only history will know the outcome. Increasing the S-corporation shareholder limit to 75 reduced the need for LLC formation, which now tips the argument in favor of the S-corporation for many new businesses who plan to have only a few shareholders.

 On the CD

A sample Limited Liability Company Organizing Checklist (document 05-18), Limited Liability Company Articles of Organization (without manager) (document 05-19), Limited Liability Company Articles of Organization (with manager) (document 05-20), Limited Liability Company Operating Agreement (without manager) (document 05-21), Limited Liability Company Operating Agreement (with manager) (document 05-22), Limited Liability Company Member Certificate (document 05-23), Limited Liability Company Consent Resolution in lieu of First Meeting of Members (document 05-24) and Limited Liability Company Minutes (document 05-25) are included on the companion CD.

Because conversion to an LLC from another type of business structure can be costly, LLCs are generally recommended more for startups than for established businesses.

One concern about LLCs, however, is that there is no unified set of tax laws because individual states created their own laws regarding LLCs, which were then copied by other states. Check with your secretary of state and the IRS to find out more about the laws governing LLCs. If you are not careful, you might set up your LLC only to find out that the IRS will treat your company as a partnership for tax purposes.

Professional Corporations

A special corporation structure addresses the needs of professionals who share a practice, such as lawyers, doctors, and accountants. The *professional corporation*, as it was initially called, provided special tax-related benefits to the participants. Many of the benefits have been reduced since 1981, however, and the growth in the number of professional corporations has declined. If you are a licensed professional who falls into this special category, check with your accountant to determine whether a professional corporation provides you any special benefits. Professional corporations use the letters P.C. after the company name to indicate the kind of corporation.

 Talking Business

A **professional corporation** is a special corporation sometimes used by lawyers, doctors, and accountants. It is often subject to restrictions related to malpractice matters.

State to State

As if life wasn't complicated enough, assume that you now want to operate your business with offices in several states. The good news is that this is possible. If the majority of your business comes from your home base in one state, you can avoid the multistate headache. The bad news is that, if this is not the case, you need to perform some filings and registrations to qualify in each state where you do business. You will have to file tax returns in each of these states as well.

Some firms specialize in setting up companies that need to operate in several states at once. Contact a law firm and get a referral to one of these firms or simply contract the law firm to perform the needed paperwork for you.

You can do all the multistate setup legwork yourself; however, this approach might become a black hole for time and effort. You are probably better off farming it out to those who do it for a living. This is particularly important when considering a name for your organization because the name must be available in all states of interest. (Read Chapter 6 for more information about names.) If you insist on doing it yourself, contact the secretary of state in each state of interest for filing guidelines and fees.

Don't forget that once you set up offices in separate states, you should begin tracking sales tax for these states along with the percent of corporate revenue derived from operations in these states. The tax collectors in each state want their "fair" piece of your profit pie, and if you don't track it carefully from the beginning, you might spend December through March of each year unraveling your finances so that you can accurately pay your business and sales taxes in each state.

Listen Up

Numerous computer software packages can automatically generate a wide variety of legal documents for you, from a bill of sale to articles of incorporation. Most packages even modify the documents to suit the state in which you do business. They usually cost under $100 and pay for themselves with one use. Check out *PC World*, *MacWorld*, NOLO Press, or *PC* magazine for an assessment of the software. Naturally, make maximum use of the forms included on the companion CD to this book. They should save you tons of money in that your attorney will likely only have to confirm the content instead of writing it from scratch.

Dealing With the Tax Man

Taxes never go away. All you can do is try to minimize their negative impact on your profits. The impact of taxes on your choice of organizational structure is worth a brief discussion. I present only general concepts here about income taxes; talk to your accountant about your specific situation. Remember, there are many other taxes your business will have to pay. You need to learn about all of them in your area—city, county, state, sales, franchise, and so on.

The company net income will pass directly to you as owner or major stockholder (of any type of business structure except for the C-corporation). You then declare it on your personal tax return and pay tax at your personal tax rate. In corporations, all salary expenses (including the owner's salary) are deducted from the company's revenues prior to determining how much tax must be paid, but the corporation pays payroll taxes on it as well. You then pay personal income tax only on your salary, just as you do for any company.

Self-employed individuals really feel the bite of FICA (Social Security) and Medicare taxes because they pay both the employee's share and the employer's share of these taxes in the form of self-employment taxes. This is a little misleading, though, in that the overall payroll tax rate is the same whether as a sole proprietorship or corporation. It is simply paid in a different way and out of different funds.

In a corporation, however, *dividends* paid to shareholders are taxed twice. Dividends are paid to shareholders out of company income after the corporate taxes have been paid. The shareholders then declare those received dividends as income and pay tax on them again. This is called *double taxation*, and it can get expensive. At the time of this writing, there is some talk about eliminating personal taxes on dividends, so make sure that you verify whether double taxation is still in effect.

Talking Business _____

A **dividend** is money paid to shareholders out of the corporation's profits (after taxes are withheld). This is a form of compensation to the shareholders for having made the investment in the corporation by purchasing shares.

Double taxation occurs when a business pays tax on its annual profits and then passes the remaining profits on to you, the majority shareholder, who again gets taxed at the personal level; as a result, the same dollar is taxed twice. There is some talk about eliminating double taxation at the time of this writing so verify whether double taxation is still in effect.

Sometimes, corporations come up with creative ways to avoid or minimize the financial bite taken out of their shareholder's dividends as a result of double taxation. Some people get so focused on avoiding paying taxes that they lose track of their primary concern: running a successful and profitable business that fulfills their personal and financial goals. We all hate giving Uncle Sam a nickel, but avoid the temptation to fiddle with your tax planning to the point that you lose focus on your business.

Individuals and corporations do not pay taxes at the same rate. You will find that the break points between tax levels differ. Depending on your situation and the company's income levels, you might be better off leaving the money in the company and paying corporate taxes instead of paying yourself a large salary and paying personal income tax. Check out the following table for the relative rates for personal and corporate taxes.

Typical Personal and Corporate Taxable Income Rates

Single		Married, Filing Jointly		Corporate	
Income	*Tax Rate*	*Income*	*Tax Rate*	*Income*	*Tax Rate*
$0 to $6,000	10%	$0 to $12,000.	10%	Not a business category	
$6,001 to 27,950	15%	$12,001 to 46,700	15%	$0 to 50,000	15%
$27,951 to 67,700	27%	$46,701 to 112,850	27%	$50,000 to 75,000	25%
$67,701 to 141,250	30%	$112,851 to 171,950	30%	$75,000 to 100,000	34%
$141,251 to 307,050	35%	$171,951 to 307,050	35%	$100,000 to 335,000	39%
$307,051+	38.6%	$307,051+	38.6%	$335,000 to 10M	34%

There are additional rates for companies over $10 million in annual taxable income, and I hope that you someday need that information, which was left out of this table.

Single people should look at this table and smile. Check out the corporate tax benefit offered to single people who earn between $27,951 and $67,700. The personal tax rate is 27 percent, but the corporation's is 15 percent. That 12 percent (27 percent minus 15 percent) can be left in the corporation for business use at a lower tax rate than what a sole proprietor must pay.

Listen Up

Your company must pay FICA (Social Security), unemployment, and Medicare taxes for each employee over and above the standard salary. This currently amounts to around 7.62 percent. The employee also pays these taxes. See Chapter 14 for more information on taxes.

Remember that if you pay the money left over in the corporation to yourself as a salary bonus at the end of the year, you have to pay the company's portion of the payroll tax (7.62 percent) and you then pay 27 percent in personal income tax instead of the corporate rate of 15 percent, which the company would pay if you just left it in the company. This means that a total of 34.62 (7.72 percent + 27 percent) percent of each corporate revenue dollar associated with your salary goes to taxes before it ends up in your pocket. On the other hand, if you need the money to pay your personal bills, you have to pay yourself and take the tax bite.

Notice that a C-corporation allows you the option of leaving the money in the corporation or paying yourself in the form of a bonus or dividend. An S-corporation or LLC takes this decision out of your hands and makes you treat the leftover corporate profits as personal income, without having to apply the payroll taxes. In this case, an S-corporation shareholder would pay at least 27 percent tax on the S-corporation net income unless that income pushed the shareholder into a higher tax bracket, which might require a 30 percent personal tax rate payment.

Here is how I suggest that you think about the tax aspect of the business structure decision:

- Determine what you expect your salary will be and assume that payroll taxes will be paid on that either as self-employment tax or payroll tax.

- Determine the amount of net income that the corporation will see if it meets your business plan projections.

- Look at the tax tables and determine whether the taxes are lower if taxed at the corporate rate or as personal income.

- If the personal tax rate is lower, then set your company up as anything other than a C-corporation. If the C-corporate tax rate is lower, then leave your company as a C-corporation so that more of the early years of net income stays in the company. You will need that money the most in the early years.

- If you expect your company to show a loss for the first few years, which is not uncommon, then you might consider being a sole proprietorship or S-corporation so that the loss can be used to decrease your personal tax liability. Note that the S-corporation has some relatively restrictive loss limits, whereas the sole proprietorship loss limits are limited only by your total income.

For Your Plan

As part of your business plan, you want to address your reasons for choosing your business's legal structure. Make sure you address

- ◆ The type of business legal structure you plan to use.

- ◆ Your primary reason for selecting that structure.

- ◆ If a corporation, where you plan to incorporate and the names of key officers and board members.

- ◆ Legal protection of the company name.

- ◆ Intentions related to opening offices in other states or countries and within specific time frames, if applicable.

- ◆ How the legal documents were created, signed, and recorded to provide confidence that the company creation documents are legally binding.

- ◆ The tax implications of the business type choice and thresholds at which various other changes, such as from an S- to a C-corporation, will be performed.

- ◆ Where the legal formation documents are stored.

Your goal with this section is to provide the reader with a solid understanding of the company's legal structure, why that structure was selected, and how that selection benefits the company and its shareholders in the future.

 On the CD _____

> The companion CD contains a ton of additional information related to selecting the right business for you. Women and those of you who qualify for minority status should definitely check out your special section titled, "Special Opportunities for Women and Minorities" (CD05-2). Those of you who think that a franchise is in your future would be well advised to read "Franchises: Paying for Their Experience" (CD05-1). And all of you should read "When to Use a Lawyer" (CD05-3) to make sure that you legally protect yourself when setting up your business. Each state and business requirement is different, so make sure that you are set up right for your particular situation.

The Least You Need to Know

◆ Editable legal forms are included on the companion CD that you can adapt to your business and then run by an attorney for final okay.

◆ Select the business structure based on your expected business goals. Each form has its own benefits; you want to choose the one best suited to your needs.

◆ Sole proprietorships, partnerships, and corporations are not the same. Choose your business structure based on operational, legal, and tax considerations.

◆ Corporations provide the highest level of legal protection but can subject dividend income to double taxation.

◆ Don't be afraid to investigate franchising; you can profit from other people's experiences.

◆ Taxes are a part of life for any business. Recognize that you have to learn about them or find competent help to pick the right business type that fits your business and tax needs.

Chapter 6

Important Corporation Realities

In This Chapter

- ◆ How to set up a corporation
- ◆ An overview of articles of incorporation and bylaws
- ◆ Setting up a board of directors
- ◆ Keeping control of your corporation

There was a sense of destiny in the air as Susan made her way to her office. She said good morning to her assistant and anxiously looked for the folder that contained the artist's renderings of their company logo. She liked the name. Her husband chose it from the final list of contenders. He beamed when she told him that they would use it. It was fun to see him enjoy participating with her in the dream she had wanted for years. It surely made life at home easier.

The artist's renderings were beautiful. The colors were just what she wanted, and the name and logo were clear enough that anyone who saw them would understand what her company had to offer. It cost around $4,000 for the public relations firm to create the name and renderings. The company was now ready to go.

At that moment Walter, the company attorney, walked into the room. He was holding a piece of paper in his hand and had a somber look on his face, even for Walter. He handed Susan the piece of paper and waited. The letter was from the secretary of state's office. It said that the name they chose was already in use by another company within the state and that their request for the name reservation was denied.

Susan's mind did a few somersaults and then landed. They were back to square one and $4,000 poorer than before they started. Why did they rush to have that logo created? Couldn't they have waited to hear back from the secretary of state? Susan's mind was racing. "I guess it's back to the drawing board again," she sighed. "But this time, let's send several potential names to the state for approval, rather than just one. I certainly don't want to waste any more time or money on choosing a name."

Creating a corporation is like creating a new business life. The corporation has the ability to make commitments, incur debt, hire employees, flourish (if successful), and go out of business (if not). You are the principal avenue through which this entity is created, and the responsibility for performing the proper legal steps involved with the corporation's birth is in your hands.

Corporations are created under guidelines established by the state in which the corporation will reside. Each state has its own regulations that govern the creation and operation of a corporation. The secretary of state's office defines these guidelines and is your contact point for initial information. In this chapter, I give you a general overview of the process.

Creating a Corporation

First, determine who is going to be a shareholder in the corporation. How many shareholders will there be? Almost always, you need a minimum of one shareholder or officer of the corporation before the state allows you to incorporate. Some states require a minimum of two officers. You are asked for the names of the president, treasurer, and secretary. These can all be you. Just like the general store owner in a small town, you might have to wear several hats in your corporation.

On the CD _____

A sample Corporation Organizing Checklist is included on the companion CD as document 06-01.

Next, determine the state(s) where you intend to do business. Many states allow you to incorporate in that particular state but locate your main offices and operations in another state. (Delaware is one state that permits this situation.)

The major benefits for "long-distance incorporation" are usually tax related. If a state does not have a corporate income tax or imposes only a small one, it is financially advantageous to incorporate there; but you still have to pay the applicable business state income taxes for the states where you actually run your business. Therefore, depending on your state regulations, it may or may not make sense to do an out-of-state incorporation.

Beware of taxes that present themselves under a different name. For example, Texas has no state income tax, but it does levy a "franchise fee" that is really the equivalent of a tax. (By the way, the fee applies to businesses even if they are not franchises). It surely feels like a tax when you write the check to pay it. Check with corporations in your state of interest to confirm the flies in the corporate ointment.

Listen Up

Unlike sole proprietorships, which typically involve just one piece of paper filed with the county clerk's office, a corporation is formed at the state level by the secretary of state.

The corporation filing fees you have to pay to the state to set up your corporation vary widely, from as low as $40 to as high as $900 or more. (California, where else? Ouch!) Unless becoming a national company immediately is important to you, you are probably better off keeping the process simple and incorporating only in your home state. Startup life is complicated enough without adding more complexity than is necessary.

If you dream of going national quickly, however, see Chapter 5 about doing business in more than one state, and plan early for the complexities.

Your corporation must have a name that serves both a legal and marketing use. The name must comply with the state's legal requirements and should also convey something about your offerings to your customers. Naming details are covered in the following "What's in a Name?" section.

Smoke Signals

Check the laws of your home state carefully. If you incorporate in another state, your state might charge stiff taxes to out-of-state corporations, negating a lot of the tax advantages of incorporating elsewhere. If you do business in more than one state, you might have to file tax returns and pay taxes in all of them. You must also track and pay applicable sales taxes for the states where you have sales or operations offices.

Talking Business

Articles of incorporation establish the structure and stock ownership of the corporation. The articles are public and filed with the secretary of state. The state will probably issue a certificate of incorporation along with a *state charter number* (the official number assigned to your corporation, like a Social Security number). This is your official record of incorporation.

Finally, you must file *articles of incorporation* with the state. The articles outline the basic characteristics of the business and become the legal framework within which the corporation must operate. The business's purpose, planned duration of existence, and capital structure, such as how many shares of stock have been issued and who owns what, are defined in the articles. (You'll learn more about articles of incorporation later in this chapter.) Once you file the articles and the fees are paid, you are incorporated!

Congratulations! You have just given birth to a business with a life and identity all its own. The secretary of state will send you the official "birth announcement." Establishing a trusty board of directors is a natural next step. Later in the chapter, I show you how to do just that.

Laying Down the Law: Articles of Incorporation and Bylaws

How do you establish the articles of incorporation and the bylaws for your company? These two documents spell out the overall intent of your corporation. You file the articles of incorporation with the state as part of the corporation formation procedure. The board of directors creates the bylaws and determines the company operating procedures. Bylaws are the private rules and operating policies of the corporation that the shareholders approve and that the corporation must follow.

On the CD

Sample Corporation Pre-incorporation Agreement (document 06-02), Corporation Articles of Incorporation for a Single Shareholder (document 06-03), Corporation Articles of Incorporation for Multiple Shareholders (document 06-04), and Corporation Stock Certificate (document 06-05) documents are included on the companion CD.

Articles of Incorporation: The Basic Ingredients

The articles of incorporation need not be lengthy. They just need to be accurate and to provide the state with the necessary information for incorporation. Most of the articles are easily created. Try this basic structure or the one on the CD as a starting place. You might also find that your particular state provides sample articles that you can use. In the following articles, type the bold sentences and fill in the italic requests.

Article One: The Company Name

The name of corporation is *(enter your company name).*

Article Two: The Period of Duration

The period of the company duration is (enter the number of years your company will be in existence, which is usually assumed to be PERPETUAL).

Article Three: The Company Purpose

The purpose of the company is to (enter the basic reasons why the company exists; most people simply use FOR ANY LEGAL PURPOSE).

You can also be a little more specific and mention the types of products or services the corporation will be selling. However, if you ever decide to change the purpose of the corporation, you might have to alter or amend your articles of incorporation. For this reason, it is best to be somewhat general.

Article Four: The Capital Structure

The total number of shares that the company is authorized to issue is *(enter the number of shares)* **at a** *par value* **of** *(enter the par value of each share)* **dollars each.**

For example, you can assume that the company is authorized to issue 100,000 shares at a par value of $.01 each. (Don't confuse *authorized shares* with *issued shares*. Issued shares are actually in the hands of a shareholder. Authorized shares are shares that can be sold by the company but need not be.)

> **Talking Business** _____
>
> The total number of shares of stock the corporation is permitted to issue is known as the number of **authorized shares.** For instance, if 1,000 shares of stock are authorized at the start of the corporation, a total of only 1,000 shares can ever be sold to shareholders—no more than that. **Issued shares** are the number of shares that are actually issued. **Par value** is an accounting term used by bookkeepers in tracking the shares issued. Its value is usually set very small.

You can even authorize and issue different classes of stock, but this is certainly overkill for the vast majority of businesses at your current stage of development. Get big and profitable enough to make worrying about multiple stock classes important, and then hire some financial wizards to help you put it together.

Keep this section simple unless you have specific reasons for creating a more compli-cated capital structure, and be sure to verify your capital structure with your account-ant and lawyer before finalizing your articles. You need to file amended articles of incorporation if you ever decide to change your capital structure. In addition, if you sell shares and then change your capital structure, you need to convert the old shares to new ones.

Article Five: Initial Capitalization

Most business transactions are not considered binding, or final, until money has changed hands. For this reason, your corporation might require some form of *consid-eration* to officially start.

The corporation will not commence business until it has received for the issuance of its shares consideration of the value of (*enter the desired amount of money or valued services amount; usually not less than $1,000*).

Talking Business

Consideration is a legal term for "something of value." That something could be money or the right to do something. Many contracts are not valid until some form of consideration has changed hands. In some cases, that con-sideration can be as little as $1 to make the transaction legal.

Notice that this initial capitalization must be paid for by corporate stock, and that stock currently has a par value of whatever you set in your articles of incorpo-ration. For example, assume that you invest $10,000 in your corporation and that your articles of incorpo-ration authorize 100,000 shares at a $1 each par value. This means that the corporation must issue 10,000 shares of $1 par value stock, or 10 percent of authorized shares, to you in exchange for the initial capital investment. Check with your particular state's authorities to determine whether a minimum per-centage must be issued to validate the corporation existence.

Article Six: Address and Registered Agent

The address of the corporation's *registered office* **is** (*enter the address*) **and the name of its** *registered agent* **at such address is** (*enter your name or the name of the person who is the primary contact for all company-related business, including legal matters*).

The address must be a street address, not a PO box.

Article Seven: Board of Directors Information

The number of directors is (*enter the number of directors, typically 1 to 3*), **and their names and addresses are** (*enter the names and addresses of each board member*).

Some corporations have a *board of directors* consisting of only one or two people, such as the owner and the owner's spouse, but then also establish an *advisory board* to give business advice and guidance. An advisory board works in the same way as a board of directors in counseling the president, helping identify new opportunities, and giving feedback on the direction of the company.

The difference is that the members of the advisory board have no financial interest in the company; they are not shareholders, and they assume no liability for the corporation's actions. In some cases, you might find that successful business people are more likely to agree to serve on an advisory board than on a board of directors because they don't want to be held liable for the consequences of the corporation's actions.

Talking Business

An **advisory board** counsels and guides the senior management of a company, much as a board of directors does. However, an advisory board has no financial stake in the company and assumes no liability for the corporation's actions.

The **registered agent** is the official person to contact for all legal matters. The registered agent may or may not be located at the principal place of business, also called the **registered office**. In some states, the registered agent must be an attorney, and in others, you can serve as the registered agent.

Article Eight: Name of the Incorporator

The name and address of the incorporator is (*enter your name, assuming that you are the person forming the corporation*).

This can be a third party with no interest in the company at all who is simply completing the paperwork for you, such as an attorney.

The incorporator, in some states, may have to sign the articles in front of a notary public. Then you file the articles, or a copy of them, with the state.

Smoke Signals

Don't issue all authorized shares of stock to yourself when you first start and capitalize your company or you might limit how you work with and sell shares of stock later.

Also, if you do not handle all financial transfers between you and the corporation as you do those with either a standard investor or employee, then you might place your corporation status and protections in jeopardy. You would document a loan made to or received from a third party, and you must do the same for yourself and the corporation.

Bylaws: The Basic Ingredients

Your corporation now exists. What is it going to do, and how will it conduct itself on a daily basis? The bylaws should explain. They are the internal rules that govern employees' and officers' actions when the directors are not there to supervise. Violation of the corporation bylaws is usually treated as a grievous offense and can be grounds for dismissal in most companies.

On the CD

A sample Corporation Bylaws document is included on the companion CD as document 6-6. A sample Corporation Board of Directors Minutes of Initial Meeting document is included on the companion CD as document 06-07.

Of course, when you're both the president and the board of directors, you can fire yourself whenever you want. If you have outside shareholders—investors other than you and a spouse or close family member—be aware that they can use a violation of the bylaws as a reason to bring in someone else to run the company if they hold a majority of the shares. If you own the majority of your corporation's shares, they probably can't fire you, but they can still cause problems for you. The moral of the story: Set up bylaws that you should have no problem living by.

The first board of directors meeting is used to adopt the corporate bylaws. The bylaws can cover any areas of conduct deemed necessary and generally include company policy in areas such as:

- When and where shareholder meetings are held

- When and how the board is formed

- How frequently meetings are held

Listen Up

If you choose to use software or the enclosed CD forms to create your articles, be sure to verify your capital structure with a financial adviser before finalizing it. The software simply works with the information you provide and does not verify its accuracy. If the information you type is incorrect, your articles of incorporation will be flawed.

- Voting rights of shareholders and directors

- Procedures for hiring and dismissing company officers and a description of their duties

- The overall handling of stock shares and dividends

- Usage of the corporate seal if required by your state

- Internal approval procedures for legally committing the company

- Definition of the company fiscal year, which is frequently the calendar year for simplicity's sake

◆ References to the articles of incorporation as needed and procedures for amending the bylaws

The bylaws contain a lot of information that helps to maintain consistency in company policy in the midst of daily pressures. Make sure that the bylaws reflect the business and spiritual integrity of the organization; then stick with what you have or change the bylaws to better reflect your mission.

Bylaws and Articles "In a Can"

Most bylaws and articles of incorporation include standard language with only minor changes for specific company-related information. For this reason, many people decide to write their own using a computer program with the standard format for incorporating, which they then edit for their own situation. I have included editable versions of sample incorporation forms on the companion CD. You can educate yourself about the process and also save some money along the way to incorporating by getting to know the various forms that apply to your business type.

Although you might be tempted to save a few hundred dollars by using "canned" forms to create your corporation, be aware that you could create serious problems for yourself down the line. You should always consider having significant documents (such as contracts and official paperwork) reviewed by your attorney to make sure you establish your legal structure the way you intend. Changing them later requires filing the changes with the state, which costs money and time.

Listen Up

Pull out your bylaws every 6 to 12 months to remind you of the direction in which you initially intended to steer the company. Daily pressures can take you off track, and this review will help you to keep company operations consistent over the long term.

Establishing a Board of Directors

It has been said that human beings are reasonable in that we can always justify and rationalize our desires and actions. Being "reasonable" in this way may be a dangerous trait when you run your own business. It is often helpful to have someone to report to, or you'll find reasons to take the company into business areas where no company has gone before—or where no company should go.

Listen Up

You have certain obligations with respect to maintaining your corporate status. There are companies that specialize in creating corporation kits for a fee. One such company is TCS Liberty Legal, located in Houston, Texas. Contact 1-800-392-3720; www.tcs-libertylegal.com. If you are not issuing stock, you probably don't need a kit, but it should cost under $100 and might be a good idea anyway.

Talking Business

The **business judgment rule** protects members of corporate boards of directors from lawsuits filed by shareholders, customers, or others if the decision that caused the lawsuit was made in the best interest of the corporation.

This is a wonderful reason for creating a board of directors and, by the way, it is required by state law anyway. A board of directors is a group of people who are often not involved with the daily operation of the business but who have a vested interest in keeping the company on track. Board members usually serve for one year, but three-year terms are not uncommon. Smaller corporations will usually have the primary shareholders as the board of directors, as a minimum.

If you plan to keep your company small, you can act as your own board. This certainly keeps arguments between the board and upper management to a minimum. If you plan to grow past the "mom-and-pop" stage, you should consider a board of directors consisting of advisers from the business community.

Directors are required to act with the best interests of the corporation and its shareholders in mind. As long as they act with integrity and make decisions that any "reasonable" person would make given the same information, they are generally protected from potential lawsuits or claims as a result of their decisions. This is the *business judgment rule* designed to protect directors from claims derived from frivolous lawsuits filed by irate shareholders who may have lost money on their investments.

For example, if a board of directors decides to stop selling a particular product because it loses money for the company and a customer becomes upset at that decision, the customer may still sue the corporation. However, the members of the board of directors cannot be sued unless the customer can prove the decision was a poor one for the company.

Directors generally serve on a board for indirect benefits, such as business contacts, prestige, and other related rewards. Typically, board members receive payment of travel expenses for attending meetings, as well as nominal payment for serving on the board. Board members are frequently majority stockholders in the corporation, which ensures that board decisions are made on behalf of the shareholders and not simply to serve the company officers. When you own all of the shares of stock, this is not such a big deal. As you involve more shareholders, the board becomes more important. In fact, most large investors want a seat on the board to have a vote in company direction and operation.

A diverse board is better than one that comprises people from the same industry or background; people with varied backgrounds bring different perspectives and contacts to the company. Board members who own shares will act in a more responsible manner because they have a direct interest in the company's success. Adding board members with financial, legal, managerial, and political experience can assist the company greatly when fast decisions must be made. This higher level of expertise shortens the information-gathering phase because the experts are often right there in the room.

 On the CD _____

Sample Corporation Subscription Agreement for Officers & Directors & Initial Shareholders (document 06-08), Corporation Board of Directors Consent to Act Without Meeting (06-09), Corporation Notice of Board of Directors Meeting (06-10), and Corporation Board of Director Minutes (06-11) are included on the companion CD.

It is a good idea to have the director stock ownership phased in over a period of time based upon participation and overall company performance. Doing so means that board members receive a small number of shares when they join the board. These shares increase over time, based on how well the company does and how much time the board members spend on company business. Setting up a stock ownership plan that takes effect over several years takes more time up front but ensures that the directors are motivated to make your company, and you, succeed.

With an advisory board, the members are still expected to act in the company's best interests and to recommend actions that further the corporation's goals, but the issue of liability doesn't come up. That's because an advisory board is much less formal than a board of directors and because the advisory board members generally receive no compensation for giving advice. In most cases, no formal, written relationship exists between the advisory board members and the corporation. As a sign of your appreciation for their time and guidance, you should probably buy them dinner once in a while, but you don't have to give them shares of stock or big payments.

Finally, make sure that all board members agree to disclose any potential conflict of interest situations that may arise. Most organizations require that all board members sign a disclosure form up front, either stating that there are no known conflicts of interest or explaining potential conflicts. Nothing breeds contempt and distrust faster than finding out that one of your confidants is cavorting with a competitor without your knowledge.

The Right to Vote

Voting rights in a corporation can get pretty complicated. In a small corporation, the topic is a little less complex but is still important if you plan to create a board of directors to help you steer your company. If you aren't careful, you can have a board of directors that steers you right out of the company. Read on and learn the pros and cons of corporation voting rights and the creation of a board of directors.

Shareholder Voting Rights

Who gets to vote on the operation of the business? Everyone may feel entitled to a say, but only specific people—shareholders and board members—get to actually vote on the company's direction.

In general, shareholders hold a single vote for each share of stock they own. Because it is not always feasible for a shareholder to be involved in daily business decisions, shareholder voting rights are typically applied to topics that affect the entire corporation, such as changing the articles of incorporation, amending the bylaws, approving mergers or the purchase of another company, and dissolving the corporation and selling most or all of the company assets. Shareholders also vote on who will be on the board of directors, although the first board is created by the company management.

On the CD

Sample Corporation Shareholder Agreement for investing shareholders with Buy-Sell provisions (document 06-12), Corporation Notice of Shareholder Meeting (document 06-13), Corporation Shareholders Consent to Act Without Meeting (document 06-14), Corporation Shareholders Minutes of Initial Meeting (document 06-15), and Corporation Shareholder Minutes (document 06-16) documents are included on the companion CD.

Shareholders also indirectly vote at the board level through the use of a *proxy*, which allows the designated board member to vote on that shareholder's behalf when choosing new board members using a process called *cumulative voting*. Cumulative voting is not covered here in detail because it usually does not apply to a small corporation, but you should learn how it works once your company gets big enough that additional board members are selected. Remember that board members vote on what you can do with regard to the daily operation of the company.

Talking Business

A **proxy** is assigned by a shareholder to a board member who then votes on that shareholder's behalf.

Cumulative voting is a voting method that enables shareholders with relatively fewer numbers of shares, called **minority shareholders,** to concentrate their board member votes. Cumulative voting would be specified as part of the corporation bylaws if applicable, but rarely used by a smaller company since the concentration of shares lies with the founder. If you think this applies to your situation, then you should really see a lawyer to understand fully what you are getting into.

Board Member Voting Rights

Decisions regarding the daily operation of the company are made at the board level. The board of directors votes on items such as the addition or removal of corporation officers (such as you), officer salaries (such as yours), dividend payment decisions, product lines, addition and removal of services, labor negotiations, issuance of shares or bonds, and other related operational activities. This voting occurs on a one-vote-per-board-member basis and is not dependent on the number of shares held by each board member.

Board member voting presents some interesting situations that you should be aware of. For example, assume that the board gets mad at you and decides to get back at you for reasons that have nothing to do with business. If the majority of the board votes to remove you as president of the company, they can do this even against your wishes. Would you normally expect this to happen from the trusted people you put on your board? Certainly not, or you never would have put them on your board in the first place. Could this happen in a close corporation where the other board members are also family members who might have a personal ax to grind? Unfortunately, yes.

Is the addition of a board of directors still a good thing? In general, I think the answer is yes if you want your company to grow. You can protect yourself from becoming personally liable for all company debts and then being voted out of company management by the board of the company you founded.

 On the CD

Sample Corporation Shareholder Proxy (document 06-17), Board Resolution to Sell Business (document 06-18), Shareholder Resolution to Sell Business (document 06-19), Agreement to Sell Business Assets (06-20), and Stock Purchase Agreement (all shares) (document 06-21) documents are included on the companion CD.

Change the bylaws to require that the president and CEO of the company (that is, you) cannot be removed from office without a shareholder vote. Because you hold the majority of the shares, you cannot be voted out of office by the board members who are almost always *minority shareholders*, unless you also vote yourself out.

Shareholder Proxy

Any fundamental changes to a corporation must be approved by a shareholder vote, as outlined earlier. This voting is done either through a *direct shareholder vote*, where each shareholder shows up and casts his or her vote (rarely done), or through a *proxy statement*, in which the shareholder authorizes a board member with a proxy endorsement to vote on that shareholder's behalf (the usual method).

Talking Business

In a **direct shareholder vote,** each shareholder shows up and casts his or her vote. More commonly, a shareholder votes through a **proxy statement,** in which he or she authorizes a board member with a proxy endorsement to vote on his or her behalf.

It is common for board members in large corporations to solicit proxy authorizations from shareholders so that they can concentrate voting authority under their specific director seat's authority. In most smaller corporations, the president is the default recipient of the shareholder proxy.

A quorum of shares (more than 50 percent of issued shares) must be represented for the vote on resolutions to have validity. In order for a resolution to pass, more than 50 percent of the quorum voters must vote in favor of it. Some states allow for nonquorum stockholder meetings to decide on resolutions if 100 percent of those present vote in the same way.

Whenever there is a major corporate decision to be made, such as the buying of another company or the selling of the one you own, it is common to make sure that the majority of shareholders are in agreement with the sale. After all, they own a part of the company as well.

On the CD

You will find two important supplemental sections on the companion CD. "Picking the Right Business Name" (CD06-2) contains information you will wish you had known when picking your business name. It is frustrating and expensive to change names once you are up and running, so read this section before you finalize your business name. "Smart Stock Handling for Small Business Owners" (CD06-1) presents real-world considerations and solutions to voting rights issues as they pertain to board members and shareholders. Just a few minutes spent with these two bonus sections may save you a bunch of money and time later on.

The Least You Need to Know

♦ Each state has its own regulations regarding incorporating. Contact the secretary of state's office in your state's capital.

♦ The incorporation process is fairly simple and inexpensive in most states, costing between $300 and $1,500 depending on the state. Only one shareholder is usually required to incorporate.

♦ Choosing the right name is crucial. Start with the name, verify its availability in the states where you'll be doing business, and reserve it until you finish the articles of incorporation. (See the "On the CD" note at the end of this chapter.)

♦ A board of directors will greatly assist your progress in developing the megacompany you envision. Look for board members from the start and choose wisely.

♦ Change your bylaws to preclude the possibility of your being voted out of your own company.

♦ Do your homework before you incorporate. It is often difficult and costly to change mistakes.

♦ Time your date of incorporation so that it includes the bulk of the tax year, or you could end up filing a tax return for a corporation that was only in operation for a few days within the tax year.

Chapter 7

Working at Home or Away

In This Chapter

- ◆ The benefits and pitfalls of working at home
- ◆ IRS considerations for home offices
- ◆ Choosing the right location for your business
- ◆ When to rent, lease, or buy

"How's it going in your corner office?" Mary called to ask.

"Great! Instead of getting up at 6:00 A.M. to drag myself downtown by 8:30, now I can leave my bedroom at 8:29 and be at work 30 seconds early," Jim explained.

"Sounds wonderful. What do you do with all your free time now?" Mary asked.

"I work! One of the drawbacks of having a corner office in the basement is that it's just too easy to keep working long after all the downtown workers have left for home. And, while I see more of my children than I used to, they can be a distraction, especially when I'm on the phone."

"So are you ready to come back to work with the big boys?"

"Not on your life!" came the reply. "I can handle the distractions, and running my own business from a convenient location is one of the most rewarding things I've ever done. Why, some days, the only reason I leave my home office is to make a deposit at the bank."

Who hasn't sat in rush-hour traffic and fantasized about working from home? What? Give up soot, smog, rude drivers, and several hours of my day to work from a spare room at home? Why do that? Simple: It sounds great. And it can be if you have the discipline to make it work. This chapter introduces you to the great and not-so-great aspects of working out of your own home and how to make the right decision as to when and where to set up a formal office.

Home Office: Pros and Cons

Take a look at some of the good and not-so-good points associated with a home-based business in the lists.

The pros of a home office:

A 30-second commute—You save one to two hours per day in time commuting, which provides more time for business and for your nonworking life.

Save money—You already pay rent or a mortgage. Save the money you would spend on office space and put it back into your business.

Tax advantages—You should be able to deduct expenses associated with the office section of your house, which otherwise are not deductible. You might actually make money off the deal. (More on this later in the chapter.)

Listen Up

You can deduct the expense of your home office even if you are employed by someone else, but the office still must be used solely for work and not as a part-time playroom for the kids. This is reported on your Schedule A (Form 1040).

Family benefits—You are closer to the family, which allows for meals at home. You might be able to rope family members into helping, on occasion. You can also work at night, after others have gone to sleep, without having to put on your shoes.

Lower-risk trial run—You can test the water regarding your business idea without incurring a lot of outside financial costs and long-term obligations. If your idea takes off, you can always move to a regular office. (More on this later in the chapter.)

The cons of a home office:

Motivational liability—You can get sidetracked into personal stuff such as cleaning the kitchen or arranging the screws in the shop. Personal phone calls can take up a lot of your day when people know you are at home. After all, "you're not at work" in their mind. You're at home. You need to set them straight on this one and be consistent about it.

No commute—On the days when you don't want to work, the commute helps to separate your home life from business. When you work at home, you might spend that extra hour on the couch. If you had gone into the office, that time could have been used productively.

Lack of peer contact—You are relatively isolated in your home office, whereas a regular office provides contact with other business owners who are not only colleagues, but also sources of leads, business, and guidance. This is an important issue to which you should give serious thought.

Been There ... Done That

I have noticed a change in the past 15 years regarding perceptions about home-based businesses. In the late 1980s, you were not "really in business" if you worked out of your house. Now, there are so many home-based businesses that some people think you are nuts to have a "real office." Go figure! If you take care of your clients by offering great value and service, few will care if you work out of your home. No need to advertise the fact, by the way. If working out of your house bothers you from an image perspective, then meet in restaurants or other public places that are convenient to them as a way of dodging the "home office" stigma.

Starting your business from home is a relatively painless way to begin either a service business (such as consulting, accounting, massage, and so on) or a small product-oriented business such as mail order or light manufacturing. You are already paying for the house and utilities. It makes sense to use these prepaid (fixed) expenses to your best benefit, but be cautious of the potential pitfalls associated with running a business out of your home.

This section deals with the financial and personal aspects of working from your home. You'll also find a section on determining the right time for moving out and whether you should lease, rent, or buy your new office space.

Keeping Your Overhead Low

As we said in the Army: "Uncle Sam can't make you do anything. He can only make you really sorry that you didn't!" Working out of your home is financially attractive in the early days, but you need to follow the proper steps to ensure that the IRS allows your available and desirable business and personal deductions.

It is tempting and reasonable to assume that all expenses associated with the business section of your house are tax deductible as a business expense. They might be, but you have to be careful how you present them on your taxes and back up the claim with paperwork.

As the judge says, "He who has the most paperwork wins!" Documentation of expenses is critical in making your case for home-office business deductions to the IRS. See IRS publication 587, "Business Use of Your Home" for details related to the tax impact and benefits of running your business out of your home. There are special regulations for those who store inventory or for those of you who want to run a day-care facility out of your home. See Publication 587 for the details if either of these apply to you.

Smoke Signals

Don't underestimate the impact of working alone. You might really start to miss those impromptu talks around the water cooler. Some people set up office in an executive suite or office building simply so that they have other people around. More than one person has closed his own business to work for someone else due to the isolation.

Here is the key: The business section of your house must be used "regularly and exclusively" for business purposes. This means that your home office must be your principal place of business operation and you cannot have another fixed location at which you do business. You must use it "exclusively and regularly for administrative or management activities of your business or trade." Meetings with clients, vendors, or others would qualify. There are all types of exceptions to each of these rules, however, so make sure that you read the rules in Publication 587 for yourself. They are worth knowing.

You must really use your home office as an office, not as a shortcut for some desirable tax deductions. The IRS is getting tighter on these restrictions instead of looser, and you must take the proper steps up front to back up your case for a home-office deduction. Beware that claiming a home-office deduction used to be a high-risk "flag" for a possible audit, so take the deductions you earned but make sure that you can back them up if audited.

The percentage of your home expenses that is allocated to your office is calculated on either a square-footage or number-of-rooms basis, assuming that the rooms are all of about the same size. For example, assume that you have a five-room house of 1,500 square feet. One room comprises one fifth of your house, once again assuming that all rooms are about the same size. Take one fifth (20 percent) of all housing expenses and allocate them to the business as expenses. You just saved money on your personal bills but gave up one fifth of your house to the business in the process.

You can also use the square-footage approach if the one room is much larger than the others are. For example, assume that the room is 500 square feet of the 1,500 square foot house, or one third. You can still take the one-third (33 percent) deduction, but you should make the case that this particular room was the best candidate for the office and is exclusively used for that purpose.

Beware of your home computer. It is not both a home and business toy when speaking with the IRS, no matter how you really use it. By the way, if you use the computer for both business and personal stuff, you probably need to keep detailed track of usage hours or you might find yourself pushing Uncle Sam uphill, which is a tough one. If you plan to use it for business, then use it for business. (You really don't want your kids playing with important business files, anyway. Can you imagine the mayhem that would occur in your house if your five-year-old son accidentally erased all your accounting records and you did not have a backup?) Keep yourself, your clients, and your family out of this minefield and keep your business and personal computers separate.

> **CAUTION**
>
> **Smoke Signals**
>
> Local zoning, building, or landlord ordinances might prohibit you from starting a business in your home. For example, if your business requires customer parking, increases street traffic, or causes wear and tear on your property, you should check with the city and your landlord for approval before investing too much money and time into working out of your home.

When Is It Time to Move Out?

You have been working diligently in your office for a while now, and things appear to be stabilizing. Clients expect you to remain in business and start providing you with repeat business. The delivery people know that your business exists and don't freak out when they deliver a business-related package to a residence. They've even learned to put delivered items behind the front swing, just as you have asked them to do since you started. Things appear to be going along well. Why would you consider moving out of the house and into a new location? Simple; to either make your life easier or to make more money—or both. The same home-office situation that saved you money when you first started can start to cost you money if it keeps you from expanding.

Typical indicators that it's time to consider a move include some of the following:

◆ When the office gets too small for the equipment and number of people you need to run your business.

◆ When the level of business activity at the house gets so high that it regularly disrupts the daily personal home routine.

Listen Up

It makes life easier to have separate business and personal checking accounts and telephone lines. This allows you to clearly define business and personal expenses along with separate telephone charges. The IRS really likes it this way, which is a good reason to do it in itself. Otherwise, you really need to log every telephone call made.

◆ When you find yourself not taking on new, good business because you are already working as hard as is humanly possible.

◆ When your clients appear uncomfortable coming to your home for business meetings, and you start feeling uncomfortable having them walk through your house to get to the office. This often happens when your clients start bringing their clients to your meetings.

◆ When you can't get temporary help because the agency won't let its people work in a private residence due to insurance reasons.

In short, you should move out when you have made it and when the problems associated with the business become operational and not financial. This means that you are no longer worried about whether or not you will be in business next year, but more worried about what you will be doing for your business next year and beyond.

Location, Location, Location

Locating your new, "real" office is a lot of fun, but it's time consuming. Just like buying a house for your family, you are setting up an important part of your lifestyle. A long commute means you are away from home more, but it might and should place you closer to your clients and prospects, which should bring in more business if you provide services. A more expensive space might present the desired image and bring in more money but with a higher up-front cost on your part. Consider all these factors when moving to an office that is not in your home. Take your time. You will likely have to sign a multiple-year lease, so you want to make sure it is something you can live with from both an operational and cost perspective.

Try these points on for size when looking at a new location:

1. If you provide a service, does it make sense to be centrally located near your clients and prospects? Probably. Is the potentially longer commute worth it on your part?

2. Are you moving to please yourself or to improve business operations? Either is fine, but understand your motivations.

3. Will you make up the commute time by being more productive while in the office, as compared to working out of your home? You might spend extra time with the commute but find that your day ends earlier because you are more productive while at work without distractions from home. On the other hand, if you are someone who works a lot at night, how will you handle that workload if you are now working out of another office?

4. Is there a competitor in the area of your new office? If so, does this hurt you or help you? Sometimes, people want to "shop around" and look for locations where competing companies are easily accessible. This applies to retail and many professional services. Will this competitor cause you to lose existing clients or make it difficult to gain new ones? If so, should you move far enough away from the established competitor so that you have a geographic advantage in your new location?

5. If you have a manufacturing type of business, does the new location make much difference to the operation? Probably not, because you ship to your clients and you can do that from just about anywhere. Once again, move to improve business operations, not to stroke your ego due to your new-found success. Make sure that zoning ordinances allow you to run your type of business from your intended location.

> **Listen Up**
>
> Renting furniture is a low-cash way to outfit your office. Rent-to-own plans allow you to make your furniture rental payments apply toward the purchase price. In general, if you rent for more than 12 months, you might as well have bought the furniture.

6. Is moving going to cost you customers? People do not like change unless it benefits them. How will this change benefit or hurt your existing clients or you?

7. How much more business do you have to create from the new location to justify the additional expense (not sales revenue, but actual profits after all marginal costs are taken out)? Is this number reasonable, and can you achieve it within the needed time frame? (See the break even analysis technique presented in Chapter 15 for details.)

8. What if you don't move? What would happen? Is there some external reason forcing the move that takes the "if" completely out of your hands and turns it into a where, when, and how?

9. Locate your permanent office in an area that allows you to keep the same phone number as the one you had at your house. In this way, you do not have to ask your clients to call you at a new number. At the least, automatically refer your old number to your new so that clients can call you during your transition period.

I'm sorry that I can't give you standard answers to these and the myriad other questions that no doubt will arise. The answers are heavily dependent on your particular situation, but here are a few rules that might help to narrow the field of confusion:

♦ Manufacturing business locations are most often chosen based on shipping, receiving, parking, space, and other operationally oriented criteria. If you primarily ship, mail, or work over the phone, it really doesn't matter where you locate your office as long as that location supports the daily operation.

♦ Service businesses that require the clients to come to you are heavily location-dependent. Why would clients go out of their way to come to your place when your competition is just down the road from their office? Get geographically close to your clients, and they will come.

♦ A nicer location might present a better image but might not necessarily generate more revenue. Don't confuse appearance with profits; they are not always equal. (Read the opposite argument next.)

♦ Basing your service business in a well-recognized location or building might increase name recognition and respectability in your clients' mind. You are associated with this respected office location, which should reflect well on you and increase trust. Trust is a necessary ingredient for any successful service business. Does the new location instill that trust without placing your company in financial jeopardy?

♦ Retail requires high-visibility frontage. Period. If your customers can't find you, they will not buy. They might not even know that you exist. Traffic is needed and encouraged in a high-visibility location such as a mall, craft and service fairs, downtown areas, and busy streets. F. W. Woolworth learned this with his first store and ended up closing after only a few months. After that, he never underestimated the value of location, location, and location.

Look at what your existing and potentially new competition is doing. Ask your customers about their reactions to your possible move. Get as much information as possible before taking the plunge. It would be a shame to take an operation that is working well from your home with its associated low overhead and place it in jeopardy by making an office move that is really only needed to feed your ego.

Here is just a quick reminder to consider important but less visible things such as adequate, lit parking for your clients. Our training center's female clients like to use the covered, lighted parking area at night. Make sure that the building is in compliance with the Americans with Disabilities Act. See ADA with Disabilities Act (ADA), which requires providing easy access for disabled persons. Check for wheelchair ramps, doorways that are wide enough to accommodate a wheelchair, and restrooms that are designed for wheelchair access. Signs should be posted in Braille for those who are visually impaired. Do the elevators operate smoothly and quietly? Is the hall lighting such that it conveys a lively impression to your clients? Does the carpeting smell or look worn? Don't forget that your clients will make a judgement about your business and you from the environment within which you and your business operate.

CAUTION

Smoke Signals

Let me give you a word of caution related to making your office space too lavish. I worked for a startup company in Silicon Valley that provided computer peripheral products to a very large computer manufacturer. We had just moved into a new building that, candidly, was palatial, gorgeous, and very expensive. In a rare move, the computer company's procurement officer came to our new location to negotiate the new contract. After seeing the fountain and gold-plated faucets, the first words out of his mouth were, "We are clearly paying you too much." That set the tone for the rest of the negotiations, which were painful, and costly, to say the least. Put the money in the bank unless spending it on your building beyond the respectable norms of your industry serves a valid business purpose unique to your particular situation.

Ask your potential clients about the things that are important to them; I never expected that restroom design would be as important to our female clients as it turned out to be. I worked with the building management to get women's restrooms on our floor upgraded before those on other floors or the men's. It paid off, and we got higher evaluation marks for our improved facilities and more business from our female clients. Your clients know best what they are looking for. If you provide it, they will come.

Lease, Rent, or Buy?

Should you lease, rent, or buy? This one is simple. Which one works out to be the financially most attractive while also serving the needs of your business? Leasing ties you into the same location for a longer period of time but provides you with lease-rate stability. Renting provides you with the monthly option of moving elsewhere, but your rent can fluctuate at any time, and the landlord has the option of asking you to vacate. Buying provides tremendous stability but with a large financial commitment on your part.

I suggest that you consider this progression for a service business:

1. Start out at home until your business warrants moving out.

Talking Business

Business incubators are organizations set up to incubate new companies from their inception, or seedling, stage just as a farmer would use an incubator to hatch chicken eggs. Incubators provide a varied menu of support services such as financing, clerical support, office space, equipment, phones, networks, and close proximity to other startup companies.

On the CD

A sample Lease for Real Estate (document 07-01), Purchase Agreement for Real Estate (document 07-02), Option Contract (document 07-03), Warranty Deed (document 07-04), and Land Contract (07-05) are enclosed on the CD.

2. Look into renting space in an executive suite of offices. Here you get the clerical support needed to operate without incurring a huge financial commitment. You can also generate contacts with other suite members. Another option is to explore *business incubators*, which provide the same level of service as executive office suites, but often with more camaraderie and coaching. This option works well for technology companies in their research and development stages.

3. Lease your own space when the restrictions of the executive suite begin to cost you time, money, or both. Or lease if the executive suites are simply more expensive than you can stand for what you get, which has been the case with me in the past.

4. Buy your own building when you have a successful track record under your belt. Many companies use the SBA for funding of this type of business-related building purchase. At the time of this writing, mortgage interest rates are about the lowest they have been in almost 50 years, so this is a great time to buy if you can afford it. But don't sacrifice your business's financial security to own the building.

If you have a manufacturing business, try this approach:

1. Work out of your house for as long as possible, zoning allowing. You might be able to do this by using third-party contract manufacturing houses for the actual production-related activities while using your home for office-related administrative functions.

2. See if you can partner with another company that already exists. Use their surplus capacity as an interim step.

3. Lease your own space when you're confident about future business, such as when you have ongoing contracts or automatic stocking-level agreements.

4. Buy when you are ready. Once again, look to the SBA for help in financing the purchase of a building.

For Your Plan

When writing your plan, it is important that you present some discussion related to space requirements. This indicates to the investors that you have thought about and have a reasonable assessment of this very important aspect of running a business.

Make sure you include the following:

- Where you are working now and where you plan to work for the startup stages of the operation.

- When you will know it is time to move to a new location.

- A rough estimate of office and manufacturing space needed for the first three years of operation, broken into the various growth phases that apply to your particular business.

- Estimated lease rates for manufacturing and office space in your business area and how these estimates were obtained.

- Any special arrangements you may have that help in dealing with space requirements and expenses.

- Why the geographic area you have chosen for your business will work from a demographic, political, financial, economic, and population perspective. This is particularly important for retail and service businesses.

- Present related zoning or other legal considerations and how your chosen location addresses them.

CAUTION

Smoke Signals

Letterhead, envelopes, business cards, and telephone listings must be changed when you move offices. Some people work from an 800 number and PO Box so that they never have to change their phone or address information when relocating. They then advertise the real ones when in their permanent location.

On the CD

Experience is the best teacher, and the CD contains a special bonus section that provides hard-learned tips for maintaining your efficiency and keeping your focus while working from home. It is titled "Maintaining Efficiency While Working from Home." Just one of these tips could keep you from falling into the same traps others have while working from home. How to handle the kids? Ways to "go to work" when your commute is only 30 seconds? The tax implications of being your own landlord? Balancing time at the pool with time closing deals? It is all there.

The Least You Need to Know

◆ Office location is important for both you and your clients. Consider your business location from your client's perspective; consider the finances from your own perspective to find the optimal blend of location and expense.

◆ Just because you run your business from your home doesn't mean that the expenses are tax deductible. Follow the IRS rules, and stay out of trouble. Read Publication 587.

◆ When you work at home, treat it just like a job. Go to work at regular hours and discipline yourself to stay on the job to get the work done even though you are only in the basement.

◆ Location is particularly important to most service and retail operations. Choosing the wrong retail location is worse than not starting at all, so make sure that you are as confident as possible about its traffic, parking, build-out, signage, and other important issues before signing.

◆ Product and manufacturing businesses are less location dependent. Their location can be based on price, space, and zoning along with access to transportation and employees.

◆ Minimize your commitments and expenses in the early days of your business until your revenue stream starts to pick up and stabilize. Gradually work your way up to leases and purchases after you have a successful sales and net income track record.

Part 3

Writing a Great Plan

Now that your business is set up and you've filed all the necessary paper-work, you need to get some customers. Here is where sales and marketing come front and center. Customers will make or break you because they bring in money. In this section, you'll learn how to use marketing to get customers and keep them. You'll also discover the basics of selling, along with information about—believe it or not—how your competitors can actually help you succeed.

You will also have to deal with employees, payroll taxes, manufacturing, operations, and your company's financials. All of these topics are presented in this part not only as a resource for you in writing your plan, but also as a reference for you to use in managing your business to success. This part includes very important information that provides an important founda-tion for your ultimate business success.

Chapter 8

Defining Your Market Opportunity

In This Chapter

- ◆ Determine your available marketplace
- ◆ Find applicable research data
- ◆ Extract and correlate facts to determine market truths
- ◆ Market characteristics greatly affect your chances of success

John stood up from his chair and walked to the window before speaking. "Of course there is a market for my product. It just makes sense that people will want it."

Jason, a potential investor, shook his head and then looked directly at John.

"All right. Let's play it this way. You say in your plan that you will sell 10,000 units next year. And, coincidentally, that gets us just over the breakeven point. What percentage of your available market must buy your product before you meet that 10,000?"

"Not that high of a number. I'm not sure, but I know I can sell 10,000."

"I don't doubt that you believe that you can sell 10,000 units. What I don't believe … scratch that … don't have a sense of is whether that 10,000 represents a small fraction of everyone who can use this product or more than really need it. Do you see my point?"

John just stood there and looked at Jason.

"John, just because you believe it to be true doesn't make it true. I have faith in you and your ideas, but the market will determine if we make money or not. We have to know more about the market."

Your customers make purchase decisions based on their needs, how your offering fills those needs, and their ability to buy. The more customers you have buying, the better your chances are of selling. The fewer customers you have buying, the worse are your chances of selling more product. This makes common sense, doesn't it? Here is the rub: How do you predict their likelihood of buying at all in general and then project their likelihood of buying from you in particular? That is the art and frustration with market and industry forecasting.

This chapter takes a detailed look at some basic forecasting and research procedures that you can use to gauge the larger market forces that shape your likelihood of success.

Understanding and Assessing the Market's Influence

It is hard to overestimate the importance of overall marketplace trends. Just as it was nearly impossible to find a winning stock in the declines that happened in the recent stock market collapse, so it is difficult to find customers to purchase your offering if the marketplace is in decline. On the other hand, if you are lucky (smart?) enough to be offering a desirable product to a hungry market, you might continually struggle to keep enough product on hand to fill demands. Under these circumstances, you only have the time to count your money a few times a year, but that is generally okay with you. Right?

Let's take a closer look at an optimal buying situation before we get into the details of forecasting market trends. Optimal buying conditions would look something like this:

◆ The overall marketplace demand for your offering continues to grow at more than 20 percent per year when measured by dollar sales levels and when inflation is low, under 3 percent.

◆ The number of units that your existing customers are expected to buy from you next year will increase and they already have your product purchases in the next year's budget.

- The number of vendors providing products to your marketplace is decreasing, which means that this increased customer demand can only be fulfilled by you and a few other vendors. Less competition is a good thing under these circumstances.

- There is no pending legislation or major social change that will undermine the great market conditions that you currently enjoy.

- Your customers have enough money to purchase what you offer.

- Your customers are convinced that they need what you offer and are ready to install it as soon as possible.

Here is a market situation that any vendor would think ideal: when you have lots of customers with lots of money, who all have a recognized demand and few vendors that they can purchase from. If you can't make money in this type of marketplace, you might as well stay at home and watch *Gilligan's Island* reruns. And if you are even lucky enough to have a marketplace like this come your way, take maximum advantage of it because it won't last very long in a global free enterprise system. Huge market opportunities create high interest on the part of other vendors who want a piece of your marketplace pie. Somebody, somewhere will create an offering that at least matches, if not exceeds, the value of yours, putting increased pressure on you to perform. This pressure usually means that your profit margins will start to shrink even if your sales continue to increase; the opportunity starts to look less attractive than it once did.

Listen Up

This forecasting process is a process of trial and error. You try to find how close you are to ideal and then, when you find that ideal isn't feasible, look to see how close you are to bleak. You are always looking for ideal but constantly watching for if and when the analysis turns substantially toward bleak. This may indicate a very poor market within which even the best of ideas simply can't succeed.

Carrying this scenario of many vendors entering a hot market to its extreme shows many vendors competing for the business of a fixed (or declining) number of customers. Now the customers are in the driver's seat regarding when, how many, and how much to pay for your offering. If you don't make it attractive enough, they will go elsewhere. As new products come onto the market that meet the customer's need, you will eventually find that demand for your product starts to diminish.

You are now in an opposite situation to that of the ideal mentioned earlier in this section:

◆ The number of new customers is stagnant or even decreasing from year to year.

◆ Industry-wide sales have flattened or even decreased from year to year.

◆ Along with this decreasing marketplace sales number comes a decrease in profit margin as well, so you are now shipping more product (on a unit sales basis) than you ever have before and making less net income than ever before.

◆ Customers invite you to provide a bid for their business but they are not sure when they will move forward and will make no commitments to any specific vendor.

◆ There are oodles of vendors selling something that looks almost exactly like your offering, making differentiation difficult, to put it mildly.

You are now in a really tough situation, and the future prospects for your company and offering look pretty grim, bordering on bleak.

Here is the question that you are trying to answer with all of this market research and forecasting work: Where does your company sit in the continuum between "ideal" and "bleak"? And on what facts do you base this assessment other than your gut feeling or hunch? Anything you can do to determine objectively where you stand will not only add credibility to your business plan but also help to decrease the uncertainty and risk associated with investing time and money in your idea.

Fill an Existing Market Need ... Don't Create One

I am going to make this section short and to the point: You can't afford to create a customer need. If you want to survive the startup stages of business, make sure that people are already ready and willing to purchase your offering if it meets their needs. You don't have the resources to convince potential buyers that they really need this new idea when they aren't sure themselves in the first place. Leave the market creation to the IBM, General Motors, and Allstate Insurance companies of the world. Make your money addressing the secondary and tertiary needs that these big company market creation efforts spawn since they rarely satisfy all of their potential customers. Even a little piece of their existing pie is better than all of a market pie that is still a figment of your imagination. See? Simple. Done.

Determine Overall Market Characteristics

This section presents some techniques for estimating (or *guesstimating*) your current and projected market conditions. There is a lot more art to this process than science, and it is heavily dependent on how lucky you are in finding the information you need. Not only are you looking for a needle in a haystack, but you also have to mentally correlate the relationship between all of the various haystacks in the hope of gleaning some type of meaningful trend that helps you predict the future.

You must make a number of assumptions when completing your market analysis. For example, the percentage of available customers that you expect will pay for your product or service, called *potential market penetration*, is a key estimate in determining the amount of money you will make if every potential customer bought from you (your *potential sales revenue*).

Talking Business

Market penetration is a measure of the percentage of total customers who have bought from you. If there are 1 million people in your market and 500,000 have bought your product, you have captured 50 percent of the market.

Potential market penetration is your estimate of how much of the total market you can capture over time.

Your **potential sales revenue** is the dollar value of sales you would achieve if everyone who is a potential customer bought from you.

Guesstimates are your best guess of something based on factual estimates and a little bit of educated hunch.

You can come up with some decent projections of potential market penetration through information from other companies who did what you plan to do or from guesstimates from people experienced in the field. No one expects you to know exactly how many sales you will make during the first year, or even the first two years, but you can provide fairly accurate estimates by making some educated assumptions. It is important, however, to make it clear when you are working from verifiable industry facts and when you are expressing your personal or professional opinion. In this way, the reader can differentiate between what you "think" is true and what is indeed an industry reality.

Listen Up

If you become careless or, even worse, deceptive on how you present the facts in this section, you may create questions about your integrity in the reader's mind. This will almost surely eliminate the possibility of obtaining the funding you require.

Is the Market Growing?

Market growth happens in two basic flavors: dollar sales and unit sales. Dollar sales deals with the estimated total amount of money spent purchasing offerings like the one you are investigating. Unit sales deals with the estimated number of units (widgets, hours, boxes, and so on) that were sold.

Here an imaginary set of market circumstances is used to demonstrate the procedure you might follow for uncovering overall market potential and characteristics.

Assume that you are interested in selling a special type of cooking dish that is used inside of a microwave oven. You have looked around and found nothing else like it on the market and are convinced that this product is your ticket to national stardom and an early retirement. Let's see if this is true.

Listen Up _____

Notice that if you take the total number of dollar sales and divide it by the total number of unit sales, you get a marketplace average of the sale dollars/unit sold. In itself, this is a valuable number to know since it now lets you know if your intended offering is above, even with, or below the industry average.

First, what do we know? The product is used in microwave ovens, which means that the only people who will use it are people who currently own, or are planning to purchase, a microwave. Let's start here.

Go to the library or cruise the Internet for retail sales information pertaining to the number of households with microwave ovens. You might even find this data in the Census or through the Department of Commerce, so it never hurts to check.

By the way, a quick Google search (www.google.com) using "Microwave oven marketplace statistics" as the search terms showed 4,160 matches and led me right to the International Microwave Power Institute (www.impi.org) where all kinds of microwave-related reports are available, for a fee of course. To really show you what is available with a simple Internet search, check out this URL: www.ammagazine.com/AM/FILES/HTML/PDF/0601shipments.pdf to see some very useful data pertaining to home appliance shipments.

From the chart referenced above, we find that 12.62 million microwave ovens were sold in 2002, and that this represents an increase of 6.2 percent over 2001. That tells us a lot already if you expect your product to be sold at the time of a new microwave purchase. We know that your total available market is 12.62 million units and that the market grew over the past 12-month period, but not everyone will buy one of your units (sorry)—this is a different story that we address in a few minutes. Read on.

What if your product is only useful in microwaves above a certain cubic footage? Then finding the breakdown of units sold by cubic footage would further help you define your available market since this 12.62 million number deals with *all* microwaves sold.

Search until you find this breakdown by cubic footage, likely on a percentage basis, and then apply that percentage breakdown to the total sales numbers you found at that last site. I went to the Wal-Mart site (www.walmart.com) to see the various microwave size breakdowns, and they appear to come in the following cubic foot sizes: 0.6, 0.8, 1.1, 1.6, 1.8, and 2.0. We now have a general idea about the sizes involved.

Next assume that we want to know what the breakdown is by geography because we feel that only people in warm climates would be interested in our product. This means that we are interested in the states in the West, Southwest, South, and Southeast as prospects. This will narrow the market even more. From The Weather Channel website (www.weather.com), I found a map that showed the average temperature by state for the year, which now enables me to pick the states of most interest.

> **Listen Up**
>
> It is tremendously important to know as much as you can about the overall characteristics of your "best" potential buyer. Using these characteristics, you narrow down the overwhelming amount of information available to just that applicable to our specific scope of analysis. Typical criteria include income, location, education, or pertinent social interests such as environmental protection.

Perhaps only people above a specific income bracket or under a certain age are expected to buy our product; that would narrow the scope even more. Starting to get the picture? Assume that from all of this additional refining of the total marketplace, we now determine that of the 12.62 million new microwave units sold in 2002, only 5 million represented viable prospect for our product. We still know a lot.

We know that 5 million microwave units are sold annually with which our product could be bundled. It is a reasonable "guess" that this 5 million units figure will increase by 6 percent or so (the national average) next year as well. We could refine this by knowing more about the percentage increases by unit types and geography and whether that 6 percent is a one-year fluke or an ongoing steady average.

You are trying to determine the total number of units you could possibly sell if everyone bought your product with their microwave, and then you can scale it back to something that is a reasonable percentage of that total market. Sorry. You are not going to sell 100 percent of the new purchasers on your great product. It just doesn't happen.

The total possible units that the market could purchase this year is 5.3 million, as shown previously. Now, assume that your company can reasonably sell just 10 percent of those new purchasers on buying your product along with their new microwave. By the way, 10 percent is usually a high number for first year introduction, but it is used here to keep the math simple. You will more likely see a 1 to 3 percent acceptance rate in the first year.

That means you could expect to sell 530,000 units which, if sold for $30 each, would translate into sales of $15.9 million. Not bad for a new company. You can adjust the percentage sold up or down from this starting point, but notice that you now have a benchmark for determining the quantity of units you expect to sell and the amount of sales revenue you expect to earn from those sales. Much of the rest of your plan will be determined by these two numbers, so you want to make them as accurate as possible.

Is the information fragment correlation process that constitutes market forecasting starting to tie together for you a little more? It is a process of curiosity, discovery, learning, and assimilation. The more you learn, the more you know about how to find that specific piece of data that will tie your entire analysis together. Remember that you are always trying to estimate just a few values that will eventually end up in your financial analysis spreadsheet:

- How many of your units can reasonably be sold?

- What will be the average price per sold unit?

- How long will it take you to get up to a certain sales level, and what percentage of the total prospective purchasing population will have to buy to make those numbers?

- How does the total marketplace subdivide and reduce as you apply the specific demographic traits of your most likely buyer?

- What is the best way to get to your prospective buyers based on their easily tracked demographic characteristics?

Keep your analytical eye on finding the answers to these questions, and the information will come your way. It always does once you are focused on knowing what you want. Take heart in knowing that if trustworthy numbers don't come your way, this analysis process will educate you to the point that you can make your own educated guess, knowing that it will likely be as good as anyone's.

You now have some credible market estimates. Next take a look in Chapter 10 for additional information on setting your price and estimating the number of people who will actually buy your product once they know about it. Combining the information from these two chapters will provide you with the sales revenue and unit forecast numbers that you will use to predict production, marketing, sales, cash flow, and other critical operational requirements.

It is always hard for me to believe that all of this research, analysis, and investigation comes together as just a few numbers on a spreadsheet. But, oh, how important those numbers are. You just can't be too careful when estimating your sales numbers because major over- or underestimating of these sales numbers can put you right out of business.

Who Are the Major Players in Your Market?

As mentioned earlier, your offering and company don't exist in a vacuum. You most likely already have competition for the type of product you intend to offer. Assume, continuing the example above, that we found out that Competitor A offered your target customer a product similar to yours and sold 4 million units per year. This information tells us that your maximum available market—before having to steal sales (and customers) from A—is 1 million units. Why? Because they are already buying from A, who must already be heavily entrenched in that market to have an 80 percent market share ([4 million/5 million] = 80 percent). You not only have to overcome the fact that you are the "new" kid on the block but also that buying from A is the customer-accepted norm.

If, on the other hand, A offers a similar but highly deficient product to yours and only sells 500,000 per year, then you might have a great situation on your hands. Competitor A might have created a market need for your type of offering, but it has done a pitiful job of filling that demand with one of sufficient quality. You might be able to step directly into that market need "void" with your higher-quality offering and sell a ton of product right under A's nose. If this happens, make sure to send A's president a box of chocolate and a thank you note after you make your second million dollars. See Chapter 9 for additional details related to assessing and dealing with competition.

How Long Will This Opportunity Last?

We all know the saying that "Nothing lasts forever." This is particularly true of a hot marketplace. At some point, it will cool down, and you don't want to be caught off guard when it does because this can undo, in a few short months, all of the success you created over the prior few years. Take a look at Chapter 10 for information related to predicting the maturity level of your particular industry. Knowing your industry's maturity level helps you determine the requirements for and time frame of the level that follows. In this way, you can be prepared for that level before it actually happens, making money right up until the last minute.

Some markets, such as the novelty gift market, are highly volatile, meaning that they explode and fizzle in only a few months. Think about the Pet Rock. Others, such as steel manufacturing equipment, last for years or even decades. Your marketing window of opportunity will vary with your industry, and you should have a somewhat intuitive sense about your particular industry's market window and its unique signs of change.

Research Data Sources Are Everywhere

One of the best ways to learn about your industry's trends is to turn to the media. Trade newspapers, magazines, reports, websites, and radio and television stations carry so much information that you can become overloaded if you are not careful. By knowing what you are looking for, you will recognize a research data point gift when it comes across your desk. Where others would read it and move on, you will read it and add it to your analysis.

The best way to undertake market assessment research is to read the following:

◆ Industry and trade business magazines and newspapers

◆ Local newspapers (and local news programs)

◆ Publications about subjects pertinent to your offering

◆ National news and business publications

◆ Related Internet materials and websites

◆ Industry association trade journals

> **Listen Up**
>
> Stop by your local library and ask the reference librarian about sources for demographic information. No doubt, you will be overwhelmed with the various sources for this commonly used information. Even better, know the specific data you are seeking and let them find it for you. That is their job, and they all seem to like a good investigation challenge.

> **Listen Up**
>
> If local company owners are unwilling to share their secrets, call similar business owners in another town or state. Since you are not a competitor, they may be willing to talk with you about what they've done that has worked—and not worked. Check out online sources such as forums and discussion groups with people who can provide advice based on their experiences.

Since you already know what you want to sell but don't know how much people will pay you for it, you could narrow the focus of your research to similar businesses in your area. Study them, read all the recent articles about them in your local library's clipping files, and talk to the owners about how their businesses are going. From their experience, you will be able to gauge a reasonable price point and acceptance level for your offering. There is really no better indicator of acceptance of an offering than to see how similar products have been purchased before. From this baseline, you can assess whether your proposed offering is more or less valuable to the customer and guesstimate this value assessment's impact on what your customers will pay.

Researching Your Plan

The deeper you get into this research process, the more you will start to appreciate your local public library and the reference librarians who work there. Virtually all the information you'll ever need to research your business idea is out there. You just have to know where to look for it. These reference librarians are masters of finding that obscure fact that you simply cannot find. And if they can't find it, it just may not be out there. Get to know these reference gurus really well, and use their important talent to its fullest extent.

The whole point of this chapter is to get you started on understanding your marketplace and industry so that you can make some credible predictions about your expected sales levels. Although you might have years of experience in the type of business you want to start (perhaps you've been working in your family's printing shop for decades), investors want to feel confident that your market instincts as well as your operational abilities are correct.

To show them that your ideas are on target, you have to give them proof in the form of reliable published articles, reports, and other statistics. Saying that you know the market for printing is growing exponentially each year is nice, but being able to back up that statement with a report from the Department of Commerce that says essentially the same thing gives you a lot more credibility—and that's what you need at this point. To accomplish this, all you need to do is turn to reliable experts, such as publications, reports, and market gurus. All are available by phone, fax, Internet, or at the library.

Listen Up

Remember that increased credibility translates into decreased perceived risk in the mind of your potential investor. The lower the risk, the more likely this investor is to take a chance on your venture. Credibility is a good thing, and it comes from objectively obtained, credibly analyzed data.

As I showed you earlier in this chapter, the growth of the Internet makes it likely that you can find much of the information you need in cyberspace. Once you become gifted at Internet searches, you might be able to avoid trouping off to the library. However, I still find that trained librarians are often able to point me in just the right direction, particularly for those difficult-to-find yet important, obscure data points that can be highly elusive. Don't be afraid to contact your local university library as well. The state universities have an incredible network of libraries that may provide just the information you need, and your tax dollars have already paid for it.

Some of the most useful databases available to help you in learning more about an industry, a company, or a group of target customers include the following:

- Lexis/Nexis
- ProQuest
- Dow Jones
- InfoTrac

The following are some helpful websites you can turn to for assistance:

- **www.fuld.com.** A competitive intelligence resource

- **www.thomasregister.com.** The Thomas Register

- **www.dnb.com.** Dun and Bradstreet

- **www.google.com.** General Internet search engine

If you're lucky, you might find that more information exists than you could ever use in your business plan. Chances are good that somebody, somewhere has compiled exactly the information you want. The challenge becomes finding it. Once you find it, you also might need help getting it in the form you want. (I know a guy who studies the sex life of fire ants. Go figure!) The point: Somebody, somewhere, is working to find an answer to your questions.

Listen Up

Subscribe to industry-specific publications and trade groups. They offer support and research that might not be available to the general public. Find a Federal Repository, frequently located at a local university, which contains all the latest government document information. You already paid for the research with your tax dollars, so you might as well use it. A listing of documents is also available from the Government Printing Office. Call 202-512-0000.

The Least You Need to Know

- Credible marketplace and industry information is out there, but you may have to add scraps together to get the overall picture.

- Use the Internet search engines such as Google to help you search. Get to know the search parameters really well.

- Play devil's advocate with your data and look for the holes in your analysis and assessments. If there is a hole, a professional investor will find it, and it might cost you your funding.

- Know that market forecasting is an art but one that is based on the predictable rules of business. Supply and demand is a law almost as immutable as gravity. Determine the demand and the supply, and you will have a solid sense of the viability of your idea.

Chapter 9

Learning from Your Competitors

In This Chapter

- How to evaluate your offering against your competition
- Determining whether you want to lead or follow the competition
- Methods for researching your competition
- Defending yourself against competitive pressure

My boss sat back in his chair and reflected for a moment. His eyes brightened, and he smiled as he moved forward in his chair.

"I was on a plane going to Minneapolis," he said, "and two guys behind me were talking about a large sale they were working on. When one guy said the name of the company and the contact's name, I realized that it was one of my customers. He then outlined the entire sale situation, including the dollars involved, the basic technical requirements, the time frame within which a decision would be made, and who would make the decision. In short, he told me everything I needed to know to steal the sale."

"What did you do?" I asked, knowing that my boss liked inquisitive people, and also because it really was a good sales story.

"I called the customer immediately after arriving at the airport and told him that I had heard he was looking for some equipment and that I had what he needed at a price that just happened to be 5 percent cheaper than the bid provided by the guy on the plane," he replied. *"I closed the deal that afternoon before the other guy even had a chance to claim his luggage."*

This is a paraphrasing of a true story (except the luggage part). There is always some competitor out there who will take your lunch away, and you might not even know how it happened! This chapter shows you how to meet—and beat—the competition.

Is the Competition Real?

It is easy to overreact when dealing with the competition. You might treat your competitors as insignificant (watch your ego on this one) or as a major threat (watch your paranoia on this one). Both of these approaches are inappropriate unless you know something about the competitor. You need an honest understanding of your competition's strengths and weaknesses before deciding how you should respond.

It is very important that you spend time in your plan discussing your competition. Any investor will know that a good idea either already has competition or will find it appearing soon after the new idea is proven viable. A plan that does not include a detailed discussion about competitive risks is a plan that was created in a vacuum. That is a scary prospect for any investor since it indicates a naïve approach on the part of the entrepreneurs.

In general, *direct competitors* (companies who sell the same product or services to the same customers as you) pose either strategic or tactical threats to your business. A strategic threat can affect you negatively down the road but might only make itself a minor nuisance at the present time. A tactical threat takes money out of your pocket today when your customers go to your competitor instead of you to spend their money. A large company that might enter your marketplace a few years down the road would be a strategic threat. A large company that currently offers competition to your offering is a tactical threat.

> **Talking Business**
>
> A **direct competitor** is a company who sells the same product or service to the same customers that you do. A weak competitor who takes up a lot of your time but really poses no threat to you is merely a nuisance.

A strategic threat can easily become a tactical pain in the butt if you don't pay attention to it and take the proper actions to protect yourself. A tactical threat, if large enough, can cause major problems for you. This is especially true when you have a small customer base that provides most of your sales. If your competition takes one customer, which they will definitely try to do, they can hurt you both today and down the road when other potential customers wonder what's so special about the competitor that they were able to take a major account away from you.

When you start your business, you are in the enviable position of having no major competitor who takes you seriously. This provides you with a tremendous amount of freedom because nobody will be aiming to eliminate you in sales situations. You know that you are doing okay when competitors start to know your name and change their marketing strategy to go after you. That's both good news and bad news at once.

Because you are just starting out, you should be collecting as much information as possible about the companies in your particular market segment. People might not yet view you as a competitor and thus might be more open with their information. Sit down with that information and imagine the picture that your prospective customers have in their minds about each of your competitors. Your competitors' marketing message and positioning generally creates this image. (See Chapter 10 for more on this topic.)

How does your offering compare to your competitors'? If you were a customer looking at the two companies, would you see them as direct competitors or as two companies in separate market segments? Does this perception come from the fact that they offer different products or services or that their marketing message presents it differently?

From this approach, you can get a first cut on who to treat as a competitor. Remember that you continually want to be training yourself to see things through the eyes of your customer. Those are the most important eyes, after all.

Accumulating Competitive Information

The Central Intelligence Agency calls it information; I call it the essence of competitive action. No matter what you call it, information is the key to making informed and appropriate competitive decisions.

Information is everywhere, and all you need to do is keep looking for it, find it, collate it, and, finally, put it into some semblance of organization and order. It is amazing how fragments of information can give you an excellent overall picture of a competitor.

Where do you start looking for competitive information? How about the Yellow Pages? Who is listed in the category you would choose for yourself? Are they also listed in another category? If so, why? How many companies are listed there? How do they position themselves in the ad? Is it a display ad or simply a small-column ad? Grab last year's Yellow Pages and compare it to this year's. Has the number of competitors increased or decreased? Did some of the advertisers advance to a display ad? Did their positioning change from last year to this year? Look at how much insight you can obtain about your market by simply looking at the Yellow Pages.

Useful sources for competitive information include the following: Yellow Pages, newspapers and magazines, your customers and your competitors' customers, annual reports, social gatherings and networking functions, sales brochures, and websites, to name a few.

Scour the newspapers and trade publications for advertisements, articles, and quotes from any of your potential competitors. Ask your friends to do the same. They might find something that you missed. Start a folder for each of the competitors. (They really deserve at least a manila folder, don't they?) Your local library might also keep files on local companies that you can scan for free. Every time you find a piece of information, write it down if you heard it, or photocopy it if you found it in print. Date and place the information in that folder. I promise that you won't exactly remember it later, and the mind has a convenient way of changing its perception of reality over time.

Smoke Signals

Beware of the tendency to spend a lot of money for market research reports prepared by professional companies that you can generally perform on your own. Having someone else perform general research hurts you on two fronts. First, you have to spend much-needed cash early in the process; second, you give up the opportunity to become familiar with the marketing information yourself. Spend the money on marketing research if you must, but try to find out some of this information on your own first. Having great research but no money to spend taking advantage of that research is poor planning.

Ask your customers what they know about your competitors. How do they like dealing with them? What do your customers like? Dislike? What is their satisfaction level? Why don't they use you for the same products and services in which they are using your competition? Notice that this discussion opens another level of communication with your customers, which is always a good idea.

Ask customers for pricing information when you have either lost or won a bid; they just might give it to you. Note that if they give you this information, they will probably share it with your competition in the same way. I have actually had clients give me a complete competitor's bid with all references to the company deleted. In this way, the information appears generic in nature and does not reveal the source, yet provides valuable insight into the competitor's overall offering. Guard this customer confidence like a diamond! It is a tribute to your client-vendor relationship when a customer opens up in this way, and you should treat it with the high degree of respect it deserves.

Review the company's own sales literature such as brochures and catalogs. Check out its website. If you don't know the website's URL, then try something like www.*companyname*.com or go to a search engine like www.yahoo.com or www.excite.com and do a search on the company.

Their website may tell you more about the people, sites, plans, products, services, policies, warranties, and pricing than you can get anywhere else. Be aware that they will also check out your website, so don't put information there unless you want it found.

Some companies specialize in accumulating information about companies for a fee. These *clipping services* review a set number of publications for information regarding certain companies. You tell them which companies you want them to watch for and which newspapers or magazines you want them to read. They generally photocopy any articles that appear and send them to you on a regular (usually weekly) basis. This service is not free, but it might pay for itself in the valuable information about your competitors that you may have overlooked.

Finally, you can call your competitors and ask for information. A lot of times, they will send it to you. Don't use a fake personal or company name. If you misrepresent yourself, you are toying with *industrial espionage*, which is really scary. Penalties for fraud and misrepresentation can be severe and can seriously damage your business and your credibility. Just give them your name, number, and address and hope that you're talking to someone who doesn't know who you are. Don't volunteer information, and only give what you're asked. This approach is probably a safe bet when you first start out and will become more difficult as your success builds along with your reputation.

> **Listen Up**
>
> If the competitor you are researching is a publicly held company, you can get a lot of information from their annual report. Call Investor Relations for the company and ask for it. If the company won't send you one upon request, simply buy a share of stock, which entitles you, as a shareholder, to the same information that any other shareholder would receive.

> **Talking Business**
>
> **Clipping services** are companies such as Bacon's and Luce Clipping Services that read thousands of newspapers and magazines on the lookout for articles about or references to specific companies. Many businesses hire clipping services to watch for articles about their company and the competition. Unless you have the time to read virtually every major business magazine and newspaper, you might want to hire some professionals to do it for you. **Industrial espionage** is the practice of collecting information about competitors through devious methods. Using public information sources that everyone has access to isn't considered espionage, but rummaging through corporate waste paper baskets after hours would be.

The secrets to accumulating competitor information are open ears, focused attention, closed mouths, and organized details. It's a job that requires constant diligence and doesn't take much time once you begin. As time goes on and you become more familiar with your competitors, you will get to the point that you know them almost as well as you know your own company, sometimes understanding their next move before it is even announced. If you get this good at predicting your competition, don't tell them. This is the type of skill that is best kept secret.

Comparing Yourself to Them

Okay, so you've played super-sleuth and acquired a wealth of information about your competition. Put down your pipe, Sherlock; it's time to get into the trenches and start analyzing the information you've collected. How do you compare to the competition from your customer's perspective? When you find the answer to this question, you are on your way to determining your own position in the marketplace.

Here's an exercise that will help you find some answers. Take out a pad of paper or create a spreadsheet to automate the easy calculations that follow:

- ◆ Divide your sheet of paper or spreadsheet into six columns: A, B, C, D, E, and F.

- ◆ In Column A, write down the top 10 criteria your customers probably use in deciding who to buy from. Characteristics can include technical competency, service, phone support, convenience, credit terms, years in business, depth of offering, price, and so on. You can add to this listing later if you want, but only use 10 for now.

- ◆ In Column B, place a number that corresponds to the amount of importance you believe a customer places on this particular item, based on your experience. Make 1 stand for least important and 10 stand for a must-have. Although these are your opinions, they are still worthwhile to note. Your chart should look something like the following figure.

- ◆ Create individual columns for each of your competitors and your company. These columns will contain a number between 1 and 10 that gives your *subjective assessment* of how well each company meets customers' needs. (See Effect Columns C and E in the example.)

- ◆ Create another column set for your company and each of your competitors. For each company and each of your competitors, multiply the subjective assessment column's number (Column C and E) by the importance number (Column B), and insert the result in each column you've just created.

- ◆ At the bottom of each column, total all the numbers in the column for your company and each competitor. This final number provides a relative weighting assessment of how each competitor compares against the others and your company.

Ⓐ Characteristics	Ⓑ Importance (1-10)	**Your Company**		**Competitor #1**	
		Ⓒ Effect (1-10)	Ⓓ Result (B x C)	Ⓔ Effect (1-10)	Ⓕ Result (B x E)
Years in Business	4	3	12	6	24
Credit Terms	7	8	56	8	56
Hours of Operation	7	8	56	8	56
Depth of Offering	6	6	36	8	48
Prior Experience with Company	8	5	40	6	48
Certification	5	8	40	6	30
Ideal	**370**	**Totals**	**240**		**262**
		Sale Price	**$75**		**$95**

In this example, Competitor #1 has a superior market position compared to your company, as indicated by the higher total (262). This higher total helps to justify the higher product price.

How does the number in your last column compare with those of your competitors? Is your number higher or lower? The same? How does your price compare with the others when compared against the summary numbers, such as in Columns D and F in the example?

In general, you want your number here to be high because it indicates how close you are to ideal for your customers. Ideal is calculated by totaling the importance column and multiplying by 10—the perfect score for each item. For example, the sum of the importance column in the previous table equals 37, which, multiplied by 10, equals 370 points for the ideal.

Divide your rating (such as 240) by the ideal (such as 370) to see how close you are from a percentage standpoint (240/370 = 65 percent). What is the proper percentage level? It's a relative setting and one that is highly dependent upon your business and customer type. In general, you should strive to be at least in the upper 25 percent or have a percentage rating of 75 percent or higher, which would give you a C or better in high school.

Numbers are okay, but I think in pictures, so I plot price and Total Relative Weighting Importance Factor against each other for my company and my competitors. Just follow the horizontal line until you get to the proper weighting factor, and then follow your result until you intersect with the proper price horizontal line. Put a dot there and label it. Repeat this process for your company and all others. You can now see graphically where you are compared to the competition. If you really want to be thorough, you can also plot the ideal weighting against a realistic ideal price to see how you compare to it.

Notice from the example that the competitor charges a higher price and also provides a higher weighting factor, which probably justifies their charging a higher price. If you keep your products and services the same and then offer a discount price, you will continue to move down along a vertical line because you are decreasing pricing and keeping the weighting the same. Keep this up, and you will be initially busy and eventually out of business.

On the other hand, decreasing services and keeping the price the same also eventually rings the death knell for your business because people will eventually stop buying from you. Your offering will be too expensive compared to what they perceive that they receive. Graphically, you move to the left along a horizontal line when you keep price the same and decrease services, which decreases your weighting.

Where do you need to beef up services? Where do you get the best weighting-factor return for the dollars spent? Offering longer hours of operation or better credit terms increases your weighting factors on two items of high importance, whereas spending money on certification provides a lower weighting-factor return.

Okay, enough of all this graphing and other technical stuff. Will you make decisions strictly by this weighting analysis and chart? Probably not. Will the results from this analysis provide you with a structured way of analyzing your competition so that you can make informed decisions? Absolutely yes. This is a good reality check and one worth performing on a regular basis, when you're not checking out your competitors.

You should now have a pretty good idea of how you stack up against your competition. You might be less expensive than they are, for instance, but now you realize that you don't offer the extra services that they do. You can deal with the lack of services either by adding services (and potentially raising your prices) or by strongly emphasizing in your marketing program that customers will get a bargain when dealing with your company.

On the other hand, if your price is too low and you have a higher total value, you might want to consider raising the price on your offering. Why leave money on the table if you don't have to?

Price Wars Hurt Everyone

Here is the worst of all business worlds: Your competition decides to gain customers by dropping their price. This often starts a *price war* where all companies try to keep their customers by matching or lowering their prices even more. This is a dangerous cycle that usually winds up with suppliers being hurt, the customer confused and dissatisfied, and substantially lower profit margins all around. The airline and computer industries go through this cycle on a regular basis. It tears the entire industry apart and takes years (if ever) to recover lost finances, and there's really no reason for it. Look at United Airlines being hurt by the pre-bankruptcy price wars but now gaining market share, after its bankruptcy, by dropping its own prices and putting pressure on American Airlines to match. It looks like other airlines might be taking turns in the bankruptcy seat.

There is a way to beat this cycle if it happens to your industry, but it takes amazing courage and fast reflexes. Instead of lowering your price, keep the price where it is. Beef up your extra services and sell the increased quality that you can provide for the higher price. Any experienced corporate business person knows you have to make a reasonable profit margin to stay in business. Instead of automatically dropping price as a reflex reaction, try this approach first, but continue to monitor your sales carefully. If you can't keep sales up, then you might just have to join the fray and hope that you survive. Look at Southwest Airlines, who maintained profit margins while the others lost billions.

Listen Up

When all competitors compete based on price and keep undercutting their competitors to get sales, they are engaged in a *price war*. As each company lowers its own price, others drop their prices to compete, resulting in profit margins in the industry as a whole falling to critically low levels. If sales volume keeps increasing for all competitors, you may be okay, but when the market simply cannot buy any more, no matter how low the price goes, companies will start going out of business. If your company has better profit margins than the others by having lower cost of operation, then the price war may work out to your benefit.

Your company is almost never hurt by continually looking for ways to keep fixed expenses low while also cutting operating expenses. If the price wars don't come, you simply make a higher profit margin than the others, which is good. If a price war does come, you have more margin to give up through price cutting before you get into serious financial jeopardy. This is also good. Keeping costs low while maintaining high levels of customer service is just plain old good business.

Are You a Specialty Store or a Superstore?

Are the other folks in your industry large companies such as Wal-Mart that have deep pockets and a wide selection of offerings? Are they smaller companies that provide a specialized, niche offering that a few people use (specialty stores such as Candles Are

Us)? It's important that you understand where you want to fit in the continuum between the two types of businesses. Note that these terms apply equally well to service or product businesses. You could be a full-service health club or a specialty massage practitioner.

If you're trying to be a superstore but don't have the money to provide the required variety and volume of products needed, you will probably go out of business. The financial demands of making a business of this size work will affect your ability to maintain appropriate inventory or personnel expertise levels. Once your "shelves" appear naked or you don't provide a proper service level, customers take their business elsewhere.

If you're a smaller business that tries to cater to everyone's needs, you will probably fail—not because you lack skills or ability, but because your customers will expect more than you can offer. In addition, your smaller quantity of purchases will keep your costs and prices higher. The superstore firms will clobber you on price alone. Think about it—if your customer can purchase the same product at 20 percent less price from one of your competitors, you must offer some other very real benefit for them to purchase from you. All things being equal, customers tend to buy the lowest price. If you plan to charge a premium, you must make sure that things are not equal and that the quality/value perception is higher on your side.

It is interesting that the superstores are wary of the specialty stores eroding their business in key areas. A specialty store can provide a much higher level of personalized service to customers than a superstore can ever hope to provide. The specialty store can also charge a little more for the service because the customer perceives it as having more value. In this way, the specialty store keeps margins high and expenses low, which is always a good way to run a business. However, you need to know your customers and offer the specialty items they need.

Bookstores present an interesting example of the smaller bookstore holding its own against the mega stores such as Barnes and Noble or Borders. These niche/local bookstores tend to know their local clientele and offer books that are specifically related to their interests. They make the bookstore not only a place to purchase specialized books, such as offering the best selection of local area gardening books around, but also a community meeting place where residents congregate as a social activity. The local bookstore becomes part of the community and is supported as such.

In technical areas, a specialty store may be one that not only sells hardware and software but also customizes computer equipment or software for the customer's particular needs. The company makes money on both the products and the services. The customer wins because she knows that her purchase will be handled in a low-risk, professional manner. Customers will pay for the service, especially if the cheaper or larger department store route has burned them.

In retail, for example, a specialty store might be one that deals only in candles and related items. The customer might be able to find a cheaper candle in a superstore, but could he find "just the right one"? Probably not, and that is the benefit of a specialty store. People expect to pay more for the added selection and service. Value is what sells; don't shortchange yourself on that count, but don't gouge your customers either. Find that right balance, and you can create a dedicated clientele.

Trying to be a superstore when you should be a specialty store is surefire trouble, as is the reverse. If you don't have the broad range of products or services to qualify as a superstore in your industry, stick with serving a small niche as a specialty store. You'll probably make more money by establishing a reputation as a specialist in a particular area, rather than a generalist who tries to do everything. And you'll probably have more fun and do a better job of it along the way. Check your ego. Make more money.

Using Market Segmentation to Your Advantage

Within every market and industry are smaller pockets of opportunity called market niches. These are a smaller, more specialized segment of a bigger market. For example, attorneys who specialize in construction industry accidents are pursuing a niche within the larger legal profession. Vegetarian restaurants are another type of business targeting that segment of the population that doesn't eat meat. Each use a niche strategy.

Larger companies don't waste their time trying to meet the needs of a small portion of the market, but you might want to. Niches can be very profitable if you have the right offering.

These market niches are often like a vacuum in that once you make your product available, everything you produce will get sucked into the niche, too. You can also easily establish a strong reputation that will make it difficult for larger competitors to compete with. Even though niches might have fewer potential customers, they are often easier to sell to.

By the way, a hot unique product in a hungry niche market means you can charge more for your offering and increase profit margins. Get a good mental picture of what this means and watch the smile grow on your face. Those elephant crumbs are looking more appetizing all the time, aren't they?

Cooperation Versus Competition

The Chinese have a saying that goes something like this: "Who knows you better than your enemies?" This also applies to business competitors.

It is not uncommon to find that you and your competitors, or even your noncompetitors, have more in common than it initially appears. They might address a particular market niche much more effectively than you do and vice versa. Combined, you might offer something that is truly more powerful than each of your individual strengths. You can cooperatively market your offerings. You can share mailing and administrative costs and aid each other in new product development activities.

For example, suppose that you are a corporate bookkeeping service that doesn't prepare taxes. It makes sense for you to align yourself or in some way partner with a tax preparation service. The benefit is that your customers perceive you as providing a higher level of service: bookkeeping and tax preparations. You send them tax leads and they send you bookkeeping leads. Each is happy as long as both parties play by the agreed-upon rules and don't start moving into the other alliance member's sandbox.

> ### Been There ... Done That
>
> As a professional speaker, I am continually on the lookout for places where I can present my keynote and seminar talks on entrepreneurship, management, and communications topics. Like any business person, I am always looking for leads. Oddly enough, a lead source has come up from other professional speakers who talk on the same or similar topics. We share leads with each other for this simple reason—our customers don't want to use the same speaker year after year. They may want a talk on the same topic but will not use the same speaker they used within the past few years. I pass my colleagues' names to my contact when I finish my engagement, and they do the same with my name when their engagements end. In this way, by sharing leads, we are helping each other out as well as our customers. Who would have thought that true?

There is a potential down side to all of this cooperation. You may have to share sensitive company information (such as your customer list) with them to a much larger degree than you otherwise do with a competitor. You need to weigh the pros and cons of doing this, but if the benefits of the alliance outweigh the risks, you should go for it.

For Your Plan

When writing the Competition portion of your plan, make sure that, at a minimum, you include the following information. Know that your plan readers will be keenly interested in both the competition and your reaction to their potential threat.

- A table that presents important competitor facts such as name, geographic location, public/private, nationally known or local guru, sales revenue, net income, number of employees, competitive products, years in business, and any other significant information.

◆ A comparison of your offering against that of your competitors. It should outline the features and where they are better than you and where you are better than them. Pricing, warranty, terms, and other significant purchase-related information should be included.

◆ Clearly outline your own competitive advantages so that the reader knows that you not only understand the scope of the competitive threat but also are ready to deal with it in a credible way.

◆ Your strategy for marketing and selling against these competitors, including the specific tactics you plan to use winning business.

◆ If your offering is substantially different from anything else out there, how do you plan to convince customers to go with you instead of staying with the established way they have previously done things? How do you plan to deal with the almost guaranteed reality that your competition will come out with a product that competes once your idea is proven worthy?

 On the CD

> Most of us would like to get a free ride at some point in our lives, and your business might be able to enjoy the same benefit. But you must be clear on whether your company is in the position to actually create a new market (making you a market maker) or, more likely, you are in the position of taking advantage of markets created by other larger companies, making you a market follower. Check out the special bonus section "Market Makers and Followers" (CD09-1) for additional information on this important differentiation and topic.

The Least You Need to Know

◆ Competition will always exist, but that's not necessarily bad. Comparing your products and services to those of your competitors helps you stay on top of what customers want.

◆ Watching your competitors provides insight into what's going on in your market and what they believe customers want. This information can help you better plan for the future.

◆ Customers purchase value, not price. Just because your competitors drop their prices doesn't mean that you have to. A price war can often present an opportunity, depending on your particular market segment, your profit margins, and product offering.

◆ You might find that working with your competitors against other common foes is a better strategy than trying to "go it alone" against everyone.

◆ Only provide competitors with information about your company on a "need to know" basis. If they don't need to know it, then don't give it to them. It's that simple.

Chapter 10

Smart Marketing

In This Chapter

◆ Making marketing support sales success

◆ The value of target marketing and demographics

◆ Pricing strategies

◆ Promotional methods

◆ Distribution considerations

Jamie, the marketing consultant, brought the company executives into the room to report her findings. The company had seen a drop in its sales, yet it was spending more money on marketing and sales activities. The president felt that they were doing something fundamentally wrong. She had always believed that the harder you pushed something, the more it moved. For the first time in her company's history, the harder she pushed by spending more money and energy, the less she got back.

"Okay. Let's start at the beginning. It appears that you have a loyal customer base and that they all come from four general industry groups. Would you agree with that?" asked Jamie. The president nodded.

"Then why are you spending all of this time and money selling into new market areas when you still have room for growth in your target areas?"

"We cannot depend on the same old customers for our livelihood. What if something happens to one of them? Then where are we?" the president inquired defiantly.

"Good point," said Jamie. "That would be true if your current customers and their respective market segments had minimal sales growth opportunity, but it appears that you are in the enviable position of having a firm market presence in a growing industry. You should first concentrate on taking care of business in your strong areas before moving into areas where you are unknown. Let me show you how a target marketing campaign to companies in your strong market segments can improve sales, decrease personnel requirements, and decrease costs. Interested?"

"What do you think?" said the smiling, yet doubtful, president.

How do you make sure your product or service is targeted to the people who can use it most? This chapter introduces you to the basic concepts of marketing and helps to round out the information presented in the other sales, marketing, and finance chapters.

Marketing and Sales: Linked but Different

Despite the fact that most people use the words *sales* and *marketing* interchangeably, the two activities really are different.

Marketing consists of strategies that help to identify your customers, figure out what they need, determine what to charge them, tell them that you have what they need, and then sell it to them efficiently. In MBA programs, those are also called the "4 Ps" of marketing: product, pricing, promotion, and place of sale, which is also called distribution. If you want to get technical, they should really be called the "3 Ps and 1 D" of marketing, but let's not get nit-picky.

> **Talking Business**
>
> **Marketing** involves selecting or defining the right product, pricing strategy, promotional programs, and distribution outlets for your particular audience, or market. **Sales** is the part of your business that involves the steps you take to get the customer to actually buy your product or service.

It is marketing's responsibility to identify the most likely customers, design the best product or service offering, set the product or service's price range, and choose the overall advertising message and presentation content most likely to get customers to buy. Specific marketing activities include market research, product or service definition development, analysis of pricing levels, creation of marketing materials and sales aids, advertising, public relations, and sales support.

Sales activities include contacting customers, making presentations, and getting the orders, among other things. The most effective marketing tells your salesperson the company type (industry or size) and contact person title most likely to buy from your company, which products they'll probably use, a viable pricing strategy, and why the customer would use your company's products or services over a competitor's.

Effective marketing and sales campaigns require that you get close to your customers and thoroughly understand their buying motivations and habits. You might not get it right the first time, but careful planning makes sure that your darts hit the board, and experience leads you to the bull's-eye.

> **Listen Up**
>
> The essence of highly effective sales and marketing is as follows: Sales efforts work best when the salesperson addresses the customers most likely to buy, with a product they are most likely to use, for a price that is within their budget, with a presentation that delivers the right message in an easily understood format. It's simple to state but difficult to do.

Who Is Your Market?

We human beings like to believe that we are all unique, and on some basic level, we are. However, in other areas, we fall into certain groups that think, act, buy, and react alike. We're not all lemmings who jump off a cliff at once, but we do have certain characteristics that bind us as a group. These characteristics are often called *demographics* and include such things as age, income level, educational level, and marital status.

Breaking down your target customers by demographic characteristics is called *market segmentation*. When marketing people discuss the *demographic profile* of their ideal customer, they are looking for the common characteristics associated with their most likely customer.

A bank, for example, might segment its customers by age because people's banking needs change during different phases of their lives. People over the age of 50 are more likely to be interested in retirement-related products than 18-year-olds, and 18-year-olds are more likely to be interested in college loan details than 30-something couples who want to buy a home using a bank mortgage. Market segmentation helps the bank to group similar customers together and develop products that they will be interested in.

> **Talking Business** _____
>
> **Demographics** is a set of objective characteristics (including age, number of children, marital status, education level, job title, and others) that describes a group of people.
>
> A **demographic profile** refers to a specific set of demographic characteristics that sales and marketing people use to target likely sales prospects.
>
> An **ideal customer profile** is a demographic description of the type of customer most likely to benefit from your product or service.
>
> **Market segmentation** refers to dividing the total available market (everyone who may ever buy the product) into smaller groups, or segments, by specific attributes such as age, sex, location, interests, industry, or other pertinent criteria.

Compiling information about potential customers is the challenge for market research companies. They gather information through mail and phone surveys and personal interviews to determine people's buying habits. As a business owner, you can then buy and use this information to develop effective marketing programs to sell to these potential buyers. Remember to use your own customer database as a starting point for the types of customers who use your products. There is almost surely some commonality among your existing customers. You just need to find it and then use it to find new customers.

Anyone can buy marketing surveys (unless a specific company paid for the survey for its use only). Check with your local library first to see if it subscribes to any of these reports. Typically, the library purchases a wide variety of these reports and makes them available to the public. Look for a federal repository, which is a library that carries a lot of federal reports and documents. These reports were created with your tax dollars and are freely available to anyone who wants to read them.

This type of information may be available for free from other sources, too. The federal government compiles information about the age, household size, and financial status of all Americans in the form of a national census every 10 years (the last census was completed in 2000) and makes it available at most libraries. The Census contains substantial information about the American public and breaks the country into areas called Standard Metropolitan Statistical Areas (SMSAs).

Target Marketing: Picking Your Customer

If you sell beef products, it wouldn't make sense to invest time and money displaying your products at a vegetarian convention. Obviously, people who don't eat meat aren't the best sales prospects for a meat product. Promoting your meat products at a barbe-cue owners convention would make a lot more sense.

Identifying your customer is an important part of the marketing process. If you don't know who will buy your product and why, you have no idea who to contact and how to present your wares. When you don't know who your likely customers are, the result is a *scattergun marketing* approach, in which you blanket the market with a general message and hope that someone sees it and calls. This is not a very effective approach because it is costly and time consuming and results in few sales.

Target marketing, on the other hand, focuses your financial and personnel resources on the people most likely to purchase what you offer. Suppose a particular geographic area has 100,000 potential customers for your products or services. A direct mail piece sent to this group at $1 each would cost $100,000. From this mailer, you might get a 2 percent response (which is a typical response rate). That number translates into 2,000 people wanting more information from you. Of those people, assume 10 percent, or 200, actually buy your product or service. For a $100,000 investment, then, you've sold your company's goods to 200 people. A little statistics and customer characteristics analysis will probably show that these 200 people have demographic similarities that propel them into a specific market segment (which I discussed earlier).

Listen Up

There are a number of government and commercial websites containing useful marketing data. Check out some of these for help in researching your market: *American Demographics* magazine (www.demographics.com), Census data (www.census.gov), social statistics (www.whitehouse.gov/WH/services), and business articles (www.reuters.com).

Talking Business

A scattergun sends buckshot in a wide pattern in the hope that it will hit something. Similarly, **scattergun marketing** sends marketing information everywhere hoping that someone will hear it (the opposite of target marketing). **Target marketing** involves focusing your marketing and sales efforts on those groups of potential customers most likely to buy your products or services.

Although promotional methods such as direct mail are discussed later, I should point out that you just spent $500 per customer to get each sale. Now, if you're selling a $10,000 item, you've done well, but if you're selling a $20 item, you've lost big bucks.

To develop a target marketing approach, you first need to define which markets contain your best potential customers. This means that you need to know something about what you're selling and who needs it most.

For example, you might find that your market segment is mostly women between 25 and 45 years of age, or that they are mostly college educated or work in specific industries. You can also use certain circumstances as market segmentation criteria; for example, businesses moving to a new location usually need new telephone equipment. To contact businesses most likely to purchase a telephone system, your first step might be identifying those who are moving or planning to move soon.

Target marketing does not waste time, money, and effort approaching people who are not good prospects. As a result, you get much better results from your marketing time and money investment. The types of results you get vary widely from situation to situation, but you will always find target marketing a more manageable and efficient marketing effort than the scattergun approach.

Make sure that you keep this next point in mind when looking at your market opportunities: As a smaller company, you are most likely serving a niche of some type, which means that you do not provide something that serves a lot of people's needs. Know and accept your niche and then serve it better than anyone else to improve your chances of marketing success for the least expense.

Name Your Price

Price is an interesting phenomenon in our capitalist society. It often represents more than just the amount of money that is paid for a product. Price is often viewed as a status symbol or a measure of worth over and above the amount that changes hands; the most expensive suit wins. Pricing a product too low can make it appear inferior and can make people avoid it, even though it's of comparable quality to more expensive models.

Ultimately, the customer pays a price that is consistent with his *perceived value* of the offering. If the customer perceives the name on the product as having high value (such as designer clothing), then he or she might be willing to pay a high price to wear those designer duds.

Talking Business

Perceived value is the overall value that the customer places on a particular product or service. This includes much more than price; it considers features such as delivery lead time, quality of salesmanship, service, style, and other less tangible items. With a perceived-value pricing strategy, you set a price for your product or service by determining what people are willing to pay, yet making sure that you can still cover all your costs. Don't let your ego dictate your product's price. Several companies with a substantial jump on the market have fallen flat because of the faulty belief that people would pay more for their product simply because it was new, different, or had a particular company name on it!

Pricing strategies fall into two basic categories: cost based and market based. You can calculate cost-based prices by determining the costs of producing a product or delivering a service and then adding a profit margin. This means that you'd better know your exact costs or this can really "cost" you the farm. You might think that you're doing great, only to find out that your costs were wrong and you are selling for less than your overall costs.

You determine market-based prices by studying pricing for similar products or services and then basing your prices on that information.

You need a lot of information about your product costs, your competitors' pricing, and how customers decide what and when to buy to accurately and comfortably determine pricing for your offerings. Here are some basic rules that will help you determine the best price for your service or products:

♦ Never price the product below your cost. You need to make a profit on virtually every sale to stay in business. Some people think that if they sell huge amounts, they'll come out okay in the end. Wrong! You can't lose a nickel on each unit and expect to make up the profit in volume.

♦ If you have a new company or a new product, you generally cannot match price with an established company with a similar offering. This is because the other company is already known and trusted and is a less risky choice for the customer. For the same price, its offering is considered a better purchase value.

♦ You generally have to price lower than the established competition until you get a foothold in the market (unless your offering is perceived by the customer as unique and more valuable because it cannot be found anywhere else).

♦ You can generally sell intangibles such as better service, deliverability, and location for up to 20 percent over a competitor's price. Over that price point, the customer will probably treat your offering as too expensive for his or her perceived value.

◆ Don't always price your offering on a cost-plus-profit-margin basis, called "cost plus pricing." Although this approach is easy to compute, it usually leaves money on the customer's table that you could have otherwise put in your company bank account. "Market-based pricing" is generally more complicated but best ensures the most possible profit on each sale. In other words, if you do a better job producing the product and lowering your costs, market-based pricing gives higher dollar profits, whereas cost-based pricing cuts your sales price with each cost improvement, cutting your profit as well. (By the way, if you understood this last sentence, you are getting this important topic under your belt. If not, keep working at it until you do.)

◆ Quantity discounts are an effective way to encourage your customers to purchase more of your product at a given time. However, watch the discount amounts, or you might find yourself selling a lot for a minimal profit.

Obviously, you can set your prices wherever you want, but your ideal price means more sales (and profits) for you because you will have figured out what your customers believe is a fair price for your goods. In return, they buy more. Knowing what your competitors' profit margin is can help you adjust your pricing strategy.

Talking Business

When your price is calculated using the cost to the company plus whatever profit margin is reasonable for your industry, you are using **cost-plus-profit pricing**. A widget that costs $1 to produce with a desired 50 percent profit margin would sell for $1 + ($1 × 0.5) = $1.50. You're simply adding on your desired profit percentage to your actual costs.

When you price offerings at a level set by what everyone else is charging, rather than by costs, you are using **market-based pricing**. With this strategy, you can generally make more money assuming your competition is charging reasonable rates and you can keep your costs down.

You must answer several key questions when determining a pricing strategy:

1. What are your competitors offering your potential customers in terms of their basic product or service price and the price of any add-on services?

2. How much does it cost you to supply the product or service desired by the customer (including those additional intangibles just discussed)? Make sure that you include variable costs, fixed costs, expected quantities, and total revenue into this portion of your pricing analysis.

3. What additional features do you offer
   your customers that your competitors
   do not, and are these features worth
   more money?

The costs associated with a product vary,
depending upon where it is in the product
life cycle. The next section provides a brief
overview of a new product's typical life cycle.
You can use this model as a guide in determining your pricing, distribution, and marketing message strategies.

> **Been There ... Done That**
>
> I have a friend who prides him-
> self on his hourly consulting rate
> of $300, but he only bills three
> hours ($900) a month. Another
> colleague, on the other hand,
> charges $110 per hour and bills
> 30 to 50 hours ($3,300 to
> $5,000) per month. If the intent
> is to make money, then the lower
> billing rate is the way to go.

Listen Up

Profit margins for a company are available, sorted by Standard Industrial Code (SIC),
from the Dun & Bradstreet Reports, Robert Morris Associates' Annual Statement Studies,
or the annual report of publicly traded, established companies. Most publicly traded
companies will send you a copy of their annual report if you call their investor relations
department. If not, buy a single share of stock, and they legally have to provide it.

The Life Cycle

Every product or service goes through a *life cycle* from its introduction until the time
it is discontinued or taken off the market (see the figure that follows). The life cycle
usually refers to products, but services go through a similar evolution.

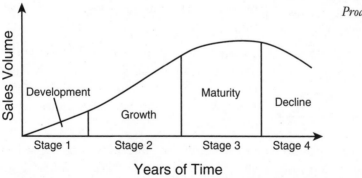

Product/service life cycle.

The life cycle is divided into four basic stages:

Stage 1: Market development (a.k.a. embryonic). The product or service is new to the market, having recently been introduced. Sales are slow at this stage, and customers take longer to make a purchase decision due to their lack of familiarity with the product. Only potential customers who have shown a willingness to experiment with new products or services are good prospects at this stage. That group of experimenters is often referred to as early adopters because they are the first to try something new.

Stage 2: Market growth. Sales are increasing steadily, and there is a general awareness of the product or service. Competition usually starts to show up at this point.

Stage 3: Maturity. Overall demand starts to level off as customers purchase the offering as a routine part of doing business. Customers have a high degree of familiarity with the offering. *Price erosion* can happen at this point due to intense competition from what is now an established market for the product or service. This is sometimes called the commodity stage since it is at this stage that products are treated as basically all looking alike.

Stage 4: Market decline. Customer demand for the product or service starts to decline due to improved variations of the product by other companies, new technology, or other market forces that make the product inferior or obsolete.

> **Talking Business**
>
> The **life cycle** is a set of four distinct phases every product or service goes through from the time it is introduced to the market to the time it is discontinued. When so many competitors enter the market that everyone has to keep dropping their prices to win sales, **price erosion** lowers the market price and profit margins. This is typical of a commodity product.

Although most products or services go through a life cycle in a matter of years or a decade, fad products such as novelty gifts (the mood ring or pet rock) might experience an entire life cycle in a very short period of time (such as a single Christmas buying season). Durable goods, such as microwaves, might have an extended life cycle caused by the level of technological sophistication and a high level of consumer acceptance.

Notice that the perceived value of your offering changes over the life cycle. In the early days, when customers are just learning about what you are selling, only a small segment takes a chance by making a purchase.

In the growth stage, with demand for your offering increasing, you might be in the driver's seat. This means you can charge a premium price because you have something everyone wants. The growth stage can be highly profitable, but it can also seriously strap your company for cash even though you are showing large sales revenue increases using the accrual basis of accounting.

By the time you enter the maturity stage, you probably encounter competitors who have developed similar products, which forces you to compete on price and service. For example, the personal computer industry is in the maturity stage of its development. Notice the rapid price erosion combined with improved performance that this industry has experienced. This is typical of an industry in the maturity stage of the life cycle.

The product life-cycle concept affects your pricing strategy. Once you determine where your product or service offerings fall in the product life cycle, you can make a better choice about your long-term strategy. The price you set for your rates as a new consultant, for example, is different from that of an experienced, nationally known consultant.

Use the three different strategies—cost, market, and perceived value pricing—to choose the price level that will generate the most sales. Then make sure that your price is consistent with your life-cycle position.

Your Marketing Message and Positioning

I used to regularly play racquetball with two guys in their 60s, and they whipped me every time. As if getting beaten wasn't bad enough, at the end of the game, I was totally exhausted, and they were only slightly winded! One time, I finally put aside my pride and asked about the secret to their racquetball success. They replied, "It isn't the speed with which you hit the ball as much as your position when you hit it."

Market positioning is everything in sports and in business. I don't mean the geographic location of your company, necessarily, but rather the way your customers perceive (position) your company in their thinking.

Take a moment and think about the hundreds of marketing-related messages that bombard you on a daily basis. How do you sift through the irrelevant ones and focus on the ones of importance to you? It depends on the way the product is presented and whether it communicates a message of interest to you. The marketing message, the essence of your positioning goal, is the key to customer perception.

The message should be simple, easy to remember, and easy to understand. The only way you can effectively position your company or your product in your customer's mind is to understand his or her thinking and lifestyle. You must know your competition's marketing approach and …

> **Talking Business**
>
> Creating a positive image in the minds of potential and existing customers is called **market positioning**. The purpose of market positioning is to have potential customers perceive your product or service in a particular way that not only differentiates it from the competition but also makes them more likely to want to buy from you.

1. Make sure that your new company is seen as different from the others, or

2. Make customers more comfortable with your totally new company or product by making it look a lot like your competition, which reduces perceived risk and adds validity to your company by association.

Here are some examples of typical positioning statements:

◆ Lower price with superior quality.

◆ More convenient and better-stocked store shelves.

◆ More fun at a lower price.

◆ Earn your college tuition in exchange for several years of training.

The range of positioning statements is infinite and limited only by your creativity. Your marketing message clearly and simply conveys the positioning benefit perception you want your customers to understand. Spend a lot of time thinking about this and try several variations on colleagues. The marketing message will appear in almost everything you produce and will create the perception your salespeople work with during the sales process. If your message is off, you are in trouble because your customers won't even think of you when they need exactly the products or services you provide!

Listen Up

Change may be a natural part of life, but it generally causes confusion when dealing with marketing messages and positioning. It takes months (or years) to create a solid market positioning in a customer's mind, and you should not tamper with it in a careless way. Confusion is a dangerous thing when dealing with customers. Decide on the positioning and stay with it unless you are absolutely sure it doesn't work. You can tamper somewhat with the message as long as all the adjustments convey the same positioning benefits to your customers.

If you know someone who changes careers on a regular basis, you know how hard it is to discuss this person's professional capabilities. She may be brilliant, but if she cannot explain her qualifications in a simple way that means something to the listener, she remains an enigma. Enigmas are interesting at cocktail parties but rarely get hired for important projects.

The same is true of your offerings. Keep the positioning consistent, and make sure your marketing message accurately conveys the customer benefits associated with the positioning. You will get tired of using the same message well before your customers will. In fact, just as you get bored with it and want to change it is when the customers start taking notice.

All About Advertising: Pushing and Pulling

Advertising is good for increasing awareness of your company and its offerings. Unless you're in retail, don't expect to close many sales directly from your advertising. The point of advertising is to firmly plant your marketing message into consumers' minds so that they think about you when they look for what you offer. Advertising also gets the company in front of a wide variety of people in a timely manner.

Marketers (or marketeers) call this *mind share*. This is the part of a person's thought process occupied by perceptions associated with your specific company. The greater the mind share, the more likely people are to contact you when they are looking for what you offer. If you have no mind share, then they won't even know to call. You develop mind share by using advertising, publicity, promotion, and personal experience with your company.

Advertising is useful for creating a *pull marketing strategy*, which means that the customers "pull" your product through the distribution channel by asking for it. A pull strategy is expensive because it requires massive marketing to your potential customers to alert them to your product's availability.

At the other extreme is the *push marketing strategy*, which requires you to convince distributors to carry and promote your product, hoping that customers purchase it. A push strategy might show faster initial results but depends on the activities of the specific distributor. Some companies begin with a pull strategy; then they are lucky enough to build visibility through customer demand. This often raises distributors' interest level, and it transforms into a push strategy.

Talking Business

Mind share is the portion of a person's thought processes that includes perceptions of your company's offerings. One hundred percent mind share means that any time a person needs your type of offering, he or she thinks of your company. A **pull marketing strategy** convinces your potential customers to request your offering through their suppliers. In essence, the end user pulls your offering through the distribution channel by putting pressure on suppliers to carry it in their inventory. A **push marketing strategy** sells your product to distributors, who then promote it to their customers. A pull strategy is driven by customers. A push strategy is driven by distributors.

Keep the following points in mind when you consider advertising:

◆ Many companies provide money to distributors for cooperative advertising. If you mention their products in specific ways in your ads, they pay for a portion of the ad. Include enough suppliers, and the suppliers can pay for the entire ad. Contact each of your suppliers for their specific restrictions.

◆ Yellow Page advertising is a must for any business trying to reach the general retail public, such as a restaurant. The phone book comes out only once a year, so you should plan in advance to be included. Check with colleagues about their success with the various ad types and sizes; take the plunge and hope for the best. Know that this contract will require payment for at least a year independent of what happens to your business. Try to not personally guarantee it if possible.

◆ Placing an ad just one time in a paper or on TV or radio is generally useless. You need to repeat your ad on a regular basis to get the best results, so plan for 6 to 10 insertions, or don't waste your money.

◆ Advertising firms specialize in making companies like yours succeed with advertising. They also have an art department that can design an ad for you.

◆ Contact each publication, radio, and TV station you are interested in advertising with and ask them to send you a *media kit*. The kit includes demographic information about the people who read each publication, listen to specific radio programs, and watch individual TV shows. Typical information includes age, sex, education, household income, and marital status. This information lets you determine whether the people who will see or hear the ad are the ones most likely to buy from you.

◆ Ask each media supplier if they have ever run ads like yours before and what type of responses they received. This might help you determine whether it makes sense to invest in advertising there.

Infomercials are currently popular as a means of marketing products and services and must be effective, based on the rapid increase in the number of infomercials currently on television. There's a lot of money riding on the success of some of these infomercials; some cost hundreds of thousands of dollars to produce, and they are generally beyond the financial reach of the conventional entrepreneur. This doesn't mean that this avenue should not be pursued, only that the startup costs should not be ignored. Producing a half-hour or hour-long commercial is extremely expensive, and on top of that, add the cost of buying the TV time. I am not necessarily recommending or refuting the use of the infomercial as a marketing tool. I just want you to know that this avenue is available and may be right for your business, but that it requires much more investigation before taking the plunge.

There are a number of new advertising tools now available via the Internet, including banner ads, site ads, and search engine listings. For people using the Internet regularly, this can be a great way to get their attention. To explore how to use the Internet as one of your marketing tools, check out Chapter 21.

Advertising can be a useful tool when used properly, but it can also drain massive amounts of cash from your company with minimal financial return. Make sure that wherever your ads appear, they are seen or heard by serious potential customers for your company's product or service offerings. It is also wise to pay for professional help when producing ads. There's no sense paying big money for ad time or space only to run an ineffective, poorly designed advertisement. Spend your money where it will count the most.

> **Talking Business**
>
> **Media kits** are prepared by the advertising departments of newspapers, magazines, and television and radio stations as a means of encouraging companies to buy ads. These kits typically contain demographic information about their audience, a rate card, and an editorial calendar for publications, which tells readers what to expect in upcoming issues.

Mail Order and Direct Mail

Do you want to take on the opportunities and headaches associated with mail order? With a mail-order system, you get the order along with its payment and then you are responsible for getting the product into the hands of the customer. You have 30 days from the time you receive the order to the time you have to ship it, which gives you plenty of time in many cases to produce or acquire needed products, instead of stockpiling a huge inventory.

> **Listen Up**
>
> Ebay, Amazon, and other similar Internet-based companies now provide a sales outlet that was not possible even a few years ago. Many people provide their products over these services, using the service itself as its sales force. The people using these services properly and to their full extent are often making large amounts of money. Things are changing in this arena, so you are cautioned, once again, to verify the nuances of their use for yourself, but you are also well served by looking into them as a viable and potentially highly profitable sales channel.

A big down side is that customers can cancel the orders after you ship them. Credit card fraud is also a real problem with mail-order sales, which means that you might never get paid for the order. Accepting credit cards is crucial for mail-order sales because you risk having even worse collection problems if you rely solely on checks for payment. Many companies wait until a check clears before shipping the product to the customer as one way to combat bad checks.

Because there are huge up-front costs required to create and mail a catalog, companies have to be confident they will receive enough orders to at least pay for production and mailing of the catalog. With response rates in the 0.5 to 3 percent range, you must have a high profit margin on the products sold to cover the initial investment.

By law, you have to ship a prepaid order in 30 days or offer a refund to a customer who doesn't want to wait any longer. Although it might improve your cash situation to produce according to how many orders you receive, make sure you can deliver in 30 days or less.

For Your Plan

The marketing section of your plan is absolutely critical, and you must spend time making it just as credible and clear as possible. Make sure that it, at a minimum, includes …

- A detailed description of your target customer, including demographic profile. Make sure that you explain where you came by this profile.

- The buying characteristics of your target customer and his or her industry.

- The synergy between your marketing approach and that preferred by your target customers.

- Your rationale for choosing the sales approach.

- Your intended positioning statement and why it was written in just that way. How does it differentiate your company and offering from others, and if it does not, why not?

- How you plan to advertise and promote your company and offering. What are the projected costs of this promotion?

- Your pricing rationale and how it stacks up with the competition. Include discussion and analysis on the profit margins required for each step in your particular marketing/sales approach.

- Tie this pricing discussion in with your offering's cost information to verify that you can maintain adequate profit margins as defined by the norms for your intended industry.

- What are your plans for expansion beyond your initial market introduction? What are the time frames for this expansion?

 On the CD

Make sure that you look on the CD for additional information related to marketing your new company. First check out "Promoting Your Company and Products" to learn ways for using the media to get free advertising. There is a proven way to work with the media so that they want to work with you, and it is included in this CD bonus section. Next, take a few minutes to read "Balancing Profit Margins with Your Selling Approach" (CD10-1). This CD bonus section helps you make sure that your distribution channel is right for your customers and also ensures that you keep your sales costs where they have to be to make money.

The Least You Need to Know

- Marketing lays the groundwork by communicating why customers should buy your service or your product. Sales closes the deal and brings in the money.

- Price is not the only buying criterion; customers look at the total value and benefits of your offering. You must remain clear on the difference.

- Create a simple, yet clear, marketing message that describes your company's market positioning, and stick with it.

- Advertising and promotion are important to positioning your company in the marketplace. A company or product's position affects how people perceive it.

Sales: The Money Funnel

In This Chapter

◆ Understanding the value of effective selling

◆ Matching sales procedures to your company's offering

◆ Evaluating direct and distribution sales

◆ Selling services

"So what happened?" asked the board member who provided the initial funding for the company.

"The sales just didn't come in as expected," said the president, a professional engineer and former operations manager. "We've been through three sets of salespeople and can't seem to find a good group. They all seem to just want more money and don't bring in the bacon."

"Have you ever been with them on a sales call?" asked the board member.

"Not really," replied the president. "I have been working with our technical people to make sure the product can do what we promised. Selling is what I have sales managers for. Why pay them if I have to do everything myself?" He knew he was on shaky ground.

"Let's make sure I understand. We have a product and a production facility that works perfectly due to your involvement, but we have nobody who wants to buy what we build. Is that correct?" Heads nodded around the room. "What is wrong with this picture, and what are your plans to correct it?"

Picture a salesperson. What do you see? A fast-talking nonlistener who is always looking at your pocketbook? A slick dresser who continually promises to do things in "your own best interest" but who is obviously only interested in selling you something—anything—whether you need it or not?

When you go into a retail store to find a particular item, do you ask the salesperson for help or tell him or her that you are "just browsing" when she offers to assist? If you are like most people who do not use the help, it may be because you have had bad experiences with salespeople before and prefer not to have something you don't need forced on you.

Understanding the sales process and what it takes to succeed at selling is important in running a successful business. As the founder and owner of your company, the sales "buck" stops with you. You are in sales when you start your own company. The only question is whether you will fully realize that fact and set up your sales operation to support your particular sales capabilities and style.

I call sales the money funnel because no cash comes into the company unless someone has sold your product or service to a customer and you have the customer's money. Selling is your lifeline to staying in business. To succeed, you must give it the attention and respect it deserves. You can stay in business if your accounting is inaccurate or if you aren't the best of managers, but you will definitely be out of business if you cannot create sales. This doesn't mean that you must do the selling yourself, however. If you lack the interest or the ability to sell successfully, find someone who can.

You need to know enough about sales to manage those actually performing the sales function and to determine when a sales slowdown represents a problem with your sales force or a problem with your company's offering or intended market.

Remember, no matter how you feel about sales, there is one undeniable fact: Without sales, you are without a business. Period.

Manipulating and Selling: Not the Same Thing

Most of us have had someone convince us to buy something we later realized was not in our best interest. We felt manipulated by the whole process and by the salesperson involved.

Manipulation has nothing to do with sales! If you manipulate people to buy your offering and they don't want it, they will resent you, your company, and its offerings for a long time. That single sale could cost you a fortune in future revenues, not only from that one customer who will never buy from you again but also from everyone he tells about his negative buying experience with you.

Sales is the process of matching your products or services with a customer who truly needs them. You are helping the customer solve a problem by providing a service or a product that will make his or her life easier. It could be as simple as selling a pair of shoes for a special party or as complicated as setting up an experiment on the Inter-national Space Station. If the customer has a need for your offering and you provide a credible product or service that meets those needs, within the budget, then the customer will buy! It is just that simple. If the customer doesn't buy, there is either something wrong with your offering, how it is being presented to the customer, or who it was presented to.

Manipulative selling might earn you a fast buck, but it also eliminates the chance for a future sale to that customer. Professional selling is the action of solving a customer's problems through your company's offerings. It is service based instead of manipulation based.

Many new salespeople have shifted from average performers who just do their jobs to outstanding performers who like what they do by simply making this conceptual shift. The difference between these two approaches is trying to sell something to a customer without caring whether she needs it (manipulation based) versus determining first whether the customer has a need that your product or service can meet (service based).

 Listen Up

If it turns out that the customer has a need for what you're offering, then the sales process begins. Obviously, more satisfied customers result from professional selling than from manipulative types of selling. You don't need to be a business guru to understand that satisfied people buy more and tell their friends to buy from you. This is good.

True business and selling success usually comes from a lot of smaller successful clients instead of a single "killing." The huge deals make good press and media headlines but really don't reflect the reality of day-to-day business success.

Getting Close to Closing the Sale

The sales process takes place in a number of stages. Look at the way you buy anything. You go through your own set of questions and investigation stages before actually forking over your money. You might evaluate the available information, read about the product in magazine or newspaper articles, ask knowledgeable friends for their opinions, flip a coin, call your mom for her advice, and eventually decide on a purchase.

Talking Business

A **close** (pronounced *cloze*) is a request by a salesperson for a specific action on the customer's part. Asking for the order is the ultimate close, but smaller closes occur at each stage of the selling process to gradually move the customer toward committing to the purchase.

Professional selling involves a sequence of small events that eventually lead to the sale. At each step along the way, the salesperson makes little requests for customer action or *closes*, which eventually lead to a sale. For example, asking to meet with someone face-to-face is a small close in that you are asking the customer to take an action that leads in the direction of the sale. If the customer agrees, you are one step nearer to getting him or her to make a purchase. Once the customer is satisfied that buying your product or service is the right decision, he or she commits naturally and on his or her own to a purchase.

People expect to be asked reasonable questions that help them solve their problem, and they also expect you to ask them to buy. If you don't ask for the order, you can't blame them if they don't give it to you.

Everyone Has to Sell, but Not Everyone Closes

Nothing is more irritating to customers than to be continually asked to buy something before they're ready. Eventually the salesperson's lack of sensitivity bothers the customers to the point that they leave simply to stop the salesperson harassment.

Everyone in your organization should support the sales process by providing information, support, service, and guidance when requested by the customer. When it is time for the final order to be placed, the salesperson takes care of writing up the sale.

Been There ... Done That

I have seen small business owners hire sales people and then basically wash their hands of the sales and marketing activities of the company. Wrong move! It must be an organizational mandate that all employees, including the owners, think of themselves as salespeople with respect to serving the customer. If the phone rings six or more times before being answered and there are employees there who could have answered it, then that customer is not being served, and a sale might be lost. That employee who answers the phone must know enough about the company and its offerings to either help the customer directly or connect that customer with another employee who can. Taking care of customers is the responsibility of all employees, and when a few drop the customer service ball, especially the owners, the entire company suffers. It is the responsibility of top management and owners to make sure that there is no question in the minds of employees that the customer must be taken care of, and not taking care of the customer will not be tolerated.

Aggressive selling is closing when it is inappropriate. Professional selling is closing as needed to move the customer forward to the next sales stage while still keeping the customer comfortable with the sales process. The moral of the story: Don't rush customers into making a decision, or you might lose them forever.

Is Your Offering a Special or Commodity Item?

Your company's approach to selling is largely determined by your market positioning and message. Offerings with plenty of competition, where the products and services are pretty much the same, require that features and benefits such as price, delivery, warranty, and stability be emphasized to set your company apart. Specialty products and services, such as high-technology electronics or tailored clothing, require a higher level of personalized service and credibility as part of the sales process because each product is so different from the others on the market.

Where does your product fit? Commodities rely more on the distribution channel to effectively get products in the hands of new customers, as well as established customers who use your product on a regular basis. There is little or no difference between commodity products (milk, white envelopes, and lead pencils), and price is a major factor in the customer decision-making process.

Specialty products require a higher level of technical and sales sophistication because the product's competitive advantage must be explained well. The salesperson has to know about the benefits of the competitors' products and services and how they compare to his own company's offerings in order to sell the customer on why one is better. It is often possible to sustain higher profit margins selling specialty products because the customer is more sophisticated regarding your particular product. This is why fine wine shops, antique dealers, and high-end stereo stores charge so much more for their products. Their products are not generally available, and the salesperson provides a higher level of knowledge and service as part of the sale process.

Is Your Customer Qualified?

All the sweet-talking, wining, dining, and fancy brochures in the world will not close a sale from an unqualified prospect (someone who is not able to buy). I have seen more new, and even experienced, salespeople invest valuable time on prospective customers who were really never qualified to purchase in the first place. Here is a list of five criteria you can use to determine whether you are dealing with a qualified customer.

Again, a qualified customer is someone who is interested in buying from you and has the means and capability to do so. If you can't answer "Yes" to these five key questions, you don't have a qualified potential customer. Get the answers, or you might waste a tremendous amount of time and energy on a prospect who cannot buy from you.

1. **Does your customer need what you have to offer?** If your customers don't need what you offer, then you can't blame them for not buying it. Would you buy something you didn't need just to make the salesperson happy? No way, and they won't either!

   Make sure you really understand your customers' needs and that they understand what you have to offer. Your challenge is to accurately identify your potential customers' needs and make sure your marketing message addresses them. If you determine that you cannot meet their needs, get out of their way.

   You might even want to help the customers find an alternate source if your offerings are not what they need. Doing this makes the potential customers feel good about your company because you are truly doing something that has no immediate reward for you (because you know they aren't going to buy from you right now). In the long run, your willingness to help find a better source might pay off with the customers coming back to buy from you later because you've already demonstrated that you really have their needs at heart. Trust is a very important aspect of an ongoing sales and business relationship.

2. **Are you working with the decision maker?** Ultimately, a single person will authorize the purchase of your offering. If you are not dealing with the person in charge of the budget, who can say "yes" and sign on the dotted line, then you are only dealing with someone who has the authority to say "no" to the sale or at best can only influence the outcome.

   Instead of wasting time and energy convincing someone who is not authorized to make a decision to buy from you, first determine who the decision maker is. This might require that you meet with nondecision makers until you find the right person. You then work to meet with that person. Meeting with anyone else but the decision maker doesn't get you any closer to making the sale and can be very expensive from a time and money perspective.

3. **Is there money budgeted for this purchase?** If there is no money available to pay for a purchase, there is no potential for a sale. It is perfectly okay to ask whether money is already in the budget for this purchase. You might find that the money is coming out of next year's budget and that the sale is on hold until the next fiscal year starts. You might also find that there is no money currently budgeted for this project, which should set off warning bells in your head. You might discover that your customer needs to spend the budgeted money by the

end of this fiscal year, which provides an added incentive on his part to move the sale forward.

4. **Is there a pending event?** A pending event is something expected to happen in the future that affects when a decision is made. The pending event drives the time frame within which a decision is required. Typical pending events include fiscal year end (when budgeted money needs to be spent or is lost), management orders, moving offices, and mergers. If there is no pending event, the customer can, and might, take forever to make a decision. Why should they force the decision when a decision is not necessary? If there is no critical deadline, you might spend a lot of time trying to convince an unmotivated customer to buy.

5. **Is your customer politically open to using your offering?** Sometimes you can have everything in place, the deal looks like it can't help but close, and then it falls apart. It is almost as though an unknown power stepped in and killed the deal. That is probably just what happened. Many companies have divisions and subsidiaries they are supposed to buy from, and if it is discovered that they are planning to buy from another company, someone might try to kill the deal. Why would a company buy from you if it has a subsidiary that offers the same product at a comparable price? It won't! Not because the product isn't right. Not because you did a poor job of selling. Simply because there's a company policy that says all purchases must first be made from an internal business partner. Period.

Try to find out about these barriers to your sales early and save yourself a lot of frustration and anguish later. You can do this by researching all the divisions of a large company to determine whether there are groups providing the same service or the same product that you are. It might also be useful to know who the company is currently buying from to determine whether you'll be able to win business away from them. Use the research procedures outlined in Chapter 8 as a starting point. Or even simpler, ask someone who works for the prospect company if there is a political conflict. That person might just tell you.

Been There ... Done That

As a new salesperson, I was working on selling some test equipment systems to a major auto maker. The contact people were always happy to meet with me and arranged the meetings for around 11:30 in the morning. Several other people would show up for lunch on my nickel. After several such fruitless meetings, I asked my boss what I could do to move the sale forward. He congratulated me on seeing that something was wrong and explained, "These guys only buy test equipment from Vendor A (a competitor). They have a game going to see how many times they can get a free lunch out of a salesperson before he or she realizes that there is no possibility of a sale."

The Nine Stages of Selling

Baking bread can be a frustrating and exhilarating experience at the same time. It is an art form, and anyone who has failed in the bread-baking process can verify this. You must follow specific steps in precisely the right order and at precisely the right time. Reordering the sequence or trying to rush the process invariably leads to a poor-tasting loaf.

The sales process is similar; a sale will go through specific stages before the deal is either lost or won. Performing these steps out of sequence usually leads to poor results, and skipping a step usually leads to disappointment. Plan your sales strategy to include moving the customer from one stage to another, with small closes along the way, rather than rushing the customer forward to the final close. I will now walk you through these stages and explain what occurs and what you should accomplish.

The Suspect Stage—Stage 1

At this stage, you have heard from a friend of a friend that perhaps Company A needs your products or services. Suppose you provide business consulting services. This is the first stage in the process, and it usually occurs as a result of your marketing efforts, such as a direct-mail letter, advertisement, or phone calls.

When you don't know much about Company A but you think it might need your services, it is considered a suspect or a lead. There really is no close at this stage other than to make contact with a person on the staff at Company A to verify that he has a need for your services.

The Prospect Stage—Stage 2

If you make contact with a representative of Company A and learn that the company does indeed need the services you provide, you have just received confirmation and can move Company A to the prospect stage. In the first stage, you just suspected that Company A had a need, and now after receiving confirmation, you know for a fact that it has a need. Company A is now a prospective customer.

Confirmation from a prospect can come in the form of a response to your direct-mail campaign, a request for additional information, or a phone call made by your sales-person. The close for this stage is to have Company A agree to an in-depth discussion about its business needs. Not your needs, but the company's needs! This discussion can occur in person or over the phone depending on geography and industry.

The Entrée Stage—Stage 3

In the entrée stage, you have your first major interaction with the prospect. This contact is often made in person. For technical sales in particular, personal contact is usually required to understand the customer's needs and to explain your company's complex products and features.

This stage enables you to learn more about the prospect's need for your services and lay the groundwork for the next stage. Here you qualify Company A regarding money, time frame, and the decision-making process. Your close for this stage is to have the prospect detail for you exactly what it intends to buy: how many, for what purpose, when, at what price, and so on. The more you know about Company A's plans and needs, the better you can convince the company that you are the best choice for this project. It is not uncommon to leave this stage with more questions than answers, which leads to the next stage, discovery.

> **CAUTION**
>
> **Smoke Signals**
>
> You do lose control when you use distributors or reps to perform the sales function for your company. Major problems can erupt when distributors make commitments or promises on your behalf that you cannot or will not fulfill. Be sure that you define up front each party's responsibilities to avoid such politically and financially costly situations.

The Discovery Stage—Stage 4

In some cases, there is no need for a discovery stage because the prospect has already indicated its needs to you and has requested a specific proposal or quote from you. When this happens, you can proceed to Stage 5, the proposal.

When you are dealing with larger companies, you might find that you have to speak and meet with several people before being ready to send a proposal. Often, this is because many layers of management need to give their "okay" to whatever business you might be trying to win. This might mean many presentations, meetings, or visits just to be sure you've spoken with everyone involved in deciding which vendor company the prospect should use. When you're meeting with numerous people, you have to repeat the process of learning and addressing each person's needs and concerns.

If you haven't already collected this kind of information in Stage 3, determine the prospect's situation, what might be the best way to improve the situation, the budget, how quickly the work must be done, and the most important factors in picking a supplier. Armed with this information, you can write a proposal that shows you truly understand the company's situation and that you can provide a solution that's also within the budget.

The Proposal Stage—Stage 5

Once the prospect's needs are defined and the overall sales criteria are established, it is time for you to present your best solution: your proposal. This can be in the form of a formal written document or bid, or you can simply tell the prospect that the shoes cost $75. In either case, you now explain to the prospect that you recommend a specific solution to improving his situation, and the cost is such-and-such.

For a large-dollar sale, this stage might involve a formal presentation to a committee of people. Make sure that you don't have food stains on your shirt or blouse and ensure that you present the benefits that the customer receives from buying from you and don't concentrate as much on your particular offering's features.

Trial Close Stage—Stage 6

In the trial close stage, you ask the prospect for his reaction to your proposal, and whether he plans to buy from you. Don't take "no" as final at this stage. "No" might only suggest that you missed something or that the prospect needs time to consider your proposal. Ask for some feedback on your proposal and just listen to what the prospect tells you. You might be surprised by what you hear. Adjust your proposal accordingly and promptly resubmit. Feedback at this stage is your friend if the prospect doesn't accept your proposal as you presented it. Thoroughly doing your homework in the discovery stage will keep you from having nasty and unwelcome surprises when you trial close.

On the CD

A sample Consignment Agreement is included on the CD as document 11-01.

Some creative sellers who work with retailers will get over the customer's commitment resistance by offering their product on a consignment basis. In this way, the retailer does not pay for the seller's product until it actually sells. If the product does not sell, then the seller simply takes back the product. The only risk to the retailer with this arrangement is the energy the retailer puts behind selling the product and the floor space used up in offering the product. The seller runs the risk of the retailer selling the product and then not paying the seller for the sold products, but this is more of a credit issue than a sales one.

The Budget Stage—Stage 7

Many large purchases must go through an approval process at the prospect's company, which can take anywhere from a few hours to a few months, depending on the company and the offerings involved. This stage is often nerve-wracking for both vendor and your primary contact who wants your offering. It requires patience. Unfortunately, all you can do is maintain regular contact with the prospect to ensure that nothing stops the positive momentum toward the sale.

For a small purchase, this stage can be as simple as running a credit card through the machine and getting an approval code.

The Close Stage—Stage 8

The close stage is when you ask for the order and either get it, find out what is missing, or simply lose the deal to another company. All prior closing stages lead to this point. If you read the situation properly, had valid information and a qualified customer, you stand an excellent chance of winning the sale. This is an exciting and scary time for both you and your customer, particularly when the sale involves a large amount of money.

If you get a "no" or a "maybe," return to the discovery stage to find out if you missed some crucial bit of information or if the prospect's needs have changed. Then go through the rest of the stages again. If the customer meets the five qualification criteria, you should either get or lose the deal (or at least know what has to happen to obtain the order).

Listen Up _____

Start tracking and forecasting your sales as soon as you receive an inquiry from a potential customer. Monitor the prospect's progression through each of the sales stages so that you can better gauge when the actual sales transaction may occur. This gives you a consistent way of forecasting sales and predicting cash inflow.

On the CD _____

The CD contains a sample Sales Contact (document 11-02), a sample Purchase Order (document 11-03), and a sample Bill of Sale (document 11-04).

The Post-Sale Stage—Stage 9

You've made the sale and the deal is closed. Everyone should be happy, right? Check back with the decision maker to make sure things are going okay. Make sure the customer is still happy with his or her choice and isn't having doubts or misgivings. This is an often overlooked and critically important stage to building long-term customer satisfaction. This is also a great time to ask your new customer for referrals to others who might be able to use your offering. A solid referral from a happy customer is golden and cannot be over valued. Don't be afraid to ask for the referral, as many new customers want to share their success with others and will happily give you the referral.

On the CD

A sample Limited Warranty is enclosed on the CD as document 11-05.

It is much less expensive to keep an existing customer than to find a new one. Your most valuable assets are your repeat customers. Guard them jealously. To ensure that they continue to be repeat customers, check back with them after each sale to confirm that they are pleased with their purchase. Show your customers that you have their best interests at heart and weren't just after the sale.

A Commodity Sale Versus a Complex Sale

The sales process varies somewhat, depending on whether you are selling a CD player at a department store, a fancy house on a lake, or a $500,000 computer system. Although the timing of each stage might differ, the sequence must be followed or the sales process gets disrupted.

For example, the department store sale stages are something like this: The customer walks up and asks for assistance. This handles Stages 1 through 3. You ask what the customer is looking for and how much he or she wants to spend. There are Stages 4 and 5. You find a unit that you think matches the customer's needs and ask whether he or she wants to buy; end Stage 6. The credit card is processed, and the customer signs the receipt and walks out the door with the CD player (Stages 7 and 8). Asking the customer how the CD player is working out the next time he or she comes into the store covers Stage 9.

The sales process becomes more complex when working with high-dollar items or services, but the stages of the sale are the same. For example, trying to charge a consumer's credit card for a CD player before he or she has agreed on a unit would definitely not work in this scenario. Why do you think that placing Stages 7 and 8 before the other stages would work when selling a $500,000 computer system?

Map out your sales cycle and expected stages to set realistic expectations about what is needed at each stage of the sales process and the time frames involved in moving a prospect from Stage 1 to Stage 8.

Been There ... Done That

Adding up the total time for all stages gives you an idea as to how long it will be from the time you make your first viable prospect contacts to the time when you can expect to cash your first customer payment checks. Make sure that you include normal payment terms in determining the time frame. This is an important time frame to know since it has a direct bearing on the amount of cash you must have on hand to fund operations until customer payments help to defray expenses.

Your Sales Channels

Salespeople are important people in your organization. Just as important, in many cases, are the people who support the sales team, such as the customer service personnel. You might want to have a few salespeople responsible for finding new customers but also have a number of support people who are solely responsible for servicing and selling to existing customers.

These two tasks, finding new customers and supporting existing customers, require different skills. The support person has a relatively routine job that revolves around meeting delivery deadlines and keeping account information up to date, but the new business salesperson must create opportunities on a daily basis.

Running an efficient and productive sales team requires focused attention, enthusiasm, and commitment. But you don't have to do it all by yourself. Hire the help you need to keep sales coming in.

There are a couple of different ways that your sales staff can reach new customers. You can use independent distributors or representatives to give your company rapid exposure, or you can build a direct sales force that deals directly with customers. Both approaches have pluses and minuses.

Distributors as Sales Agents

Using *distributors* or independent representatives removes you and your sales force from direct customer contact. The advantage is that you now have an in-place sales force of hundreds or thousands selling your product or service. A disadvantage is that it is more difficult to get customer feedback because you have a barrier between your company and the customer. Plus, remember that the customer will deal with the representative on your behalf, and if the representative does a poor job of dealing with the customer, it will definitely reflect poorly on you.

It is critical to get customer feedback so you can accurately determine whether you should be developing new products or services. It is also important for you to know how happy your customers are with the distributor, rep, and your company. Can you trust the distributor or rep to make that assessment for you? In most cases, the answer is no, so you have to decide whether the additional sales from using this independent organization is worth giving up direct contact with customers. You might have to add personnel to your staff to acquire the information you would otherwise have obtained from your sales force.

> **Talking Business** _____
>
> A **distributor** is a company that purchases products from you at a reduced rate and then sells those products to its own customers. Distributors are commonly used in commodity industries. Money is made on the difference between the sale price to the customer and the cost of the materials as purchased from your company.
>
> A **manufacturer's representative** is a person or company who sells your products on your behalf. Reps do not purchase the products; they only sell them to their existing customer base. They make their money on the agreed-upon commissions earned from successful sales.
>
> A **consignment** sale is one where the retailer does not pay the manufacturer or distributor for products displayed until it actually sells.

Using distributors usually means you need to hire fewer salespeople to cover a comparable geographic area or market, allowing you to keep your personnel costs down. However, you need to interview and qualify distributors as carefully as you would a full-time salesperson because that distributor is going to represent your company. Make sure you are comfortable with that. Plus, you will be giving up a percentage of each sales dollar to pay for the sales rep or distributor fees. That percentage will vary between industries and product lines. In essence, you are trading a fixed cost (your own employees) for a variable cost (the commissions), the total amount of which varies with sales.

Should You Use Your Own Sales Force?

When is it time to set up your own direct sales force instead of selling through distributors? That is a good question, and one each company must make based on its own set of circumstances.

Here are a few things to consider when making the choice:

1. The overhead associated with an internal sales force is substantially higher than with distributors. Those overhead costs eat into your profits every month, whether the sales are there to support that overhead or not.

2. You gain more control over your customer relations when you sell direct. This provides you with better management information for decision making.

3. Selling direct does not take advantage of established customer relationships your distributors may already have in place. Your direct sales force must generate its own contacts and relationships, and that can take a longer time to develop, delaying sales in the process.

4. An internal sales force you can fully train is often better able to handle sales of highly technical products and services and will be less likely to make promises your company can't keep.

5. Some companies start out selling direct on a smaller scale until they determine the proper sales strategy for their offering. They then approach larger distributors about introducing their products or services through the distributor's sales channels.

Listen Up

Perhaps a blending of in-house and distribution selling is the right approach for your company. You might sell directly in your local geography but choose to use distribution in more remote locations such as other states or in foreign countries.

You have more control and flexibility with an internal sales force, but you also have higher expenses. You need to examine your marketing strategy to decide which approach makes more sense for you right now.

Selling Services Instead of Products

Services provide an interesting sales situation. The customer is buying something of value, but when the project is completed, he or she might not have anything tangible to show for it. For example, the result of your service contract with a customer might appear in the form of a new organization structure, better-trained staff, a new logo design, or a piece of software. These items clearly contribute to the company's success, but they are less obvious to the customer.

You have to keep in mind that services solve people's problems through your expertise and experience. Because the customer doesn't walk away with a tangible product, he or she must walk away with the belief that he or she benefited from using your service. Benefit-oriented selling is an important part of any sale, but it is critical when selling services such as consulting or training.

Clearly defining the *scope of work* from the beginning is critical to success when selling services instead of products. Because the customer might not have something tangible at

Talking Business

The agreement on exactly what services will be provided to a customer is the **scope of work**. For instance, the scope of a project might be writing a press release. Mailing out all the press releases is beyond the scope of work, meaning that those activities were not included as part of the agreement and would have to be paid for separately.

the end of a project, it is important to clearly define at what point the project is complete. More than one company has been left holding the bag when they submit an invoice that the customer feels is too high or should not be paid at all because the customer doesn't feel he got his money's worth. The company providing the service may have done everything it was asked to do, but if the customer thought he or she was getting something else, it becomes difficult to get paid.

To avoid such situations, the best policy is to get adequate detail about what is to done in writing. In your proposal to your potential customer, state clearly what you are offering to do and at what price. Make the desired outcome as specific as possible, preferably including the delivery of a final report. If there is nothing tangible you can provide to signify the completion of a contract, such as with service contracts and warranties, set a specific time period during which your services are offered. After that period is up, your services stop.

On the CD _____

A sample Project Agreement is enclosed on the CD as document 11-06.

Always avoid vague, ambiguous statements such as "We will edit the new corporate brochure until the customer is happy with it," which is a time bomb just waiting to explode. What happens after you've done 25 versions of the customer's brochure and he just can't make up his mind? Is your work done, or do you have to continue to edit and re-edit until the customer is satisfied? If you state exactly how many rewrites you provide as part of the agreement, the answer is probably no—you don't have to keep working forever—but with vague statements, you will probably never get paid.

Talking Business _____

Milestones are important target dates or goals that help you track how well you're performing against your long-term business goals. Milestones can indicate that a specific percentage of a project has been completed, once a certain step has been taken, or it can provide evidence that the project is completed. These smaller percentage completion divisions enable you to bill for portions of the project as they are completed instead of having to wait until the entire project is finished.

Instead, use carefully chosen and specific wording, such as the wording I used for a sales brochure design proposal: "We will provide an initial concept design followed by a professionally created first draft and then a second final version of the brochure that includes any requested customer changes from the first draft." Establish *milestones*— that is, measurable targets or events that demonstrate that you have provided the service and reached your objective.

Advance payments (retainers) or down payments are always good, but they are particularly valuable with contracts for service. People have convenient memories, and a little cash on the line always seems to keep the memory of both parties active and on track. It's also an excellent sales qualifier. Any prospect who is unwilling to pay a percentage of the total project cost is not someone you want to do business with. A charge of 25 percent is the suggested minimum, and 35 to 50 percent is not out of the question. Submit invoices regularly (determined in agreement with your customer) if you are billing on an hourly basis so you receive regular payments for your work.

 On the CD

The CD contains a sample Software Licensing Agreement (document 11-07) and a sample Contract Drafting Checklist (document 11-09).

For Your Plan

When writing the section of your plan dealing with sales, make sure that at a minimum you cover the following points:

- Explain whether your offering's sales process will be routine (commodity-like) or more complex (such as a technical sale).

- Define the required skill set and preferred personality type of your sales force (whether direct or through distribution) and why the direct/distribution decision was made. How will these people be trained not only in your sales process but also on your offering?

- How will customer service issues be handled once the deal is closed and the next stage of business relationship begins?

- Explain the timeline for a typical sale and the various actions that will be taken at each stage of the sales cycle.

- Explain the compensation and commission structure that you plan to use for paying your sales force. Include as much information as you can about travel and other sales-related expenses.

- Outline the sales tracking and management procedures you intend to follow and how that procedure will be used for sales reporting to upper management, boards of directors, and investors.

- Explain how leads will be generated, how they will be followed up, and how lead tracking will be coordinated. Will your company use telemarketing, and if so, how?

◆ Lay out a contingency plan to cover the possibility that the initial sales plan does not work and how the determination will be made to move to your contingency "Plan B."

◆ Outline how your sales force will implement the marketing plan's strategy for winning sales from competitors. Deals will have to be won on more than your smiles, nice as they may be.

The Least You Need to Know

◆ Sales are necessary for a company to survive. If you are not highly sales motivated, then you should hire someone who is.

◆ Selling is a process, not an end in itself, and all company personnel must be sales oriented even if they are not officially in sales.

◆ Every sale must go through nine specific and sequential stages before the customer is willing to make a commitment.

◆ Closing and selling are not the same thing.

◆ Don't waste time on a prospect who doesn't meet the specified qualification criteria.

◆ Selling direct or through external sales representatives fills different needs and requires different approaches.

Chapter 12

Production Planning That Gets Results

In This Chapter

◆ The importance of your production plan

◆ Production considerations for product and service companies

◆ Production personnel issues

◆ The importance of automation

◆ Setting expectations

The activity level on the manufacturing floor properly impressed Vickie. Tony, her friend and the business owner, had taken his company from the idea stage and turned it into a full-blown production house.

"Wow," she said. "You really have something going on here. Stuff is stacked everywhere, and you literally have people climbing the walls to get at your products. This sure looks good!"

"Well, looks can be deceiving," replied Tony with a somber look in his eye. "The reason those people are climbing the walls is because I did not allocate enough space for inventory storage of finished products. We had to put a shelving system in place so we could stack our finished inventory along walls instead of in an inventory storage area as I initially wanted."

"Why are the wall storage areas color coded?"

"The red areas are for products that have not passed in-process inspection. The blue areas are for finished products that did not initially pass final inspection, have been reworked, and are now awaiting reinspection. The green areas are for finished products that are ready for sale and shipment," explained Tony.

He paused for a moment and then continued. "Not properly planning and realistically estimating the required square footage forced me to hire three people who do nothing but shuttle things from the walls to the production floor and back again."

"It is pretty crowded in here," was Vickie's comment, reality now sinking in. *"And the activity level is pretty intense. Why not just move to another facility?"*

"I got a great lease rate by signing up for a three-year minimum. I have 12 more months on the lease that I would have to pay even if we moved to another facility. The money analysis just doesn't justify the move. So here we are: one busy, big, bustling, occasionally irate family waiting for our lease to expire. This is a mistake I will never make again."

No matter what you plan to do, whether it is produce products or provide services, there is some type of process that will be involved. The more efficiently you plan and manage this process, the more easily you will be able to grow as your sales grow and the lower your costs of production will be.

If you plan to sell gizmos, then whoever funds your project must be convinced that you can build the gizmo you plan to sell and to the prescribed specifications. As a result, it is important to understand the production aspects of your business because if you can't produce, you won't get paid.

Production in Product and Service Environments

Think of production as the process of combining raw materials, labor, and manufacturing equipment into a finished good that can be sold.

For example, if you are building music CDs, you have a few components that add up to your finished product: the CD itself, the jewel case in which the CD is shipped, the paper inserts, and a plastic wrapper. You must combine all these pieces so that the final product can be sold in a music store. The process does not vary from one CD to the next. As a result, you can look for ways to streamline the assembly process and develop processes that make this repeatable assembly as efficient as possible.

This type of production involves routine tasks that do not vary much from one CD to the next, except for perhaps the specific insert and CD. The more CDs that are produced, the better the assembly people become with the process and the more efficient the production process becomes. This increased efficiency translates into decreased manufacturing costs, which provide higher profits if you can keep your prices constant.

This process seems pretty straightforward for a product-based business, but what happens when you provide services, which is what most small business owners start out doing? The equation shifts: Materials become a very small portion of the process and the expertise and labor portion becomes dominant.

Product businesses are based on a process that is relatively independent of the people performing the tasks; service businesses often get their work because the client wants a specific person performing the task. The process and ingredients are different, but some similarities make the analysis of the production process easier to handle.

Service businesses rely heavily on the expertise of the personnel. The jobs typically performed by service personnel are nonroutine in nature, meaning that each job is potentially different from the next. This doesn't mean that there aren't similarities, but to use the CD-packaging analogy presented earlier, the jewel case might be a different color, the CD a slightly different shape or more than one in a case, the cover literature might need to be edited for each CD, and special handling instructions may be required. The overall process of putting it together is the same, but the specific steps required in making it all fit will likely involve tweaking for each CD.

The similarity in developing product and service processes is that you always want to find the common tasks involved in each process. This commonality presents an opportunity for applying automated, money-saving strategies to this stage of the process. Of one thing you can be sure: You will never reach high production volumes if everything you produce is a custom act of creation—you must take this into account when establishing your offering prices.

Been There ... Done That

If you look at a doctor's office, you see a blending of routine and nonroutine tasks and how they are delegated to the proper personnel. For example, taking temperature, blood pressure, and weight and performing other routine tasks are handled by a nurse, whereas the nonroutine tasks—the examination and evaluation of each patient—are performed by the doctor. The patient might be in the office for an hour, but the doctor might only be with the patient for 15 minutes. In this way, the doctor can see four patients in an hour instead of only one, which would be the case if she performed all the routine tasks on her own.

Here are some key points to remember when defining your production process:

- The more times you do something, the more efficient you become at doing it.

- Increased efficiency usually translates into reduced costs and increased profits.

- The more routine (repetitive) the task, the less skilled the personnel must be to perform it and the easier it is to ensure consistent quality.

- The more tasks vary each time they're performed, the higher the personnel skill level required.

- Production in product-based businesses tends to be more routine, making mass volume efficiencies the goal.

- Service-based businesses tend to be more time dependent because the overall project variations can fluctuate from one time a task is performed to the next. It is difficult to estimate the amount of time something will take if you have never done it before. You can guess, but knowing for sure is not likely.

- Service-based businesses should look for a methodology that makes the nonroutine tasks more routine, allowing less skilled personnel to perform the tasks without compromising quality. More skilled people can then focus on the nonroutine aspects that more fully utilize their higher skill level.

- Personal customer contact and relationships are critical to a service business (would you go to a doctor you don't like?), whereas product performance and quality are critical in a product business. (Have you ever met the designer of your Sony Walkman?)

Are You a Mass Producer or a Job Shop?

It's time to add another level to the analysis process. Hang in there with me because this evaluation procedure becomes second nature after a short while. The more you understand your operation, the more likely you are to make it as reliable, efficient, and profitable as possible without sacrificing the overall quality of your offering.

This section compares *mass producer* to *job shop* environments. If you are continually producing the same thing, you are a mass producer. For example, a company that produces candles is a mass producer in that once set up to make candles, the process might make thousands, or even millions, in a single run. Can you imagine how good you get at something after you have done it a few million times?

Job shop environments require more customization to complete each job. This doesn't mean that the same underlying technologies are not used. It only means that they are used in a different way for each job. For example, creating a custom software package is a job shop environment in that the software is developed once for a specific customer. You are not going to take the same software and resell it to others since few other people will need *exactly* what you developed for earlier customers. You might still perform the software programming operations using a specific programming language, but the software application itself is customized for each customer. Now, if you create the software and then package it for sale on retail shelves, the software creation process is nonroutine, but the process of packaging the software and shipping it to a retail outlet is routine for each software box shipped.

Talking Business

Mass producers continually produce the same products (routine). **Job shop** operations require more customization to produce each product (nonroutine).

Been There ... Done That

I have some friends who run a small business that specializes in custom injection plastic molding of very large parts. Once the process is set up, they might produce only one, two, or three parts for a customer. This is clearly not a mass production environment, but they have a unique process methodology that allows them to create the required parts in a reliable and efficient fashion. If they based their pricing model on mass production economies, they would be out of business. They realize that their offering is unique and charge the premiums needed to ensure that the customer does not get gouged, yet they cover the costs associated with a job-shop environment.

Linking Purchasing, Production, and Marketing Forecasts

Get ready; here comes an automation speech. If you have ever worked in a product manufacturing environment that did everything by hand, you understand the importance of automating your purchasing and inventory processes.

This can get pretty complicated, but it is really important, so bear with me. You need to order parts from your vendors before you can build your product. This means that you must have quantity projections about the products to be built. In addition, each of the components that you include in your product has some delivery lead time requirement from your vendors. This lead time can be as short as overnight for a standard part, such as a screw, or as long as several months for a custom casting part, such as the frame of a bicycle. This means that before the components can be purchased, you must know how many you plan to build, which means that you must know how many your sales and marketing people plan to sell. And more specialized parts are generally more difficult to find and more expensive to purchase.

The service equivalent or a specialized part is finding a person with the unique skill set needed to address your customer needs. You must either hire a person with the required skills, hire a less capable person and train her to have the required skills, or train one of your internal personnel to have the proper skills. In any case, lead time involved with getting the right person with the right skills must be considered. You even have a lead time involved if you already employ someone who has the proper skills. Why? Because if you are operating profitably, that person is already busy on another project and might have to finish it before he or she can start on the new one.

Oh, by the way, you also need to ensure that you have the financial means to purchase the components (or hire the personnel) because there will be some manufacturing lead time on your side before the product gets out the door and into customer hands and you receive the payment. Before you flip out, take a look at Chapters 16 and 17 and reaffirm to yourself that cash is king, credit is queen, and luck is the joker.

Most of the accounting software packages I have seen, such as QuickBooks, allow you to track purchasing, inventories, and sales but don't integrate forecasting. Most of the canned sales support packages I have seen, such as ACT!, allow you to track contacts but really don't allow you to track manufacturing forecasts.

How can you manage the critical gap between your sales forecast and your production and purchasing requirements? You either need to handle this gap in a rigorous, yet manual, manner at first, pay someone to develop custom software, or scour the industry for a software package that addresses your specific company needs. These packages are out there, but you might pay thousands of dollars finding the package that is right for you. They are generally referred to as manufacturing requirement packages (MRP).

Is an MRP software package worth the initial investment? It depends on how large you plan to grow and how substantial your initial funding is. Paying a lot for the right production control software package could deplete your cash reserves to the point that you jeopardize the company. Clearly not a good idea. But those of you with aspirations of growing a large manufacturing company want to take a hard look at automating with an MRP system from early on in your company's life. If you don't, and you are successful, you will likely lose sales, customers, profits, and sleep as you deal with the intense demands that arise from rapid manufacturing growth. Make sure that you hitch your MRP wagon to a solid software product provider who will be around in the future to keep your software purchase reliable and contemporary.

In keeping with my "automate from the beginning" philosophy, I suggest that you either buy a package (if possible) or train yourself to think of your company as a process. It starts with the sales lead to the order and continues through purchasing, production, shipping, receipt of the product by the customer, receipt of the payment check from the customer, to the final cashing of the check. Ultimately, it also includes generating the operational and financial reports on a periodic basis.

Ask another manufacturer in your area for a facility tour just to see how it deals with its particular production environment. If you are building the same type of products, such as electronics, you might be able to learn from each other. Ask the manufacturer about the software it uses for MRP. It might save you headaches down the road.

> **Been There ... Done That**
>
> Make sure that you spot-check your MRP reports to ensure that the numbers flowing from sales to production to purchasing make business sense based on your experience. The longer you are in business, the more accurately you will be able to estimate your sales forecasts, which better ensures proper production goal setting. But periodically spot-check the accuracy of your operational systems.

Create a Production Flow Chart

You don't have to become a process engineer to build many products, but you should have an idea of how the process flow works and what sections need special attention. This involves a big sheet of paper, or the use of a software package such as CorelFLOW, Microsoft Project, or other flowcharting and project management software packages.

Map out the entire process on a piece of paper, and note which steps are routine or nonroutine. Also map out the weak links, or *gating items*, in the process. These are the items that restrict your ability to produce in higher volumes (mass production) or produce in less time (job shop). Making these gating items more efficient always pays huge dividends later, and you need to watch them like a hawk, for these are the items that can also put you out of business.

> **Talking Business**
>
> A **gating item** is an item that limits the overall efficiency of the process. If this item's efficiency is increased, the overall process generally becomes more efficient. Track these carefully.

For example, a large airplane manufacturer recently went through a huge sales growth spurt where its sales and marketing people sold many new planes to several foreign governments. Good news? Not for this company. They couldn't get many of their critical parts from their vendors in time to meet the production schedules. They had to shut down their plant for a few weeks in 1997 while they waited for the gating item parts to arrive. Here is a company with a stellar sales record and a black eye simply because it outsold its production capability due to gating item parts.

Finally, look at your process map, and determine the amount of space needed for each stage of production. Don't forget that the raw inventory parts you receive from your vendors need storage space along with the finished products. In addition, products that go through many stages of production need interim storage space along with those products rejected during the production process. If you don't take a detailed look at the space requirements early, you might end up like our friend in the opening story who had employees literally climbing the walls.

On the CD

A sample Notice of Rejection of Delivered Goods is enclosed on the CD as document 12-01.

Successful Project Management

I am not going to go into the details of project management in this chapter, other than to point you in the direction of understanding basic project charts and tools. By the way, another book in this series called *The Complete Idiot's Guide to Project Management, Third Edition,* is an excellent introduction to project management. I suggest using it to add meat to the skeleton outline provided in this section.

A *Gantt chart* shows you the relationship between the various project components and their required completion sequence (see the following figure). I create my Gantt charts using a spreadsheet package such as Microsoft Excel with the tracked items listed in the left column and the column headings labeled as the weeks, or days, on which each stage of the project is to be completed. I then note the dates for completion with special symbols such as "M" for milestones or "S" for start and "F" for finish for tasks that take a period of time to complete.

The *critical path analysis* allows you to determine the process bottlenecks so that you can keep an eye on them. Project management software packages perform this critical path analysis for you. You don't have to go overboard on all this stuff in the beginning, but if you don't get a realistic picture of your space and time requirements, you can be seriously hit later when you get into actual production. Plus, it is a waste to plan your production around a higher level of throughput and then not ensure that you have enough capability to handle the required critical path items. It is hard to say too much about the importance of knowing and managing properly your critical path items.

		12/23	12/27	12/29	1/2	1/5	1/9	1/12	1/16	1/19	1/23	1/26	2/2	2/6	2/9	2/13	2/16	2/19	2/22	2/25
CIG to Starting Your Own Business, First Edition																				
Project writing schedule - Gantt Chart																				
cigtimng.xls																				
Milestones																				
	25% Completion					MM														
	50% Completion										MM									
	100% Completion															MM				
	Author Review																	XX	---	XX
Chapter No.	Introduction																	XX		
1	So, why go into business...			▓																
2	Preparing the business plan		▓																	
3	Strategic vs. tactical planning				▓															
4	Which business form to choose						▓													
5	Additional corporation considerations								▓											
6	Effective marketing makes selling easier									XX										
7	Dealing with competition										XX									
8	Without sales, nothing happens										XX									
9	Making sure that you are making money					▓														
10	Working with banks...											XX								
11	Cash is more important than you mother										XX									
12	Setting up for credit card sales							SS	▓											
13	What to do if they don't pay						▓													
14	Complicating life by adding employees													XX						
15	Simplifying payroll....														XX					
16	Other stuff...															XX				
17	Using automation																XX			
18	Dealing with success																XX			
Appendix A	An actual business plan									XX										
Appendix B	Glossary																		XX	
Legend:	Milestone	MM																		
	Proposed Completion Date	XX																		
	Duration of Completion	XX	---	XX																
	Completed Item	▓																		
	Slipped Item	SS	▓																	

A sample Gantt chart.

Talking Business

A **Gantt chart** is a method of displaying and tracking project items where one item's completion is dependent upon the prior completion of another item.

A **critical path analysis** is a project management technique that maps a process flow and then determines the items that limit production. These items become gating items.

Throughput refers to the total amount of product being manufactured within a given period, usually a work shift or day. The higher the production levels, the higher the throughput.

By the way, the more detail you have in your planning, the more likely you are to get money from your investors. The details show them that you have thought through the steps and understand what you are doing. Without the details, you are winging it with their money. Think about it. Would you rather give money to someone who has spent the time thinking about the details or to someone who says, "Trust me; it will be okay"?

Maintaining Quality

Nothing will put you out of business faster than being a new company that gets a reputation for bad quality. Happy customer referrals are critical to the success of your business, and if you let the quality suffer, your referrals will become negative instead of positive. Ouch—then bye-bye!

I recently gave a speech to a group of quality professionals on the importance of instilling quality in small business environments. It forced me to formalize some of my thoughts on the topic. The talk was well received and they encouraged me to pass my thoughts on to my readers. So here is a synopsis of the high points from my talk for your consideration and specific application to your company environment and plan writing:

♦ Know what you sell and what your customers buy. Make sure that you or someone you trust inspects the critical qualities that your customers expect from your product or service before your customers see your offering. This applies to both product and service companies. If your company offers massage services, get a massage by each of your massage personnel every now and then to ensure that they meet your standards. If you offer tax preparation services, have one of your senior people randomly spot check the returns to ensure that they are accurate.

♦ Never let your customers become your final product inspection team. Make sure your product or service meets your expectations before you let them see it. Customers never forget that you sold them deficient goods.

♦ *Underpromise* and *overdeliver*. This is where I see many small businesses suffer. Because you are small, you might feel that you have to overpromise to compete with a larger company. You know that you are overpromising when your evenings and weekends are tied up doing extra stuff for a customer, and you are cursing yourself for having promised things that are not part of what you normally offer. If what you promised must be there as part of the standard offering, then make the proper production changes and set up to include it as part of your normal operation. If not, do not overpromise unless you have a lot of free time. Just be careful to not "underpromise" so much that you lose deals that you credibly should have won. Keep looking for the balance, and you will find it.

♦ Never *overpromise* and *underdeliver*. You can deliver exactly what all of your brochures promote and still have an unhappy customer if the customer was promised additional items that were not delivered. This is an easy problem to fix. Promise only what you can deliver or realize that you and your company will continually be jumping through hoops complying with "loose lips" promises.

> **Been There ... Done That**
>
> Cisco Systems, the communications products manufacturer, has set up annual surveys of both customers and employees as a way of gauging satisfaction. Employees are paid a bonus or raise based on the results of their respective quality surveys. In typical Cisco fashion, they automated the survey process to make it simple and fast. Perhaps there are a few lessons here for your company as well.

◆ Personally spot-check the products or services before they leave your business, and let everyone know that you do it. This tends to keep employees on their toes and ensures that your toes don't get stepped on. Perhaps you should set up some type of financial incentive system that is tied to acceptable quality levels.

◆ Work with customers up front to establish their expectations. This is particularly true for service agreements, or you can find yourself working for a client forever, with the best of intentions, not getting paid for it, and still having an unsatisfied customer even though you delivered what you thought the customer wanted. For example: "My Company agrees to supply Your Company with a draft of the document, circulate the draft to the client for comments, and then incorporate those comments into the final draft." Notice how only one level of revision is included in this agreement; this means you do not waste time and resources endlessly revising your work.

◆ Define specific, concrete expectations, and do not leave them general. General: "To deliver a product or service to the customer's satisfaction." Concrete (Recommended): "To deliver a product that meets the specifications as outlined on product specification sheet 01-A, dated 09/27/2000."

Talking Business

When you **overpromise,** you make a commitment to a customer that exceeds what your company is set up to deliver. When you **underdeliver,** you deliver less than that which was promised. This behavior is almost guaranteed to generate a nasty phone call and possibly a poor recommendation from your customer.

Savvy business owners may **underpromise**—that is, promise to deliver less to the customer than they actually intend to deliver. People don't get mad when they receive more than they expected for the same price.

For Your Plan

When preparing the production portion of your plan, make sure that you consider the following points:

◆ Make sure that you understand the routine/nonroutine aspects of your offering and adjust your operation and personnel accordingly.

◆ Spell out how and where you intend to perform your manufacturing and production activities.

◆ Estimate the product and labor costs associated with your offerings, taking into account the cost decreases that typically come from higher volume and more experience. This information is critically important to setting your prices and maintaining healthy profit margins.

◆ Present any labor- or skill-related issues that directly affect the production process.

◆ Explain how you intend to define and maintain an appropriate level of quality for your intended customer audience.

◆ Present a flow chart of the operational process from order receipt until the offering is received by the customer. Specify the gating components, skills, or operational steps associated with your production environment and how you plan to address these critically important concerns.

◆ It is common for the production plan to present the details associated with lead generation, order receipt, processing, invoicing, and collections. They are all part of the production process associated with a healthy business. Including this in your production section instead of in the marketing sales section is not uncommon and is recommended by some.

◆ Include an explanation of how you intend to finance and create new offerings, whether service or product oriented. At some point, a new offering must come along to take the place of the ones you initially offer, and it is good to present some thought in this regard.

The Least You Need to Know

◆ You must understand how your company creates and delivers its offerings and then ensure that the quality that makes you successful is an integral part of the process.

◆ Understand the routine and nonroutine aspects of your business, and assign appropriately skilled personnel accordingly.

◆ Automate as much as possible from the beginning (again!).

◆ Map out your production process and specify the personnel, raw materials, space, time, and equipment needed at each step of the process.

◆ Underpromise and overdeliver.

◆ Know the relationship between the time needed to produce your offering in relationship to when and how your customers buy.

◆ Spot-check quality yourself and never let your customers do your final quality inspection.

13

Lions and Tigers and Employees, Oh My!

In This Chapter

- ◆ Why adding people to your organization can be a good thing
- ◆ The value and risk of a personnel manual
- ◆ Effective and legal interviewing procedures
- ◆ When a contractor is really an employee
- ◆ Test-driving employees before hiring

"Tell me this again," said Julie. "Didn't you smell it when you went by her desk?"

"Sure I did," said Bill, the company lawyer. "But so what? There's nothing in your company procedures manual that covers drinking on the job."

"Because of that, I can't fire her?" asked Julie. "She carries a bottle in her purse. She takes a nip in the bathroom on a regular basis. I have even accidentally picked up one of her coffee cups to find that she was drinking Irish coffee. She's drunk on the job, and I want her gone!"

"That is understandable but not legal. Has her drinking affected her job performance in any way? Can you definitely point to business lost because of her drinking? Has it disrupted the normal flow of business in such a way that has cost the company money?"

"I know that it must have happened, but I can't point to a specific instance," said Julie. "So you're telling me that I'm stuck with her because firing her would open us up to a wrongful termination suit based on our not having a no-drinking policy in our manual."

"Pretty much. You need to watch her closely and look for signs of poor performance that can then be documented. Then you can let her go for poor performance. In the interim, you should never mention the drinking problem to her and act as though nothing is wrong. Otherwise, you play right into her attorney's hands when you finally let her go. Sorry."

Adding employees represents a great leap for your business; there is so much demand for your product or service that you need to expand your staff. Yet managing other people brings with it a number of issues that you don't have to deal with when you work alone. In this chapter, I'll show you how to manage and lead your employees—successfully.

When You're Successful, You'll Need Help

If you follow all the great advice I'm giving you throughout this book and add your own special flair, you will probably become so successful that you just won't be able to do it alone. At that point, you need to add employees to your organization. It might be only a clerical person who handles billing and answers the telephone or a complete staff of people who handle all those new projects you just brought in as a result of your incredible marketing skills.

In either case, you need to address the new challenges associated with running an organization that now has staff members. There are lots of ways to find employees, but before I jump into how to find the right employees, how to manage them, and all that detailed stuff, let me present a few bigger issues for you to consider:

1. You have been on your own, and possibly working alone, since you started your company. Make sure that you actually need an employee for functional reasons, not simply because you want someone around the office for business companionship. Have you gotten to the point that you are losing business because you don't have enough help? That is a cost justification for hiring a new employee.

2. Employees cost money and must pay for themselves either today or in the near future. Once you hire an employee, you assume the responsibility for paying him regularly, no matter what the business's financial condition is. Even if you have a really poor month, you still have to sign those paychecks to your employees. Are you ready to absorb that expense, or would it be smarter to push yourself a little more for a short while and build up a nest egg? Is the lack of that employee costing you money yet?

3. When you add people to your organization, you inherit a responsibility for their financial support. If you aren't making enough money to support yourself, you probably can't afford to support someone else.

4. You become the last employee to be paid if the company has cash flow problems. Are you ready to accept not getting a paycheck for a week or two (or three or four or ten) without resenting the other employees who have gotten paychecks?

5. Employees take up space, use telephones, and make decisions; you must expand your business operations to include them. They need to take responsibilities from you to help the company grow. Are you ready to let go enough to use them effectively?

6. Have you ever managed people before? Are you familiar with the challenges of encouraging and leading employees? Do you need to take some classes in effective supervision before taking the plunge? Even if you have managed workers before, a refresher is probably a good idea.

7. Know that a small business is different from a large corporation in that one employee out of a total of two makes up 50 percent of the personnel. If that person has troubles, 50 percent of the company operations are in trouble. Be aware of the large effect one person can have on your business, your customers, and your earnings.

8. If you are in a service business, make sure that your employees reflect the proper attitude and image you have worked hard to establish. A few weeks of poor telephone attitude toward your customers can unravel years of consistent service on your part. If you are really lucky, one of your established clients will tell you about the problem first, but few customers ever complain; they just leave! Teach your employees early about the level of service they are expected to provide and reinforce it with your own actions.

9. Your customers will need to adapt to working with someone on your staff. Make sure that the new employee maintains the same level of concern and dedication to customer satisfaction. The best thing that could happen to your business is for your customers to like working with your employee as much or more than they liked working with you. Now you can focus on other business issues besides customer satisfaction. It is a good sign when customers want to work with your employees instead of you, assuming that you and the customer are still on good terms. This means that you are successfully transferring your unique style throughout the organization.

10. Don't forget that employees can always (and probably eventually will) find another job. This is your business, and you will be around long after they are gone, unless you are very lucky and find the right long-term fit with an employee. If an employee leaves, you inherit her decisions. This means that commitments made by an employee can obligate you long after that employee is gone. You, on the other hand, can't just leave and find another job because this is your job. Period. Find that balance between delegation and monitoring that provides the employee with effective freedom to make decisions while ensuring that the decisions made will work for you as well.

11. There are legal issues related to having employees that you could ignore when it was only you working at the company. Some form of a personnel policies manual would help you avoid situations such as the one Julie has in the introductory scenario. On the other hand, personnel policies that are too elaborate can get you into unnecessary trouble.

CAUTION

Smoke Signals

You might be tempted to hire a friend or relative so you'll have someone on your staff whom you can trust; be sure he or she is qualified for the job. Don't let trust be the primary reason you hire him or her or your company will suffer. Go over the details of what you really know about him or her, compared to what you have simply assumed or heard since you first met. The last thing you want is a surprise that causes you to fire a friend or relative, which disrupts the business, ends a friendship, and makes holidays even more stressful than they already are.

I have had both excellent employees and poor employees work with me over the years and have found that poor performers have a much bigger impact in smaller companies than they do in huge corporations. Larger companies can afford the luxury of one or two poor performers; smaller companies cannot. If you find employees with performance problems, such as employees who can't seem to do the work right or at a reasonable pace, let them go quickly before they do serious damage to your business.

Unfortunately, the tendency in small businesses is to take care of employees as if they were members of your family. I say unfortunately because small business owners tend to keep employees on for a much longer time than do larger corporations.

Never forget that you started this business. It is yours, not your employees'. Try to let go of the daily decisions so that they can carve a place for themselves in the operation of the business, or you will wind up with morale problems down the road. Remember, however: You sign the checks, co-sign all company debts, and ultimately make the big decisions. They might also need to be reminded of this as you give them increasing responsibilities and they naturally take more initiative. How you do this is a matter of style; don't be too heavy-handed because an overbearing boss can easily drive away a good employee. (Besides, they obviously know that you own the company.) It is an interesting balancing act to promote employee initiative while also making sure that the employee doesn't get you into financial trouble.

Smoke Signals

> If the company only makes money when you are there, then a vacation becomes much more costly than the trip itself. You're really paying for the actual vacation expenses, lost company revenues as a result of not being at work, and the time needed to get caught up once you return to the office. The solution? Set up your pricing so that the times you work cover the times that you are off. You could also define your operation so that the business makes money even when you are not there. This solution could involve outsourcing of routine operational components, hiring employees, or possibly more effective use of the Internet.

Once employees take on more responsibility for the company's activities, you might wonder how you ever did everything yourself. There isn't a more satisfying business experience than to find a series of orders, invoices, projects, and bank deposits that your employees created without your involvement. To call in from a well-deserved vacation and find thousands of dollars worth of revenues and profits coming into the company while you are gone is the essence of small business success.

Been There ... Done That

I tend to set dollar thresholds under which employees can make decisions within their business area before they have to contact me. For example, I might let an office manager make any decision under $250 on his or her own, up to a total of $1,000 in a month. I then review the purchases with the employee at the end of the month. In this way, I let the employee know what I expect and teach him or her how to make decisions that I would have made on my own.

This is beneficial to the employees in that they get to work with some autonomy, and it is better for me because I don't get bothered about each expense. If money is tight, I drop the thresholds. Or I start the employees at $100 per purchase and $400 per month, and increase the limits as I become more comfortable with their decision-making ability.

Your business needs to be able to create revenue without your involvement, or it will never grow beyond your own abilities. That can only happen when employees get involved and have the freedom to act on their own, within certain guidelines you set.

If you want to keep your company small, then you might never need another employee, other than an occasional relative or temporary helper to handle clerical stuff. If you want to grow so the company works on a relatively independent basis, then you need employees. Accept that as a reality and plan for it in advance. That way, you can be on the lookout for the right person and get him or her onboard when the timing is right.

Good Help Isn't Hard to Find

Depending on your personnel needs, there are a few avenues you can take when you begin seriously looking for employees. First, you can try out potential employees through a part-time employment arrangement before making a full-time hiring commitment. You can also hire candidates for a specific project, as *independent contractors*, and see how they work out. Finally, temporary help agencies can serve as excellent sources of candidates who have already been screened for your particular job opening.

Other sources include college and university co-op programs where students learn on the job through structured programs that help them apply what they've learned in their course work, as well as high school programs that match interested students with part-time employers. Many colleges and high schools also encourage students to apply for internships during summer and winter vacations, where they work for an employer full-time during those breaks from school. Although internships are generally shorter term than co-op programs, you can have a student help on some important projects during a summer vacation. All these options are excellent ways to give students a chance to gain real-world experience while benefiting from their efforts at your company. You will typically use them for more routine tasks.

Talking Business

An **independent contractor** is a temporary worker hired on a per-project basis. Often the contractor will sign a contract specifying the length of the project, the work that needs to be done, and the payment for that work.

As your operation becomes more stable, you will want full-time employees on your staff so that you are not constantly having to train new hires that may only be around for a few months. Take your time finding the right people.

Start out the hiring process by getting a clear picture of what you want this person to do. Write out a detailed job description. Then picture the personality type you want in that job. Ask other business owners about personnel that they have worked with that might be right for your job opening. Place ads in the paper and prepare yourself for hours, or days, of reading resumés and interviewing applicants.

Independent Contractors

Independent contractors come in all shapes and sizes (literally). As with temporary agencies, you hire a contractor for a particular job, and you let him or her go when you are done. Contractors expect to be let go at some point, so the parting is rarely accompanied by hard feelings. Typically, the length of a project is specified in a contract when a contractor is brought in, so there are no surprises about what happens when the work is done. (She leaves unless you want to hire her to work on a different project.)

Generally, these folks have an area of expertise such as accounting, computer graphics training, or specific business skills you know your company needs. You must qualify a contractor on your own and decide whether that person is the best for your specific project. The working relationship is between your company and the contractor directly, but she works as a consultant to your firm, not as an employee. You have no ongoing obligations to the contractor.

 On the CD

A sample Independent Contractor Agreement is included on the CD as document 13-01.

One of the major differences between working with a contract employee and a temporary employee is that your company directly hires the contractor to do a specific task. A temporary employee is actually an employee of the temporary agency, and this agency "rents" her to you for a fee. With independent contractors, you spell out up front exactly how long they are asked to work, on what project, to do what specific types of activities, and at what cost. It is also a good idea to spell out the risks that you expect the contractor to assume, such as liability insurance and all associated payroll taxes.

Temporary employees, on the other hand, really don't have any part in setting the terms of their work with you; their employer discusses those with you and then provides the individual best suited to help you out. In many cases, temporary employment contracts are open ended, so you can end them whenever you want. With an independent contractor, you work out the specific end date of the project up front.

Expect to pay more for the contractor than a temp. One reason is that the contractor is operating as a business owner, too, and must cover all his business costs with each project. Typical price ranges for writing services start at $15 to $30 per hour, document layout and design contractor fees range between $20 to $75 per hour, and professional services such as attorneys range from $65 to $250 per hour. The beauty of working with a contractor is that the person comes in with well-developed skills that are immediately applied to your situation with little or no training needed. You get the desired results quickly and efficiently. They may also have extensive expertise in a given area that you can use long after the contractor is gone.

I generally learn a lot from working with a professional independent contractor. The good ones know their stuff and put it to work quickly. Finding a good one is a lot like finding a prince: You have to kiss a number of toads before you find the right one. When you find the right one, he or she appreciates working for you on a regular basis, and you are relieved to have someone you trust and professionally respect.

Fellow business owners are a tremendous referral source for specific contractors who do their jobs well. Start asking for referrals even before you have a need to use their services so that when the need arises, you have a list of qualified contractors from which to choose. You will probably need these people when some type of emergency arises, so it helps to have the relationships already established before the crisis.

When hiring an independent contractor, remember that the IRS has specific criteria that determine whether a person is a contractor or an employee. If you hire someone as an independent contractor but the IRS decides later that she was really an employee of your company, you might be liable for past payroll taxes, Social Security payments, and penalties. Be clear up front about how the IRS would characterize your relationship before taking chances with an independent contractor. See the "When an Employee Is Really an Employee" section later in this chapter for a detailed list of criteria.

Putting Retired Folk to Work

Here is an idea for you: Tap into the huge reservoir of people who have professional experience but who no longer work outside the home. This includes housewives and househusbands who now take care of their children during the day. It also includes retired men and women who might want to earn some extra money. Frequently, these workers bring substantial expertise to their work and present few personnel headaches.

In exchange for these talents, these employees require that you be pretty flexible on their work hours. People taking care of their kids need to work around school schedules, and the retired don't want work to cut too deeply into their free time. I have found these groups easy to work with and a great personnel financial investment as part-time workers. Check with the local PTA for people who are active with the schools and ask around. You might just be surprised who you find.

Take Your Employee for a Test Drive

Just as you can date for a while before deciding to get married, you can test potential job candidates before making a long-term commitment. There are several intermediate steps you can try before taking the plunge.

Because everyone is always on his best behavior during job interviews, it is very difficult to determine whether a person is a good fit for your company in that setting. You need to observe the job candidate in other situations before deciding whether to hire him.

Part-time employment is a great "try-and-buy" approach where you get to test the water with the prospective employee. Use the employee 20 to 30 hours per week, and see how you work together. If it works, you have someone who comes on full-time with a lot of background and who would otherwise need training at full-time rates. If it doesn't work, you can count your blessings and let him or her go.

Checking out college and high school students through co-op programs where the student works for you a set number of hours per week for a semester or during a summer vacation is another option for testing potential full-time employees. After working with a student for several months, you can decide whether to offer him or her a full-time job after graduation.

At a minimum, you should establish a 90-day *probationary period* that every new employee must endure. A probationary period is a time for both you and your new employee to decide whether this is the best job for him or her. Before the 90 days is up, you must let this person go, or he or she automatically becomes a full-fledged employee, which means entitlement to any of the benefits you give your other employees. In other words, on day 91, this person automatically becomes an employee.

There's no reason to rush right into hiring full-time employees if you feel more comfortable taking it slowly. Try some of these approaches to checking your potential employees before making a big commitment to them.

On the CD

A sample At-Will Employment Application is included on the CD as document 13-02.

Listen Up

Small business owners have one major problem when it comes to employees: They are fast to hire and slow to fire. This means that they tend to hire people without thoroughly checking them out and then, once an employee is determined wrong for the job, small business owners tend to be very slow to let them go. Be smart: Be slow to hire and fast to fire. It may sound heartless, but trust me when I say that it will save you heartburn along the way.

Talking Business

A **probationary period** is a length of time (usually 90 days) during which both you and a new employee have a chance to see whether the employee is right for the position and vice versa. Before the 90 days are up, the employee is either let go or hired on an official basis.

When an Employee Is Really an Employee

It is incredible how complicated it becomes to determine whether a person is an independent contractor or an employee. The same person performing the same work under slightly different circumstances can be considered an employee, costing you much more financially than an independent contractor.

The IRS tends to lean on the side of finding workers as employees, not independent contractors, because it means they get more in employment taxes from you, the employer. Be sure you're clear on whether you have an employee or independent contractor working for you.

The basic test to determine whether someone is an employee is whether you control the person's daily activities or whether she makes those decisions herself. A person is an independent contractor if she is held responsible only for results, and if her methods, hours of work, location at which the work is performed, and tools are under her control and not dictated by you.

Listen Up

Call the IRS office (1-800-TAX-FORM) to request its Publication 937 on independent contractors to determine whether you have employees or contractors, or check out the IRS website at www.irs.gov.

Does the person perform services for more than one company? Is she responsible for her own profit and loss and is she used for specific expertise applied to specific projects instead of just showing up during specific time frames? The more restrictions that you apply to a contractor relationship, the more likely that contractor is considered an employee.

The IRS has a set of criteria that they consider when defining an employee's status. Use these criteria to substantiate your claim that a person is a contractor instead of an employee.

Make sure you have a written subcontractor agreement with the person that clearly spells out the separate liability relationship. A sample contractor agreement is included on the companion CD. Make sure that the contractor provides his own liability insurance and worker compensation insurance, or you might find yourself the recipient of a nasty legal suit if the contractor gets hurt on the job.

More Employees, More Restrictions

All companies are not created equal. Depending on the state where you are doing business and how many employees you have, you will be affected by different rules and regulations. One way to deal with these various state and federal government regulations is to develop a *company policy manual*, or employee manual, for everyone's reference.

A company policy manual spells out what the company expects of its employees and what they can expect in terms of benefits and other topics related to employment. New employees receive a copy of the policy manual and are responsible for adhering to these policies. A well-defined policy manual clears up employee confusion because everyone is given the same information. It also helps specify who should be contacted with follow-up questions. For smaller companies, the policy manual becomes the personnel policy manual. Know the laws of your individual state, and create the proper policy manual to address those state laws.

A few personnel issues apply to all companies, regardless of the number of employees. You should clearly spell out the number of company holidays provided to employees each year and the amount of vacation and sick time a person is eligible to take during the year. If you have other company policies that employees need to know, state them in the policy manual.

Drafting your own handbook is cheaper than having an attorney write it, but a legal review is essential to make sure you haven't made significant errors.

Talking Business

A **company policy manual** spells out what the company expects of its employees and what they can expect in terms of benefits and other topics related to employment. New employees are given a copy of the policy manual and are made aware that they will be held responsible for adhering to these policies.

State and federal laws kick in at different company-size levels:

♦ If you have fewer than four employees (depending upon the state), you are the master of your domain and can hire, fire, and reward pretty much as you see fit.

♦ As an employer, you have to worry about a wide array of federal laws that address discrimination and other important personnel-related issues.

♦ If you have 50 or more employees, you need the same level of policy manual as IBM or General Motors. It must include policies on family and medical leave, harassment, drug-related issues, discrimination, and virtually any other workplace-related issue, such as smoking.

On the CD

See the Employee Handbook Checklist (document 13-03) and Receipt of Handbook (document 13-04) documents on the CD.

My recommendation regarding your personnel policy is this: Until you need a comprehensive manual as outlined in the previous paragraphs, simply include those items that you absolutely want and intend to absolutely enforce. A few of these might be no drinking on the job, no smoking in the workplace, excessive tardiness or absenteeism as grounds for dismissal, no sexual harassment, no discrimination in the workplace, no stealing, and other rules that you know will be enforced.

Smoke Signals

If you write a policy manual, make sure that you comply with the written policies. It is a good idea to leave out statements regarding policies that don't apply to your company yet because of its size. Whatever you state as a policy, you must be prepared to follow.

Make sure that new employees get a copy of the personnel policies manual as part of the hiring process and that you expect strict adherence to these policies. In this way, if someone is caught drinking on the job, you can let him go for being in violation of the company policy, even if his performance has not suffered. (Thus you can avoid Julie's position as outlined in the chapter opening.)

Beware the "policies in a can" approach, which uses a standard software package or standard forms to define your personnel manual. They are probably overkill for your small organization and could open you to unnecessary exposure to legal action.

Medical Insurance

As the business owner, you have always had your medical insurance paid by the company. Now you have an employee. Does this person get company-paid insurance just like you? What is the law?

To start with, the law covering medical and life insurance benefits is the Employee Retirement Income Security Act (ERISA) that was passed by Congress in 1974. This act does not require employers to provide medical, retirement, or any other benefits of any kind. It only regulates how these benefits must be handled if they are provided. Employers typically offer benefits as a way to attract employees to their company and as a way of improving everyone's quality of life.

The snag comes in when you offer benefits to certain employees (such as you and members of your family) and don't offer the same benefits to other employees. In general, it is better for business and morale to offer the same benefits to everyone. The safest way to avoid this situation is to verify benefit offerings with an attorney or a benefits specialist.

The policy manual helps keep misunderstandings regarding employment benefits to a minimum, which will help you avoid possible litigation later due to unfulfilled expectations on the part of employees.

There is another potential snag depending on the type of company you own since medical insurance premium expenses may be deductible for employees but might not be deductible for employee owners. This is an area where it pays to talk with your tax professional.

Determining the right medical insurance plan for you and your employees is a potentially confusing and time-consuming process. For starters, you generally must have at least two employees (you and one other) before you qualify for most group plans. The coverage may apply to local incidents, but not cover incidents that occur out of town. Does the plan allow you to choose your doctor, or must you use doctors who are members of the plan you choose? The world of medical insurance is interesting and complicated. I suggest that you ask a few other business owners how they worked out their medical insurance situation; you might save yourself a lot of legwork.

Do your homework and don't jump at the first plan you see, or you might find yourself changing plans on a regular basis.

> **Listen Up**
>
> Smaller companies are exempt from many employment laws. For example, hiring relatives or friends over others is, by definition, discriminatory. This would make most small businesses in violation of federal and state laws. Call your local department of labor or your local chamber of commerce for guidelines when you begin preparing your policy manual.

> **Been There ... Done That**
>
> At one time, I (on and off) had only one other employee in my company. This meant that I was regularly having to go on and off the group policy due to the two-person minimum. (I guess one person doesn't comprise a group.) My agent let me know that I could set up a policy for myself, and then allow my employees to join my policy and set their own coverage levels. I upped their salaries enough to cover the employee's insurance premiums and insulated myself from having to define a blanket plan that applied to everyone or changed when I was back to running a solo operation. This worked pretty well. Some plans now allow you to have only one employee, so check around as new products are coming along all the time.

Sexual Harassment

Picture this: Your company is sued for sexual harassment. You know nothing happened, but you are in front of the judge, who asks about your internal policy regarding sexual harassment. He wants to see it in writing. Oops. It has been verbally expressed to all employees but never in writing. He and the jury decide in favor of the person filing the suit on the grounds that if you really meant it, you would have put it in writing. If you did not specifically state that sexual harassment is prohibited, then the opposite must be true; you must condone sexual harassment. This actually happened! I'll bet this section now has your undivided attention.

If you do not put such important policies in writing, you are in potential trouble. But if you are a small company not currently bound by the sexual harassment laws because of your size and you have a statement in writing, then it can also be used against you. Be safe, rather than sorry, and discuss the information provided in your handbook with an attorney to be sure that you are not opening a can of worms with certain statements. It's always a good idea to discuss your sexual harassment policy with your attorney as a preventive measure.

Is there a lighter side to all of this? I have looked for it and can't find it. It is unfortunate that working with employees has become so dangerous, but it appears to be the nature of the beast. The best prevention for a nasty lawsuit is to avoid it in the first place. Treat all employees as people who perform a function for you. Mentally neuter them (and yourself) when you are on the job and treat them as company assets who perform a function. Nothing more.

 On the CD

A sample Sexual Harassment Policy is included on the CD as document 13-05.

Avoid the temptation to become friends with your employees. Keep the proper amount of professional distance between them and you (while never being unfriendly). They work for you. You sign their checks. No matter what, you are never going to be one of the guys or girls. It will become difficult to handle personnel situations with authority if you spend every evening socializing with your employees.

I've talked to several business owners, both male and female, who think of employees as nuns and priests as a way of attaching no gender at all to their employees. In all conversations, they relate as though they were talking to a member of the clergy so that no inappropriate remarks are made. This might seem a little extreme, but it seems to work for them.

You might not have to think of your business as a monastery, but don't forget that the primary reason for having employees is for them to perform a job function that makes money for them, the company, and you. Anything more than that might be misinterpreted and should be treated with caution.

Solicitation and Competition

How could these former employees do this? You spent three years building up that account, and they stole it away within 90 days of leaving your company. Their overhead isn't as high as yours, so they undercut your price by 30 percent. What could you have done to prevent this? A *noncompete clause* might have been one way to go. A noncompete clause is an agreement that your employees sign, saying that they won't steal your business ideas or methods and go to work for a competitor or become competitors by starting their own firm.

Although noncompete clauses are treated differently from state to state, you should definitely look into them as one way to protect yourself and your company from ex-employees stealing your ideas and opening a business across town. When an employee signs a noncompete agreement, he or she essentially agrees not to compete with you in a specific geographic area (such as in a particular city or region of the country) for a specified period of time (such as one to two years) by performing the same function for another company that he or she did for you.

Talking Business

A **noncompete clause** is an agreement that your employees or suppliers sign, saying that they won't steal your business ideas or methods and go to work for a competitor or become competitors by starting their own firm.

On the CD

A sample Employee Covenant Not To Compete is included on the CD as document 13-06.

The theory says that your director of sales couldn't quit and go work for your competitor right away in a sales-related position. The reality of an employee noncompete is that it cannot keep a person from making a living in his or her chosen field. In other words, you really cannot keep a person from taking a job as a sales manager or design engineer with a competing firm. You can, on the other hand, keep that person from using any privileged, confidential, or proprietary system information in his or her new job because this information belongs to your company. A salesman can still sell; he or she just can't use your customer list. An engineer can design; he or she just can't use design procedures that are proprietary to your company.

Enforcing an employee noncompete that keeps a person from being able to earn a living in their selected field is a difficult, and usually fruitless, endeavor. You are better served making sure that people know that contact lists obtained at your company stay at your company and are not to be removed when the person leaves. Company confidential documents, which you should make sure are marked as such, cannot be removed from the company premises. Diligence on your part during hiring and while protecting sensitive information is the best defense you have against an employee using your information against you.

Think of an employee noncompete as a mechanism for keeping honest people honest.

Some states treat signed employee noncompete agreements very seriously and prevent a former employee from taking a job at a competing company if you file suit to that effect. Other states take the view that noncompete agreements limit where a person can work, and don't uphold them. Check with an attorney who specializes in employment law to find out whether your state supports noncompete agreements. If it does, work with an attorney to write an agreement that protects you rather than do it on your own. You might just create more headaches for yourself down the road if you handle this stuff yourself.

You cannot keep someone from making a living in his or her hometown. A noncompete clause signed as part of the employment process essentially says that a person cannot earn a living in the same town as your business because he or she agreed not to compete with your company when he or she joined on. However, few courts in the country will uphold a company's rights to keep a person from making a living.

They will, however, uphold a company's rights to retain its customers without worrying about a former employee stealing those customers away. This is called a *nonsolicitation clause*, which says that the employee agrees not to pursue your existing customers for business that is related to your company. This agreement lasts for a specific period of time, usually one to two years. Former employees are restricted from using the customer contacts acquired while working with your company to aid another company, including their own.

The best way for you to cover yourself in this situation is to have the employee sign a noncompete agreement as part of his or her employment. This is particularly true for an employee who has regular customer contact. It makes you seem a little paranoid, but it might also save thousands of dollars of business from walking out your front door. When a customer starts to wave cash in front of a former employee, his or her loyalty to you will be severely tested. Without the noncompete agreement, you might end up with a personal disappointment and a financial loss without legal recourse.

By the way, if a newly hired employee starts sharing confidential information about his or her last employer even though he or she signed a confidentiality agreement with that employer, then you should reasonably assume that he or she will do the same with your information when he or she goes to the next job.

Talking Business

A nonsolicitation clause is an agreement that your employees sign, saying that if they leave your company, they will not pursue your existing customers for business that is related to your company.

Interviewing Techniques

There are some questions that should never be asked of anyone because they are inappropriate, illegal, or both. You would probably never ask your best friend why she married that louse of a husband, or you risk losing a friend. Similarly, you should never ask certain taboo questions when interviewing people for a job.

Why? Simple. If you ask an illegal question and you don't give the interviewee the job, he or she can use the fact that you asked the question as grounds for a discrimination suit—even if the question was asked purely as a conversation starter, such as "Did your children enjoy the Christmas holidays?" or "How old are they now?" The problem is that the topic should never have come up, and now you need to show that you don't have discriminatory hiring practices.

 On the CD

Sample Pre-Employment Questions (document 13-07), Employment Letter (document 13-08), Employment Contract (document 13-09), New Employee Procedures (document 13-10), and Employee Non-Disclosure (document 13-11) documents are included on the CD.

Some people try to determine information from secondary questions. For example, asking why a person moved to your city might indicate that he or she came with a spouse who was transferred. Asking if working on Sundays is a problem might raise information about the person's religious activities.

You should avoid using secondary questions to solicit the disclosure of information that could be considered prejudicial. The purpose of an interview is to determine the employee's ability to do the job—nothing else. Don't trifle with potentially discriminatory questions; nothing the interviewee reveals is worth the cost of defending an employment discrimination lawsuit!

Start any job search with a clear definition of what you want in the ideal person for the job. Create a *job description* that includes areas of knowledge the person must have to perform the job. Education and former experience must be clearly defined; develop objective criteria by which candidates can be screened. The more clearly you know what job you want them to perform and the kind of expertise you need, the more likely you are to find the right person to fill the open position. Be specific in your requirements if you want to minimize the amount of training this employee will require. For example, "must

Talking Business

A **job description** is a detailed listing of the duties to be performed by the person filling the job, also including the required skills, education, and certification levels, and other criteria directly related to the job.

know Word for Windows styles operation" is specific, whereas "computer operation required" is general. If you are willing to train the employee, then you can make the requirements more general, which broadens the candidate field.

In reality, and in the eyes of the law, you are trying to find the right person for the job, regardless of race, sex, marital status, or other criteria. The suggested interview procedures help ensure that you find the information you need without jeopardizing your company in the process.

Never bring up the following topics while conducting the interview:

- Marital status

- Veteran status

- Race

- Religion

- Nationality

- Children

- The interviewee's age

- Sex and sexual orientation

You need to know answers to many of these questions after the person is hired because emergency and medical information might pertain to children and spouses, but do not include them as part of the interview. In addition, make sure that you provide no verbal agreements about the length of employment or reasons for future possible dismissal. The person being hired might later construe these as commitments. These verbal commitments might be used against you later if problems arise with this person's performance that cause you to let him or her go.

Here are several things that you should consider doing with new employees:

- Let the applicant know the good and bad of working for you and your company.

- Avoid questions that deal with marital status, kids, religion, politics, sexual preference, and other areas that could be construed as potential ground for discriminatory treatment.

- Never lie about the company or things that might have been in the news. If you don't want to talk about it simply say so, but don't misrepresent the facts.

- Avoid talking about childcare.

- Keep notes during the interview as they relate to this person and the job.

- Make sure the applicant confirms that the items on the job description are things he or she can and will do.

- Make sure the applicant gets a copy of the employee manual. Question the applicant on its contents and have him or her sign the form indicating receipt.

 On the CD _____

> Sample Disciplinary Notice (document 13-12), Termination Letter (13-13), Employee Severance Agreement (document 13-14), Employee Information Release (13-15), Family and Medical Leave Act Request (document 13-16), and Employee Physical Accommodation Notice (document 13-17) documents are included on the CD.

- Keep your notes on a separate piece of paper and not on the resumé just in case someone else sees it, so that your thoughts cannot be construed as having prejudiced the others who interview.

- Have the applicant tell you about prior work experiences.

- Be consistent with how you interview, telling everyone the same information and asking what are basically the same set of questions.

Present the most positive aspects of the company in the most consistent manner. Your final intent is to find the best person to fill the job opening—period. If you mislead an applicant about company-related problems, you can find an employee making a substantial career change under false pretense, which can only lead to management troubles and a possible lawsuit.

 On the CD _____

> There are three great bonus sections included on the CD specifically related to employees and personnel issues. "Hire to Complement Your Existing Talents" (CD13-1) shows you how to make sure that the employees you hire add capabilities to your company. "Making the Most of Temporary Agencies" (CD13-2) lets you in on the secrets related to using temporary agencies to your best advantage. "Plan to Grow Beyond Your Own Capabilities" (CD13-3) helps you understand how employees fit into your overall business growth plans. You are missing a lot of great information if you don't check out these special bonus sections.

The Least You Need to Know

- No man or woman is an island when it comes to succeeding in business. You must have the assistance of others if you want the company to grow beyond your capabilities.

- Create an environment where employees can grow professionally and financially. Allow them to feel like a part of the process, and you will reap the rewards associated with having a successful business that operates without you. But don't give employees free rein until you are sure they will act in both the company's and your best interest.

- Give potential employees a tryout before making a permanent commitment. Use probationary periods or temporary assignments to find out how they fit with your operations.

- An ineffective employee in a large organization can be disruptive, but in a small company, he or she can be disastrous because of the effect he or she has on others and on customers.

- State and federal laws kick in at different company size levels, based on the number of employees.

- Set up your minimum personnel policies to cover you on the "must adhere to" issues and add others later as needed.

- Make sure you conduct interviews in a legal and effective manner.

Chapter 14

The Tax Files: Payroll Taxes

In This Chapter

- An overview of payroll taxing procedures
- Deposits and reporting deadlines
- When to consider an outside payroll service
- Rules to live—and pay tax—by

I'm a professional engineer, thought Kevin. I should be able to understand something as basic as payroll taxes. After 15 years of working and receiving paychecks, it's hard to imagine that it could be this complicated.

Okay. Deductions are made from the employee's paycheck based on earnings and several tax types. What is this FICA thing? And then there's unemployment. This is for both the state and federal taxes. I can handle that. The deposits are made quarterly for the state and annually for the federal. Or was that the reporting procedures?

Forget about that for now. Let's get this company portion of the payroll deductions under control. Hey. Wait a minute. These numbers are the same as the employee ones. Did I make a mistake, or are they supposed to be equal? Maybe the company pays it all? No, that can't be.

Wow. Now I know what a dog feels like when it chases its tail. Time to take Jill up on her offer to explain this stuff to me. It's clear that it's really unclear, and I just don't have the time to figure it out on my own.

"Hi, Jill? This is Kevin. Have I got a deal for you. What are you doing for lunch today, and were you serious about explaining payroll tax procedures to me?"

Your business won't grow without employees, but adding employees means adding responsibilities, including the need to manage payroll tax deposits. More than one company has gone under due to improper management of payroll taxes, and figuring this maze out for yourself can be costly and legally compromising. This chapter introduces the payroll process and outlines the IRS guidelines for making tax deposits. Learn this well and save yourself money and grief.

Payroll Taxes: You Can't Avoid Them, So Learn How to Deal with Them

Unless you intend to be a sole practitioner all your life, you will have employees at some point, and with employees come payroll taxes. No one I know thinks payroll taxes are fun or interesting, but as a business owner, you need to have a basic grasp of the legal requirements. Otherwise, you can get tangled up in bureaucratic red tape and headaches that make asking for a loan sound pleasant by comparison. You don't have to be a rocket scientist to calculate payroll taxes, but you do have to pay attention to the details. By the way, as a sole proprietor, you still need to pay self-employment tax on your salary, so you really don't get around it even then.

As you read through this chapter the first time, you might feel kind of overwhelmed. Don't worry. Over time, this feeling will pass as you become more familiar with all the rules. Eventually, it will make perfect sense. You will have to decide if that is a scary thought in itself at that point.

Here's one of my favorite business secrets: Just because you have employees doesn't mean that you have to do the accounting for your payroll. That's what staff (and service bureaus and accounting software) is for! Read on for an introduction to the regimented, deadline-filled world of payroll tax accounting—so that at least you can find out what you'll be delegating to someone else.

> **Been There ... Done That**
>
> Delaying your understanding of payroll taxes simply delays the inevitable and puts your company in financial and legal jeopardy. Spend the time today to get this information soundly under your belt because payroll taxes and the IRS are like gravity: They always win. The penalties for delaying payroll tax deposits are substantial, so don't even think about going there.

Payroll Tax Overview

Ever talk to someone from the IRS? To picture a typical payroll tax auditor, imagine that IRS representative without a sense of humor, and you're likely to be pretty close to the mark. The first thing you need to know is that all taxing jurisdictions (federal, state, and local) have their own requirements and filing deadlines that they take very seriously indeed. If you file all the right forms on time, you most likely won't have many problems.

That leads to the next question: How do you figure out which forms to file and when to file them? The three basic types of payroll taxes are income taxes (which you withhold from wages), Social Security and Medicare (you pay half, the employee pays half), and unemployment (you pay it all).

◆ States and some cities have income taxes, as does the federal government, so you need to consult both the federal guidelines and relevant state and local guidelines to determine how much to withhold and when to pay it over to the taxing authority.

◆ Social Security and Medicare are easier to figure out because they are only federal taxes and subject only to the federal rules.

◆ Unemployment is subject to both state and federal rules, with potentially complex interactions between the rules, requiring even more detailed record keeping.

To find the federal rules, contact the Internal Revenue Service (IRS), which has a package of tax rules and guidelines for businesses, including Publication 15, Circular E, *Employer's Tax Guide*. It's not the most fascinating reading in the world, I'll admit, but it's something you need to know about if you have employees and handle your own payroll tax accounting. The website has a wealth of information, including the forms and instructions, and is located at www.irs.gov.

CAUTION   **Smoke Signals** _____

> Don't rely on your computer alone! It's a good idea to manually verify tax liabilities if you typically use a software package to calculate your tax payments. If the software package is off in its calculations, you still owe the money. Depending on whether the mistake is in your favor or not, you may find yourself with more money than expected or owing more than you can pay. Software packages make mistakes, and cumulative payroll tax payment mistakes can put your company and you in serious financial trouble. The same applies to any payroll tax service you might use. Check their work occasionally as well.

For the state rules that apply to you, contact your state Department of Revenue (for income tax withholding information), Department of Labor (for unemployment tax information), or Secretary of State (in case you can't find the right bureau to answer your question). Look in the blue pages (governmental section) of your phone book under Federal or State Government to find out where to get the information.

Your employees will give you information about their tax status, number of dependents, and withholding allowances on a federal Form W-4. You can use this employee-provided information to look up the right withholding dollar amount in the tax tables or apply the right percentages for your state's formula. Some states have their own version of the Form W-4, which might contain different information from the federal form. In fact, some states don't have personal state income tax at all. You must check the rules for your particular state and proceed accordingly.

However, just because you figure it out once, don't think you're done for the year. If your employee's pay rate, marital status, dependent status, or address changes, the withholding amounts may also change, and you also have to be aware of the relevant ceilings ("wage base" in IRS lingo) for Social Security taxes and unemployment taxes.

On the CD

A sample Cover Letter to IRS for Employer ID (form SS-4) is included on the CD as document 14-01.

Providing detailed, repetitive calculations is what payroll tax reporting is all about, along with weekly, monthly, quarterly, and annual reporting requirements. If you like this sort of stuff, you will be in heaven. I, on the other hand, use a software package to keep me out of trouble.

Talking Business

Your **employer identification number (EIN)** is a number given to any company that has employees, whether it is a corporation or a sole proprietorship. You need to complete IRS Form SS-4 and submit it to the IRS to get an EIN. You can do it over the phone by calling 1-866-816-2065 with the information required to complete SS-4. Additional EIN information is available in IRS Publication 1635, Understanding Your EIN. You can even get an EIN from the IRS website, wwww.irs.gov. If you have employees, you must have an EIN to ensure that all your tax payments are credited to the correct account, which is indicated by your unique EIN. Call the IRS to get your Federal Tax Deposit Coupon book (IRS Form 8109). You need a bank through which you make these tax deposits (Federal Depository). They are not mailed in.

You've filled out the forms and followed the instructions; now you just drop them in the mail and relax, right? Wrong! Federal taxes and some state taxes are subject to depository requirements, and you can't just mail a check with your return. In essence, you deposit the taxes at your local bank either using a payroll tax coupon with your *employer identification number (EIN)* on it or by paying electronically. The depository schedule might not be the same as the reporting schedule (this depends on several factors), so read the regulations carefully.

Breakdown of Payroll Tax Payments

Tax Type	Employee Portion	Company Portion	Total	Threshold
Federal Income	As determined from the W-4 form	None	10%, 15%, 27%, 30%, 35%, or 38.6%, depending on salary level	Depends on Tax filing status
State Income	As determined from the W-4 form	None	Determined on a state-by-state basis	Depends on Tax filing status
Social Security	6.2%	6.2%	12.4%	$87,000
Medicare	1.45%	1.45%	2.9%	Unlimited
Federal Unemployment	0%	6.2%	6.2% less the state percent	$7,000 payment
State Unemployment	0%	Depends on the state	Depends on the state	Depends on the state

Fudge on these taxes, and you will pay big time and without mercy. It is one thing to be late on a payment to a creditor. It is another to be late on payroll deposit payments to the IRS because you are essentially playing with the employee income deductions. The employer is a trustee of these trust fund taxes and as such has fiduciary responsibility to make proper payment to the IRS. The IRS will eat you alive in late payment fees and interest if you delay, so make sure that you read the next section and file on time. Think of it this way: You are holding the employee payment portion for the IRS, so if you do not make the payment, you are essentially stealing from the employee. That puts a little different spin on it all, doesn't it?

Filing and Paying Payroll Taxes

You have performed the calculations, made the payroll deductions, and paid the employees their well-earned paychecks, but there is still more for you to do. You now need to report the deductions to the IRS and make a bank deposit or electronic deposit to ensure that the IRS gets the money you've so carefully deducted from everyone's paycheck. Refer to "IRS Publication 509, Tax Calendars for 20xx" for additional information.

Tax Deposits and IRS Form 941, Employer's Quarterly Federal Tax Return

Make your payroll tax deposit with a company check at your local bank along with the Federal Tax Deposit Coupon that tells the IRS which company is making its deposit. The coupon should have the deposit amount filled in, along with the box associated with the quarter to which the deposit is to be applied and the type of tax based on the particular IRS form number (in other words, 941, First Quarter). The bank will give you a standard deposit receipt in return.

You deposit the federal payroll taxes on either a monthly or semiweekly basis, depending on the size of your payroll. If your total tax deposits exceeded $50,000 in the prior four quarters, then you probably have to deposit semiweekly. If not, you can deposit on a monthly basis on or before the fifteenth of the month. The IRS will let you know, but you are ultimately responsible even if the notice was not received. It is a good idea to keep tabs on the amount of tax you pay. In general, you deposit taxes on a monthly basis for your first year. Your payroll tax service should be able to provide you with this historical (or projected) information, or you can simply pull it from your accounting package. This scheduling is a little confusing at first, but get it on your calendar and stick with it so it simply becomes part of doing business.

Make sure that you get your payment into the bank before the end of the banking day. There is a time difference between the end of the banking day and the time the bank closes. Be sure you know when the banking day ends. For example, the banking day might end at 2:00 P.M. even though the bank closes at 4:00 P.M. The deposit must be in the bank by 2:00 P.M. in this situation.

The IRS has moved into the twenty-first century and set up the Electronic Federal Tax Payment System (EFTPS). The plan basically dictates that employers who must make total combined deposits of employment, excise, and corporate income taxes in the prior year of $200,000 or more must make electronic deposits. Once again, the IRS will notify you if you must comply with the electronic filing requirements, but you probably shouldn't trust them on this one either. You must complete and return to the IRS an enrollment form at least 10 weeks before you plan to make your first electronic deposit. (For more EFTPS information, call 1-800-555-4477 or 1-800-945-8400 or go to www.eftps.gov.)

If no wage payments are made in a month, no deposits are needed. If the fifteenth falls on a holiday or weekend, you can deposit on the following business day and still be on time.

Listen Up

Depository banks don't have to accept checks from other banks for payroll tax deposits, so when you are choosing your business bank, make sure that it can accept payroll tax deposits.

Semiweekly depositors must stay on top of things. If you pay your employees on a Wednesday, Thursday, or Friday, then your tax deposit must be made by Wednesday of the following week. If payday falls on Saturday, Sunday, Monday, or Tuesday, then deposits are due at the bank on the following Friday. There is a special three-day rule that adds a day to the deposit deadline for each day that a holiday falls between the payday and deposit date.

You report all the deductions you've taken from the payroll to the IRS for a given calendar quarter on IRS Form 941, Employer's Quarterly Federal Tax Return. This is for payroll tax information only. The form must be in the mail and postmarked by the last day of the month following each quarter. For example, for the first quarter (January through March), you must complete and mail the 941 form by the last day of April.

At this time, you should evaluate the amount of money you owe in taxes and what you actually paid throughout the quarter. If the amount you still owe is less than $2,500, which it should be if you are calculating and depositing your payroll taxes properly, simply enclose a check for that amount with your Form 941.

Listen Up

The semiweekly and monthly deposit designations have nothing to do with when you pay your employees. The IRS expects to receive payroll deposits monthly or semiweekly (depending on the size of your payroll).

The following table summarizes the payroll filing procedures for you.

Payroll Deductions Made	When Payroll Checks Are Written
Federal bank deposits required	Either semiweekly or monthly, depending on deposit levels. Deposits are made with IRS coupon form 8109 or electronically.
Payroll deduction form 941 completed and postmarked	On a quarterly basis on the last day of the month following each calendar quarter.

continues

continued

Payroll Deductions Made	When Payroll Checks Are Written
State unemployment reporting and payment	Usually quarterly, but the last day of the month following each quarter.
Federal unemployment reporting payment	Annually, using IRS form 940 and deposit coupon form 8109.

Payroll tax calculations, deposits, and reporting are initially confusing but become a routine part of operation in a short period of time. Ignore them, and you will pay stiff penalties, so step up to the table and do it right from the start.

Based on how you pay your employees, you might annually have to also file Form 945, Annual Return of Withheld Federal Income Tax. This gets pretty arcane, so check with your tax professional to see whether you have to file this form as well.

Here are a few additional forms to think about that will be obvious to you once you see them: You must furnish employees with their Form W-2, Wage and Tax Statement by January 31 of the calendar year following the tax year in question. You then send the IRS a copy of the W-2 forms along with a Form W-3, Transmittal of Wage and Tax Statements, by the following February 28. Similarly, you must provide contractors with their Form 1099 (such as 1099-MISC, Miscellaneous Income) by January 31 of the calendar year following the tax year in question. You then send a copy of these 1099s to the IRS along with Form 1096, Annual Summary and Transmittal of U.S. Information. Notice that the W-2 and 1099 are to provide payment record information to the employee and contractor, respectively. The W-3 and 1096 are to inform the IRS about those payments. I think of them as a way for the IRS to close the loop on who received payments from your company. You are required to provide these forms, so just do it and don't let anyone talk you into not providing a 1099 to them if you paid them more than $600 in the tax year.

State and Federal Unemployment Taxes

This part gets easier. After you've been accruing unemployment payments with each payroll period, your state will make you complete a reporting form and deposit the required funds on a quarterly basis by the last day of the month following each quarter. For example, you make first quarter (ending March 31) payments by the end of April. The federal reporting is done on the IRS Form 940, which you must complete annually by the end of January of the year following the reporting period and mail along with a check for the proper amount remaining that was not paid throughout the rest of the year.

The state tells you what rate you must pay for unemployment, based on historical unemployment benefits paid to past employees. This unemployment rate indicates their assessment of the amount of risk your company poses to the unemployment fund. If a number of your employees leave your company and file for unemployment compensation, you see your unemployment tax rate increase. Tax rates reflect expected costs for your industry but are adjusted based on your specific experience. If no one leaves your company and files for unemployment, after a few years, your rates might even decrease. Sure. I believe in the tooth fairy as well. Sigh.

Rules to Live (and Save Taxes) By

Here are a few rules that I learned the hard way. I relay them here with embarrassment and with the hope that I can save you from the same mistakes:

1. Report your payroll taxes—yes, all of them on all of the nice little forms—when the reports are due. That's right—on time!

2. Make sure that your deposits are accurate and on time. Only an act of God can save you from IRS penalties and fines if they are levied against you or your company.

3. Use a payroll software package such as QuickBooks, which includes a payroll service to ease the payroll process. If you don't use a software payroll package, then investigate a service to handle payroll for you. If you only have a few paychecks, you might try manually determining and entering the data yourself using the tables supplied with IRS Publication 15.

4. Find someone who understands the payroll tax calculation and reporting process. Have them show you their completed forms and walk you through the process when you first start issuing payroll checks. If there is anything nonstandard about your payroll process, then have a professional verify your approach and your first few paychecks and deposits.

5. Stay on top of things, and always include the additional payroll tax expenses when considering an employee raise. Perhaps you should offer your employee additional benefits instead of a raise because a raise has the additional payroll taxes attached, and certain types of benefits do not incur the incremental taxes.

The payroll tax reporting and deposit procedures will eventually become second nature to you, but it is definitely confusing when you first start out. I had a tough time finding all of this information in one spot and made some serious blunders that cost me thousands of dollars. Don't make the same mistake. Get the right advice early in the process and follow it. The late fees are tough to swallow.

Listen Up

Your unemployment tax rate fluctuates, depending on how many employees have ever filed for unemployment. If former employees file for unemployment benefits, you see your unemployment rate increase, unfortunately.

As a final note, don't fiddle with these taxes. If you look at where the money comes from, you can see that you are holding your employees' money until deposited. If you are delinquent in making these deposits for any length of time at all, it might be viewed as theft, and you can get yourself into serious legal trouble that you really don't want. Don't take chances with payroll tax liabilities. If your company goes under, you still owe these taxes, so pay these guys before you pay everyone else. Have I made myself perfectly clear on this matter? It is really important.

Using a Payroll Accounting Service

You always have the option of giving this task to someone else. Your accountant will generally do payroll tracking for you as part of a standard service offering. Outside payroll services specialize in nothing but payroll accounting. This might be too much for what you need at this time, but you might ask your fellow business owners about how they handle their own payrolls. These payroll services have also been adjusting their service offering to accommodate businesses with a small number of employees. The payroll tax process is an important concern for all business owners regardless of size and age; experience is a good guide in this area.

The Least You Need to Know

- Employee-paid payroll taxes include Social Security, Medicare, and federal and state withholding. The company and the employee pay equal amounts of Social Security and Medicare. The company pays all the federal and state unemployment tax.

- Payroll tax deposits are required semiweekly, monthly, or electronically, depending on the size of your company's payroll. The first year you will probably make monthly payments unless your payroll is large.

- Federal payroll taxes are reported on a quarterly basis using IRS Form 941. Similar forms are necessary for state payroll tax reporting.

- Federal unemployment taxes are paid quarterly if the unpaid liability exceeds $100. Otherwise, they are reported and paid annually using IRS Form 940.

- Don't be late on reporting or deposit deadlines because the penalty fees are huge!

Making Sure You're Making It

In This Chapter

- ◆ Why you need to understand accounting procedures
- ◆ Basic accounting principles
- ◆ An overview of balance sheets and income statements
- ◆ Cash flow analyses
- ◆ Comparing cash flow to accrual income statement
- ◆ When to use an accountant or CPA

Jake, who lived in Tulsa, was in Chicago for a business seminar and was excited about seeing his friend Dan. They had worked on cars together in high school and now owned their own auto repair businesses. It was great to talk about business; they shared the same problems and could be honest with each other because they were not competitors. Dan's business was in its fifth year of operation. Jake started his about two years ago and was clearly not making it. Things were tough, and this seminar was his last shot at turning things around before he had to "bag it" and get a "real job."

"I don't understand," said Dan. "You're a great mechanic and you love working with people. What's wrong with your business that you aren't making ends meet?"

Jake looked out the window and back at Dan. "Good question. I'm busy as all get-out and often have to turn business away, but at the end of the year, my accountant tells me I don't have enough money to pay myself what I need. Something's wrong, and if it doesn't get fixed soon, I go back to work for the dealership."

"What is your percentage profit margin?" was Dan's initial question. "And how does your pricing compare with the competition in town?"

"I have the lowest prices around," said Jake proudly. "I dropped our prices 20 percent last year, and that was when things really cut loose. We're doing more work than ever, and my sales are twice what they were last year. I even had to add space to my garage to handle the new business."

Dan smiled and then looked Jake squarely in the eye. "High sales and profits do not always go hand-in-hand. If you can't keep your profit margins where they need to be, you're in trouble. What's your percentage profit margin?"

"I don't know," replied Jake. "I let my accountant take care of all that financial stuff for me. I do cars; he does numbers. I just tell him what I want our prices to be and he takes it from there. That's what I pay him for."

"So he makes your financial decisions? What does he know about the car business? Does he care if you don't make money? You really don't review your financial statements more than once a year? I have a bad feeling that you're a great mechanic who never made the transition to being a business manager. Let's get a copy of your financial statements and compare them to mine. I bet we can get an idea of where things are going wrong," said Dan warmly. "Your business means too much to you to let it go under due to bad pricing and financial decisions."

Jake nodded with a somber look on his face, silently hoping that Dan would buy lunch. He started to realize that managing the business like a hobby instead of a business might have hurt his dream of independence. This time, he would stay awake during the seminar's financial analysis segment.

Like Jake, most business owners treat accounting as a necessary evil. I understand that attitude completely because I did the same thing. And because I did not treat the accounting aspects of managing my company seriously, I made a few financial decisions based on bad information, much to my regret. I now believe in the value of accurate accounting, and I encourage you to learn from my mistakes.

This chapter won't make an accountant or bookkeeper out of you. Relax. It will, however, introduce you to important accounting terms and methods so that you will learn enough to manage an accountant in a way that is valuable to your own business situation. Remember that your accountant works for you, not the other way around. Get him involved early so that he understands your needs, but remember that you inherit the financial impact of your decisions, not your accountant.

Accounting 101

Communication is a wonderful thing—when it works. Communication takes on a new importance when it's about money. Money is a basic necessity of life, and most people treat threats to their money as threats to their person. Accounting procedures and statements provide a standardized way for people to communicate about financial and business situations.

The purpose of the highly structured world of accounting is to provide business managers and others with the information they need to manage a business or evaluate their investments. Accounting is how business keeps score, and, just like keeping score in baseball, there are numerous rules and procedures to accurately reflect the results of the actions on the field.

You need to accumulate information that is timely, reliable, and useful, and you don't want to take valuable time away from making money. Fortunately, accounting principles and policies can make accounting for your business easier. Several software packages are now on the market that make accounting a much simpler task than ever before. We talk about them in more detail later in the chapter.

> **Listen Up**
>
> If you're publishing financial information for use outside of your company, you need to consider an additional set of special accounting rules (called *GAAP*, or *Generally Accepted Accounting Principles*) when you prepare your financial statements. For managing a business, however, you only need to make sure your accounting system makes sense to you and to your financial advisers.

The following sections provide some basic accounting concepts so that you can understand the considerations involved in setting up and maintaining your accounting systems. Time spent up front planning and developing good accounting procedures can save you countless hours of frustration down the road.

Accounting Periods

Accounting periods are periods of time, such as months, quarters, or years. Keeping records by accounting periods allows a company's financial reports to be compared from one time frame to another. It's a good idea to review your company's performance on a regular basis so you can become aware of potential problems, such as running out of cash, higher product or fixed costs, or lower sales figures, before it's too late. Watching how your financial condition changes from one period to the next provides important *trend* information that tells you early on if you are doing better or worse than before.

Accounting periods also provide a basis for comparing company performance from one period to the next, from quarter to quarter, or from year to year. Additionally, to file your tax returns, you have to determine in what month you want your year to end so you can report your profit or loss for that year.

For starters, you need to determine when your company will evaluate its financial performance. Most companies, small and large, look at their basic financial statements at least quarterly (every three months) to measure their progress toward long-term goals, and most managers review their financial statements on a daily or weekly basis. It's always good to know where your sales are coming from and how your money is being spent.

The next question is, "When does your company's financial year begin and end?" A year in a company's history is a *fiscal year*. Unless there is some reason to do otherwise (as recommended by your accountant), keep your fiscal year the same as the calendar year, from January 1 to December 31. This means your quarters will end on March 31, June 30, September 30, and December 31.

Of course, you need to consider whether the IRS has any relevant rules before you can comfortably select a fiscal year end. The good news is that you can always change your fiscal year after you have been in business for a while, so you shouldn't worry too much about this selection. Start out with a standard calendar year and change it later if needed.

Talking Business _____

Accounting periods are set calendar time intervals (months, quarters, or years). Keeping your records up-to-date by accounting period will allow you to compare one period to another. A year in a company's history is called a **fiscal year.**

When the company's financial reporting period is the same as the calendar year, which extends from January 1 to December 31, it is called a **calendar fiscal year.** Most companies use a calendar fiscal year, and you should, too, unless told otherwise by a tax professional.

Sales and Costs

Assume that your client pays you today for work you intend to perform in 60 days. First off, kiss this customer and keep him happy; this type of client is rare, indeed. Second, take a look at whether you should declare that payment as earned income. (In other words, can you spend the money today knowing you won't have to give it back, or should you wait?)

Talking Business

Income is the general term for money received from selling a product or service to a customer. Any money paid to you before the product or service is fully given to the customer is **unearned income**. If the customer can cancel his or her contract and get the money back, you have not truly earned it.

Sales revenue is the first item on your income statement and represents the total amount of sales that your company earned during the accounting period. Income doesn't become sales revenue until it is earned.

Net income is the amount of money left over after *all* expenses have been deducted from the sales revenue figure. **Earnings** is another term for net income.

Trend analysis compares today's results to those experienced in the past or projected into the future. You can learn a lot more about today's performance if you compare it to how you did before. You do this intuitively anyway, so why not make it part of your standard procedures?

The **cash basis** of accounting recognizes sales and expenses when cash is actually received or spent. The **accrual basis** focuses on the earning process and matches sales revenue and expenses required to earn that sale to the period when the earning process is completed.

On the other hand, money you have received for work performed or for products provided is known as earned *income*. You've done everything the customer requested, according to some formal or informal agreement. You can consider the money yours since you have no situation that could create a legal obligation to return it. At this point, the transaction can be considered a sale and booked as *sales revenue*.

In the *accrual* accounting world, when you receive payment from a customer for work that hasn't been completed yet, for accounting purposes, you need to show that payment as *unearned income* until the work is done. When the earning process is complete, the accrual basis of accounting reports that transaction as Sales Revenue and eventually Income. Accrual accounting is discussed in more detail in a few more pages.

If the customer can cancel his order, then the money really hasn't been earned yet, has it? You are essentially holding the money for him until you complete the work. In short, if you haven't finished earning the money by meeting all the terms of your contract with the customer, you shouldn't consider the revenue from those sales as truly yours. Many businesses hedge on this requirement and eventually get themselves into trouble.

If you have a noncancelable contract along with a nonrefundable advance, then the money you received is yours. At that point, you can include it as sales revenue.

If you use the *cash basis* of accounting (described in the next section), you don't need to know the difference between collections and earned income. In the cash-based accounting world, everything you receive from sales is considered income when it is collected, and you don't make any special accounting entries to show when it is earned.

My company runs on the cash basis. I usually recognize the sales revenue at the time of invoice generation unless the dollars involved are so large that they can make a material (important) difference to my company's financial well-being.

Cash or Accrual: Which Accounting Method Is Right for You?

Here's a fundamental accounting question: When do you actually incur an expense? Is it when you use the product or service, or when you pay for the product or service? The answer is different depending on whether you use the cash basis or accrual basis of accounting. These are two approaches to accounting, and you need to know a little about both to effectively manage your business.

The cash basis of accounting recognizes sales and expenses when money (cash) is actually received or spent. The accrual basis of accounting focuses on the earning process and matches sales revenue to the period when the earning process is completed, not simply when the cash is received. The accrual basis also matches expenses incurred to generate those sales to the period in which the income is reported. It is often said that accrual accounting recognizes an expense or income at the point where a commitment (agreement) is made, not necessarily when cash actually changes hands.

If your business has inventory, the IRS says you must use the accrual basis of accounting, so that decision is made for you. However, if you run a service business, especially if you are a small business, you might find that keeping your books on the cash basis is much simpler.

Here's an example to illustrate the differences between the two methods.

Assume that you run a small consulting firm, and you're working on only one project right now. Last month, you spent $400 on supplies and office expenses, paid your staff $1,000, and billed your client $2,500 for the project. This month, your client pays the bill (and the check clears the bank!). Under the cash basis of accounting, you show a loss of $1,400 last month because you paid for the supplies and salaries then, and you show a profit of $1,100 ($2,500 − $400 − $1,000) this month because you collected the payment now. Under the accrual basis, you match the expenses incurred last month with the revenue earned last month and in that month show a profit of $1,100 ($2,500 in revenue less $1,400 in expenses). Note, however, that this does not mean that last month you put that $1,100 in the bank. This is the scary part of not understanding the implications of accrual accounting statements. You may see a positive net income on your statements but have no money in the bank. Why? Because your customers owe you the money and have not paid you. Their earned income is accruing and continues to accrue until they pay you. If they never pay you, that accrued income never turns into cash, which ultimately is what you really care about.

If you have a fairly simple business, with expenses incurred close to the time sales revenues are collected, the cash basis of accounting might give you information that is accurate and timely enough to let you run your business. However, most larger businesses use the accrual basis of accounting, for some or all of the following reasons:

◆ They have inventories, so the IRS makes them use accrual accounting.

◆ There are long lags between the time expenses are incurred and the time customer payment for sales are collected, and the business managers feel that cash basis accounting gives them a distorted picture of operations.

◆ The business sells a small number of large items, and showing earnings based on collections results in dramatic swings in reported performance from month to month, even though the underlying operations might not be fluctuating nearly as much.

◆ The business has more than one owner, and the owners want a clear picture of the earnings of the business, not just the cash collections. (Cash-basis accounting gets particularly messy when partners split up.)

◆ Their accountant talked them into it. (Accountants often believe the accrual basis of accounting provides better information on the results of business operations, even though an accrual-basis system might be more complicated or costly to maintain.)

CAUTION

Smoke Signals

Beware tracking part of your business on cash basis and part on accrual. This can get very confusing when reading financial statements. And it is guaranteed to make your banker question the validity of the rest of the numbers. But if you use the cash basis of accounting, you must make a nearly obsessive commitment to tracking what your customers owe you along with when and how they pay. All this accounting stuff is important and interesting, but your business success starts and ends with creating sales, collecting customer debts, and keeping your company able to pay its bills. Never lose your emphasis on creating sales and collecting customer payments no matter what accounting procedures you use.

The Cash-Basis Accounting Method

How do you track money owed to you when you're using the cash basis of accounting? Very simply, you complete work for customers and you bill them. In some businesses, you receive payment right away, such as if you are running a restaurant; customers pay after they eat. You keep track of who owes what by having waiters and waitresses use order slips. At the end of the night, you total the amount on all the order slips collected and match them with the amount of money in your cash register. You then deposit most of that money in your bank account and keep some in the register to use as change the next day.

If you run almost any other kind of business, however, you probably have to wait to receive payment. You might bill a customer on the first of the month and have to wait 30 days until the check arrives. To keep track of who owes what, create a file of all the invoices sent to customers. As customers pay, you deposit their checks in the bank and take their invoice copies out of the file. You can always check to see whose invoice is outstanding by looking in your file. Once more than 30 days has passed, you want to give the customer a call and find out if there is a problem. (See Chapter 18 for more important information on collections.)

The Accrual-Accounting Method

Accrual accounting imposes an additional accounting step; now you have to use the accounting system to track when a customer is billed as well as when the collection comes in, and you might be (and probably will be) making accounting entries at times when no cash has changed hands.

Furthermore, accrual accounting might report handsome profits while you have no cash in the bank to pay suppliers—because all those sales show up as revenue but your customers haven't actually paid you yet. When managing any business, large or small, remember that cash is like air, and track your bank balances and expectations about cash flows using the techniques discussed later in this chapter. Many businesses have shared the sad experience of running out of cash before all the bills have been paid; try not to join them!

Accrual accounting might also impose tax complications. No one likes paying taxes on reported income before the cash from those sales has been collected, but that can be the way accrual accounting works. Your accountant or tax adviser can give you suggestions on techniques to minimize this source of pain. I'll bet that last statement got your attention.

The following table summarizes the advantages and disadvantages of cash-basis and accrual-basis accounting.

Cash Versus Accrual Accounting

Cash Basis	Accrual Basis
Advantages	
Relatively simple to use	Provides a conceptually more correct picture of the results of your business operations
Understandable to anyone who has balanced a checkbook	Consistent with the way bigger companies report their financial results
Reports income when you have the cash to pay the taxes	Accepted by the IRS if your business has inventory
	Simplifies accounting during change in ownership
	Makes reporting to outsiders (bankers, potential investors, and so on) more comprehensible because they are used to accrual-basis statements
Disadvantages	
Can distort the results	Can be costly and time-consuming of operations, possibly leading to bad business decisions
Not acceptable to the IRS if your business has inventory	Might not match reported income and cash availability
Not comparable to the way bigger companies report their financial concepts and their reported results	Requires some thought and expertise to understand the accrual accounting system
Complicates accounting during changes in ownership	
Can make your company's financial condition appear worse than it is if you offer credit terms to your customers	

Understanding Financial Statements

Settle down in a comfortable chair and make a pot of coffee; it's time to learn the language of accounting. It's not nearly as fun as the language of love, but stick with me. Even if you intend to use an accountant to manage your records, you still need to understand basic financial terms so you can make reasonable financial decisions on your own. And if all of this understanding makes you tons of money, you will love it. Trust me.

Understanding financial statements isn't difficult. Yes, even you can pick it up. Using financial statements effectively along with a valid sales forecast gives you a preview of good and bad times before they hit, so you can take proactive measures if necessary.

This section introduces you to financial statements and explains their basic purpose. There are three basic financial statements: the *income statement, balance sheet*, and *statement of cash flows.* The income statement shows you the sales revenue, expense, and net income level of your company during a specific accounting period, which is usually a fiscal month, quarter, or year. The balance sheet shows you how much you own and how much you owe at a particular point in time, which is usually calculated at the end of a fiscal quarter and on the last day of the year. The statement of cash flow shows exactly how much cash you actually received and how much cash you spent on a periodic basis. You really need to watch your cash flow statement carefully. Your cash flow statement keeps you informed about how much money you actually have in your bank account to pay all your bills.

Talking Business

There are three basic financial statements. The **income statement** reflects all income and expenses for a particular period of time (usually a month, quarter or year). The **balance sheet** shows your total assets and liabilities on a given date, usually the end of the accounting period. The **statement of cash flow** (or **cash flow analysis**) shows exactly how much cash you received and how much you spent on a monthly basis. This statement helps you understand the cash reality of the accrual basis income statements.

The income statement and balance sheet will have different numbers for the same accounting period if you create these reports first using the cash basis and then again using accrual accounting. Modern accounting packages enable you to report using either technique. If you understood why the accrual- and cash-basis reports for the same period will have different numbers, you are starting to understand this section. If not, keep reading this section until you get it. This topic is simply that important.

A Chart of Accounts

One of the procedures accountants use to make record-keeping easier and more understandable is summarizing transactions so that similar transactions are grouped together. They do this by using a *chart of accounts*, which lists all the possible categories of transactions and organizes them to make producing financial statements easier. Accounts that summarize the assets and liabilities of the company are grouped together to form the balance sheet. Accounts that summarize the sales and expenses of the company are grouped together to form the income statement. Those statements, taken together, describe the total financial condition and results of operations for the company. The statement of cash flows uses information from both income and balance sheet statements.

It is critically important to set up these accounts so that they are not only useful for tax purposes but also so that you can get the financial management information (reports) you need to make effective financial decisions. Remember, you don't get to report any taxes on income if you do not manage your business successfully enough to have a positive net income at the end of the year.

For example, tax accounting only requires that you know the amount of revenue received and the total costs associated with earning that revenue. From this information, you can calculate the net income on which income tax is owed. Management accounting may additionally, for example, track the revenues and costs associated with specific product or business areas, so that management can determine which business activities are profitable, and which are losers. This has nothing directly to do with tax preparation but has a lot to do with profitably managing your business. The specifics of setting up these management accounting categories depend on your particular business, but the importance of setting up these management accounts early in the process applies to all businesses.

Don't feel that you need to reinvent the wheel when creating these accounts. Try to get your hands on a copy of the chart of accounts for a company like yours, and you will likely find almost all of their accounts will apply to your company as well. Make life easier for yourself.

If you are using the accrual basis of accounting, you also need a financial statement that details cash flow activity, which is likely to be different from the activity shown on the income statement. Cash-basis companies might not need as elaborate an analysis to generate a good understanding of their cash flows, but they should still be aware that lags between billing and collection could adversely affect their cash position.

The Income Statement

Your income statement (or *profit and loss statement*, or *P and L*) tells you whether your business is profitable. The income statement totals the amount of *revenue* and then subtracts the expenses associated with making that revenue. The result is the *pretax profit* and, after taxes are paid, *net income*.

Income statements show you how much you sold and how much it cost you to create those sales during a particular period of time. Most businesses prepare year-end income statements so they can see how they did during the year. You can also prepare income statements for any period, such as monthly, quarterly, or year-to-date.

Expenses fall into two categories: *cost of sales* expenses and *operating (fixed)* expenses. Cost of sales expenses (also called the cost of goods sold, or COGS) are those directly related to producing your product or providing your service. These generally include the cost of raw materials, the cost of labor to run the machine that produced the widget you sold, and other expenses required to obtain or create the product or service.

Talking Business _____

A **chart of accounts** is a list of all the categories used by a business to organize its financial expenditures and sales. These accounts will be defined so that they track the way you run your business even though many of these accounts are standard between most companies.

Revenue is the total sales amount received by the company. **Pretax profit** is the amount of money left over after all expenses, except for tax payments, have been deducted. **Cost of sales** expenses are the costs directly linked to the production or sale of a product or service (raw materials, labor, and other expenses). **Operating expenses** are those expenses associated with running your company (salaries, rent, utilities, and so on).

For example, suppose you sold a coffee mug for $5.00 and it cost you $3.00 to purchase it. The cost of sales is $3.00, which is what you paid for the mug. The *gross profit* calculation associated with this single mug's sale is revenue – cost of sales = gross profit, or $5.00 – $3.00 = $2.00 gross profit. Because the total costs of producing your total product sold change depending on how much you manufacture at a time, cost of sales are called *variable expenses*. The cost to your company of providing products for sale varies with the quantity sold, or is said to "vary with sales." Just as things usually cost less when you buy them in bulk, producing a product in large quantities works the same way. Generally speaking, the more you produce and sell, the lower the cost to produce each product and the higher the gross profit. This sentence is important enough for you to digest it until it make sense.

Talking Business _____

Your **gross profit** (also called gross margin) is the amount of money left after you cover the cost of sales: gross profit = revenue − cost of sales (also called cost of goods sold, or COGS). Out of gross profit, you pay your operating (also called fixed) expenses. Sorry for the jargon confusion, but I wanted you to see the various terms here first.

Operating (fixed) expenses are those expenses associated with running your business. You still have some amount of these expenses regardless of how much you sell in a month. These include your salary, your rent payment, the cost of the electricity in your office, insurance, administrative salaries, commissions, and other similar costs of operating the company. Operating expenses are paid out of the gross profit.

Notice that operating expenses include commissions that vary with the sales level, so they are not strictly "fixed" expenses but are often treated as such when performing financial analysis.

Now that I've given you an overview of what the income statement provides for you, take a look at one.

Remember the earlier coverage of accrual- and cash-basis accounting? Look at the income statement that follows in the next section and notice how the relationship between expenses and revenues is linked directly to profit calculations. Unless the two are synchronized, there is no way to accurately determine if you made money during the time period that you're examining.

The Balance Sheet

Whereas an income statement reflects the flow of money in and out of a company during a specific time frame (as videotape records events over a period of time), the *balance sheet* shows the amount of company assets and liabilities at a particular point in time (a snapshot of how things are at a particular moment). The balance sheet is based on a fundamental equation of accounting: Assets = Liabilities + Owner's Equity.

Assets are those items of value the company owns, such as cash in the checking account, accounts receivable, inventory, equipment, and property. The value of an asset is based on its initial purchase price minus any applicable *depreciation* (the accounting-tracked decrease in value that occurs as an asset ages).

CAUTION **Smoke Signals** _____

When you are analyzing the depreciation of an asset, don't confuse book value with market value. For example, your 10-year-old car might have $0 book value. Does that mean that the car is no longer worth anything? Not necessarily. The car probably has some market value in that someone would be willing to pay you something for it. The market might think that an asset has value even after it is fully depreciated.

For example, cash is an asset. You obtain the cash either from selling stock, obtaining a loan, or selling your services or products. Cash is money you can spend on the spot. It is called a *liquid asset;* you can use it immediately to pay off a debt or to purchase items. Other common liquid assets include accounts receivable and inventory. Liquid assets are part of current assets and represent those assets that you expect to be converted into cash within a year.

Talking Business

Assets are items of value owned by the company, including cash, property, and machinery. The value of an asset is based on its initial purchase price minus any applicable **depreciation** (the decrease in value that occurs as an asset ages).

Liquid assets include cash and anything that can be quickly converted into cash in less than 12 months (such as inventory and stock and bonds). **Fixed assets** are those that are difficult to convert quickly, such as buildings or machinery.

The **book value** of an asset is its purchase price less the total amount of depreciation that has already been applied to the asset.

The **market value** of an asset is what someone would pay for the asset, even though it may have been partially or fully depreciated.

A typical income statement.

A Simplified Income Statement
Jackson Surveying—Income Statement
For Fiscal Year Ending December 31, 20XX
Income Statement

Item	Dollar Amount	Description of Its Income Statement Function
Sales	$250,000	All revenues
Cost of Sales (variable costs)	$95,000	Variable costs associated with the revenues
Gross Profit (Gross Margin)	$155,000	Sales - Cost of Sales
Operating (Fixed) Expenses:		All nonvariable expenses:
Salaries	$65,000	Usually administrative and executive salaries
Rent	$18,000	What you pay to keep your doors open
Marketing and Sales	$55,000	What it costs you to sell your offering
Total Other Expenses	$138,000	Total of All Other Expenses
Pre-Tax Profit	$17,000	Gross Profit - Total Other Expenses
Federal/State Taxes	$5,950	Taxes due on the Pre-Tax Profit
Net Income	$11,050	Pre-Tax Profit - Federal and State Taxes

Fixed assets have a longer life and are more difficult to convert into cash quickly. Typical fixed assets include buildings, machinery, and land. The net *book value* of an asset is based on its initial purchase price less any depreciation. Different fixed assets have different depreciation terms, or depreciable lives. Check with an accountant to determine the proper depreciable life of a given item.

Liabilities are amounts that you owe. Typical liabilities include accounts payable, which reflects amounts owed to suppliers, loans, credit cards, taxes, and other people or organizations to whom you owe money. *Short-term liabilities*, which are paid back within 12 months, are also called *current liabilities*. Long-term liabilities include the portions of mortgages and equipment loans that are not due in the next 12 months.

Owner's equity is the portion of the balance sheet that displays what is left over when all liabilities are subtracted from all assets. Take what you own, subtract what you owe, and you are left with owner's equity. This is the number that you want to maximize because it can reflect the book value of your company. The initial investment of your company stock and accumulated retained earnings are added together to calculate owner's equity.

Talking Business

Liabilities are amounts that you owe, including loans, credit cards, and taxes. **Short-term liabilities** (those due within 12 months) are also called **current liabilities. Owner's equity** is what is left when you subtract your lia-bilities from your assets. **Net income** is money left over after all com-pany expenses, including taxes, have been paid out of revenues.

The amount of *net income* (see the sample income statement earlier in this chapter) determined at the end of the year is added to an equity account named retained earn-ings. You add the current period's net income to the prior period's retained earnings to calculate the company's retained earnings at the end of the period in question. A negative retained earnings is often a flag for a company in financial trouble. If you think about it for a second, it will make sense to you. The only way that the retained earnings can become negative is if there are negative net income values added to it, which means that the company lost money during the period that created the nega-tive net income.

The following table is an example of how to organize your accounts in preparation for making your balance sheet.

Typical Balance Sheet Accounts

Assets	Description
Cash	Bank accounts, petty cash, investments.
Accounts Receivable	What other companies (customers) owe you on a credit basis, to be paid usually within 30 days.
Inventory	Raw materials, finished goods, products being built, retail merchandise, product manuals, and so on.
Fixed Assets	Land, buildings, machinery, office equipment, depreciation expense.

Liabilities	Description
Short-Term (Current) Liabilities	Must be paid in less than 12 months. Includes accounts payable to suppliers, unpaid wages, taxes, credit card debt, short-term loans, and long-term notes with less than 12 months left on their term.
Long-Term Liabilities	Due over a period that is longer than 12 months. Includes mortgages, equipment loans, bank loans, and other long-term financial obligations.

Owner's Equity	Description
Equity Equation	Assets – liabilities = Owner's equity.
Capital Stock	Owned by shareholders. Includes common stock and preferred stock.
Retained Earnings	Current and cumulative year's net profits or losses as accumulated from prior- and current-year income statements.

So here you are with accounts and numbers. Now look at the following figure to see how to put them together to create a balance sheet.

As your company grows, the numbers on your assets and liabilities and equity lines usually will grow larger and larger because you'll be purchasing new equipment, increasing your accounts receivable because of higher sales, or improving your cash situation. Companies just starting out will typically have a small number on their assets and liabilities and equity lines. Focus on having a positive net income, which will create a positive and growing retained earnings, thereby increasing your owner's equity.

```
              A Simplified Balance Statement
              Jackson Surveying—Balance Sheet
                 Period Ending December 31, 20XX

Current Assets
Cash in Bank                              $15,000
Accounts Receivable                       $25,000
Inventory                                 $18,000
Other Current Assets                       $7,000

Total Current Assets                      $65,000

Fixed Assets
Land and Building                        $250,000
Machinery                                 $75,000
Office Equipment                          $35,000
Accumulated Depreciation                ($25,000)

Total Fixed Assets                       $335,000
Total Assets                             $400,000

Current Liabilities
Credit Cards                               $3,000
Wages Payable                              $9,500
Taxes Payable                              $3,000
Line of Credit                             $5,500
Accounts Payable                           $4,500
Total Current Liabilities                 $25,500

Long-Term Liabilities
Mortgage Loan                            $185,000
Machinery Loan                            $55,000
Equipment Loan                            $30,000

Total Long-Term Liabilities              $270,000
Total Liabilities                        $295,500

Owner's Equity
Common Stock                              $45,000
Retained Earnings                         $59,500
Total Owner's Equity                     $104,500
Total Liabilities and Equity             $400,000
```

This typical balance sheet shows the format for organizing all your balance sheet accounts.

Listen Up

It is common for small business owners to manage their business so that they show a negative net income and, as a result, pay no taxes. Since privately owned companies do not have to face the scrutiny of the public investor marketplace, like that of a publicly traded company, there is minimal pressure to show a positive net income. You can also take this approach with your business, but be prepared to answer some pretty tough questions if you ever need to present your negative income financial statements to outside investors such as bankers, venture capitalists, or the like. Or worse, the IRS.

Owner's equity, your company's net worth, is calculated by subtracting the liabilities from the assets. This means that as your assets (what you own) increase and your liabilities (what you owe) decrease, your equity increases. This makes logical sense, and the balance sheet puts it into a form where it can be calculated precisely. Realize, however, that your owner's equity usually does not reflect your company's market value. Setting the market value for an ongoing company is usually a complicated matter and heavily industry dependent.

Although your balance sheet might not change drastically from week to week, it's a good idea to regularly review whether you are taking on more debt or increasing the equity of the company. Most financial software packages can easily provide you with a balance sheet and income statement whenever you want to look at it. Always make sure to know if you are looking at an accrual- or cash-basis report.

Cash Flow Analysis

A cash flow analysis can be your most important financial statement because it tells you whether you have enough cash to pay your bills. Never forget that cash is as important as air for your business. Period. Although tracking your assets and liabilities is important over the long term, when you're just starting out, the key challenge is keeping more cash coming in than is going out.

A cash flow analysis, or statement of cash flow, looks a lot like an income statement (see the following figure). The major difference is that your income statement focuses on earnings from operations, whereas the cash flow analysis also reflects investments, borrowings, repayments of loan principle, and other balance sheet changes. Cash flow from operations might also be significantly different from reported earnings, especially if you are using the accrual basis of accounting. Remember also that your income statement might be based on accrual accounting methods, whereas your flow statement is based on actual cash in and out flows.

Listen Up

You can and will spend cash in ways that will not show up as an expense on your income statement. For example, the interest that you pay on a loan is deductible as an expense, but the principle portion (the part that decreases the amount of outstanding loan balance) is not an expense. You pay cash to reduce the loan payment, but it does not become an expense. For this reason, the statement of cash flows will not match your income statement.

The reason you need both an income statement and a cash flow analysis is that you might have a really good month of sales followed by a really bad month of sales. So bad, in fact, that you have to get a loan to cover your expenses. By watching your cash flow analysis, you can see in advance when you will start to run out of cash during that month. However, because an income statement based on an accrual basis of accounting records when obligations are made, not when the cash is either spent or received, the good months and bad months often even themselves out. You wouldn't know by looking at your income statement that August almost put you out of business due to lack of available cash, but your monthly cash flow analysis would alert you to potential problems before they become real problems. You should now see that you must use all three financial statements to get an accurate picture of your company's financial condition.

It is also a good idea to become good friends with your receivable aging report. This is the report that tells you who still owes you money and how far past due they are with their payments. If you offer net 30-day terms, and you see most of your clients paying in 45 to 60 days, then you are providing them with additional credit for the extra 15 to 30 days. In essence, you are taking out a loan to cover for their delayed payment. If that is okay with you, then you are more generous than most small business owners I know are. Get your collections in order, and you might find your need for cash decrease accordingly. See Chapter 18 for actions you can take if they don't pay.

	January	February	March	April	May	June	July	August	September	October	November	December	2003
Revenues													
Product Sales	$1,200	$1,620	$2,187	$2,952	$3,986	$5,381	$6,995	$9,094	$11,822	$15,368	$19,979	$25,972	$106,556
Services	$300	$405	$547	$738	$996	$1,345	$1,749	$2,273	$2,955	$3,842	$4,995	$6,493	$26,639
Net Revenues	**$1,500**	**$2,025**	**$2,734**	**$3,691**	**$4,982**	**$6,726**	**$8,744**	**$11,367**	**$14,777**	**$19,210**	**$24,973**	**$32,465**	**$133,195**
Cost of Sales													
Product Cost	$300	$405	$547	$738	$996	$1,345	$1,749	$2,273	$2,955	$3,842	$4,995	$6,493	$26,639
Services Cost	$45	$61	$82	$111	$149	$202	$262	$341	$443	$576	$749	$974	$3,996
Total Cost of Sales	**$345**	**$466**	**$629**	**$849**	**$1,146**	**$1,547**	**$2,011**	**$2,614**	**$3,399**	**$4,418**	**$5,744**	**$7,467**	**$30,635**
Gross Margin	**$1,155**	**$1,559**	**$2,105**	**$2,842**	**$3,836**	**$5,179**	**$6,733**	**$8,753**	**$11,378**	**$14,792**	**$19,229**	**$24,998**	**$102,560**
Overhead Expenses													
Salaries	$3,500	$3,500	$3,500	$3,500	$3,500	$3,500	$3,500	$3,500	$3,500	$3,500	$3,500	$3,500	$42,000
Payroll Taxes and Benefits	$700	$700	$700	$700	$700	$700	$700	$700	$700	$700	$700	$700	$8,400
Advertising and Promotion	$300	$300	$300	$300	$300	$300	$300	$300	$300	$300	$300	$300	$3,600
Depreciation	$150	$150	$150	$150	$150	$150	$150	$150	$150	$150	$150	$150	$1,800
Supplies and Postage	$100	$100	$100	$100	$100	$100	$100	$100	$100	$100	$100	$100	$1,200
Professional Fees	$175	$175	$175	$175	$175	$175	$175	$175	$175	$175	$175	$175	$2,100
Printing	$200	$200	$200	$200	$200	$200	$200	$200	$200	$200	$200	$200	$2,400
Telephone	$250	$250	$250	$250	$250	$250	$250	$250	$250	$250	$250	$250	$3,000
Equipment Rental and Repair	$50	$50	$50	$50	$50	$50	$50	$50	$50	$50	$50	$50	$600
Travel	$650	$650	$650	$650	$650	$650	$650	$650	$650	$650	$650	$650	$7,800
Miscellaneous	$225	$225	$225	$225	$225	$225	$225	$225	$225	$225	$225	$225	$2,700
Office Space	$900	$900	$900	$900	$900	$900	$900	$900	$900	$900	$900	$900	$10,800
Total Overhead Expenses	**$7,200**	**$7,200**	**$7,200**	**$7,200**	**$7,200**	**$7,200**	**$7,200**	**$7,200**	**$7,200**	**$7,200**	**$7,200**	**$7,200**	**$86,400**
Net Income (Loss) Before Tax	**($6,045)**	**($5,641)**	**($5,095)**	**($4,358)**	**($3,364)**	**($2,021)**	**($467)**	**$1,553**	**$4,178**	**$7,592**	**$12,029**	**$17,798**	**$16,160**
Provisions for Income Tax													
Federal Income Tax	$ -	$ -	$ -	$ -	$ -	$ -	$ -	$ -	$ -	$ -	$ -	$ -	$0
State Income Tax	$ -	$ -	$ -	$ -	$ -	$ -	$ -	$ -	$ -	$ -	$ -	$ -	$0
Total Tax Provisions	$ -	$ -	$ -	$ -	$ -	$ -	$ -	$ -	$ -	$ -	$ -	$ -	**$0**
Net Income (loss)	**($6,045)**	**($5,641)**	**($5,095)**	**($4,358)**	**($3,364)**	**($2,021)**	**($467)**	**$1,553**	**$4,178**	**$7,592**	**$12,029**	**$17,798**	**$16,160**

Note: Tax deductions not included to simplify analysis.

A typical cash flow analysis.

On the CD _____

More important information about financially managing your company is included as bonus sections on the companion CD. "Using Financial Statements" (CD15-2) helps you more effectively use the information contained in your financial statements so that you can make more profitable decisions. "To CPA or Not to CPA" (CD15-1) helps you understand what you really get from using a CPA for your accounting requirements. For many smaller businesses, a CPA is overkill, but for the right circumstances, a CPA is a great professional to have on your side. One tip from these sections could pay for the entire book, so make sure you check them out.

The Least You Need to Know

- Accounting is the tool used to determine the financial health of your business. It is a necessary and integral part of your business, and you should pay close attention to it from the start.

- Financial statements include an income statement, statement of cash flow, and balance sheet.

- Accrual- and cash-basis accounting provide different profit and loss information for the same accounting period. Make sure that you always track your cash and don't always believe the accrual-based income statement.

- Bookkeeping is basically clerical in nature once the procedures are set up; financial accounting involves analyzing financial performance and comparing current results with prior accounting periods.

- When in doubt, get an accountant. You might not need a CPA right away.

- Automate from the beginning and make sure that your software package can handle growth in areas such as receivable tracking, inventory, and accrual accounting.

Part 4

Running a Healthy Business

Your business plan is an important step in getting your business up and running, but you will need additional information and skills to make your business successful once it is alive. Your business will need cash as much as you need air. And cash availability is tied directly into your credit policy. Which is tied directly into your policy on collecting bad debts from people who don't pay. This part tells you what to do in these important areas.

It also helps you work with your commercial banker and explains how to set yourself up to take full advantage of automation in general. The prior parts got you going. This part helps you continue on that road to sustained success.

Chapter 16

Cash Is More Important Than Air

In This Chapter

- ◆ The value of cash in your organization
- ◆ Turning receivables into cash
- ◆ How rapid sales growth can jeopardize your business
- ◆ Using credit to your advantage
- ◆ Determining total cash requirements

Laurie stared in disbelief at her conference room table. She had heard of this happening to other companies; she couldn't believe it happened to hers.

"We're out of money," she said. "I can make payroll, but I don't have enough left over to pay our suppliers."

"That's impossible," said Philip, the VP of Sales and Marketing. "We just had three of our best months this quarter. In fact, our current revenues are triple that of last year at this time, and our income statement clearly shows a profit for this quarter. What gives?"

"The earnings are right, but we haven't collected on those large sales over the past few months. And remember, we've had to pay our workers and suppliers even though our customers haven't yet paid us. It'll be great when all those sales are collected, but if we keep growing as we have been, we're likely to need even more cash."

"So are you trying to tell me that our marketing success has put the company in jeopardy?" cried Philip.

"Not at all," said Laurie. "We simply did not plan for the rapid increase and came up short with our lines of credit and other ways of getting cash into our bank account. It was my and Jerry's responsibility to plan for this, and we blew it. We need to tell our vendors our dilemma. I think honesty is the best policy. Let's just hope they will let us stall our payments. We can't let it happen again!"

Everyone nodded his or her head at the seriousness of the situation. They had been so happy about being successful that they had forgotten that cash is like air for your business.

Keeping the cash flowing into your business is key to growth and expansion, not to mention paying your bills in a timely manner. This chapter will help you develop strategies for keeping the money flowing into your business so that you don't run into the same trouble Laurie's company did. It also shows you how to determine the amount of cash you will need to keep afloat.

When You're Out of Cash, You're Out of Business (Usually)

Love may make the world go 'round, but it's cash that keeps the lights on while you are spinning. Try to retain an employee when you cannot pay him, and you will understand that cash is the business equivalent of air. Lose your employees, the good ones, and you have substantially hurt your business. Once they're gone, they're usually gone for good.

Take a look at your vendors. How long will they keep providing you with the materials you need if you cannot pay your bills? About as long as a snowball would last in a west Texas desert. Once again, you cannot blame them for putting a stop to your credit line. Guess who is paying employees out of his or her own pocket because her or she gave you credit and you can't pay? Your vendor! Your vendor has to cover his or her own behind just like you do.

Now, what about you? What happens if you cannot pay yourself? How long will you keep the business alive and pay your employees when you are not being paid? A few months, maybe, but when it becomes a way of life, you will be seriously tempted to pull the plug and "get a real job," not because you don't love what you do, but simply because that's what an organism does when its air supply is taken away.

A cash problem hurts your employees, your vendors, and you personally. Lack of cash might cause your usually professional employees to become disgruntled, might cause the quality of your product to decline, and might lead to your own loss of enthusiasm. The result is that your customers will be affected, and they probably won't like it. Their opinion of your company might drop as employees become snippier over the phone or in person. Unfortunately, customers don't really care why the quality has declined; they just recognize that it has, and they might decide to take their business elsewhere if it continues.

All this because you forgot that cash is king! Income is great. Equipment is wonderful. Receivables are heartwarming. Inventory gives you something to count on boring weekends and at the end of the year. But cash is the oil that makes it all work smoothly on a daily basis.

How Success Can Kill Your Business

How good can it get? Here you are with a 300 percent increase in sales over the past six months. Your people are flying high, and you just can't seem to do anything wrong. As a matter of fact, the projects coming your way are larger than you ever thought you would have, and it looks like you'll get them all! Your initial dreams have come true, and you're on the verge of becoming unbearable to everyone around you. Don't worry. Life is about to humble you, unless you have taken the proper steps to deal with the growth.

Have you ever met someone who told you that he was so successful, he went out of business? If not, you should look for such a person and buy him dinner (or a drink, depending on how he dealt with the loss). Just as you don't need to go through a windshield to learn that seatbelts are a good thing, you don't need to go out of business to learn the dangers of rapid growth.

Picture this scenario: You used to provide $10,000 per month in services, and all your customers paid cash on delivery or by credit card. When you completed the sale, you got the cash and it went straight into your business checking account. Everyone was happy. Then customers began asking for credit terms. After all, your competitor offered them credit, and they have consistently used your company instead. It wasn't such a big deal, and they were stable. Why not offer them credit? So you did.

Take a look at what happened when you agreed to offer credit payment terms instead of cash. You delayed the cash payments you would have definitely received this month for at least a month. You, however, still need to pay your employees and vendors at the end of *this* month. Where is that money going to come from? Unless your company has a lot of cash on hand (and wouldn't we all like that situation?), it will have to come from you, the owner. When the customer pays, you will simply pay yourself back the amount you loaned the company and all will be fine. So far, so good. Sort of ….

> **Smoke Signals**
>
> Don't put all your eggs in one basket. As dangerous as it is to grow your company quickly, it's even more risky for that growth to be the result of a relationship with just a few customers. Keep trying to expand and diversify your customer base while managing your growth.

Now let's be really successful and bump your monthly sales to $30,000. Wonderful! Who is going to provide the cash needed to cover the month-end bills? You? Do you have the $30,000 on hand to lend the company? Even if you do have the cash at $30,000, you might not when monthly sales hit $50,000 or $100,000. What about if customers start to take liberties with the net 30 day payment policy and start paying in 60 or 90 days instead? Can you now come up with the $60,000 to $90,000 it will take to cover the cash flow during that delayed payment period? Now I have your attention.

My point is this: Someday you will no longer be able to personally provide this kind of cash advance to the company. Uh-oh! There go your employees and all those wonderful vendor relationships. When they leave, they place everything that made you successful in jeopardy. In short, the whopping success that you enjoyed has just put you precariously close to being out of business. Isn't it amazing how a few short (or very long sleepless) weeks can turn your business on its ear? That is exactly what will happen if you don't take steps to avoid a cash crunch.

I'm not trying to talk you out of making your business as wildly successful as you can imagine. I'm just trying to convince you to open your eyes to the fact that success can destroy all that you have built if you don't also deal with its potential risks. Use the information in this chapter in conjunction with that in Chapter 18 to ensure that your credit and collection policies are rock solid, which will minimize the cash pressure on you and your business.

Factoring, Credit Terms, and Loans

Here you are, all dressed up to go to the dance with a hot date and no cash to pay for the cab. Now what do you do? You go to someone and borrow money against your next paycheck or income tax refund. Well, the same thing can be done with a business, and it's called *factoring*. With factoring, a company gives you a percentage of what customers owe you, sort of like a short-term loan using what is owed you as collateral.

You can also improve your cash situation by providing your customers with an incentive for paying their bills early (or even on time) and delaying payments to your own vendors with whom you have credit. This improves your cash position (for the short term) by decreasing the *float* between when you must pay your bills and when you receive money.

Finally, you can get a short-term loan that is secured by your receivables from a bank or other funding source. This technique is less expensive than factoring and provides greater stability, along with other benefits such as improving your lending relationship with your banker.

Talking Business

Factoring is the process of receiving money now for payments your customers are expected to make to you in the next few weeks. There is a cost for having that money now, however, which is paid in the form of a percentage fee to the factoring company or factor. It is expensive to do on a regular basis but can be effectively used if needed. But you must plan ahead with the factoring company to factor your receivables. **Float** in this context refers to the time frame between when you earned the money due you and when it is actually received. It can also mean the time frame between when you actually receive money and when portions of the money are due payable to others.

Factoring Receivables

If you need cash now to cover business expenses, there are companies out there who will provide you with cash for your receivables in exchange for a fee. Here's a general outline of how factoring, or discounting, of receivable notes works. (Use this as a way of understanding the process and verify the percentages with prospective factoring companies.)

1. You close the deal and the customer agrees to pay you for your product or service.

2. The company that plans to factor your receivables issues an invoice to the customer (usually on your letterhead), which the customer is to pay.

3. The factoring company immediately gives you cash worth between 80 and 95 percent of the receivable value.

4. The factoring company then gives back a portion of the fee (usually up to 10 percent of the initial 5 to 20 percent discount) if the customer repays within the specified time frame.

For example, assume that a client contracts from you $10,000 worth of your product or service. Assume that you can realistically expect to receive that money within 45 to 60 days, which can put you in a bind depending on your company's cash situation. You could factor the note using the previously outlined procedure and have the numbers work out as follows:

1. You close the deal for $10,000.

2. The factoring company issues an invoice to your customer for $10,000 and indicates the terms in which the payment should be made to the factoring company.

3. The factoring company writes you a check for between $8,000 and $9,500, depending on the factoring company.

4. If the customer pays within the allowed 30 days, then the factoring company writes you another check for around 10 percent (or $1,000) when payment is received. (The longer it takes for your customer to pay the factor, the less of the original invoice amount you get back.)

On the CD

A sample Receivables Purchase Agreement is included on the CD as document 16-01.

Assuming that you receive an 85 percent factoring rate with a 10 percent additional payment received within 30 days, you see $8,500 immediately and $1,000 within 30 days. You give up 5 percent, or $500, to get your money up front instead of later and for pushing the collections issue over to the factoring company. Collection becomes their problem, not yours.

If you are in a cash crunch, factoring can save your hide. However, here are the down sides, and they are not trivial. If you used a line of credit, interest only payments, at 5 percent per year interest rate, then borrowing that same $100 for one month would cost you $100 × 05/12 = 42 cents instead of $5. When you receive the $100, you pay off the line of credit. Simple. Wow! That's big bucks for the convenience of having your cash earlier instead of later. On the other hand, if you need it, you need it.

You can minimize the sour taste that factoring percentages can create by performing your own factoring services. If you have substantial personal resources and you own a corporation, you can use your own money to replace the need for factoring. You can buy the receivables from your corporation with your personal funds and provide the same terms as a factoring company. At least, the interest is going into your favorite account (yours!) instead of some other company's. You will, however, need to declare the interest income on your personal tax return. After all, it is income that you earned as a private individual even if the money did come from your own corporation.

Unfortunately, you can only factor up to the limit allowed by your personal resources. You then must look for other options.

Using Credit Terms to Enhance Your Cash Position

Timing is the secret to success, and that is particularly true when working with money. The time that money is in your hands, or in someone else's, either makes you money or costs you money. You must make every possible effort to turn your sales into cash as quickly as possible, paying as little as possible to get your money faster, such as by factoring or offering fast-payment discounts.

You have an excellent opportunity to improve your cash flow by simply changing the way you pay your bills and collect receivables from your clients. If you must pay in 30 days and your clients must pay in 60 days, you have a problem. On the other hand, if your customers pay in 10 days and you pay your vendors in 45 days, you are in excellent shape. You accomplish this by simply offering your customers a discount (such as 2 percent of what they owe you) for payment within 10 days. Many companies will jump at the chance to save the 2 percent, and it's certainly cheaper for you to offer this discount than to pay a factoring service 5 to 15 percent for the same result! From your customer's perspective, they are saving 2 percent off of their product costs (which improves their gross margins) by simply paying early, which may not be a problem for many of them. You will hear this credit policy referred to as "2 percent in 10 days/net 30 days" credit terms.

On the CD

Sample Credit Application (document 16-02) and Credit Information Release Authorization (document 16-03) documents are included on the CD.

Listen Up

Don't tell the IRS that I told you this, but you can improve your cash position for a two-week period by holding your monthly payroll taxes until the middle of the month, assuming your payroll situation allows you to do that. Sometimes, providence will shine on you when that big check you've been expecting arrives just in time to make the payment. If not, you better be ready to come up with the cash needed to make the tax payment. Remember, this is a very last resort action because delinquent payroll taxes can land you in big trouble with serious legal consequences.

Think about it. Plot out on a piece of paper the timing of payments made and received. Assume that a $10,000 sale is made today. Mark on a calendar when you expect to provide the products or services, when you plan to receive the payment made under your credit terms, and when you have to pay your vendors and employees. Notice that the arrows for money going out and money coming in have a delay between them that usually doesn't work in your favor. You must pay the suppliers before you receive payment. Now mark where payment would be received with a 2 percent discount in 10-day incentive. Isn't life easier when the cash is in your hands, instead of in your customer's account? Plus, when you have the money, you don't have to worry about it becoming uncollectable, which is a horrible circumstance in which to find yourself.

Buying on Credit

Your grandmother may have always told you to stay debt free because a person in debt is a person in trouble. Well, that might be true for certain people, but credit is the lifeblood of a growing company. Credit in itself is not bad. It is how you use this credit that can either save your hide or hang it out to dry.

Try this technique for increasing your cash situation. Instead of paying $25,000 in cash for that bunch of computer equipment you intend to buy, why not go to your bank and have them give you a loan secured by the equipment? The bank will probably want 20 percent ($5,000) down and the rest financed over 24 to 36 months at the going interest rate. Notice that your monthly expenses go up, but you have $20,000 cash in your bank account to handle unexpected cash shortfalls. Heck. Some vendors are even offering, at the time of this writing, "buy now, no interest or payments for up to two years" payment terms. This is really pretty scary from a customer perspective because you could take full advantage of this offer, run up a huge debt to this vendor, spend the customer payments on growing your business, and find yourself unable to pay the debt when due in two years. It takes a lot of self-discipline to manage this type of debt/credit opportunity properly and not put your company in jeopardy.

 On the CD

Sample Security Agreement (document 16-04) and Guaranty (document 16-05) documents are included on the CD.

Even your grandmother would agree that paying your bills while keeping some cash on hand is a healthy state of financial being.

Taking Out a Loan

You can imagine that every business has the same problems in turning its receivables into cash. It should not surprise you that people, even banks, provide loans designed to cover exactly this short-term timing situation. It is essentially a line of credit secured by the receivables, and you are expected to pay it down as quickly as possible. The interest rate is some variation of prime plus a few percentage points annually, instead of 60 percent, and you establish a credit history with your bank. That always pays off in the long run because the bank can become an integral partner as your success requires higher and higher borrowing levels.

Applying Break-Even Analysis to Determine Startup Cash Requirements

A thriving, dynamic business always has something new happening. It might be the business itself when you are first starting up, or it might be introducing a new product line. In either case, it is important to get a solid idea of when and whether your business or new offering will make money. The financial technique used for estimating that time frame and likelihood is called *break-even analysis*. Notice that knowing the break-even point is important to determining the amount of cash you need to have on hand. The further out your break-even point, the more cash you need to keep you solvent until you get past break-even and start making money. The closer your break-even point, the less demanding your cash requirements. Without knowing your break-even point, you are simply guessing, which is scary.

In a nutshell, a break-even analysis tells you how much you have to make in dollars or products sold to cover all your costs. Obviously, your goal is to do much better than that, but start first with ensuring you can at least pay for the products or services to be produced. When you operate at break-even, it is not costing you anything to keep your doors open, and when you are over break-even, you are actually making money.

A break-even analysis takes into consideration three pieces of information:

Talking Business

A **break-even analysis** is a calculation of how much sale revenue you must create to cover your basic fixed costs of doing business. This dollar sales value can also be translated into a unit sales level. Above that level, you're making money. Sounds like a pretty important number (and initial target) to know.

- The average sale price of what you sell, which can be either products or services. Just estimate how much your typical sale will be and divide it by the number of units (or hours) you sold to earn those sales.

- The average variable cost to you to produce what you sell, or how much it costs to produce your typical sale. Once again, add up your total estimated variable costs and divide them by the number of units (or hours) involved to create those total costs. Ideally, you want the number of units used in this step to match the number used to calculate the average sale price. This is your average variable cost.

- Your total fixed costs per year (and then per month), which are your total expenses for the year that you have to pay no matter how much you sell. This includes things such as rent, your phone bill, insurance, tax, employee salaries, and utilities.

Your break-even point in units is calculated by dividing

Fixed costs ÷ (1 – average variable cost/average sale price)

Remember that when calculating your average cost of producing products, you will have to add all of your expenses associated with manufacturing, such as raw material costs, labor costs, and waste and dividing it by the number of products produced. That's your average. Some individual units may have cost more than others to produce, and some less, but over time and larger quantities, the cost evens out to some average.

Similarly, the average price of your product can be determined by adding your anticipated sales for the next year and dividing by the total number of units you expect to sell. While you may sell some for higher or lower prices, this calculation averages them into a single number, which simplifies the analysis.

For example, if you have annual fixed costs of $30,000 and sell software programs that are priced at an average of $100 and cost $20 to produce, your break-even in dollars is $37,500:

$30,000 ÷ (1 – 20 ÷ 100) = $30,000 ÷ .8 = $37,500

This means that you must have sales of $37,500 a year just for the business to break even (pay its fixed expenses and product costs). To calculate the number of software programs you have to sell, just divide $37,500 by the price of the program, which is $100:

$37,500 ÷ 100 = 375 units

These example numbers will mean nothing to you, but if you put in some estimates of your average sales price, cost, and total fixed costs, you will get an idea of what you can expect for your company. Once you figure out the break-even in dollars and units, think about whether those figures seem high, low, or reasonable for your particular business environment. (This is a marketing question, isn't it?)

For those of you starting a service business who think there's no way to figure out an average sale price, here are some pointers. Keep in mind that calculating your break-even point isn't supposed to be exact at the moment. You're just trying to get a rough idea of whether you can ever sell enough of your product or service to pay all your expenses and make some money.

If you're not selling a product, there are other ways of estimating your break-even point. If you are thinking of becoming a consultant, for instance, you determine your hourly rate and divide your fixed costs by your hourly rate. That tells you the minimum number of hours you need to bill each month to break even. (*Note:* It is common for consulting businesses to have very low variable costs since they provide only services and not products.) If you come up with 10 or 11 hours per week, or 40 per month, you're doing well. The average number of hours that a new consultant bills weekly is around 14;

this number should get up to around 24 to 30 hours per week once the company gets up and going. If you're having trouble choosing an hourly rate, call some of your competitors and ask what their rate is; that is a guide for what local clients are willing to pay.

Even if you are selling a product and you can't figure out the average price, just take the prices of all or most of your products and calculate an average. If you own a restaurant, you can estimate the average meal price by taking the average price of an appetizer and adding it to the average entrée price and drink price. This number may run anywhere from $5.00 at McDonald's to over $100 at an upscale eatery. Now estimate your average cost of providing those appetizers and entrées. Subtract that average cost from the average price to get the average gross margin (gross profit) per meal. Now divide your estimated monthly fixed costs by this average gross profit per meal number. This final quotient tells you how many people you need to feed each month just to keep your doors open and the lights on. Does it look feasible given the number of hours you'll be open and your neighborhood? Remember that if your restaurant is in an industrial district, you might not have many customers outside of breakfast and lunch. These are the types of questions you're trying to answer with this exercise.

> **Listen Up**
>
> When you perform a break-even analysis, be sure to divide the average cost by the average price first, before subtracting the number from 1. This gives the answer in dollars, not units. You then calculate the number of units needed to break even, which is also very important to understand.

If you come up with a number that is much higher than you think you could ever reasonably achieve, your business may have serious problems staying financially solvent. Are there ways you can reduce your fixed costs, such as by setting up a home-based office or putting off hiring employees until later? Those are the kinds of decisions you need to make to create a successful business. However, if your break-even appears well within reason in terms of sales, look again at your numbers to be sure you haven't forgotten to take something into consideration. If your calculations appear accurate, then you are in luck and are well on your way to starting a successful business.

Break-even analysis is one of the most valuable and simple to use financial analysis tools available, and you should get to know its usage. It will pay off for you well into the future.

Knowing When Enough Is Enough

There are worse fates than having a business fail miserably due to a single, catastrophic event. One of them is having it fail gradually so that it slowly bleeds your reserve funds and energy. It never really takes off, but it never really is bad enough to close the doors. Beware because the steady drip-drip-drip of cash leaving the company on a monthly basis will keep you around while draining your finances. When this happens, you find yourself digging into your personal savings each month to keep the company afloat, all the time believing that it will turn around. The problem is that both you and the company may eventually go bankrupt.

For this reason, I suggest that you set some time frame and financial guidelines for when and how you will evaluate your company's performance. These milestones should include desired, or even required, levels of personal income and time investment required to keep the business running. If you exceed these goals, then you and your business are successful. If you are below those goals, then you need to make some goal adjustments or business management adjustments. At that time, you can choose to either recommit to the venture or decide that it's time to call the idea a bad one and move on by either closing, selling, or restructuring the business to meet your desired goals.

Get your family involved in this goal-setting process. It is important that they know the sacrifices on their part are only in place for a set period of time, after which things will be reevaluated. If the business does well, you'll all benefit; but if it never takes off, your family can take comfort in knowing you'll shut it down after a certain period of time and try something else. Believe me when I say that your family is afraid for you and for themselves if the business goes under.

The hardest question to answer is, "How long do I keep investing in the company before I can expect a profit?" This is a tough question, but you can expect to lose some money for at least 18 to 24 months, and you should be making a decent living between 36 and 48 months. It is certainly common for the owner to pay all of the bills during this period of time and not take home a salary. (These are simply rules of thumb based on discussions with other business owners and do not represent scientific findings.) If you have a smaller service-oriented company that you can operate out of your home, then you might make money much sooner because your overhead is low. Are you starting to appreciate this tight relationship between your sales price, your variable costs, and your fixed costs? They are inextricably linked. In summary, the more you can reasonably charge your customers, while keeping your variable and fixed costs low, the sooner you will take home the money needed to support yourself and grow your business.

Listen Up

Assume that you need to cover at least six months of personal living expenses before the company becomes profitable enough to pay you a salary. Expect that it may take 18 to 24 months, but use 6 months as an absolute minimum. If you plan 18 and it takes 6, you are ahead of the game. If you plan 6 and run out of money at month 7, you are out of business. This is a sobering thought, so don't be too aggressive in your sales and profit projections.

Projecting Startup Cash Requirements

Your income statement summarizes how much money you made and how much money you spent for a specified period of time, which is typically one year but will be broken out on a monthly basis for the first year of operation. It allows you to look at the big picture of how much money you expect to make (or lose) over a period of time.

Use a balance sheet to determine the value of what you own (your assets) and what you owe (your liabilities) at a particular point in time, usually the last day of the year. Bankers are interested in this statement because it gives them an idea of what your business is worth and whether you can pay off your loan by selling all your assets.

Now for the clincher: Remember that your income and balance sheet might be based on accrual accounting and may not reflect cash received. You can look good on these two statements and be completely out of cash, which happens to more of my clients than you want to know. You really want to know the total amount of cash that you will require during the startup phase to cover not only initial startup costs but also the net cash outflow that will happen monthly until you make it past break-even.

Remember that each month of cash-basis negative net income (net cash outflow) increases your total cash requirement, and each month of cash-basis positive net income (net cash inflow) decreases your cash requirement. Adding the inflow/outflow from one month to the next tells you the total you need (cumulative) over the period of time of your analysis. (See the "Typical Cash Flow Analysis" chart included in Chapter 15 for an example of a cumulative cash flow calculation.)

This cumulative cash flow requirement is so important that it is hard to over emphasize. This is the total estimated cash you must have available to pay all of your bills while you are ramping up your sales to break-even and beyond. You can have this money in the form of cash on hand, ready loans, equity partners willing to buy in, or any number of other, creative ways. But you must have it available, or you may find yourself running out of cash at the very moment when your business is poised for success.

For Your Plan

Any investor knows that cash is the air supply of your company and will want to understand the uses of your cash, how you plan to manage it, and how much you need to stay afloat. Make sure that your plan presents the following information:

◆ A monthly cash flow (loss) projection for the first 12 months and then annually for years two and three.

◆ The amount of cumulative cash you will need for your venture, including a detailed description of the sources of this cash.

◆ Your intended cash management strategy, including the use of factoring, bank lines of credit, or other sources.

◆ Your intended credit management policies and your justification for why you set them up the way you did.

◆ Your expected break-even point from both a sales and units perspective. These numbers will be used in the marketing and operations portions of your plan.

◆ How these break-even projections tie in with the marketing and sales plan, which must be designed to create sales sufficient to exceed the break-even within prescribed time frames.

The Least You Need to Know

◆ Cash is the lifeblood, or air supply, of an organization. Without cash to pay employees or vendors, you are out of business.

◆ Cash will become scarce at some point in your business growth; of that you can be certain. Set up credit lines today that will help you when it happens.

◆ Factoring is a convenient, yet expensive, way of turning receivables into cash.

◆ Banks will give you short-term lines of credit secured by receivables, but the amount of credit will vary from month to month.

◆ Don't be afraid of credit. Purchasing capital equipment items with credit instead of cash shifts the purchase from a large cash outlay to smaller monthly payments, which improves your cash position as long as you don't go overboard.

◆ Understand the cumulative cash requirements of your company to make sure that you are not caught short on cash just when your company is ready to take off.

Chapter 17

Charge: Making Credit Card Sales Work

In This Chapter

- Comparing standard terms with credit card sales
- How much do credit sales cost you?
- Protecting yourself from fraud
- Telephone sales versus in-person credit card sales
- Determining the right credit card policy for you

Jamie was pumped up! Sales were going through the roof, and things appeared to be financially on track. Why did his accountant want to talk with him? What could possibly be wrong? His trusty accountant, Raymond, was smiling but also shaking his head.

"Jamie, how would you feel about having another $500 in your pocket this month without lifting a finger?" asked Raymond. He knew Jamie well enough to already know the answer.

"Sure, and what's your cut for bringing this opportunity to me?" asked Jamie.

"Not a nickel. This one is on the house. Do you remember those two large training contracts you signed last month? The one for $17,000 and the other for $15,000? Well, guess what? The clients decided to charge the sales to their American Express card, and American Express charged you 3.5 percent for processing those charges! These clients both have great credit records and probably would have jumped on the 2 percent discount we offer for payment within 10 days. In short, you gave up at least 1.5 percent of the sale price because your salespeople wanted to get credit for the sale before the end of the quarter!"

"Hmmm," Jamie thought, punching numbers into his calculator. "3.5 minus 2 is 1.5 percent. And 1.5 percent of $32,000 is $480. The sales reps just cost me enough to pay for a great evening out on the town for me and that wife of mine that I never see! What do you suggest?" asked Jamie.

"Let your salespeople know that credit card sales cost the company extra money because the credit card company charges a processing fee. Cards should be used only for sales under a certain dollar level and limited to specific situations, such as new customers without a solid credit history with our company. If you don't set some limitations on credit card sales, you give money away to credit card companies when you can have the cash in your pocket. Credit cards are an excellent way to avoid collection problems with new customers, but they get expensive with established customers who you know will pay."

"Thanks, Raymond," said Jamie as he walked out the door. "You can bother me with this kind of feedback any time you want."

Credit cards may well be the new form of legal tender. I know people who carry credit cards and an ATM card but little or no cash. You simply cannot ignore the implications of credit cards on your business no matter what type of business you run. It is important to consider whether offering your clients the opportunity to pay using a credit card, instead of cash or a check, is a good thing. This chapter shows you how to make that decision.

The Way Credit Cards Work

If you plan to go into a retail business, you have no choice but to offer credit cards as a payment option, or you risk losing sales. Period. However, if you'll be selling consulting services to companies and billing tens of thousands of dollars, a credit card is probably not the best way to get paid. Instead, request a completed credit application and a company check to verify that they will pay, and save the credit card processing fees.

A person obtains a credit card from a bank, which provides a line of credit to the person whose name is on the card. The credit card is issued as a Visa, MasterCard, Discover, or some other brand name. (American Express produces its own card, which requires payment in full each month for most charges unless other special arrangements are made, and provides its own credit processing operations, which I discuss in more detail later.)

You, as a business owner, set up your own merchant account so that you can process credit card sales and then have money deposited into your account. You are issued a *merchant number* by your credit card processing company that helps them identify exactly who you are, the applicable processing fees to charge, and where your money should be deposited.

> **CAUTION**
>
> **Smoke Signals**
>
> Some credit card processing companies have restrictions that prevent them from authorizing certain types of businesses. If you fall into any of these categories, be aware that you might have to do a little more shopping around to get a good deal: home-based businesses, mail-order firms, start-up businesses (those less than a year old), and business done primarily over the phone.

The customer's credit card is generally *unsecured*, meaning the bank has nothing that it can take and sell to repay the person's debt if the person defaults on payments. The only recourse is to cancel the card, destroy the person's credit record, and bother him until he pays. Fortunately for you, the business owner, you get paid whether your customer pays his or her bill to the credit card company or not. That's what you pay the credit card companies for. They absorb the risk of their credit card holder not paying the credit card balance, not you.

When a person purchases something from you and pays using a credit card, he is using his line of credit from the bank. The bank is essentially agreeing to pay the person's obligation to your company and takes the responsibility for obtaining payment from the person whose name appears on the card. In short, the bank is giving the person a loan that he uses to buy a product or service from you. In return for taking the responsibility (and risk) for collecting payment from the cardholder, the bank charges you a fee. Of course, you still get paid even if the credit card company doesn't, but you did give up a percentage of your total sale amount to them for absorbing this risk.

You can generally think of a buyer who uses a credit card as someone with a line of credit from a bank. The company whose name appears on the card, such as Citibank or Chase, handles the cardholder credit application and marketing of the card. You process a customer's purchase using the credit card and signed receipt. In return, the bank deposits the amount of the purchase (minus the fees) into your bank account.

The company that processes and clears your company's credit card transactions, debiting the charged amount from the proper credit card and then crediting your bank account, is called the *card processing company*. Such a company can be an independent business just like yours, and thus not affiliated with the credit card issuer. On the other hand, some banks now have their own credit card processing units.

PaymenTech (1-800-619-1982) is one credit card processing company you might want to contact. Another is Nova, which is a subsidiary of US Bank (1-800-432-9413) and the third-largest processing company in the United States.

> **Talking Business** _____
>
> A **merchant number** is a number given to your company that is used to identify which account should be credited when a customer makes a purchase. It also verifies that you're allowed to accept credit cards in payment. When you call your credit card processor for authorization to charge a customer's credit card, he or she asks for your merchant number, the customer's card number and expiration date, and the amount of the purchase before giving approval with its associated authorization code. An **unsecured** line of credit is a line of credit that is not backed by some form of collateral. The interest rate on this type of credit line is usually much higher than a loan secured by something of value other than your good name and promise to pay.

The Costs of Credit

Sounds pretty simple, doesn't it? Run the card through the credit card machine, punch in the purchase amount, and press Enter. You've just gotten paid. Too cool! Too easy! What's the catch?

The catch is that there's a cost to this great service. Take a look at who gets a piece of that simple transaction.

For the purposes of this discussion, I assume you are processing the transaction electronically as opposed to manually. With a manual system, you have to call and request authorization by voice, rather than let the credit card machine dial automatically by modem. The processing company also typically charges a higher fee for manual processing. Electronically is truly the way to go unless you only process a few credit transactions per month.

Terminal Fees

First is the cost of the equipment used for processing the cards. It is sometimes called a swipe machine because you can either type in the numbers on the keypad or swipe the card through the slot on the top of the unit. The machine comes from a *credit card transaction processing company*, a company that is often a bank or a bank's sales representative who acts as a liaison between your company and the credit card processing network. The machine is essentially a small computer terminal that connects you directly to your credit card processing company. This can also be computer based for those of you who intend to incorporate the credit card processing in with your billing or accounting system.

The credit card processing company typically charges you an application fee ($65 to $100) and a programming and installation fee ($35 to $50). For these fees, you can accept payment by Visa, MasterCard, and probably Diner's Club and Carte Blanche, but not American Express or Discover, both of which have their own special requirements.

American Express (1-800-445-2639) has its own processing network called the Electronic Draft Capture (EDC) network. This is AmEx's way of processing customer purchases made using its card. Once American Express receives and completes your application request, you must contact your terminal provider (the folks who are renting you the credit card processing machine) and make sure that they program your machine to process American Express transactions.

American Express strongly recommends that merchants set up their processing to be electronically based since it is easier for them and less expensive for the merchant. Of the organizations I worked with in setting up my accounts, American Express was by far the easiest to work with.

Talking Business

A **card processing company** is one that processes and clears your company's credit card transactions. Card processing companies are independent businesses, not affiliated with a credit card issuer. A **credit card transaction processing company** acts as a liaison between your company and the credit card processing network.

Smoke Signals

Trying to avoid hassles by not going electronic will probably cost you money. Everyone is better protected with electronic processing because you lessen the chances of mistakes and omissions. You should probably just take the electronic plunge from the start or expect to pay higher discount and transaction fees.

But wait, there's more! The Discover Card also has its own network and requires the same actions. Call Discover at 1-800-347-6673 to start the process and get the electronic terminal.

Should you simply buy your own terminal instead of renting one? Good question. The answer depends on your volume, monthly rental fee, and current cash situation. Rent for a few months and see how it goes. If after six months you start to resent the monthly charges, you should either go back to a hand processing system (in which you manually call each charge for verification) or buy your own electronic terminal. Typical costs for such new terminals are $500 to $800.

Here you are with your credit card terminal and some customers, ready to sell your product or service using credit cards. You thought the analysis was over, but it is really just beginning. In addition to the setup charges and terminal costs, the credit card companies also want a percentage of the transaction amount and often a per-transaction fee as their compensation for guaranteeing the charge. Read on to find out how much you have to pay for this privilege.

Monthly Fees

First, you pay a monthly fee for the electronic terminal rental ($25 to $55) that is automatically deducted from your bank account by the service company. You are also going to pay a monthly service fee ($5 to $10) for the reporting of your account activity during the month. This is also automatically taken from your company checking account.

> **Listen Up**
>
> Here are a few statistics that will fit in with your incentive to accept credit cards. Consumers already use credit cards for 25 percent of all of their spending, and these consumers typically spend more on a transaction if it is by credit card than by check (204 percent more) or cash (20 percent more) since they are not limited by the amount of cash that they have on hand. To pay a few percent in transaction fees to increase the transaction amount by 20 percent or more is a simple justification to make, don't you think?

The credit card company then charges your company a percentage of the transaction amount for each purchase. This fee varies between service providers, credit card companies, the type of transaction involved, the size and frequency of the transaction, and whether the transaction is processed electronically or manually. The bank charges you a transaction fee for each deposit made to your account. The following table shows typical discount and transaction fees for the various credit card types.

Typical Discount and Transaction Fees

Credit Card Type	Discount Rate (Percentage of Purchase Amount)	Transaction Fee (Cost to Deposit in Bank Account)
Visa	1.6 to 3.0%	20 cents
MasterCard	1.6 to 3.0%	20 cents
American Express	2.95 to 3.5%	None
Discover	(Would not disclose.)	

Keep in mind that home-based businesses may have special requirements to qualify for full merchant account status. Have your marketing literature ready to prove that you are a real business.

Here is what you get for the fee and how the process works when you have an electronic system:

1. You run the card through the credit card machine (called swiping the card). The terminal reads the card number and card type off the black magnetic strip on the back of the card.

2. The credit card terminal requests the transaction amount and expiration date of the card. You type both when requested and tell it to process the transaction.

3. The terminal dials the card processing company and sends the information to the computer, which then confirms the card isn't stolen and the cardholder has enough money available on the card to process the charge.

4. If everything is okay, the computer responds with an approval code that you write (or is printed) on the sales receipt. If your machine is connected directly to a printer, the receipt prints automatically when the transaction is approved, just as you see in most restaurants and high-volume retail stores these days.

5. The credit card processing company deducts the proper percentage from the purchase amount and deposits the rest in your business checking account. You essentially get the money right away instead of waiting for 30 days and taking the risk that the customer won't pay. Make sure that your bookkeeping system is set up to track these charges if you plan to do a lot of these. Check with your processing company to see if it has a point-of-sale system that is right for your particular situation and requirements.

6. Most banks charge businesses a transaction fee for each deposit you make, so you are also charged by your bank for credit card deposits.

Listen Up

Find a company that provides access to Visa, MasterCard, Discover, and American Express as a single service. If your company doesn't want to do this, at least find out how to set up your machine so that it processes all the different credit cards you expect to accept from your customers.

7. The processing company sends you a summary statement every month that outlines all transaction dates, sale amounts, credits applied (product returns), discount rates applied, and net deposits. This statement is handy for reconciling your bank deposits, invoices, and receivables when you have customers paying by different methods. Your bookkeeper definitely needs this statement, so don't throw it away. Many modern electronic processing machines can provide you with a summary statement of transactions processed, which helps in verifying the statement provided by your processing company.

Covering Your Legal Bases

We are always happy to sell our products or services and receive payment, but what happens if the client later contests the charge and refuses to pay? What if the person using the card isn't supposed to be using it? You could be stuck with a huge bad debt that takes a large number of healthy sales to correct. The following table lists a few things you can do to minimize the chance of those situations occurring.

Credit Card Sales Protection Procedures

When Someone Charges Something in Person	Actions and Reasons
Check the expiration date to make sure that the card is still valid.	Look at the Valid From and Good Through dates on the card to make sure that the card is still valid. Check that the information is embossed and not just printed.
Look for a hologram or other security mark.	These emblems are difficult to duplicate. If you can't find one, you might be holding a fake card.
Disclose the terms of the sale and get a signature, if possible.	The more that's in writing and signed by the customer, the harder it is for him or her to contest the charge. Make sure terms, conditions, and return policy are easily spelled out on the receipt.

When Someone Charges Something in Person	Actions and Reasons
Run the card through an imprint machine or electronic terminal, fill out the sales draft completely, and get a signature.	Take the customer's card and run it through an imprint machine or electronic terminal using the proper sales receipt. Make sure it is legible and completed with all pertinent information included. Verify that the signature on the card matches that provided by the customer on the sales form. Don't accept an unsigned card.
Get an authorization number for each transaction.	Run the card, amount, and expiration date through the electronic terminal to receive a sales authorization from the service company. Write the authorization number on the sales draft.

The preceding information is taken from the December 1992 issue of the Agency Inc. Newsletter, Volume 3, Number 12 and is applicable today.

If you plan to take orders over the telephone without seeing the customer and getting his signature, you can still take a few steps to better protect yourself. Because the chances of getting burned over the phone or by mail are much higher than in person, the credit card companies will probably charge you a higher discount rate for this type of transaction. These types of transactions are often called mail order, telephone order, or Internet (MO/TO) orders.

When processing a telephone transaction, follow these steps:

1. Get all credit card information and repeat all numbers, dates, and names that appear on the card. Write "MO" or "TO" on the signature line to indicate that the customer was not present.

2. Enter the transaction immediately into your electronic terminal to verify that it is a valid card and that the card is authorized for the amount of the purchase. Get an authorization number and write it on the receipt.

3. Verify the card's CVC2/CVV2 validation code that is printed on the card if it is a Visa or MasterCard. American Express uses a Card Identification Number (CIN) as part of its validation checking procedures.

4. Verify the person's billing address using the address verification system (AVS), which is only available for cards issued within the United States. AVS will verify whether the address given by the purchaser matches that on record for that particular card.

5. Get customers to come by to pick up the merchandise. Have them sign the sales form at that time. Or have them complete a signature card that indicates their willingness to have your company transact charges against their account.

If you are processing a credit card sale by phone, if at all possible, fax the customer a copy of the invoice including all credit card information. Request that he sign the invoice and return it to you by fax for a rough "signature on file" agreement. A signature on file agreement means the customer agrees to pay you for all future charges against that credit card by the same customer. A formal signature on a file card includes the agreement duration of effectiveness, the names and sample signatures of all persons authorized to charge against this credit card, an imprint of the credit card, credit card expiration date, termination stipulations, and change-related conditions.

What to Do If a Charge Is Contested

Unfortunately, even if you have a credit card payment approved, you can still run into problems. There is a lot of credit card fraud floating around these days, and certain people take advantage of situations if given the chance. Your established customers are not usually the problem. New customers or those you will never see again can leave you with a bad bill or a contested charge that can cost you a lot of money.

This is really important, so stay awake for this paragraph: When a transaction is challenged by the customer (called a *chargeback*), the burden of proof that the transaction actually occurred falls on the merchant's (your) shoulders, not the customer's.

> **Talking Business**
>
> A **chargeback** happens when a customer contests a charge and you as the merchant have to prove that this person did indeed make the purchase indicated. If you do not have the right paperwork, this customer could get your product or service and you won't get paid.

Taking the steps outlined here might seem like a hassle, but you will have a fighting chance with the credit card company if the charge is ever contested or disputed by the customer. If the customer signed the sales draft, saw the terms and conditions, and clearly knew what was being purchased and the proper amount, you have an excellent case in your favor. The more of the transaction that was handled in writing, the better the chance you have of keeping the money. Caution and procedures make the solution to this possible trouble area. Define credit terms, stick with them, and fight for your money when the time comes. And make sure that you comply with the filing and contesting deadline time frames set by the credit card companies, or you could lose the sale proceeds even if the facts are on your side.

Smoke Signals

Beware of how discount and transaction fees affect your profits. Accepting American Express for a $10,000 charge from a solid account customer, for example, puts $295 to $350 in American Express's pocket instead of yours. In that case, you might be better off persuading the customer to pay by other means. Using American Express instead of net 30-day payment terms with solid credit customers can cost you thousands in unnecessary credit protection expenses.

Responding immediately to any inquiries from your credit card companies is essential to maintaining your merchant status. For many retailers, losing merchant status would be disastrous. Don't test the system. Answer their questions, provide any information requested, and enjoy the additional sales you're earning because you are able to accept credit cards.

Listen Up

Credit card processing companies can help you deal with what you think might be a fraudulent or otherwise suspicious credit card purchase. They call these Code 10 Procedures. Call your processor to ask for a Code 10 authorization, and it will lead you through the process, which might involve keeping the card. Don't risk taking the card if the customer may become dangerous, but know that you have avoided a fraudulent purchase if a Code 10 authorization showed up a stolen card. Contact your processing company for more instructions on dealing with Code 10 situations.

The Least You Need to Know

◆ You probably have to accept credit cards in one form or another or risk losing customers, especially if you run a restaurant or retail store.

◆ Electronic processing is the easiest and least expensive way to process credit card transactions. Investigate a point of sale system that might inexpensively make your credit card processing easier and more accurate.

◆ The various credit card companies charge between 2 and 4 percent of the transaction amount in exchange for their guarantee of payment, which can be very expensive when applied across the board to all transactions.

- Treat each sale as a legal agreement. Get signatures and transaction details to back up any claims made by the customer at a later date that he or she never made that purchase.

- Telephone and mail-order credit card sales are more expensive due to their higher likelihood of fraud. Fraud deterrent procedures are mandatory if you plan to accept credit cards over the phone or by mail order.

- Get an authorization number from the credit card company for each transaction. This, along with a signature, is your best protection for your credit card sale transactions.

18

Collecting Customer Debts

In This Chapter

- ◆ Requesting payments—without losing customers
- ◆ How overdue customer payments impact your business
- ◆ Recommended credit and collection policies
- ◆ A review of your legal options

"What do you mean we are out of cash?" shouted Judy. "Our books clearly show sales of about $60,000 for last month, so how can we be out of cash?"

"We have this problem with a few of our major accounts that make up around $35,000 of our monthly sales. They have recently started paying us in 60 days instead of 30, which affects our cash flow," remarked Judy's accountant. "We didn't authorize the change and also didn't notice customers were taking longer to pay before it was too late."

"Where do we stand in the cash department?" asked Judy.

"We owe payroll and our vendors, and our annual licensing fees are due. Those total around $45,000, and we only have $30,000 on hand. How are we going to make up the $15,000 shortage?"

"I guess I will give the company a short-term loan of $15,000 and not take a salary for this month," answered Judy. *"Remember, I can't keep doing this, or I will be out of business and we all will be out of jobs. Get those receivables on track, and get me involved personally if this doesn't start to improve immediately."*

Billing customers for products and services you've sold is only part of the process of getting paid. Staying on top of payment due dates is also critical to ensure you're paid promptly. This chapter will teach you strategies for collecting from customers, as well as tips for dealing with customers who don't pay as promised.

Collection Problems Come with the Territory

It is an unfortunate fact of business life that some people do not pay their bills on time. For the most part, they are not trying to avoid their obligations but simply think that spending the money on something else is more important than paying you.

This doesn't do you much good and provides no consolation when you are writing checks from your own checking account to cover their delayed payments.

Been There ... Done That
Credit is a business fact of life. You will either want it from another business or another business will want it from you, or both. It is very difficult to run a growing business on a debt-free basis. Offering credit helps your customers grow, and using credit payment terms with your vendors helps you grow. It is simply what most growing businesses do. Define your credit policies early on to make sure that you do not exceed reasonable credit limits as either a borrower or lender. And then stick to your policies.

Even worse, some people simply are deceitful and intended from the beginning to use your products or services without paying. These people can cost you a lot of time and money trying to recover the agreed-upon payments. In addition, you rarely get the total amount due because collection fees, court fees, and a lot of your time are often required to make it happen.

The major problem with delayed payments is the impact it has on your cash situation. You have to pay your employees and vendors on time, which means that you need to collect payments from customers, or you are quickly out of business. This means that you are writing checks to cover the float provided to your customers, which is the time lag between when you have to pay your bills and when your customers pay their bills. Repeatedly being forced to pay your own bills on time while everyone else takes more time can lead you into serious financial problems. If you're growing quickly, you might be affected even more by slow-paying customers.

Plan from the start to have an effective credit and collections policy, and stick to it. Prevention is the best protection from collection problems. Not handling credit and collection properly can put you out of business, even though your sales exceed expectations.

Avoidance Is the Best Remedy

Just as avoiding saturated fats is a great way to minimize the likelihood of a heart attack from clogged arteries, avoiding deadbeat clients is the best way to avoid business problems from depleted cash reserves.

Implement policies from the beginning that address the need for credit. Ensure that you stick to the policy, that your employees understand the policy, and that you do not make exceptions to the policy without good reason to back it up.

Listen Up

Every time you extend credit, you are giving someone a loan. Make sure customers are worthy of the trust you are giving them. Deadbeat customers hurt a business by not only robbing it of cash that has been validly earned, but also by creating a frustration and distrust within the company that sometimes infects the way that the company deals with future customers. You haven't had a miserable business day until you have chased clients who promise to pay and then don't, so at the end of the day you do not have enough cash to cover the company's bills. Because they don't pay, you don't take home a paycheck. Now it becomes personal. Only provide credit to credit-worthy customers.

Avoid giving credit to new customers without first having them complete a credit report. Many times, you can get a customer to pay for the order with a credit card if the amounts are relatively small. Over that, you can always ship products Cash On Delivery (COD) or only after you receive a check or money order, although you will find these methods difficult to implement in nonconsumer (commercial) sales environments.

Retail sales environments have a pretty simple credit policy. People pay cash or charge their purchases on a credit card and are there to personally sign the receipt. You receive the money at the time of purchase.

Some companies set up credit approval arrangements with finance companies so that consumers can easily purchase high-ticket items on credit. This approach is common with companies that sell appliances or furniture. The buyer completes a credit application at the store, which is sent to the finance company for approval. Once approved, the consumer receives a loan to purchase the items in question, the retailer receives money from the finance company, and the consumer goes home with the purchase. Everyone wins.

One way to avoid payment problems with customers is maintaining close contact with them to be sure that they are happy with what you provided them, whether it was a product or service. Don't just deliver the goods and send out the invoice. Follow up with a phone call to let your customers know that you care that they were happy with their purchase. This way, if you find out there was some problem or they are not satisfied, you have the chance to fix the problem. Once your customer is happy, your chances of being paid rise significantly. It might be worth adding a dedicated person to ensure that customers remain happy and don't complain by not paying their bills.

It is common in service contracts to stage payments based on job completion levels. In this way, you have gradual payment for services provided and also have checkpoint milestones where you can gauge the customer's satisfaction level. It's better to find problems halfway through the project than to complete it and find out they don't want to pay.

Another important step is timely follow-up after you've sent out the invoice. Be friendly but firm as soon as the payment is due. You don't want to ruin your relationship with your customer by screaming and shouting over a late payment if there is a reasonable explanation why it is overdue. Always give customers the benefit of the doubt if they have a history of purchases from you and have paid promptly in the past. Also be firm in asking for a date when you can expect payment, and follow up on that date. By being friendly with customers but getting across the point that payment is expected, you increase the chances of keeping that customer, rather than losing him over some angry words. However, if you've spoken with a customer two or three times and a promised payment has still not arrived, it's time to get tougher. Your loan to them (the purchase on credit) is in serious jeopardy.

> **Smoke Signals**
>
> If your business is growing quickly, your expenses are also growing quickly, giving you even more reasons to pay closer attention to your collections. If you aren't receiving customer payments in a timely fashion, you may soon be bankrupt.

You do not want to provide a service or sell a product to a customer only to find out that the customer cannot pay. If you run the financial numbers, you will find you must sell three or more of what you originally sold to recover the profits you would have received from the deadbeat order. However, you can never really make up for a customer sale that never gets paid and turns into a bad debt expense.

For example, at a 50 percent profit margin, a $20 sale costs $10 to produce; you make a $10 profit on the sale. When that client does not pay, you lose not only the profit but also the initial cost of the product, or $20. To recover that $20, you must sell two more items that make you $10 each in profit to recover the initially lost $20 sale, and at this point, you still haven't made any money. Add to this cost the collection fees, court costs, employee expenses, and interest expense on the loan you took out to cover the delinquency, and you can easily see that nonpaying clients are an expensive problem you need to avoid. The moral of the story is that no matter how hard you work, you can't make up for lost profits or cost of goods sold.

Some people treat the first deadbeat sale as a *sunk cost* and only look at recovering the $10 cost to produce the product as what they need to break even. I prefer to consider the cost of the entire lost opportunity, which makes me more respectful of the value of good customers and more leery of offering credit to companies or people I don't know.

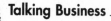

Talking Business

Money already spent that cannot be recovered is called the **sunk cost**. Sunk cost does not take into account opportunity cost, or how the money could otherwise have been spent.

Products Versus Services

In no way would I want to jeopardize your friendship by turning you into a lawyer, but a few legal issues are nice to understand before you start offering products or services to your customers.

All product sales transactions are covered by the Uniform Commercial Code (UCC), which are laws developed in the 1940s to ensure uniform sale transaction laws across the country. Although UCC rules are complicated, I will try to simplify them for you here.

A thorough understanding of contract law is critical to understanding business because you are really selling an agreement, or contract, to perform a service or sell a product. In its simplest form, the customers agree to buy what you agree to sell, with all of the mutually agreed upon contingencies attached. The contract usually only comes into play when something has gone wrong and the parties involved cannot work out their differences among themselves.

The UCC only covers the sale of products ("goods" in UCC terms) and does not cover the sale of services. According to the Statute of Frauds section of the UCC, if you are selling goods with a sale price of $500 or more, then you must have a written contract before you can go after someone for a breach of contract. Under $500, a verbal agreement is enforceable, but it is still a good idea to get it in writing. After all, if a customer is afraid to commit to the sale in writing, what makes you think that he or she won't hedge on paying you later? If a client is serious, he or she will sign an agreement that outlines what is to be provided. If you think about it, the agreement protects both sides and helps prevent the possibility of a misunderstanding.

To have an enforceable agreement or contract, you must at least have …

1. The seller and buyer specifics, such as name, address, and phone number.

2. The specifics regarding the products in question, such as quantity, price, and description.

3. Specific delivery and payment terms.

This might sound like a lot, but if you think about it, you couldn't really provide the product unless you knew this information anyway. Most importantly, both parties must sign the agreement.

Listen Up _____

If you ask to have a business agreement formalized as a written letter of understanding and the other party denies the request, you should think long and hard about continuing with the agreement. If there is nothing objectionable, then a written agreement should be agreeable to both parties. Not signing the agreement could indicate potential payment problems later.

If you plan to provide services, then you should have some type of written agreement between the client and you that outlines the services to be provided, the amount of up-front expense involved, the total amount of the service contract, when services are to be performed, and when payment is expected. Once again, if a customer hedges on signing a simple agreement with this basic information, then he or she will probably hassle you when it comes time to pay.

Listen Up _____

Send a card to your customers' accounts payable departments once or twice a year thanking them for prompt payment. Positive acknowledgment works well on all types of people.

Getting some type of nonrefundable deposit up front (somewhere between 25 and 50 percent) is also a good idea as an indication of the client's seriousness and might help minimize the possibility of the client changing his or her mind after you have already started the project. It is also a good idea to have clear, objective completion milestones that trigger partial payments.

For example, assume that you are an architect designing a house for a client. You might request 25 percent payment upon signing of the agreement, 25 percent upon completion of the first artist renderings, 25 percent upon completion of the final drawings, and the final 25 percent upon acceptance of the plans by the local building authorities. Notice that each of these steps provides the customer with a clear picture of the overall project, you get paid for the work done to date, and you built in quality checks to make sure that everyone is happy. Happy customers pay. Unhappy customers gripe, complain, take up time and energy, and often don't pay.

Cash First—Credit Later

Possession is nine tenths of the law, and this is particularly true when it comes to cash. Whoever has the cash is in the catbird seat, and more cash is almost always better than a lot of receivables from customers who can choose to pay at their discretion.

There are various ways to receive cash instead of dealing with credit of any kind. Cash comes in its standard green form (which is almost never used in nonretail businesses), personal or company checks, bank drafts, cashier's checks, or letters of credit (which is typically used when dealing with international shipments).

Bank drafts and cashier's checks are like cash because the issuing financial institution took money from the customer or an account before issuing the draft or check. There is a warm fuzzy feeling that you get deep in your pocketbook when you get a check that you know will go into default only if the issuing bank goes out of business.

When accepting a personal check, make sure the person giving you the check signs it and that the signatures match, and get two forms of identification, such as a driver's license (for identity) and a major credit card (which indicates acceptable credit). Make sure it is not postdated or written in two different colors of ink. Compare the signature on the check with that on the credit card or driver's license and make sure that they match. Subscribe to a check verification service that can automatically and quickly verify sufficient funds in the checking account to cover the amount of the check.

If you are burnt by a bum check, start a list that shows the bad checks received and from whom. Some companies post the bad checks for public display. This is not necessarily legal, but peer pressure is often a strong motivator. Make sure all your employees know the procedures for accepting checks. You don't want a great customer irritated by having to wait while an employee finds you to verify that customer's check.

When shipping products, you can request COD, usually provided by United Parcel Service (UPS), which means that the customer must write a check to the delivering driver before the product is left. There is a COD processing fee for the service. UPS then sends you the customer's check for you to cash.

Letters of credit are used frequently for international transactions. The customer's bank issues the letter of credit, which ensures that the funds in question are available for transfer once the company receives the desired products or services it ordered. The funds are then transferred from the issuing bank to your bank, and everyone is happy. (See Chapter 22 for additional information on international credit.)

Credit cards come in all shapes, colors, and sizes. The most common are Visa, Master-Card, American Express, and Discover. Make sure the name on the card matches the name of the person making the purchase transaction and that the signatures match between the card and the credit receipt, and then run the card through the approval process. At that point, the funds should be transferred to your bank account and only lost if the customer disputes the charge. (See Chapter 17 for more information about credit card sales.)

There is some disagreement on whether you should prefer credit card or check trans-actions. A check is a legally binding agreement between the issuing company (person) and your company. If the check is bad, you have a strong case for collecting on the check through the courts (assuming that you can even find the person who wrote the check). Credit card sales that have been approved are credited immediately to your account but can still be contested by the customer later. In those cases, you end up arguing with Visa or MasterCard about the charge. If there is a question about how you processed the sale, you could find yourself on the losing end of that battle. There are also credit card percentage fees paid.

Selling products or services using credit terms (such as net 30 days) is at the bottom of the credit ladder when dealing with consumers. Most larger commercial transactions are handled on a credit basis, meaning the customer has a specified time frame within which he or she can pay, which is usually 30 days. After 30 days, the account is consid-ered delinquent, and collection procedures are started. (See "Know Your Rights When It Comes to Collections" later in this chapter for more about collecting from delinquent accounts.) Attaching a late payment penalty and interest for late payment helps keep commercial accounts current, although in some states, it might affect your collection position should the company become insolvent and declare bankruptcy. Check this out in your state before making this decision.

You probably need to offer credit terms to your standard customers, just as you want credit terms from your regular vendors. It is just a part of doing business that most people accept as a standard requirement. Here are some suggestions for handling credit transactions:

◆ Set an amount above which you require a credit application and credit back-ground check before extending the credit. Zero dollars is a good number, I think.

A sample credit application is included on the companion CD or is available at most office supply stores. Make sure that you ask for at least three credit references as part of the application, and then call the references to verify the prospective cus-tomer's credit standing. Make sure that you ask about the relationship of the cus-tomer seeking credit to the reference. They are often related and won't tell you if not asked.

♦ Do the background check before you issue the credit, or risk being disappointed later. Customers understand your need to protect yourself. Let them know that credit checks take time (two to three days) and that they should submit it before the purchase when they will request the credit.

Some of the bigger credit information agencies include EquiFax Credit Information Services and TransUnion Credit. A credit report costs a few dollars but can save thousands if it keeps you from making a poor credit extension decision.

♦ Offer customers early payment benefits, such as a 2 percent discount for payment within 10 days of invoice receipt. I know of one business that always takes advantage of these 2 percent terms; the owner claims that they save a lot of money doing that.

For example, if you pay $20,000 each month to vendors and each offers the 2 percent early payment discount option, you can save $.02 \times \$20,000 = \$400$ monthly, which could be the monthly payment for another piece of equipment.

♦ Separate the sales process from the credit decision. If the salesperson is paid commission on sales revenue and not on paid accounts, then there is an incentive for the salesperson to provide a liberal credit policy because it makes it easier to sell. The salesperson gets his or her commission and you get a possible bad debt. Avoid this conflict of interest by separating the credit and sales decisions, unless you plan to do both yourself.

♦ Make sure that you run a credit check on your larger companies, and perform your credit checks every 12 months or so because company situations change. You are always looking to verify the "three Cs" of credit: character, collateral, and cash. If you know that company to be one of integrity, it passes the character test. Collateral and cash tell you about the company's current ability to pay the debt it is incurring. You can often verify the cash situation by calling the company's bank and verifying that it has enough cash to cover the credit it is requesting.

> **Listen Up** _____
>
> You can reach EquiFax on the web at www.equifax.com or by phone at 1-888-202-4025. TransUnion Credit can be reached on the web at www.transunion.com or by phone at 1-312-466-7363.

Financial Reports and Their Limitations

The industry standard for business information reporting is Dun and Bradstreet (D&B) at www.dunandbradstreet.com or 1-800-234-3867. A D&B report on a company contains payment history, business officer names, addresses, phone numbers, revenues, number of employees, high and low credit balances, payment histories, and other pertinent financial information.

To receive these reports, you need to be a regular subscriber to the service, which involves a yearly contract fee along with a per-report cost. The overall cost is often too high for a small business to justify because you might only need a few reports each year. Their plans change, so it may be worth stopping by the site to see what they are offering today.

Of course, as you're reviewing some of the credit reports, keep in mind that a lot of the data is self-reported, so don't use any one report as your sole source of information. If time allows, you might also want to make some phone calls to colleagues to see what they know about your new customer or scan some newspaper clippings on the company. (Your local library probably collects them.) Using additional information sources improves your knowledge of your prospect so you can make a better informed decision about giving credit. Ultimately, if you feel uncomfortable providing a customer with credit, don't do it without more verification.

No credit reporting agency or technique is perfect, and you want to take as many precautions as are reasonable before lending money to a new client. After all, extending credit to a company is the equivalent of lending it money.

Collection Letters

Okay, you've decided that offering credit to your customers is a good thing. What can you do to best ensure they pay as agreed?

First, make sure your clients understand the credit policy when they initiate the transaction. This means being clear about when payment is due, what the interest rate is for late payments, and whether there are any additional fees or penalties for late payments. Put this information on your sales order and invoice so that the customer clearly knows it is there, without being obnoxious about it. Do not hide the specifics because this only contributes to later misunderstandings. You are extending the credit, so you get to specify the terms you can live with. Customers can either accept the terms or negotiate new ones. Try not to do custom terms too often, or it gets confusing to administer. Check to see if your accounting package will let you enter custom terms and use it to its best advantage if it will.

On the CD

A sample Collection Letter is included on the CD as document 18-01.

Also, make sure that you follow up on and enforce your credit policies. If customers start to believe that you really won't follow up, which happens, then they will put you on the back payment burner list. You must set up a procedure that ensures follow-up on collections, or you will live to regret it.

Second, give them an incentive to pay early. Offer a small discount (2 percent) for payment within 10 days. This gets the cash into your hands more quickly and provides them with a financial incentive to pay earlier instead of later. And it is cheaper than a credit card in some cases.

Third, call customers 3 to 5 days before the 30-day point (or whatever payment due date you've set) to verify billing information and to remind them the payment is due in a few days. It is also a good idea to ask if there will be any problems with timely payment. If they say yes, this gives you a chance to be informed earlier so you can take proper actions.

Finally, once the account goes past the payment due date, it is time to begin the collection process. Your customer has broken his agreement and should be handled as a delinquent account. If you are prompt with the follow-up, the customer will probably pay more promptly in the future to avoid the embarrassment.

Try this collection letter issuance procedure on for size. You must include invoice number, past due amount, date of order, and information about how to pay in each letter. I often include a copy of the invoice so that there is no question about what is due.

- ◆ At 6 days past due date, send a "friendly reminder" and thank them for the payment if already sent.

- ◆ At 21 days past due date, send another letter firmly reminding them that the payment is past due and that they need to contact your firm to make payment arrangements. A blue inked stamp that says "Past Due" in big letters is one of the best investments I ever made and should be used on this letter.

- ◆ At 36 days past due date, send another letter that lets them know that their account is seriously overdue and now a cause of concern, and that they must contact your office to arrange payment. A red-inked stamp that says "Seriously Past Due" in big letters should be used at this point.

- ◆ At 50 days past due date, send a final letter that lets them know that, without contact on their behalf, their account may be put into suspense and possibly turned over to collection. Face it—at this point they are pushing 60 days past the due date and the likelihood of your getting paid is dropping by the day in most cases. If you want to really push this issue, you could buy a red-inked stamp that says "Delinquent" in big letters for this letter. There is no question that this stamp will get their attention.

A standard accounting report, called an accounts receivable aging report, shows you the customers who currently have credit, the total amount they owe you, and the number of days (I hope it's not months) the account is past due. Most computerized accounting packages can easily provide an aging report that you can use as your trigger for focusing on trouble accounts. Run the aging report at least every two weeks, and make sure the collection follow-up is prompt, consistent, and professional, yet firm. Collecting outstanding debts is an interesting balancing act as you keep your customers on track with their payments without offending them.

Also remember that your sales reps will likely not get paid commission until their customers' invoices are paid. This gives the reps a multiple incentive to help with collections: 1) their credibility is on the line in that they recommended that your company do business with this questionable customer, 2) they don't get paid if the invoice isn't paid, and 3) they may know the customer better than you do and have a personal interest in keeping that customer relationship healthy. Plus, will you believe them the next time that they recommend a client as a good credit risk if the past few have substantial unpaid bills? Likely not, and your reps know that, too.

If you are not currently using a computer software package to handle your accounting, you should seriously consider it. You'll find it much faster and easier to print reports regarding your customers' payment records. By the way, you need this receivables aging report if you decide to apply to your bank for a loan secured by your receivables.

Know Your Rights When It Comes to Collections

The unfortunate has happened, and a person is clearly not going to pay you. This should not happen very often, but when it does, you need to decide if pursuing the deadbeat customer is worth the time and effort. Make every effort to resolve the disputed amount before pushing things into court. Once the legal gavel falls, the conversation becomes stilted and often nonproductive. Get all agreements in writing to build your case if you ever have to take legal actions.

Small claims court is provided for resolving smaller dollar disputes in the $500 to $7,500 range, depending on the state you're in. (The filing fee ranges from $5 to $100. If you want to sue for under a few hundred dollars, the small claims process might not be worth it.) Small claims court is designed for nonlawyer types, and the rules are a lot less strict than seen on Perry Mason. Larger dollar disputes are handled in other courts and usually require the assistance of an attorney.

On the CD

A sample Complaint for Lawsuit document related to small claims court filing is included on the CD as document 18-02.

You will need two trips, minimum, to file a small claim: one to file the claim and the other to appear in court. You have to file in the county where the events occurred or where the deadbeat is resident. If you are suing a company, you need to file suit in the county in which the company is doing business. Unfortunately, it is much easier to win a judgment in small claims court than it is to collect the money. The judgment in your favor is a necessary first step and might be ego gratifying, but it is the cash that will bring you satisfaction.

Just because you won doesn't mean that you will be paid! It is your responsibility to collect the money involved, not the court's. Your basic collection options are

- ◆ Wage garnishment, where the employer is instructed to remove a specific amount of money from the deadbeat's paycheck.

- ◆ Nonwage garnishments, where the money involved is deducted from a company bank account.

- ◆ Property attachments, in which physical property is confiscated to pay the debt.

- ◆ Attaching the bank account, which means the company has to pay you first before paying any other bills. This might work if you are suing a business and know the company's bank account number.

Of course, none of these are options unless and until you have a judgment in your hands.

You can also file a lien against property owned by the nonpaying party. This lien is officially recorded and secures the debt with the prescribed property. The property cannot be sold until all liens are removed. Liens may be recorded with the Country Clerk and Recorders Office and possibly with the Secretary of State's office.

Numerous books on the market deal with the detailed intricacies of collections in general and the small claims process in particular. The best medicine for bad debts is to avoid them if at all possible using some of the techniques covered earlier in this chapter.

Working with Collection Agencies

When all else fails and you still want to pursue a deadbeat customer, then you should consider a collection agency. Whether the agency is national or local in coverage depends on your specific situation. Both kinds of agencies are listed in the Yellow Pages of your phone book. No matter where you find the agency, you should get a few references from their existing clients before you let them represent your company to your clients (even if they are deadbeat clients).

A collection agency charges a fee for their services, usually between 25 and 33 percent of the amount they collect for you. Higher fees might be charged for specialty accounts that require more extensive involvement by the agency.

Get a written contract from the agency and check references before proceeding. A collection agency could do you more harm than good by threatening customers in an inappropriate way or by getting your initial money and alienating customers through the use of threatening practices. The contract should have specific performance objectives on the part of the agency, and if those objectives are not met, you should be able to terminate the contract. The collection agency should provide reports on a regular, mutually agreed-to basis for you to evaluate their performance.

In addition, make sure the agency conforms to collection procedures outlined in the Fair Debt Collection Practices Act. These practices were designed to regulate collection agency activities, but companies performing their own collections should consider adhering to the same principles.

In general, the act states that threats to property, persons, or reputations are not allowed; obscene language and telephone badgering are not allowed; publicly humiliating the person by a printed list or other public statements is not allowed; and sending documents on misleading letterhead or threatening legal actions is not permitted, along with numerous other practices.

Collections is a tough business and one full of frustration. As a collection agency manager friend of mine puts it, "I don't like to talk on the phone. I think it comes from all those years of being lied to over the telephone."

 On the CD _____

You cannot know too much about collecting money from customers who refuse to pay. For this reason, I have included two bonus sections on the CD specifically related to collecting bad debts. "Bad Debt Ratio: Assessing the Deadbeats" (CD18-1) presents ways for you to determine what is a reasonable level of bad debt you should expect for your particular industry. "Taxes and Bad Debts" (CD18-2) explains the tax implications for your company related to customers who don't pay. Unfortunately, deadbeats who don't pay are a part of business. Take a few minutes to check out these important bonus sections.

The Least You Need to Know

- ◆ Customer credit should be earned, not treated as a right. Make customers prove they can repay the debts they plan to incur.

- ◆ You have to sell multiples of your product to make up for the lost cost and profit associated with the one not paid for. Make sure you get paid the first time.

- ◆ Avoid credit problems by using a credit application and evaluation procedure before extending credit to ensure that you will receive the payment when agreed.

- ◆ Just because you win a small claims court judgment doesn't mean you will collect. You still have to go after the customer for the funds.

- ◆ Be polite yet firm when first requesting an overdue payment. Anyone can overlook a payment. Few people resent being reminded of their commitments; most people resent being called a thief.

Business Banker Realities

In This Chapter

- ◆ Your banker is an ally, not an enemy
- ◆ A banker's perspective on lending money
- ◆ The importance of your business plan to bankers
- ◆ Working with the Small Business Administration

"These guys have absolutely no vision," said Bill. "This is a great idea, and all I need is $25,000. That's nothing to a bank their size, but NO-O-O! They want all of this supporting documentation before they will even consider the loan. Why do I bother with banks in the first place?"

"They have money, and you need money. Isn't that right?" asked Bill's father.

"Sure, but why make it so complicated? It makes me want to pull my account and take my business to another bank that appreciates a good deal," said Bill. "I know this business. They have no idea what they're throwing away."

"That might be the key to your problem," his father said quietly. "If they don't understand the opportunity, can you blame them for not seeing its value? After all, whose job is it to convince them to give you money? Theirs or yours?"

This might seem obvious, but at some point in your company's life, you will have to work with a bank. The relationship might involve something as simple as a checking account or might be quite complicated. One thing is for certain: Your relationship with the bank is easier if you understand how bankers think.

This chapter introduces you to the banker mentality along with an overview of the services you can reasonably expect from a bank.

I wish someone had told me this stuff when I started my business. Read, learn, understand, and move past any preconceived notions you might have about banks.

What Does a Bank Bring to the Table?

In a word: money! As your company grows, its need for cash also grows. Banks are storage houses for money, which is the one element most lacking in a new company. To get an idea of what it is like to be a banker, think about the last time you lent someone money and they were slow in paying you back. How does it feel to be a banker? Are you going to be more cautious the next time you lend someone money? Keep that feeling in mind when you talk to your banker, and you will have a much better understanding of that side of the desk.

Where does a bank fit into a new business's life? In the beginning, you will most likely have to turn to sources other than a bank for business financing. When you are just starting out, the bank has no experience with you, and your company has little or no financial track record. On what basis is the bank going to lend you money? Your good intentions? Your smile?

Initially, expect the bank to provide checking services and accept wire transfers, federal tax deposits such as payroll, and credit card deposits, along with other standard banking services. Over time, the bank will see your record of frequent deposits and a growing bank account, thus documenting solid growth and financial performance. Then, the bank will be more willing to risk loaning your company money. When you want a line of credit or a loan secured by a business asset of some type, you will likely want to work with a bank.

Listen Up

Banks must report to federal regulators who then insure the deposits made at that bank. For this reason, banks must make certain that their lending programs meet clearly defined federal guidelines, or they could lose their insurance coverage, which is a very bad thing for a bank. Sometimes banks can't lend you money due to those guidelines.

Banks exist to serve customers, but as the old joke says, "The only way you can get a loan is to prove you don't need it." Consequently, many startup companies have difficulty getting a loan from a bank—even if they have the best idea in the world. This is where your personal credit becomes very important.

You will have to deal with a bank in some way. Period. It's a good idea to start early to develop a good relationship with your bank—and with the loan officers at your branch. Why? Well, one of these days your business will be well established, and a banker who understands your company can be a great resource in supporting your profitable growth.

Start now, long before you ask for money, to lay the groundwork that will convince your banker that you are a solid customer and a good business risk. Besides, bankers see a lot of different businesses, and you might be able to get some good business advice from your banker at the best price: free! And getting free stuff from a banker is a really good feeling.

Why don't banks lend to companies just starting out? The banks have to be convinced that they will get their money back, with interest, when it is supposed to be repaid. Startup companies are notoriously bad about paying loans back on time, if at all, and after the turmoil in the banking industry with the savings and loan crisis of the mid-1980s and the uncertainties of the past few years, loan officers tend to shy away from risky situations. Yes, they might be missing a golden opportunity to support your business in the early stages, but they also miss the opportunity to lose the money they loan you if your company doesn't work out the way you hope.

The Loan Officer Is Your Friend. Really.

To whom would you rather give money—someone who treats you with contempt and antagonism every time you meet, or someone who appears to appreciate you for what you have to offer? Would you give money for a risky venture to someone you barely know, or to someone you have known for a while and trust? The answer to these questions is simple, and my point is probably already made. Meet the loan officer responsible for your account when you first open the account—before you need money. Keep him updated on your progress and help him become more familiar with your company. You'll find that bringing him into the loop early will make him an ally when you need to ask for a loan. Don't wait until you're desperate for money to bring him up to speed on your activities.

Listen Up

Get to know several loan officers at your branch so if your main contact leaves, you don't have to start from scratch getting to know someone else. It is also a good idea to get to know your loan officer's boss.

Make sure that this first meeting goes well—no matter what! Appear to know what you're doing, even if you're feeling doubtful. The doubts will pass, but the initial impression on the loan officer will stay. Look and act like the president of your own company, like someone who deserves as much money as you want! This meeting doesn't have to be lengthy, but you must leave a positive impression so the loan officer will remember you when you need to borrow money.

Don't underestimate the value that this loan officer brings to your business. As with any bureaucracy, it is really good to know someone inside who can steer you through the maze and support your cause when needed.

Banks Will Give You Money Only When You Don't Need It

Banks make money by lending it to individuals and businesses. The loan officer's obligation to the bank is to make loans to the businesses that are most likely to pay the bank back.

The lending policies of nationally regulated banks are monitored by the state's Office of the Comptroller of Currency, or OCC. (You can recognize a national bank by the word "national" or letters "NA" in its name.) The loan officer of a national bank must walk the line between pursuing the best business opportunity for the bank and complying with regulatory agencies such as the OCC. Private and community banks, on the other hand, have more discretion about their lending policies.

From a bank's perspective, lending money to a small business provides risks and advantages that are different from those associated with a large company. Take a look at some of these risks and advantages.

Listen Up

When you request a loan for an amount greater than the loan officer's lending authority, the loan officer must get approval from her supervisor or from a loan committee that makes decisions regarding larger loans. Plan to invest some time learning your banker's lending authority to potentially make both of your lives easier.

The smaller business loans have a higher risk associated with them because the business is usually newer and might have fewer assets to be used as collateral. The newer business has a limited profit track record as well. These risk factors will increase the interest rate the small business must pay, which in turn increases the revenue banks receive. Small businesses are also attractive as loan customers because funds from a loan can usually be covered by money from company checking and savings accounts at the bank. Because small businesses are likely to keep their money in only one bank, banks are becoming more willing to lend them money.

Larger companies have large lending needs that require extra attention from the bank—401(k) plans, a lock box, and so on. These lending services generate fee income for the bank, but the loans are priced at a lower interest rate because the larger customers are in a better negotiating position. However, larger businesses rarely have all their money in one or two accounts; it's invested in several other places.

To get any lender to provide you and your company with money, you must sell them on your company, your ideas, and on you, or this money may go to other, less risky ventures. Be prepared to present a case to your banker on why you should get the loan.

In addition, it is generally safer for a bank to invest money in several ventures, rather than all in one basket. Several small business loans spread the risk over several businesses so that even if one business owner starts to have trouble repaying his loan, the whole bank is not threatened.

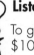

Listen Up

To give you an idea of how much a default costs a bank, consider a company with a $10,000 loan that defaults. The bank has lost the $10,000 plus the interest on the loan, which is generally 2 to 3 percent in profit to the bank. To make up that loss, the bank has to lend an additional $333,333 just to get its money back within a 12-month period. A $333,333 loan would generate close to $10,000 in net interest income to the bank in a year assuming a net 3% interest rate.

The primary reason banks have conservative lending policies is that loan defaults are expensive. Consequently, banks only provide loans that are acceptable risks in the eyes of their depositors and the regulatory agencies to which they report. They are not in the business of providing high-risk, high-profit potential venture capital loans.

As a small business owner, you must create a personal and business track record in advance that will qualify your company for a loan when you need it. Here's what you can do:

♦ Keep your personal and business financial situation healthy by using standard accounting practices and watching your personal cash flow. Try to get your debts as low as possible and your cash reserves as high as possible before starting your business.

♦ Try to get a small line of credit early on to get your credit established with the bank. A business line of credit is usually increased when you pay it off on a regular basis.

Banks often use tax returns as the basis for determining a business's and individual's financial (and consequently loan) status. Keep both your company and personal returns in order to improve your loan chances with the bank.

Calling your loan officer and saying, "I need the money tomorrow" is a red flag that something is out of control with the company and its management. A panic situation raises questions about your managerial ability. Plan ahead to make sure that you can get a bank to lend you money when you really do need it.

You can also expect to personally guarantee any loans given to your company by a bank. Every bank that I have ever worked with has wanted the same thing, and the first time you sign the papers giving the bank the right to go after your personal stuff should the business loan go into default, you can feel your skin crawl a little. It just comes with the territory, and you should not take it personally. On the other hand, more than one business owner has worked those extra hours with the image of his banker sitting in the other room monitoring loan payment status.

Bank Loans You Can Get

Now you understand the world of finance from the bankers' perspective. How does this translate into your ability to get money when you need it? Here are some loan options for you to consider.

This is really important: Banks are always coming up with new ways to make money lending to others. A tight economy and heavier dependence and respect for small business is making otherwise tight financial organizations and the governmental agencies take on more risk than they would under better times. Don't make any assumptions about what a bank can or cannot do. Get to know your banker and let him or her see if there is a program out there that is good for both your company and the bank.

An unsecured line of credit can be given on a personal basis to the company officers. This is essentially a personal loan to officers (based on the personal credit history of the individuals), who then loan it to the company. The bank does not give this loan directly to the company because the company has not proven it can pay the loan back. The officers then arrange reasonable repayment terms with the company. If you are an officer of a corporation, make sure the loan conditions, such as the interest rate and the term of the loan, are similar to those you would see in normal business transactions.

A secured line of credit is the next best option. In this scenario, the bank loans the company money to purchase an asset, such as new equipment or a new building. The asset is then used to secure the loan until the company pays it back, just like a house secures a mortgage, which is simply another kind of loan. In this case, the company typically must provide at least 20 percent of the purchase amount. (A $50,000 purchase requires $10,000 invested by the company and $40,000 by the bank.) If the loan can't be repaid, the assets are sold to recover the bank's investment. Liquid assets, such as a certificate of deposit, a receivable note, or inventory are the most desirable and easiest to loan against because they are the easiest to sell if the company defaults on the loan. Next best are fixed assets such as equipment and computers.

You might also be able to get *short-term loans* (under a year) by using receivables or inventory as your collateral. This type of loan is really a line of credit with special provisions. You provide a summary to the bank showing that your company has a certain level of liquid assets—accounts receivables from customers, inventory, or CDs—that can be used as security on the loan. The bank will only loan 70 to 80 percent of the value of the assets, which is recalculated each month. The danger is that if your assets decline from one month to the next, you might have to shell out some additional money. The nice part about this type of loan is that it generally requires interest-only payments, but the entire balance must be paid off at specified periods, usually quarterly.

That is the strict letter of the relationship. Now, here is what usually happens in reality. You talk to your banker and show a historical record of receivables, inventory, and receivables aging. From the amounts and aging, you and your banker agree on a reasonable amount of liquid asset value, and the bank opens a line of credit for that amount. The 70 to 80 percent rule still applies, and my experience has been that this keeping of the loan no more than the agreed-upon 80 percent value is handled on the honor system. My banker only asked for my receivables value at the one-year anniversary but reserved the right to investigate them monthly if desired. Your banker will probably only exercise this right if he or she believes that the note or the company is in jeopardy.

Listen Up

The value of assets is usually discounted when used as security for a loan. As my banker says, "We are in the business of lending money, not selling items to recover debt."

Notes, or loans, secured by larger assets such as major equipment and property are considered long-term and can have a 36- to 60-month repayment period. When calculating the value of your inventory, bankers use 50 percent of the retail price as the value. They don't consider the inventory worth the full price you paid for it because the bank must sell it for much less if you go out of business.

For example, assume that you secured your line of credit last month with $50,000 in receivables, giving you $35,000 in credit (70 percent of $50,000). If your receivables drop to $40,000 the next month, your collateral is worth only $28,000 (70 percent of

$40,000). The $7,000 difference between the $35,000 and the $28,000 value of your assets must be paid to the bank immediately to meet the terms of the original loan agreement. This can be a tough check to write if you haven't planned for it. Will you get caught if you try to stretch the situation? Probably not. Is it worth the risk? I think not, because if you are caught, you are in violation of a banking agreement, which can torpedo any prospects you have for keeping that banker on your side. Plus that would likely make the bank call the entire note altogether, which can really put you in a cash pinch.

Sell Your Banker on Your Company

People naturally avoid risk, and bankers make risk avoidance an art form. There is only one issue ever discussed with a loan officer: How will the bank get the money back if the loan defaults? Where will the money come from? A new company has no established source of cash. The entire business is assumed very risky. The only thing the loan officer has to refer to is the business plan.

Your bank wants to be sure you've thought through all aspects of your business and believe it can work. If you don't believe in it, why should they? Can you imagine giving $50,000 to people who are wishy-washy about where they plan to go, how they'll get there, when they'll arrive, and how they'll pay you back? I can't! I've done that and been burned. Remember, your business plan is your opportunity to explain what you want to do and how you intend to succeed.

The bank is going to expect something from you before it gives credit. First, you must do your homework and prepare a comprehensive business plan with realistic sales and expense projections. Next, you must provide personal financial statements to give the bank an idea of your own financial situation, separate from the company. People with 20 percent or more ownership in the venture are required to personally guarantee the debt, meaning that they agree to repay all of it personally if the company defaults. Period. Later you will have more negotiating room, but early on, this is the norm.

Your challenge is to convince the bank that you are credit worthy. As a new business owner, your personal credit history along with a well thought-out business plan are the best cards that you can play. My banker told me that the loans I received in my second year of business were based on my personal credibility, personal asset value, and the strength of my business plan. So far, so good!

Banks will evaluate you based on the five Cs of lending:

◆ **Character.** What are you like? Confident? Ethical? Self-assured? This is treated as a very important consideration when first starting out. Make the initial meetings count!

- **Capacity or cash flow.** Can you repay the debt? Do you have the cash flow to support the monthly or periodic payments required?

- **Collateral.** What can the bank take if the loan defaults? Make it clear that you don't intend to default, but that the bank is covered should the worst happen.

- **Condition.** What is the general economic condition of the area, and what is the intended use for the money?

- **Capital.** What is the company's net worth or equity?

Remember that banks make their money by lending money, and they are always looking for solid loan prospects. If banks don't lend money, they don't make money. Interesting, no? If you have a clean financial report, both personal and business, and a company with a solid, proven financial record, you can get money from your bank. Notice that you must perform to a certain level before your bank will consider lending you money, and only for minimum risk opportunities.

Commercial Checking Accounts: A Different Animal

Balance your commercial checking account just as you do your personal checkbook— but do it more often! Your company writes checks and makes deposits as you do in your personal checking account, but the rules are slightly different, as is explained a little later. You can shop around and find a better deal on fees and transaction costs on business checking accounts, but make sure the rules and requirements fit your needs. Don't overlook the important factors of convenience and security; after all, you hope to be taking a lot of money to the bank, so make sure the bank you select is accessible and safe.

Keep the following in mind when you set up a commercial checking account for your company:

- You are charged for your commercial account based on the number of transactions and the average account balance.

- You can expect to pay a fee for each check you deposit, along with a transaction fee for the deposit. (Can you believe it? Only a bank would bill you for giving it money!) At some banks, the rate billed for each check varies according to whether it is local, in state, out of state, or from your cousin Vinnie!

- You are also billed for each check you write.

- You receive a statement from the bank that outlines the charges billed to your checking account for those transactions. This statement is in addition to the basic checking statement listing all the checks and deposits that have cleared. The formal term for this is an *analysis statement*.

Talking Business

An **analysis statement** is a statement from your bank that outlines the various bank charges and credits incurred with respect to your business account. An **earning credit** is a credit offered by the bank in the place of earning interest because federal law does not allow you to earn interest on a business checking account.

- Banks charge transaction fees for each deposit you make and check you write, but they also give you an *earning credit* on the money in your account, which you can use to pay those transaction fees. By keeping enough in your account to offset transaction fees, you save some money.

- Verify the bank's policy on handling international transactions and letters of credit. This becomes very important when dealing with foreign customers.

- Talk to the bank about the services it offers related to conventional and Internet-based processing of credit cards.

You should shop around to get the best overall services package that is right for your company. It will be based on your expected number of checking transactions and the other business services that you will need. Do your homework up front to ensure that you get set up with the right bank from the start. It is really a drag to cultivate one bank only to find that it cannot serve your needs as you grow and you have to start building that relationship all over again from scratch with another bank.

Enter the Small Business Administration (SBA)

When nobody else will help, the Small Business Administration (SBA) comes to the rescue. Maybe. It used to be difficult to get an SBA loan, but the SBA has changed and might be able to help if the loan amount is under $100,000. What used to generate a one-inch folder of paperwork is now down to a two-page application as part of the LowDoc loan program. This is good news, but you should understand the process to see how the SBA can help you in the early days.

The SBA doesn't give you money. A bank actually issues the check. The SBA just guarantees the bank that the loan will be repaid and charges you a 2 percent fee for the insurance policy. A guarantee from the SBA that the loan will be repaid makes the loan very attractive to a bank.

Why would the SBA lend you money when a bank won't? Because the federal government thinks that small business must flourish for the domestic economy to grow, and its guarantee is the SBA's way of putting its money where its mouth is. The SBA lets the bank do the legwork and then either approves the guarantee or not.

Not all banks are SBA lenders, and you should check with the bank before starting the process. Some banks are in a position where the SBA will always approve a loan guarantee request from these banks. Call the local SBA office for information regarding these banks.

Don't assume that you need an SBA guarantee to get a loan. Fill out a loan application at the bank of your choice, which will require your personal financial information and a business plan. Should your loan not meet the bank criteria for lending (the five Cs), the bank can then turn to the SBA for a loan guarantee. If the SBA approves, the loan is funded from the bank with a guarantee provided by the SBA. The bank approves the loan if the SBA provides an 80 to 90 percent repayment guarantee. Quite often, banks would rather give you the loan themselves instead of involving the SBA because it makes working with the loan more complicated for the bank.

> **Smoke Signals**
>
> The SBA requires that you keep thorough records. The bank and the borrower must account for all funds disbursed. The record-keeping load is substantial, so be ready for it.

There are several different SBA loan types, and they change on a regular basis. Contact your local SBA office and sit through one of their introductory talks (around one hour long). The talks provide a solid basis for understanding the procedure and how to work with a bank to obtain a loan. Preferred SBA vendors do a lot of business with the SBA, so get a listing of them and work with one of the preferred banks from the beginning.

> **Listen Up**
>
> Think of the bank as the initial approval gatekeeper. The SBA only considers giving you a guarantee if three banks have already rejected you for traditional financing. You must go to banks first to get rejected and then to the SBA, which relies a lot on the bank's assessment of your situation.

Big Banks, Small Banks

Which is better—a small bank with easy access to the lending managers or a big bank with deeper pockets and higher approval levels? The answer: It depends.

All banks have lending guidelines, but the internal policies are more flexible with a small bank. The officers are more likely to bend the rules in a small bank than in a big one. With a small bank, you get to know the officers better and quicker, but the loan amount that can be approved might be smaller. This means that you should check out the bank's philosophy of operation and verify that it actually does what its marketing literature says it does. Ask for a few references of companies in your size range, and then call these references and ask them questions.

Start with the banks where you already have a relationship. If the big banks give you grief, go to a smaller one. You might look like a large fish in a small pond, so beware that the pond might not be deep enough as you grow.

Average small business loan amounts are in the $25,000 to $50,000 range, which is well within the reach of any bank. Be aware that because it takes just as much paperwork to process a $25,000 loan as a $250,000 loan, most banks prefer to process the larger amount, where they earn more interest on the loan.

The Least You Need to Know

- ◆ You will almost certainly need the assistance of a bank as your business succeeds and your cash requirements increase, so get to know the officers of your bank now.

- ◆ Your personal credit history and business plan are your best selling points when trying to get money in the early stages.

- ◆ Banks make money by lending money, but they have to lend a great deal of money to make up for a loan that goes into default.

- ◆ The five Cs determine your credit worthiness. Make sure that you have effectively addressed all of them to increase your chances of success.

- ◆ The SBA requires the same amount of preparation for a loan guarantee that a bank does. Apply for a loan at a bank first, and if you are turned down, the SBA might be able to help get it approved by guaranteeing repayment for you.

Chapter 20

Automate from the Start

In This Chapter

- ◆ Using technology for your benefit
- ◆ Automating your business
- ◆ Applying computer and telephone technology
- ◆ Planning for technology obsolescence
- ◆ Networking your company

"So why hasn't the newsletter gone out?" asked Frank. "We intend to do this on a regular basis, and it shouldn't be such a big deal."

Todd, the marketing director, looked frustrated at the question and did his best to give a diplomatic answer. "The database of names is in an old format, and we do the mail merge for the labels in our word processing software package. Making the two work with each other is a headache. Why didn't we just stick with the package we started with?"

Frank thought back. He had taken all of his customer contact information to a typing service that entered it into a computer program. Then they gave him a disk and told him the name of the software package they used, so he bought it to make things simple. His now ex-brother-in-law had upgraded the database to a more powerful and capable "fully relational" one, whatever that meant. Now Frank couldn't even print out mailing labels and didn't feel so powerful. He wondered if he would ever be able to create a telephone list using the new package. It just shouldn't be this hard.

"I guess the latest and greatest is just not so great for us, is it? Let's call a temporary agency and see if we can get someone in here who understands how all of this stuff works. Maybe we should send one of us to a training class to learn how mail merging operates. One day in a class would certainly pay for itself if we could avoid a situation like this again," said Frank.

"Maybe we can get some training on that fax and electronic mail program, too," said Todd. "We mail out 1,000 pieces per month at around 50 cents each to our local customers. That is $500 per month in postage and printing that would be completely saved by using fax or e-mail distribution instead of the mail. I know how much you like to save money. What about giving me some time and money to get trained on that, too?"

"Five hundred bucks a month? Not bad! I wonder how else this computer equipment can save us money and time."

There is simply no justification for your not using whatever reasonable technology you can afford as early in your company's life as possible.

The major reason to invest in a technology right off the bat is that over time, you will set up certain ways of performing office procedures. Many companies start by doing certain tasks by hand because it is cheaper than buying equipment. There are a few problems with this approach: (1) as your business grows, you will eventually find the paper system hampering your growth, (2) having contact information on a computer enables you to *mine* that database for information that helps you learn about and better serve your customers, and (3) the more you do by hand, the more employees you must have, increasing overhead costs and hassles and decreasing profits.

You will not be able to operate for very long without having a computer and other technology as part of your operation. Budget technology into your plan and always keep an eye and ear out for how technology can be put to better use in your company. Just beware that you don't set up your company such that the technology starts to run your company instead of it being used to support your company goals. You are in business to make money, not to buy more technology. That means you geeks as well. Just because you want it and it is "cool" is not a business justification for a major technology purchase.

I can promise you this: If you use technology to its best advantage, you will work fewer hours, have happier customers, and employ fewer people. That has to be enough reason for you to seriously consider technology as part of your business plan.

Automate the Routine and Savor the Creative

Picture this: You are moving a little screw from the left side of your desk to the right side of your desk and then back again. Repeat. Now, repeat again. Again. And again. Get the picture? Boring!

If you like this type of work, you are probably not cut out for the crazy world of entrepreneurship. Most entrepreneurs I know hate routine tasks such as paperwork, filling out expense reports, doing the bookkeeping, and completing tax forms. For this reason, paperwork, expense reports, bookkeeping, and tax forms are often done late or not done at all.

It's a big problem that you can pretty easily avoid. Computer programs already exist that can handle most of this boring stuff for you, and many of them cost under $200! Pretty cheap once you own a computer.

You can find a software package to automate most routine office tasks such as word processing, making payroll and tax deductions, keeping spreadsheets, maintaining customer contact information, and more.

As mentioned in previous chapters, you can buy software to set up your company's corporation articles and bylaws and even create a policy manual. Check out the handy table at the end of this chapter that summarizes all these software packages; this should save you some legwork.

Setting up similar systems by hand requires a lot of paper, printed spreadsheets and charts, bound reference material, a calculator or adding machine, note cards, and a lot of pens and pencils. Furthermore, all your manual record keeping is not as accurate or useful as a computerized system. Consider the amount of money you would have spent on supplies and add that to the extra time it takes to track simple customer and financial information by hand; then use that as a rough budget for your computer purchase. I'm sure you can see by now that buying a computer makes a lot of sense. Just as word processing is better than a typewriter, automated business procedures are better than manual ones. Get it?

Talking Business

Mining refers to the process of investigating available data and using it for a specific purpose. You would mine your customer database for buying patterns, geographic location trends, average deal sizes, or payment tendencies, among any number of other important information points. Use (mine) your database for information directly applicable to your own business before paying others for general information that may not be pertinent.

The weeks (yes, weeks!) you would have spent setting up these manual operations on your own are instantly eliminated for a small investment! Play your cards right and automate from the beginning.

Typical Automation Strategies

Everyone has his or her own opinions about automation, computer systems, and software. Because it's always useful to hear others' opinions on important subjects, here are my recommendations for automating your business. It might turn out later that my suggestions are not perfect for your particular situation, but they should work well enough to get you started:

1. Look for the routine areas of your business operation that don't require creativity; doing the same task over and over again is a sure sign of a routine activity. Typical areas include, but are not limited to, generating invoices, sending mass mailings (like newsletters) to clients, generating proposals, pricing calculations, tracking customers, sorting employee performance evaluations, and handling payroll tax-related clerical tasks, accounting, and bookkeeping.

2. Ask other business owners how they handle routine tasks. Guess what? They have the same problem. Why not learn from their experience?

3. To handle tasks such as invoicing, bookkeeping, financial report generation, payroll check generation, and tax reporting, look at accounting and payroll packages such as QuickBooks that are compatible with the other software packages you put on your computer.

4. Pick a *suite* of computer software packages that all work with each other to provide word processing, spreadsheet, database, and presentation capabilities (for example, Microsoft Office or WordPerfect). A suite package combines several different software packages in one, rather than having you buy them separately, which typically costs much more. The most popular suite product sold today is Microsoft Office Professional, which includes Word (word processing), Excel (spreadsheet), Access (database), and PowerPoint (presentation graphics). I am personally not crazy about the Outlook (e-mail and scheduling) portion of this suite, but it works and is certainly better than nothing.

5. Take a training class on the software packages that you will use regularly. Every day you spend in class will probably save you five days of working on your own. Trust me on this one; I see it all the time. Most people use only a fraction of the total capability built into their already installed applications. Start to use all of that capability, and make your business more efficient from the start.

6. Organize the various working files you create on the computer into meaningful directories, and use meaningful filenames to identify them, just as you organize information in a filing cabinet. If you are not the person who creates and maintains this information, make sure you understand the filing system of whomever creates it. Avoid embarrassing situations because this person has called in sick or decided to quit without notice.

7. Make a backup of that data on a daily basis, if possible. Computer hard disk drives fail. When they do, you end up losing your data or paying a lot of money to someone who will probably only recover a small portion of it. Look into backup programs that handle this for you automatically. They're not expensive and will help safeguard all your valuable files. Set up a backup regime and stay with it.

8. **Keep it simple, S**imon is the KISS principle. (Okay, so the last "s" didn't stand for "Simon" the last time you heard this one. You caught me!) Anyway, keeping it simple is a good thing. You don't want to end up spending hours and hours on your computer. You simply want to get your invoices and letters out as easily as possible. Create form letters, standard invoices, and credit letters. Try not to customize everything, and you'll save a lot of time with standard letters and packages. The computer should support your business needs, not the other way around.

9. Resist the temptation to apply new technology before someone else has tried it first. Keep away from the leading (or bleeding) edge of technology unless you specifically have the expertise to know what you are getting yourself into. A simple technology snafu can cost you tons of time, money, and aggravation. Let someone else work out the technical bugs.

10. Always invest in printers or copy machines that create high-quality results. The printed page is what your customers see and provides the impression you leave. A laser printer is almost a mandatory investment in today's business world, although inkjet printer quality is usually superb if the laser printer is out of your price range. Don't be afraid to experiment with color printing, as the costs have come down a lot and it adds that extra "punch" that separates you from the competition.

11. Ask yourself if technology, such as a website, would improve the way that your customers interact with your company. For example, tech support information placed on a website is available 24 hours a day and can help your late-night customers who get themselves into trouble using your products.

Listen Up

When a computer prints a bunch of numbers, people seem to think they must be true. This can get you into trouble if you make mistakes. Every now and then, spot-check your entries (by hand if need be) to make sure things are accurate.

Get Connected: Computers and Phones

Marketing and sales will make or break your business. Sales efforts involve keeping customer information, answering telephones, and responding to the mail. The more people you contact in a professional, timely manner, the more likely you are to increase your sales and the closer you are to retiring early. Computer and telephone equipment are part of doing business, and you should take steps to use them to their full capacity.

Computers: Buy or Rent

The sooner that you include a computer into the operation of your business, the easier it will be to grow and make money. In many cases, equipment and technology can make it easier or faster to accomplish routine tasks, making it possible for you to get more done with fewer employees. You don't need the latest and greatest, but you need enough capability to do not only what you need today but also what you expect to need over the next 18 months or so. At that point, you will likely be ready for new equipment anyway.

Listen Up

Factor in the cost and time associated with getting trained on your important computer software application packages. You don't need to be a geek but you need to understand enough about what can be done to know when it is time to call the geek and then manage their natural geek tendencies.

On the CD

A sample Equipment Lease Agreement is included on the CD as document 20-1.

If you don't have the money to invest in a new computer right now, then maybe you should consider leasing or purchasing one from a used computer store. With a lease, you pay a regular monthly fee for the use of a computer for a particular period of time, and at the end, you give the computer back or buy it for a small fee. Computer leases work a lot like car leases. Once you start a lease, you have to finish it or pay for the equipment anyway, so don't start on a lease unless you are serious.

I know several companies who no longer purchase any of their computers and lease everything for three years or less. Their rationale is simply that computers become obsolete too quickly. These companies feel that they are better off leasing so that they can simply turn in the old for the new every few years.

In addition to getting around spending a big chunk of cash all at once, leases (or rentals) also give you time to check out different computers to help decide which is best for you and your business. Of course, this is really only an advantage if you get a relatively short lease to test run the computer. If you sign up for a lease of many months, or years, you're effectively locking yourself in to using that type of computer.

You are still able to switch to something else at the end of the lease, but several months down the road, you have all your files set up and know a lot of the programs for that kind of computer. At that point, you're probably not going to want to start over from scratch.

There may also be financial benefits derived from leasing since the entire lease payment is deductible as an expense. If not leased, the deductions come in the form of interest payments on equipment loans and depreciation, which may never truly recover the capital cost of the computer. Run the numbers and include the tax impact to see which is the right approach for you, but buy something. You cannot exist for very long in today's business climate without using computer technology.

Treat Your Phone Like a Lifeline—It Is!

As for telephones, you can try using your personal line for business calls, but you'll quickly discover that this approach is inconvenient for your customers, for your family, and your business. Not to mention that it simply appears unprofessional to have your six-year old answer the phone. Naturally, your local telephone company charges you for the privilege of adding a telephone line, so economics plays a part in how many separate phone lines you can afford. In my opinion, you need to have that separate business phone line if you plan to be in business.

Having a separate line also allows you to separate your business and personal life. If you have young children, it is imperative that they not speak with customers. You appear unprofessional if your children answer calls or can be heard screaming in the background. So have a separate business line installed.

Listen Up

To ensure that you rarely miss any calls, consider getting a cellular phone with voice mail as one of its calling features. Forward your business line to your cellular phone when you are not in the office. When your cellular phone is on, you receive calls without the caller knowing the difference. When your cellular phone is off, callers are forwarded to your voice mail system where they can leave you a message. When you turn your phone back on, you are notified that you have a message that you can then retrieve. Cellular technology is so developed now that you can have calls automatically forwarded to you if you are in another city, or even another country. The advantage is freedom, but the disadvantage is that it is harder to get away from clients, which is rarely a real problem.

You will find that one- and two-line phones are common and inexpensive. Start out with one line and make it the primary phone number listed in the phone book. When you need a second line, have it roll over to the second line when the first is busy. This means that calls to the first line ring on line one if the line is free but ring on line two if line one is busy with a call. You might also want to consider installing a separate phone line to handle your fax and computer modem connection. Even in today's e-mail crazy world, you will still need to send and receive faxes at all hours, and you save yourself hassles by simply dedicating a separate line to fax transmissions. This point is particularly important for those of you desiring to work internationally. When they send faxes during the day, it might be midnight where you are. You should expect that online connections will continually become a more important part of your business life, which means mentally and financially preparing yourself for that dedicated fax/modem line.

Unfortunately, you might still want to have this fax line even if you have DSL or other high-speed data access since you may still need to receive faxes, and that high speed line won't help you in that regard.

When you need more than two incoming lines and are still operating from a home office, you may need special wiring, which means you'll have to shell out some money. The capabilities are greater, but the added expense can be substantial if you are not careful. You will likely at this point have to invest in a "key" system that enables you to have many user telephone stations within the company who all share the incoming lines. You can, for example, have 4 incoming telephone lines and 10 phone stations sitting on people's desks.

Voice mail is so common these days, it's almost become a mandatory business tool. There will always be a continuing debate about whether a live answering service is better than electronic voice mail. There are advantages to each. You need to decide what works for you based on your workload, number of phone calls, and cost.

I lean toward the electronic approach because the messages are usually more accurate and the cost to receive and record them is less. People who call me and find that I can't answer the phone can simply leave a message with a specific question or answer. Without an answering service running interference, there is little chance of miscommunication or misunderstanding. However, many people hate talking to a machine and hang up where these people would leave a message with a person.

I suggest that you look at handling your phone-answering procedures this way. First always have a live person (you) answer your main phone line. The phone should be answered by the third ring or then be answered by voice mail. The greeting on the voice mail must be friendly, clear, specific, current, and brief. Answer voice mail messages within the same day that they are received and within 24 hours at the latest. If you are out of the country and unable to reach voice mail, say so on the greeting so customer expectations regarding a return call are set. If you are out of the office, use the forwarding technique presented earlier to answer those calls using your cell phone. Don't give people your cell phone number. Just give them your office number, which forwards to your cell, so you can change cell carriers without having to notify people of a number change.

As you add employees, they should all be well aware that answering the phone by the third ring is a company priority, and not working to fulfill that goal is considered a serious breach on their part. An unanswered call may really be a lost sale or lost customers.

At first, you can forward your office line to your cell phone. But as you add employees, this phone etiquette of answering by the third ring will have to happen at the office, so train employees in this policy from the start.

Listen Up

Don't expect your computer fax card to replace a fax machine. You will have paper documents to send, such as those requiring a signature or correction with a pen. You need a regular fax machine in these cases. The plain-paper fax is, I think, a better option than the standard rolled fax paper as the received faxes last longer without fading and you have fewer hassles with the paper, such as cutting, rolling, etc. Using your computer for outbound fax-blasting is a great idea, and using a package like WinFax Pro will make this process incredibly easier and less time consuming.

For people who want to respond immediately to calls, you can also add a pager to the list of communication tools. Pagers can be set up to buzz or beep when a message is left in your voice mailbox so that you know to check it right away. You can then use your cellular phone to return the call. I use my cell phone as my "pager" in that once I turn on my phone, I am automatically notified of any messages.

Each new phone line and feature costs money, but the telephone is not a place to skimp financially. One lost call can mean a lost customer. How much is one sale worth to your company? How many new customers are needed to pay for this investment in technology? If the number is small (one or two in a month), which it usually is, then it is probably a good investment.

Been There ... Done That

One final word of caution is due here related to the phone number itself. When you are promoting your business, you will also be promoting your address and phone number. Once that number is embedded in your customers' minds, speed dialers, and contact management software packages, you really don't want to change it. Jealously guard that phone number and your phone service so that your customers rarely have to change the number and *never* get a message that could be interpreted as your having gone out of business.

I know of some companies that promote an 800 (or other toll free number) and then route that number to whatever wireline or cellular number they choose. In this way, they can relocate their phone service, and the relocation is transparent to customers. They pay more long-distance phone charges but treat it as a strategic expense of doing business. By the way, toll-free service is not that expensive anymore and offers business benefits that you might not have considered. In today's world of 5 cent/minute long-distance charges, toll-free service is simply not the big customer deal it used to be. In this case, toll free is helping you out more than your customers.

Local Area Networks, Electronic Mail, Faxing, and Security

In the past, only major corporations had local area networks, which are also referred to as LANs. But the large number of computers out there and the benefits of using a LAN are so substantial that demand for LAN equipment went up, the costs went down, and the ease of installation improved. In short, you can now easily install and benefit from a LAN in almost any environment with more than one computer.

The two traditional LAN benefits are: (1) you can share the same printer between all LAN users, and (2) all company data can be stored in a single location (file server), which improves data security and also makes data backup easier. A third and relatively new but important benefit of using a LAN is derived by those companies needing access to the Internet. A single Internet connection can be installed to the LAN, using a router/hub combination, and then all LAN users can simultaneously have access to the Internet as well. Installing DSL, a cable-modem, or another high-speed Internet connection to this router opens up the world of Internet opportunities to all employees for minimal cost.

Assume that you have a few computers in your office. Your LAN will likely be implemented using some type of 10/100Base-T networking equipment such as computer cards and hubs. The wiring will be Cat5e type, which is now pretty inexpensive and as easy to install as a modular connection for your telephone. Setting up the software, however, is not that simple unless you are really lucky, so try to find someone to get you up and running at first.

Electronic mail (e-mail) allows you to send a message (such as an electronic letter) to another person who also has an electronic mailbox. You can also send whole files from computer to computer. In this way, you can share information with others without using paper or overnight delivery services. The process is much faster and often less expensive. You can have this e-mail capability on your own LAN for internal communication purposes, and you can use it to communicate with your external clients and other partners as well.

Commercial services, such as EarthLink, MSN, America Online, and most other ISPs, provide you with Internet-based electronic mail you can use to contact people (if you know their e-mail addresses). Your internal corporate e-mail box may not, and likely will not, be the same one that you use for your personal e-mail. Sorry.

Fax still remains a great way to maintain contact with your local clients and save money. It costs you at least 37 cents in postage, plus printing costs, to mail something via the U.S. Postal Service to your local clients. It costs you nothing more than the charge for a phone call (which could be zero, zip, nada, if your customers are local and you have unlimited local phone service). Instead of 100 customer contacts costing you $37 or more, it is now practically free!

Software packages on the market such as WinFax Pro automate the fax sending and receiving procedures. You create, on the computer, the documents that you want to fax and decide who should receive them by extracting their fax numbers from your contact database. Start the program and go home while the documents are faxed to everyone. The fax program also sends documents overnight while you sleep. The following morning, your clients receive this new information from your company and you got a good night's sleep ... for free if you have unlimited local service! Yes, this is definitely worth investigating.

Of course, you should definitely check out your state's "junk" fax laws before deciding to send unsolicited information by fax. Some laws in place prohibit you from sending information by fax that someone has not requested. Although companies can send junk mail through the U.S. Postal Service, they generally can't do the same by fax. Make sure that your faxed documents provide instruction to those receiving the fax regarding how they can have their number removed from your fax list. You can lose a customer by disregarding their no-fax instructions, so beware.

> **Smoke Signals**
>
> Avoid fax overload. Your clients are happy to hear from you when you have something to say, but don't annoy them by wasting their time and fax paper. Use fax technology properly, and you can save money while maintaining better customer contact.

Security is an unfortunate requirement of today's Internet-connected business world. Know that there is a very real possibility that someone out there will try to either infect your network with a virus or break into your network, destroying data as part of the invasion. Make sure that you invest in a virus checker for your systems and network and don't connect to the Internet without ensuring that you have an effective firewall in place to keep unwanted prying Internet eyes from seeing your network.

Planning for Obsolescence

Technology is great stuff. That is the good news. It is also expensive and constantly changing. That is the bad news. Whatever you buy today will probably be a boat anchor in three years, or less. That's right! Three years at most!

This rapidly changing technology situation is not unusual when dealing with computer equipment. You typically see a major technological advancement every two years and software upgrades every 12 months, which means that you might find yourself constantly investing in newer, better equipment just to keep up.

Buy what you need for today because you need it now. Accept that almost every technology will decrease in value, and get the most use out of it today. Never buy brand new cutting-edge technology unless you absolutely need it. Use the old stuff until it slows down your business's efficiency and bottom line. Then upgrade. You can't guess what new features will be available even months from now; computer technology just changes too fast. In addition, you don't want to be the one who finds all of the problems with a new technology, unless that is what your business does. Let others work out the problems and then benefit from their work.

Most of my computer systems are pretty boring since I keep my production systems as simple as possible. I just cannot afford to have some "new and improved" software package of technology bring down my system or network, and my business along with it. Keep it simple really applies to the use of technology. If you need to make it complicated, then make sure you are ready for the complexity.

In a Nutshell

Just to keep all this software information in one place for you, I created a handy table that summarizes the packages I talked about and provides some phone numbers and price ranges to get your automation investigation on the right track.

Business Planning Related Software Products

Software Name	Company	Retail	Function Performed	Contact Info
QuickBooks	Intuit	$299+	Business accounting	www.intuit.com
Act!	Symantec	$190+	Contact management	www.symantec.com
GoldMine	Goldmine Software	$190+	Contact management	www.goldmine.com
WinFax Pro	Symantec	$99+	Fax management	www.symantec.com
FrontPage	Microsoft	$169+	Website creation	www.microsoft.com
Microsoft Office	Microsoft	$269+	Word processing, spreadsheet, presentation, and more	www.microsoft.com
WordPerfect Office	Corel Corporation	$169+	Word processing, spreadsheet, presentation, graphics, and more	www.corel.com
Norton Personal Firewall	Symantec	$49+	Firewall software	www.symantec.com
McAfee Firewall	McAfee	$29+	Firewall software	www.mcafee.com
Norton AntiVirus	Symantec	$49+	Virus checking software	www.symantec.com
VirusScan	McAfee	$59+	Virus checking software	www.mcafee.com
TurboTax Home and Office	Intuit	$79+	Tax preparation software for sole proprietorship	www.turbotax.com
TurboTax Business	Intuit	$99+	Tax preparation software for corporations	www.turbotax.com
TaxCut Platinum Home and Business	H&R Block	$49+	Tax preparation for sole proprietorship and corporations	www.taxcut.com
Quicken Lawyer Business	Intuit	$49+	Legal forms software	www.intuit.com
Kiplinger Home and Business Attorney	H&R Block	$29+	Legal forms software	See retailer

continues

Business Planning Related Software Products (continued)

Software Name	Company	Retail	Function Performed	Contact Info
Backup Now!	NewTech Info Systems	$69+	Backup software	See retailer
Norton Ghost	Symantec	$69+	Backup software	www.symantec.com

 On the CD

The CD contains even more information about how you can use technology to benefit your new business. A detailed comparison between the Apple and PC-based computer types is included in the bonus section "Comparing the Apple and PC Hardware Platforms" (CD20-2). "Automating Your Accounting" (CD20-1) information teaches you how to find the computerized accounting package that is right for you. And to close more sales, you should check out the section "Finding the Right Contact Management Software Package" (CD20-3). The information contained in these extras will kick your business's efficiency to a whole new level.

The Least You Need to Know

◆ Automate from the start.

◆ Only use technology that is proven. Don't invest big bucks in the latest and greatest untested product.

◆ Find someone who you trust to be your technology adviser and "go-to" guy for trouble. These folks are not too expensive if you make them a regular part of your business and they know your operation.

◆ Expect that your computer technology purchases will become obsolete in three years, which means you'll need to upgrade your current computer or buy a new one.

◆ Spend time planning out the communication flow between your customers and your business. Make sure that you know how telephone, e-mail, fax, standard mail, and other communication methods will work before your customers let you know with a complaint.

Chapter 21

Making Great Use of the Internet

In This Chapter

- ◆ Understanding Internet terms and benefits
- ◆ Giving your website a marketing emphasis
- ◆ Effectively using Internet technology
- ◆ Managing the Internet opportunity today and in the future

"How did you come up with these copyright forms so quickly?" asked Howard.

"Simple," said James, one of Howard's employees. "I went out on the Internet, did a search on Google, accessed the government's website, and downloaded the PDF file. It all took about 10 minutes."

I couldn't even walk to the library in 10 minutes, thought Howard. To have the form in my hand and never even leave the office is pretty cool. Howard all of a sudden got a little depressed. Here he was, the owner of a successful small business, only in his mid-40s, and already feeling like an antique.

"Heck. You could learn how to do this, boss. You just need to get over your fear of doing something wrong. Oh, by the way, you are paying for the connection, and the logon is in your name, so why not use it?"

Howard took a deep breath and looked at James. He took to the Internet so naturally, it was a little disconcerting. But, on the other hand, perhaps other people James' age also took to the Internet this easily.

"I hear that some companies actually allow their customers to retrieve information and even place orders over the Internet. Is that true?" asked Howard.

James lit up like a Christmas tree. "You bet," he said. "I just ordered a new stereo from some guys in California and regularly check out our competition's websites to see what they are offering to their customers."

Now Howard was interested. The Internet had just moved from being a cool toy that kids used to a business tool. If his competition was already doing it, he had better check it out or risk being lost in the cyber-dust.

"Could you help us get set up to provide information to our customers? Do you think that they are also using the Internet? How long will it take, and what do you think it will cost?"

"I've been working on this at home, on my own time, just because I like it. Let me loose to create our website during work time, and I will have a demo for you within a week. How about them apples?" responded a very pumped-up James.

Well, thought Howard, you spend money to make money. Let's see how this works out. "You're on, James. Let's meet later so you can fill me in on how the process works."

At this point in the book, you might feel like you have a ton of different balls to juggle, and if you drop any of them you might seriously hurt your business. Well, you're right about that. The trick is to make sure you pay special attention to the ones that can put you out of business, but that is often easier said than done.

As if you haven't had enough, I am now going to introduce you to the Internet and the opportunities presented by this marvelous technological revolution.

"Why should I care?" you might be asking. Well, here's why. There's a whole world out there that might be able to use your products or services. Getting hold of these possible prospects who may live on the other side of the United States or on the other side of the world might seem like a daunting task. Oddly enough, it just doesn't have to be that complicated any more. You have a natural connection in the Internet.

Your prospects and competition are probably already using the Internet to research personal and business matters. If they aren't, they will be soon.

The Internet is an integral part of modern life, both personal and business, and will definitely become more important in future years. You should already be thinking about ways to take advantage of this shift. This chapter moves you in that direction.

Internet Unique Realities

To take advantage of the Internet, you first have to change your thinking. Electronics, which is the mechanism of the Internet, operates at high speeds (almost at the speed of light). Although traveling from New York to Los Angeles is a trip of several thousand miles and several hours by plane, an electron travels that distance in a small fraction of a second. Japan is only a little farther.

As a result, time and distance, as we know it on an Earthly level, do not have the same meaning with the Internet. For all practical purposes, you can connect to a computer in Switzerland or in New Zealand just as quickly as you can connect to a computer in Chicago. Many of the barriers that separate two Internet-connected systems have been removed so that all users and computers share a common technological language through which communication and business can flow. In fact, some sites now automatically translate the written language from one nation's language to another. This presents a unique communication and business tool that has really never existed before, which is pretty exciting in itself. Now take a look at the business opportunities that this reality opens up for you.

If you think that doing business with Australia would be expensive due to the long-distance charges, you need to shift your thinking. For an Internet user in Sydney, a computer system in New York is only a local Australian phone call away. The Internet provides the connection between Sydney and New York, and it usually does it for a flat fee, independent of how many hours the connection is used. If that computer supplier has a local Australian outlet, the shipping is even a local process. And if the customer wants software, he or she can easily download it directly over the Internet, which means that no physical package ever touches a person's hands. As far as the Internet is concerned, software downloaded from New York to Chicago is identical to software downloaded from Bangkok to Chicago. In fact, many companies have their customer service and support functions performed by people who actually live on the other side of the globe for just these reasons.

Get the picture? Whereas before you had to let people in Sydney know that your company existed—which meant getting a Sydney mailing list, preparing a direct-mail piece, mailing the piece, and following up with a phone call—you can now allow Sydney residents to see your information over the Internet at minimal cost to both you and them. Not only can someone in Sydney see your site, but he or she can also place an order for products. Are you ready to handle that order? Check out Chapter 22 (located on the CD) for information about handling international business situations.

Been There ... Done That

A little while back, I had a chance to teach a group of Russian networking technology professionals on the operation of Windows NT, a computer program. They couldn't speak any English, but they understood the icons and menu selections, even when presented in English. Think about this. We couldn't say "hello" to each other without a translator, but when we worked with the Internet, we could discuss things in broken, technology-based English terms and via images and icons.

I once heard Steve Jobs, the founder of Apple Computer, interviewed on a radio talk show about the Internet. He commented that one of the most fascinating aspects of the Internet is that a small company can look just as large as IBM on the Internet. Nobody physically visits the company's building, but rather only sees what an owner puts on the Internet. Do a good job on your company's Internet presentation (a.k.a. your website), and you can play with the big guys. He also mentioned that the Internet and its associated technology represents a major step in the direction of a universal language that is spoken around the world.

Is there a technological challenge associated with making this leap into the Internet? Yes. Can you jump these hurdles? The answer once again is yes, and you can do it yourself if so inclined or hire someone to do it for you. In either event, you must address this important business tool or be left in the electronic dust.

Can you expect to make money directly off your website and other Internet-related activities? Probably not in the short term. You should think of your Internet activities such as a website or electronic mail as the modern-day equivalent of a business card. Have you ever made money directly from your business card? Probably not. Is transacting business easier because of your business card? Absolutely.

Once your clients get trained to use your website for information and mail, you can present them with the electronic commerce features that allow you to process orders online.

Been There ... Done That

I successfully kept my publishing business's employee headcount to a minimum through effective use of the Internet and outsourcing. Providing product information about our courseware and related services is a routine task, and many of our clients needed this information after business hours since they taught classes during the day. We set up a website at www.edpaulson.com that allowed our clients to obtain course outlines, pricing, development strategies, and other pertinent information. When they wanted to place an order, they called a 1-800 telephone number or sent a fax order form that they obtained from the website. A fulfillment center then processed the order. This arrangement was good for my customers and good for me as well.

Setting Up Business on the Internet

Several components compose an Internet site. This section presents some of the major terms that you will encounter and shows you how you can use Internet technology in your own business. This section is not designed to make you a technical geek (or expert). It does, however, give you an overview of the language and technology of the Internet so that you can fully appreciate the business opportunities it presents.

To make a connection to the Internet, you will need a computer, modem, Internet connection software, and an agreement with a company that provides the actual connection to the Internet. This may be through some type of high-speed connection such as DSL or cable modem or via a local telephone number for slower dialup Internet access. This process used to be pretty complicated but now is about as simple as software installation. Don't be scared off by the technology. My mother uses the Internet through her AOL account. Heck. She is in her eighties and she does it. You can, and should, too.

Web Jargon

Think of the World Wide Web (the web, for short) as a huge network of interconnected computers. If you draw lines between all of these computers, you have something that looks like a spider web. Picture the web as an interconnected, or internetworked, group of computers.

These computers are connected for all types of Internet-related services. I am going to concentrate on the components that you control, create, or purchase for use by your company on a daily basis.

Your home computer that accesses information from the web primarily deals with computers that host, or act as the home computer, for a website. A website is an electronic location on the web where a company stores and displays the information that it wants seen by others.

Like an individual's street address, all websites have addresses, known as *domain names*. For example, if you type an address such as www.edpaulson.com (my web address), your computer looks for the web location with a domain name of edpaulson.com.

> **Talking Business**
> A **domain name** is a unique name given to your Internet location that is used by people who want to view your Internet site. Most business domain names end with ".com". **Hypertext Markup Language (HTML)** is the language used by Internet websites. **Uniform Resource Locator (URL)** is the official name for an Internet address, such as www.edpaulson.com.

If all of this seems like a lot of jargon, just think of it this way: Your computer needs all of this information to not only find the web address but also to establish a communication session that both computers understand.

Here is the really cool and magical part: Every computer in the world that uses a *browser* (a software tool used to surf the Internet) can read a file stored in *HTML* format on a website location. Every computer connected to the Internet has some form of browser associated with it. This means that anyone who has access to the Internet can access your website and perform any number of standardized operations—such as reading site information, placing orders, providing feedback to the site designers, and paying for purchased products. Starting to get the picture? Your customers are already equipped to purchase from your website.

Finding an Internet Service Provider

All this talk about websites is good, but how do you even get onto the Internet in the first place? Well, you can set up your own Internet access by purchasing a computer, setting up the network connections, spending weeks in training classes, and losing hairs off your head. If you are into that kind of "challenge," then have at it and call me from your asylum room on visiting days.

An easier way is to rely on an *Internet service provider (ISP)*. Your ISP is the company that connects you to the Internet through a high-speed connection such as DSL or cable modem, or a much slower speed dial-up telephone number that is accessed by your computer's modem. Your ISP will likely also offer to host your website for you, probably for no additional fee but with limited amounts of storage space and capability. More on that later.

There are numerous ISPs, and you probably have local ones that provide specials for your local area. A few of the national ISPs include FlashNet, AT&T WorldNet, and EarthLink. Just open your local newspaper to find advertisements from ISPs in your area.

Other vendors that provide their own private networks along with Internet access include America Online (AOL) and Microsoft Network (MSN). With these services, you can send mail and messages to other users who are members of the same network, use custom services that are only available to that network's members, access the Internet, and also send and receive electronic mail from other Internet users.

Let the ISP worry about the latest and greatest methods of connecting to the Internet. You just worry about connecting to your ISP, letting your customers know about your e-mail and website addresses (more on that later), and keeping your website up to date.

Smoke Signals _____

Your **Internet service provider** (ISP) is the company with which you contract so that you can get your connection to the Internet. This company provides you with a local phone number and a browser that you should use for the connection. The service is usually billed for a flat monthly fee and for a number of connection hours.

An ISP will **host** your website, which means that it will make sure that your website is available to Internet visitors around the clock. The ISP provides the computer, software, and support needed to keep your site visible. You still need to create and maintain the site content unless you pay the ISP an additional fee to do that as well.

High-speed Internet access is the term used to generically describe technology that enables you to connect to the Internet at speeds that are substantially faster than you get with a modem and a dialup connection, such as DSL or cable Internet.

A **browser** is a software tool that runs on your computer and interacts with the website documents. The browser reads the HTML and other related codes embedded in the website documents, translates them, and then displays the page on your screen. Two popular browsers are Microsoft Internet Explorer and Netscape Navigator.

How do you choose an ISP? This choice really depends on your specific situation, but here are a few rules to get you started:

♦ Choose a provider that charges a flat connection fee per month, independent of the number of connected hours. (The flat monthly fee is usually in the $15 to $29 range.)

♦ Make sure that the ISP has 24-hour, 7-days-a-week access.

♦ Make sure that there is a customer service line that you can call when you need help.

♦ If you travel and want to retrieve your electronic mail messages while on the road, or even in another country, then make sure that your ISP has local access numbers in the cities that you visit most often. If it does not have these local access numbers, then you inherit the toll telephone charge back to your home city so that you can access the network.

♦ Make sure that your ISP provides enough hard disk space for you to store your anticipated electronic mail messages and website information if applicable. Verify that the number of e-mail accounts you will need is offered or is included with your ISP's offering.

♦ Check to see if the ISP for your electronic mail service also provides website hosting services. You can often get the two features in a single package for a discount rate.

♦ Get the name of a few customers who already use the ISP's services, and find out how often they receive a busy signal when trying to connect. The answer should be "rarely" or "never" or you should look somewhere else.

♦ Ask about your ISP's capability to offer *high-speed Internet access*, which means you can transfer information anywhere between 10 and 50 times faster than using a standard modem. This is a big deal once you become Internet addicted.

Naming Your Domain

The domain name is the address that people go to when they want to find your company. Your domain name is how Internet people learn to recognize you. For example, Microsoft uses www.microsoft.com, which makes sense and is easy to remember. Plus, Microsoft owns the name, which means that nobody else can put themselves on the web as Microsoft.

> ### Been There ... Done That
>
> When we first tried to find a domain name for my company, Technology and Communications, Inc., we struck out because other companies had taken all the names related to our own. Surprising? Not really, when you consider that a domain name must be unique on the entire Internet. We finally tried edpaulson.com and found that it was available, so we took it. You can use the WHOIS feature of the www.internic.net site to see if a domain name is available for use. Good luck—you can expect this name discovery process to take some time and ingenuity.

You can obtain your domain name from InterNic (www.internic.net) or any number of other organizations that provide this service, including your ISP, who will handle this registration for you. Just know that you need to find a domain name that is not taken and then have your ISP register the name and then set up a website location using that name. The fee for this registration service is usually under $30. Just remember that there is a difference between the domain name registration, which is paid yearly with the organization that reserves the name for you, and website hosting, which is paid monthly by you to your ISP.

You can have a domain name that is related to another vendor, such as jones-inc. worldnet.att.net, which means that your website is hosted by AT&T on its WorldNet service. This is the simplest and least expensive way to establish a website—even though the name looks complicated—but it also has its drawbacks. Suppose that you promote your AT&T-associated website for months, and all your customers are accustomed to visiting this site when they need information or want to place an order. Now also suppose that you decide to change to another network provider, such as AOL or EarthLink. You will probably have to change your domain name because it was previously associated with AT&T and you no longer use their services. This means that every time that you change Internet website hosting providers, you have to give your customers a new web address. This is not a good idea since you will likely change ISPs as your needs evolve.

I set up my company's domain name so that it would be separate from any website-hosting provider. I can change providers without having to change my domain name or retrain my customers. This might seem like a small point, but it can be incredibly important if you want to change website providers, so I highly recommend that you set up a domain name that is independent of the underlying provider and tell your customers to use this site.

Once you establish an Internet-based electronic mail account with your ISP, talk with your ISP about registering a non-ISP specific domain name that is hosted by your ISP. In this way, you can minimize your headaches, use the same ISP for both your electronic mail and website hosting, and write one check for both services. I am now contacted through author@ edpaulson.com, which I then forward to whatever e-mail system I choose. In this way, I can change my e-mail provider without having to retrain my customers.

> **Listen Up**
>
> Internet domain names are a hot commodity. You should think of a name that you like, that is catchy, and that accurately depicts your company and register it right away. Use the WHOIS feature at www.internic. net to verify name availability, then go to your web hosting provider to get it registered.

> **Listen Up**
>
> It is a good idea to take the time and incur the added expense associated with owning your own domain name that is independent of your provider. This way, you can change providers without having to notify all your Internet customers of the name change.

Creating Your Website

Just look at you now—with your new ISP connection, your hot e-mail address, and your own personal website location. Oops! There isn't any information on your website! When people connect to your website, they get a blank screen or an exciting message such as "site under construction." Ugh! This is a really bad thing!

You fix this situation by creating *website content*, which is displayed when someone accesses your site with a browser. Content is actually a bunch of HTML-coded pages that display on your computer monitor, in a specific way, when the browser downloads and translates the information.

Talking Business

Your **website content** is the text and visuals (graphics) that are displayed on your website. Typical content includes company history, company logo, mail and phone addresses, products and services offered, and sales or marketing contact information.

HTML code is pretty cryptic for the uninitiated. Early website designers had to live with direct HTML coding to make any kind of attractive site. HTML is still around, but the software world has made it easier for normal people like you and me to create content by developing automated content-creation tools such as Microsoft FrontPage, ClarisWorks Internet Edition, and ColdFusion. These tools work similarly to any Windows graphic design utility, but the final output is an HTML file that can be placed on a website for viewing with a browser.

These content-creation tools are not for the computer novice, but they are also not so complicated that you need three college degrees and a pocket protector to create an attractive and functional website. Some people pay a contractor to create the initial site and then use it as a tool/example for training an employee so that the next round can be created internally.

All of this website technology is pretty impressive. But just wait until I talk about links. A *link* is a section of your HTML page that refers to another Internet location, such as another website. For example, assume that your company sells widgets for the XYZ Widget Company and that your website refers to the BANGO product also produced by XYZ Widget. Your website can include a link to the www.xyzwidget.com website location for additional information about the BANGO product. Your site is referring, or linking, the browser to the other website that you don't control. You are now taking advantage of XYZ Widget's website development effort by automatically sending your users to its site when they click the link. (Oh, by the way, your site may be in New Jersey, and the BANGO information may be on a site in Tokyo. It is all automatic to the person viewing the information and clicking the link.)

Talking Business

A **link** (short for *hyperlink*) is a section of a displayed web page. When clicked by the user, the link connects the user to the Internet site (or page) associated (or linked) with the clicked selection. Note that site visitors don't move around a site in a logical sequence but, instead, move around on an almost random basis depending on their interests.

Links can also refer to various locations in your own website, which is common when your site becomes longer than a few pages. In fact, the majority of your links refer to other pages within your own site. Links are easily created, tested, and managed using the technology built into the content-creation software packages mentioned earlier.

Here are a few words of caution regarding website creation strategies:

- Never forget that the site is a sales tool first and not some place to show "cool" stuff that does not contribute to your sales and advertising goals.

- Snazzy design is important, but not as important as providing the information that your clients want.

- Make your site easy to follow and user friendly.

- Keep the site information current and display the date that you last modified the page contents. If you do this, make sure that you regularly, such as monthly, update the content and the revision date to keep the site from looking outdated.

- Keep page sizes such that they can download in less than 20 seconds at slower modem speeds of 28.8 kbps. High-quality graphic images (such as of fine art) are an exception to this rule since the viewer will expect a high-quality graphic to take longer to download.

- Ask around for sites that people like, and model your initial site after what already works.

- Graphics (visual images) download slowly from the Internet, so keep the number and size of graphics on your site to a minimum. Make sure that your site designer knows about this requirement.

- Make sure that the content-creation software you use does not lock you into a specific browser type that excludes all others. As a result, people might not be able to view or use your site. For example, make sure that the content you create will at least work with both Microsoft Internet Explorer and Netscape Navigator.

- Anything you put on your site can also be viewed by your competition. Don't put it out there unless you want it found.

- Talk to your ISP about ways of obtaining site statistics so that you can determine how many people visited your site, where they went after visiting your site, and other important information.

- Also realize that people leave your site with a simple click of a mouse button. It is your job to make your site attractive and useful enough for them to stay.

What if you don't feel up to writing and designing your own website? Luckily, website design services are all over the place, and the competition is pretty fierce. Some are good, and some just don't get it. Make sure that you work with someone who understands that the site is first a business and sales tool and second a cool technology play toy.

For around $1,000, you should be able to get a decent site design that is functional. The monthly hosting of the site by a service provider should run between $15 and $1000, depending on the level of advanced services required and the size of the site.

As your website uses expand and your needs increase, you will need to align yourself with a site development company that can add highly sophisticated features to your site.

> ### Smoke Signals
>
> I have seen some cool, trendy sites that just did not get used. "Why?" you might ask. Simple. It took a lot of large graphics files to make them look flashy, and graphics take forever to download. In addition, they allowed content to suffer in favor of form. Even though the sites were flashy, they weren't very useful. Remember to make your site a useful business service tool for your customers. Check out tennis pro Andy Roddick's website (www.andyroddick.com) for an example of a site that is graphic intensive, handles a large volume of visitors, and has sophisticated features while providing its visitors with a high-quality experience of having "visited" Andy.

E-commerce is a natural extension of Internet access in that customers can both get information and order at the same time. Adding e-commerce to your site will greatly increase the site development costs and also expose your company to liability that you should be aware of. When you simply provided information, you did not obtain anything of a proprietary nature from your customers. And if someone hacked (electronically broke into) your site, he or she really couldn't do too much damage. Once you have credit card information, addresses, names, and other customer-confidential information entered into your site, you may become a hacker target. If successfully hacked, someone could obtain a lot of financial information about your customers that, if used illegally, could put your company in a precarious legal position.

Have a long talk with your e-commerce developer and ISP regarding hacking safeguards to make sure that any confidential customer information remains confidential. If you are not comfortable with their responses, you may want to put off your e-commerce venture or find other suppliers. Always check the privacy agreements published by service providers instead of taking someone's word for it. The written agreement is what is legally binding.

This section was designed to introduce you to the processes involved in creating your own website. The early process is not that difficult, and it can really be a lot of fun. Once your site is set up, you are sure that your customers are receiving your sales and marketing information in the way that you want. Start early on establishing a relationship with a developer, such as the ones who did the Andy Roddick site. In this way, you and they develop a realistic assessment of what will be involved to move your company's use of the Internet to its next and most profitable level.

Being Found on the Internet

Once you've got a beautiful, informative site, how can you ensure that surfers will find your page among the hundreds of thousands of sites out there? Luckily, *search engines* help web readers find the sites related to subjects that interest them.

Popular search engines include Yahoo! (www.yahoo.com), Google (www.google.com), and Excite (www.excite.com), among hundreds of others. You can go to one of these sites, type the subject you are interested in (business or parenting or stamps, for example), and you are given a list of links to sites that meet your criteria.

How do the search services collect all those lists? They use search engines to scan the Internet for new sites and determine the content of those sites.

You want to make sure that search engines can appropriately categorize your site. You can do this by learning a lot about the hidden *meta tags* that are used by search engines to categorize your site. (A hidden meta tag is information that is part of your content but is not visible on your site.) If you do not use meta tags properly, you can create a great site and nobody will know that it exists.

Talking Business

A **search engine** scans the Internet for new sites and determines how they should be categorized. Search engines make this determination based on a site's section headings, page content, and the site's hidden meta tags, also called metafields.

A **search service** is a website location where users can search for information on specific topics that may be contained on Internet sites. These services use search engines to scan the Internet for information.

Hidden **meta tags or metafields** include information embedded in the website content that is not displayed to the user. Search engines read them so the site can be properly categorized. Check your content-creation software for information about adding meta tags.

Finally, you should know that the search engines will make special arrangements that ensure that your name appears at the top of any search list result. This will cost you something but might be worthy of a discussion. This area of website relationships and cross-marketing is constantly evolving and becoming ever more complicated. There is an art and science involved in being listed at the top of any search related to your category. This is like being in the beginning of your section of the Yellow Pages, independent of your company name. Finding an expert in this area of search engine registration and placement services is not a bad idea if the Internet is planned to be an integral part of your business plan.

How do you find people who provide these services? Go to Google (www.google.com) and search on "search engine registration and placement services" or something else like that until you find companies that match your needs.

For Your Plan

If your company will provide web-based services as its core functionality, then the Business Description portion of your plan will present your idea in detail. The following points are intended primarily for companies who plan to use the Internet as an adjunct to their primary business operation, but these points in most cases apply to a web-based services company as well.

- ◆ Specify how you plan to name your site, your rationale for choosing that name, and verify that it is not only available but that you have already reserved it for your business.

- ◆ Explain how and when you will develop your first website, making sure that you outline the major functions that you expect this early design to provide to your customers. Attach a budgetary estimate for this step. Graphical mockups of the proposed site help at this stage.

- ◆ Outline the phases through which you expect your site will progress, detailing how and when this capability will be required and who will do the development. Include a budgetary estimate for this step.

- ◆ Explain your plans related to providing e-commerce and other advanced features to your site capabilities. This point ties in with the one just preceding.

- ◆ Provide links to competitor sites and then explain how your site will improve upon that already in place by the competition.

- ◆ Cover the technology background of company personnel as it specifically applies to Internet technology and how this background/technology synergy can facilitate internal company efficiencies.

On the CD

Once you have your domain name registered and your ISP selected, you need to create your website and learn how to effectively use all of this great Internet technology. Three bonus sections are included on the CD to help you make the most out of your Internet technology investment. The basics of how your browser works are included in the file "Browsing the Internet" (CD21-1). More advanced website design advice is provided in "Getting Fancy with Your Website " (CD21-3) and relating your e-mail needs to your ISP is explained in "Electronic Mail and Your ISP" (CD21-2). If you want to make the most out of your Internet presence, you should read these important bonus CD sections.

The Least You Need to Know

♦ The Internet is a computer-based public communication network with connections that span the globe and which can be used to promote and sell your company's offerings.

♦ Simple websites can be created easily using content-creation software, but you will need professional help to create more advanced site capabilities.

♦ Make sure your website is clean, clear, and up to date. Remember that it is primarily a sales and marketing tool for your business.

♦ You want to own the rights to your website and e-mail addresses so that you are not locked into using any particular service provider.

♦ Effectively using Internet-like technology will reduce personnel costs, improve customer communication and service, and increase technology spending.

The Kwik Chek Auto Evaluation Business Plan

Recommendations for Using This Business Plan

What follows is an actual business plan I wrote back in the late 1980s for a used car evaluation service business called Kwik Chek. I wrote this plan to determine whether the idea would fly as an independent investment with national franchise potential or whether I should go back to the drawing board and find a new idea. I did not want to actually operate one of the Kwik Chek services myself, which is important to understanding the conclusions. It is included as a model to help you write your own business plan for your own business.

Don't get lazy and try to use this plan as is. It won't work for you or your idea, even if you have the same idea! You will clearly need to do your own research, write your own content, create your own financial analysis, and fill in the sections in a way applicable to your particular business idea.

Although I did not implement the plan, it served its purpose at the time it was written. The plan showed that the idea wasn't right for me since I did not want to be doing the work on the cars myself, and the analysis shows that owner/operator management was the way to go. Notice that the plan did what was expected of it. It told me that this idea did not fit my criteria

Listen Up _____

The flow, format, style, analysis process, and presentation are what you should be looking at when you review the plan.

Don't get put off by the plan's data being from the 1980s. The analysis process is still very valid.

for a business venture that I wanted to sink my time and money into. For the right person who is willing to do the work required, this plan could easily be modified for presentation to investors or could be self-funded. (Make sure that you update the numbers for the current marketplace and verify that it still makes money before taking the plunge. Many of the referenced sources are still in existence and can be consulted for contemporary data.)

Use this plan as a road map for the development of your own plan, and don't take the specific plan content literally. Think of it as a sample shell into which you will pour your own content.

Remember also that your plan should address the questions of the intended readers—this means that sections can be added or deleted as needed. Your levels of detail, section flows, and writing style will differ from that presented in the Kwik Chek plan. That is okay. Just make sure that you include an executive summary, the business description, competition, marketing plan, organization personnel, operations, funding requirements, and financial statements sections. The industry analysis, market analysis, and conclusion section contents will vary based on the market familiarity of the intended readers. The more familiar your reader is with the target marketplace and its unique attributes, the less detailed these sections need to be. The less familiar your reader is, the greater the need for detailed explanations in these sections.

These next few points are very important.

1. Write the Executive Summary after you have completed the plan. This sequence keeps you from writing something that meets your "picture" of how things should be as opposed to how they really are as supported by plan data and analysis.

2. The overall plan contents should support the conclusions outlined in the Executive Summary.

3. The appendix should support the overall plan contents.

Remember that this Kwik Chek plan should serve as a model as you prepare your own business plan, but it should not, as written here, become your business plan. Your levels of detail, section flows, and writing style will differ from that presented in the Kwik Chek plan. That is okay. Your plan is just that: *your* plan for *your* company. No single sample plan can do justice to the numerous business opportunities and entrepreneur styles that exist. Read this plan as a guide, and make your plan your own. Good luck, and start writing.

Cover Sheet

(Do not include this "Cover Sheet" text on your actual cover sheet. They will know it is the cover sheet.)

Plan Number: _____   Presented to: _____   Date: _____

Kwik Chek, Inc.

(A Texas Corporation)

(Corporate Office)
123 Balcones Drive
Austin, TX 78751

Phone: (512) 555-5555
Fax: (512) 555-5556
Web URL: www.kwikchek.com

Primary Contact: John Doe, President and Founder

The management of Kwik Chek has prepared this business plan for the expressed purpose of securing funding from the parties to whom the plan is presented. This business plan and all of its contents, methods, data, procedures and other proprietary information are company confidential information. No part of this plan may be revealed, copied, or duplicated in any way without the expressed written permission of Kwik Chek management. Copyright © 1989 by Kwik Chek. All Rights Reserved.

Table of Contents

(Include page numbers on your final plan.)

Executive Summary

This plan presents Kwik Chek, a mobile used automobile inspection service, to determine whether it is a profitable business venture to pursue as either as investor or owner/operator. The report begins with a brief description of the service concept and then proceeds with an in-depth look at the services proposed, an in-depth look at the used car market for purchasing characteristics, an operational analysis of the requirements for providing the service, and a financial analysis of the cash flows expected over the first three years of operation.

The results of the study show that Kwik Chek, when treated as an absentee owner investment only, requires over $100,000 in cash to accommodate negative cash flows in the first year of operation and doesn't show a positive return on investment until Year 3 of operation.

Further analysis shows that Kwik Chek, when treated as an owner/operator business, still requires $70,000+ in cash, but it shows a positive return on investment in less than two years instead of three and shows a substantial positive cash flow in Year 3 and beyond. The return on investment time period is reduced by one year.

There is already competition in the used automobile inspection area, but there is substantial market share to be had by each entrant. The Kwik Chek analysis assumes that only 20 percent market penetration is achieved by Kwik Chek to achieve the goals outlined—this is reasonable given the anticipated competitive environment.

The owner/operator scenario requires less initial investment, it shows a positive return in two years instead of three, and also provides increased cash flow in Year 3 and beyond. For these reasons, Kwik Chek should be offered to mechanic/investor groups who want to own and operate the business while establishing themselves for the long term as a service to the used car industry. The number of used car customers will continue to grow as the number of licensed drivers continues to grow, and the expected life of automobiles continues to be extended through higher quality manufacturing.

It is not recommended that an absentee owner pursue Kwik Chek as strictly an investment because the return on investment period is over three years and the longer-term positive cash flows are nominal. It is, however, recommended as an investment for an owner/operator who can serve as both owner and inspection technician with another family member working as dispatcher. This scenario provides the family with an opportunity to generate in excess of $100,000 in household income by the end of Year 2.

A Description of the Proposed Kwik Chek Service

Kwik Chek is a user vehicle inspection service designed to provide prospective buyers with objective information about the mechanical condition of the vehicle that they intend to purchase. The inspection is performed at the vehicle's location, and a complete report of the mechanical and electrical condition of the car is provided. Kwik Chek inspects automobiles and light trucks.

To schedule an appointment, the customer telephones a local Kwik Chek office and schedules a time and location for the inspection. In this way, the customer does not have to "borrow" the car to bring it to a mechanic and the vehicle seller does not run the risk of someone unknown driving the car around town. When the inspection is completed, the customer is provided with a sheet detailing the condition of the vehicle. In total, approximately 90 points are inspected. The customer can be assured that the major vehicle components will be inspected and that any major defects will surface during the inspection.

Listen Up

Notice that this description not only provides details about the service being provided but also presents the major customer benefits derived from using the service. The reader not only knows what Kwik Chek is about but also why someone would be interested in using the service. Notice that everyone has experience with buying or selling a car, so you can assume a certain level of familiarity with the need for this type of service. Gauge your description to your reader's experience level with respect to your industry. The detailed listing of inspected vehicle components simply adds credibility to your story by showing that you have thought out the details.

A detailed listing of the inspections performed during a Kwik Chek inspection is included in the next section.

The inspection time takes around 40 minutes once the mechanic is set up. Each Kwik Chek technician is an experienced mechanic. The equipment in the Kwik Chek van is designed to streamline the inspection process as much as possible. (See Exhibit X for a detailed listing of van equipment.)

The primary benefit being purchased by the user is the peace of mind associated with an objective, informed, third-party opinion of the purchase. Most people want to know what they are buying and not be surprised by major defects later when the vehicle is theirs. The Kwik Chek information can also be used by both buyer and seller as a negotiating tool to achieve a more equitable price for the vehicle.

A major benefit of using Kwik Chek over the existing method of inspection (that is, bringing the car to a mechanic) is the convenience of having the car inspected without borrowing the car or interrupting the customer's day to have the car inspected.

In essence, the benefits associated with the Kwik Chek service are peace of mind and convenience. The major marketing questions are how many people are willing to pay for the service, and at what price? The Market and Industry Revenue Potential Analysis section addresses these important marketing-related issues.

Kwik Chek Tests Performed

Engine Diagnostics

Compression

Rotor

Cap

Capacitor (as required)

Points (as required)

Electronic ignition

Oil leakage

Spark plug fouling

Spark plug wires

Belts

Exhaust for age and leaks

Oil consumption/burning

Suspension and Steering

Tire wear

Shock absorbers

Alignment (from tire wear in front)

Torsion bars tightness

Cracked leaf springs

Spare tire condition

Brakes

Check pads/shoes for wear

Check one rotor/drum for wear

Check for pulling when breaking

Check emergency brake

Accessories

AM/FM radio/cassette

Power windows

Power locks

Power seats

Air conditioning

Heater and fan speeds

Gauges

Speedometer/odometers

Cigarette lighter

Windshield washer

Windshield wiper operation and blade condition

Transmission

All speeds

Clutch slip and adjust (manual)

Reverse

Lights

Headlights (low/high)

Turn signals

Hazard lights

Backup lights

License plate lights

Dome lights

Instrument cluster lights

Outside lights

Fluid Levels and Condition

Oil

Transmission

Differential

Clutch

Brake

Coolant plus hoses for leaks

Battery

Washer fluid

Steering

Hydrometer test of coolant for anti-freeze

Electrical

Alternator charging

Battery load test

Slow leak test

Body

Undercoating

Accident repairs

Rust

Fading/peeling paint

Proper closure of doors and windows

Mirrors (inside and out)

Trailer hitch hook-up residuals

The Market and Industry Analysis

The automobile marketplace has been in a state of transition since the beginning of the 1980s. There has been a trend in recent years away from purchasing new automobiles and toward purchasing an automobile on the used car market.

It has recently become common knowledge to the general public that a new car purchased from a dealer loses a tremendous amount of its resale value almost immediately. This amount of initial loss is generally financed and paid for by the owner over a three- to five-year period and consequently does not get amortized as quickly as the

Listen Up

This section presents the big-picture case for the service. It helps the reader understand the nuances related to the marketplace and its trends over the past decade or so. In this way, the reader learns that this is not a temporary opportunity but one indicative of a longer-lasting nature.

car loses its money. A used car, on the other hand, does not lose value as quickly after purchase because the bulk of the "new car" depreciation has already occurred by the time of purchase.

Data from the 1988 Motor Vehicle Manufacturers Association Facts and Figures, as shown in the following table, shows that the total number of registered vehicles on the road today has increased steadily from 1980 to 1988, and the mean and median ages have also increased.

Registrations and Vehicle Ages

	1980	1988
Registered vehicles	150 million	180 million
Mean age of vehicles	6.6 years	7.6 years
Median age of vehicles	6.0 years	6.8 years

There are many possible reasons for this recent trend. The increased need for fuel-efficient cars, combined with difficult financial times for the public at large, have made people more cautious about how they spend their money. They are tending to treat an automobile purchase as an investment decision, rather than an impulse buy.

The major problem with a used automobile is that the buyer generally purchases the vehicle in "as-is" condition. The buyer is typically unaware of the mechanical condition of the vehicle and consequently purchases the vehicle on faith that it does not have major mechanical or electrical problems that will substantially increase the overall cost of ownership.

The current alternative to buying on faith is to take the car to a mechanic for a complete mechanical review. This action takes time and money on the part of the buyer, and trust by the seller. In addition, the scheduling of the mechanical inspection is typically done during the day when the buyer is at work. In essence, it is a hassle. Consequently, even though everyone agrees that an independent inspection is a good idea, few people actually have the inspection done.

From the seller's perspective, it is valuable to have an independent inspection report of the mechanical condition of the vehicle to assure potential buyers that there are no hidden defects in the vehicle.

This procedure is similar to that done when a person buys a house and arranges an inspection of the physical condition of the house. In some states, it is a legal requirement to have a house inspection before the house can be sold. Because a house and a car are typically the two largest purchases the average person makes in a lifetime, it stands to reason that they should both be treated with the same level of care.

It makes intuitive sense that a service that offers reliable mechanical inspection of vehicles in a convenient way and for a reasonable price would be well received by the used-vehicle buying public.

Market Opportunity Estimate

It is assumed that the Kwik Chek service proposed would be most applicable to used car purchases because new car purchases come with a warranty, providing the purchaser with post-purchase security. This report concentrates on the used car market as the potential opportunity for Kwik Chek. It initially looks to verify the business concept in the Austin, Texas area and then expand it across the country if shown viable.

The Scarborough Report on Austin Automobile Purchases for 1988 shows that 31 percent of all adults in Austin are planning to purchase an automobile, and 47 percent of those are planning a used car purchase. This implies that 14 percent (47 percent of 31 percent = 14 percent) of all adults in Austin are planning a used car purchase within the next year. (See Exhibit I.)

There are 569,000 adults in the Austin SMSA according to the most recent Census data. Fourteen percent of this number (those estimated to be looking to purchase a used vehicle) indicates that it can be estimated that 81,190 (569,000 × .14) used cars will be purchased each year. (See Exhibit I.)

The Scarborough report also shows that, on a national basis, 23,386,400 used cars were purchased in 1988. Of these, 7,607,172 (33 percent) were purchased from dealers according to the Wards report. It is then assumed that the remaining 15,779,228 (67 percent) were purchased on the open market. (See Exhibit I.)

Listen Up

Notice that this section so far helps the reader understand not only the total number of used cars that will be purchased in Austin over the next 12 months, but also that 67 percent of these cars will be purchased on the open market, with the remaining 33 percent being purchased from dealers. Also note that the reader is clearly made aware that 67 percent/33 percent national average ratio being applied to the Austin market is a clearly stated "assumption" on my part. They may not agree, but there is also no sleight of hand here.

For purposes of analysis, it is assumed that the 33 percent dealer/67 percent open market ratio outlined in the previous paragraph of used car purchases is indicative of the entire nation, including Austin, in determining the number of used cars purchased from dealers or on the open market.

Referring to Exhibit II, it can be seen that Austin should be purchasing more used automobiles than indicated in Exhibit I because the total purchases divided by the total registrations indicates a holding period of 4.6 years per purchased vehicle. This is more than the 3 to 4 years indicated by the *Medical Economics Journal*, February 6, 1989, page 174.

Listen Up

These last two paragraphs provide justification to the reader that I am not being too aggressive with my estimates. In fact, I make the case that, if anything, the number of used cars that could use the Kwik Chek service is actually larger than that estimated here. This is always good news to investors who want you to have more people to sell to instead of fewer. Makes sense to me.

The estimated new car purchases are assumed accurate because they come from manufacturer data. An increase in the total number of used cars purchased would decrease the holding period for vehicles and indicate a larger turnover than estimated for this analysis. A larger turnover would decrease the holding period and make it closer to the 3 to 4 years estimated. Consequently, it is assumed that this analysis is conservative and reflects a slightly pessimistic case for analysis.

These unit market potential estimates will be tied in with the pricing and other pertinent data to present Kwik Chek's projected financial performance.

Pricing of Kwik Chek Inspections

Exhibit III reflects the price demand curve for the Kwik Chek service at different prices. The curve is derived from data obtained from a survey of prospective purchasers of the service. The curve indicates that only 70 percent of prospective customers would use the service at any price and that with a service price of more than $110, none would use the service. The curve is most flat in the $40 to $60 range, with most people saying that $49 sounded "about right." It should also be noted that some mentioned a tendency to price the evaluation service at a percentage of the purchase price of the vehicle in question.

Verification of the $49 price came from the Credit Union National Association *Guide to Buying and Selling a Used Car*. The guide indicates that "If you think this is a car you want, hire a mechanic or car care center to evaluate the car. You can usually do so for $40 or less."

Based on the added convenience of performing the evaluation on site instead of having to take it to a mechanic as is assumed in the Credit Union guide, a $49.95 price seems reasonable and justifiable. A graph of Exhibit III data indicates that with a price of $49.95, the available market of potential users of the Kwik Chek service becomes 37.5 percent of the total number of used car purchasers.

In summary, Kwik Chek proposes to offer its service to the general public for $49.95 and expects that 37.5 of all possible used car purchasers are viable prospects for using the service at that price.

It should also be noted that national purchases are somewhat seasonal in nature, as indicated from the Scarborough report data shown in Exhibit IV. The peak buying season appears to be March (9.6 percent of purchases) through August, with the end of the year and the beginning of the year relatively slow (6.98 percent of purchases according to Exhibit IV). It is recommended that Kwik Chek be introduced to the buying public in January to allow familiarity with the concept in time for the March to August buying peak. The moderate Austin climate may reduce some of this seasonality, but it should be assumed pertinent in areas that experience cold winters.

As mentioned previously, 33 percent of all used cars are purchased from dealers. Kwik Chek can provide a similar service to the dealers as it intends to provide on the open market. The dealers will probably want a discount of 20 to 25 percent off the retail price, based upon past experience of Kwik Chek management. Kwik Chek can justify this discount because of the ease of inspection of many vehicles in the same location, instead of many locations all over the city. The reduced travel time reduces time and travel expenses, which enable the lower dealer price. The dealers will use Kwik Chek so that their mechanics can be working on more expensive and complicated repairs.

It is assumed that there will be two classes of service: (1) the dealer service at $39 per inspection, and (2) the open market at $49.95 per inspection.

Listen Up

Notice that this pricing discussion is based on "real world" feedback in the form of personal interviews and then verified with a reality that already exists in the marketplace. This type of confirmation helps to add credibility to your estimates and assumptions. It accepts a mid-range price as a way of getting more customers and selling more inspections.

Listen Up

Notice that the plan has now laid the foundation for a total revenue potential analysis. The assumptions related to the total number of unit sales are presented, as are the dealer and open market pricing estimates. It is now time to do the math and see where the national and Austin revenue potential winds up. These estimates are shown in the next section.

Market Sales Potential

Exhibit V indicates that at the $49.95 price, and with estimated 37.5 percent of the used car buyers as potential customers, the total U.S. revenue potential is $438M. This exhibit also shows that if 20 percent of national potential customers use the Kwik Chek service, $87.6M in sales will be generated. It is assumed by management that Kwik Chek cannot obtain more than 20 percent penetration due to competition. Note that this exhibit and Exhibit VI do not include a breakdown for dealer/open market inspections. This breakdown is presented in Exhibits VII and VIII.

Exhibit VI indicates that the Austin market alone has a total potential market of $1.5M at the $49.95 price, and that a 20 percent penetration of that market will generate $304,000 in annual revenues.

Exhibit VII indicates that the national potential revenues with 20 percent penetration of both the dealer and open markets is $76M, down from the previous $87M estimate but still a substantial number.

Exhibit VIII outlines the same breakdown as mentioned in the previous paragraph, but for the Austin area. It is seen that Austin can be expected to generate $282,000 in revenues and perform 6,090 inspections per year with 20 percent potential market penetration.

Listen Up

We now have total possible revenue projections for the Austin marketplace and for the nation. These projections are based on market conditions, *not* what I think should be true, other than the assumptions that are intrinsic to the analysis. It is now time to determine if Kwik Chek, its owners, and investors can financially survive with these revenue projections and to assess its competitive challenges.

Competition

Kwik Chek already has two competitors in the Austin area: Auto Chek and No Lemons. In addition, a potential competitor named CheckOut may be about to launch a national franchise.

Auto Chek

Auto Chek has been in business for almost one year. The president is a successful entrepreneur who recently sold another company and started Auto Chek a short time afterward.

The president has every intention of making Auto Chek a national franchise and has already sold the franchise rights to an organization in Dallas and San Antonio.

Auto Chek wants an initial franchise fee of $25,000 and an 8 percent royalty on sales. It has advertised a great deal in Austin, but an informal survey of people regarding the service showed that there is awareness of the service but not the name of the company. There is a potential free rider opportunity available to Kwik Chek.

Auto Chek charges $49.50 for its services and checks 90 points on each car, making it comparable with the Kwik Chek offering.

No Lemons

No Lemons has come onto the market in the past month. It charges $59.50 for its service and claims to inspect 120 points, but it inflates the number a little (by treating each tire as an inspection point, wipers as two inspection points instead of one, and so on).

Rumor around town is that many dealers are shying away from doing business with No Lemons. We intend to find out more about what these problems may be between No Lemons and the dealerships to determine if there is an opportunity here for Kwik Chek. It is definitely in the market and already out there with a van and providing the service. No Lemons is planning to franchise nationally. Fees and royalty information were not available.

CheckOut

CheckOut is an inspection company in New Jersey that has been providing services for over five years but is confined primarily to the New Jersey/New York area. It charges $59 for its service and checks around 90 points.

CheckOut is rumored to have started a national franchise, but to date, I haven't found evidence of that being the case.

Marketing and Sales Strategy

The most powerful tool for promoting Kwik Chek's success is positive word of mouth where one satisfied user tells several friends about the value received from using the service. This applies equally well for the dealer and open market segments, with the dealer segment involving a much smaller number of people. The most difficult initial problem is increasing the public's awareness about the service availability and benefits. A special referral reward system should be established where a person can earn a free inspection for recommending 10 people for the service. Vouchers can be used to track the referrals.

A monthly marketing expense of $2,500 is assumed, and it should be spent in the following areas:

Monthly Yellow Pages advertising	½ page ad at $1,200 per month = $1,200
Direct-mail pieces to dealers	200 pieces at $1 each = $200
Direct-mail pieces to households	$400 as an insert in a bulk mailing pack
Commissions for part-time sales	$700 per month at 10 percent of partial revenues

It is also assumed that around $10,000 will be spent during the first few months on radio and newspaper advertising. In addition, special promotions should be set up with the dealers around town in conjunction with radio simulcasts where free used car inspections are provided if you bring your car in for inspection while the radio station is broadcasting and on-site.

Given the more ready access to the dealer market and its decision makers, a special sales push will be applied to the dealer segment during the first few months of operation. The special emphasis to the dealer will be that using Kwik Chek to inspect the cars is less expensive than them paying their own mechanics to perform the check. This is justified by the assumption that the dealer pays around $70 per mechanic hour, including overhead and benefits, and a 40-minute inspection would cost the dealership $47 and revenue lost by that mechanic not being able to repair a dealership customer's car. At $39 per inspection, Kwik Chek should be attractive to the dealership.

Listen Up

Notice that this plan not only presents details with respect to advertising and sales activities in the first few months of operation, but also provides a rationale as to why this approach is taken.

Operations Plan

Exhibit IX outlines the logistical analysis used to determine the total number of vans that would be required to address Austin at the 20 percent penetration rate. Twenty percent was used to determine the state of the company when working at its peak efficiency.

It is assumed that inspections are provided 11 hours per day, 7 days per week. Dealer inspections will occur during the week, and open market inspection will occur additionally on the weekends and evenings. Initially one person may try covering this number of hours and, if successful, a second person should be added to reduce hours to a normal work week for both.

It is assumed that a dealer inspection will constitute 33 percent of inspections. Using the estimated 40-minute inspection time per vehicle, dealer inspection of each vehicle is expected to take 0.67 hours (40/60 minutes). The open market inspections cannot be scheduled closer than 1.5-hour (90 minute) intervals due to 45 minutes of assumed travel times between appointments and other unforeseen circumstances.

Listen Up

Notice the level of detail included with this operational assessment. There is a quantifiable justification for the analysis and its findings, which is substantially different from just projecting hunches. With these numeric estimates, the reader can make his or her own determination as to the validity of the analysis, and you have something concrete and specific to discuss in coming to agreement. Notice the comment related to adding another driver to cover part of the 77 hour work week. This is a decision usually made on the fly, but at least you start with some concrete idea of requirements.

Based on these assumptions—and the 33 percent dealer/67 percent open market split mentioned previously—a maximum of 272 inspections can be performed by one van in one month. The chart indicates that at the 20 percent penetration rate, an average of 1.9 vans will be needed to meet estimated maximum demand in Austin.

It is recommended to start out with one van with Mr. Doe performing the inspections and then add a technician along with progression to a second van when the number of inspections warrants the addition, sometime in Year 2 of operation when the total number of monthly inspections approaches the maximum per van of 272 indicated in Exhibit IX. (See Exhibit XI and XII for inspection rampup details.)

The initial plan is for the Kwik Chek office to operate out of Mr. Doe's home, which is assumed acceptable since customers will never have to visit the office. All inspections take place at the customer's location and not at the Kwik Chek office.

The van driver/mechanic will carry a cellular phone and also have a two-way radio so that scheduled appointments can be passed to the driver on a real-time basis. It is important that drivers and the dispatcher/office telephone operator be in regular communication with each other to ensure that customer schedules are kept and delays are immediately acted upon and relayed to the customer.

The Management Team

John Doe is the author of this plan and the president of the new company. He has worked as a mechanic for over 10 years and has experience repairing both domestic and imported automobiles. He has served as the shop foreman for the local Ford dealership for the past two years. His foreman duties also include profit and loss projections for the service segment of the local dealerships operation. Mr. Doe will be the initial inspection technician, with others hired as business grows.

His wife, Judy, intends to work as the secretary/dispatcher to make the initial Austin, Texas operation a success and to improve their income from the business. She has experience as both a switchboard operator for a large corporation and as an executive secretary.

Mr. Doe has a wide network of mechanic colleagues who are interested in working with Kwik Chek once the idea proves successful.

Financial Analysis

This section presents a detailed financial analysis of the Kwik Chek business idea. It first looks at the variable and fixed costs associated with the business operation. This section includes a profit analysis for each van, determines the break-even number of inspections needed to support the van and its driver, and then ties the pieces together into a complete profit and loss analysis over a three-year period.

Fixed- and Variable-Cost Analysis

Exhibit X outlines the fixed and variable costs associated with the operation of Kwik Chek.

It can be seen that the van with its equipment has a cost of $24,140. If financed over a three-year period at 10 percent interest rate, this becomes a payment of $779 per month. It is also assumed that a technician/mechanic is dedicated to the van with a salary of $1,800 per month, which is initially paid to Mr. Doe. Adding in paging, service, and maintenance, the fixed costs associated with operating a van are expected to be $2,925 per month.

The general overhead cost is outlined in Exhibit X to be $7,191 per month. This number assumes that most equipment such as computers, copiers, and so on will be financed over a three-year period at 10 percent for a monthly payment of $336. It also assumes a secretary who doubles as an appointment scheduler and earns $1,500 per month and $2,500 in monthly marketing expenses. The general overhead number also includes a $417 monthly amortization of a franchise fee of $15,000 that is equally divided over 36 months. All appointments for inspection are scheduled through the main office operator/dispatcher. This $7,191 figure includes 20 percent margin for error to allow for things that were not initially anticipated, so it should reflect a maximum amount.

Exhibit X also shows that the variable costs associated with dealer inspection is $10, and it is $11 for the open market inspection because gas mileage is involved. Included in this cost is a $5 incentive to the mechanic for each inspection performed and paid for by the customer. This is to keep the drivers motivated to complete as many inspections as possible while assuring quality work.

It can be seen from Exhibit X that total contribution to overhead for operations when at 20 percent (and working with 2 vans) is $16,475 per month. The total overhead (fixed cost) is expected to be $13,040 (2 × $6,520), which leaves the net profit before taxes at $3,435. Up to this point, there has not been any allowance for owner income other than the income earned by Mr. Doe as the test technician. At this point, it appears that the maximum before-tax income to the owner of the Austin Kwik Chek franchise would be $3,435 per month or $41,220 per year. If the franchise were owned as a subchapter S-corporation, the owner would still need to pay taxes on this amount.

Listen Up

Notice also the level of detail included in this analysis. There is a lot of information here, and a case can be made for it being a reasonable projection of the future. The breakeven numbers provide initial operational goals to shoot for so that, at a minimum, the business is paying for itself with Mr. Doe at least taking home some salary.

It is also seen from Exhibit X that the inspection break-even for the entire operation with 2 vans is 402 inspections and that the incremental costs associated with another van are covered with 90 inspections.

Overall Financial Analysis

Exhibit XI shows the financial results expected from Kwik Chek operation when the owner is not involved with the inspections. Exhibit XII shows the expected financial results when the owner actually performs inspections from one of the vans. The owner/operator actually makes the $20,000 allocated to the van operator and retains whatever profits are left over at the end of the year.

Listen Up

Look at how important that cumulative cash flow number is to the total attractiveness assessment of this business venture. Notice also that the company hits its break-even point somewhere between month 12 and the end of Year 2. If the break-even quantity is reached earlier than in month 12, then the amount of cash required to open the business is reduced and the return on investment improves accordingly.

It is assumed that Kwik Chek acquires one percent additional market share for each month it is in operation. At the end of the second year, Kwik Chek is assumed to be at the 20 percent penetration target.

The chart also indicates that there is a substantial negative cumulative cash flow during the first year. The peak negative value is $102,026 for absentee owners and $72,000 for the owner/operator. The profits derived by the second year of operation begin to erode the negative cumulative cash situation. Kwik Chek is still in a negative cumulative cash flow situation by the end of Year 3 for the absentee investors but shows a positive turn for owner/operators. Absentee owner/investors begin to show a return on their investment beginning in Year 4.

The chart shows that the company operates with a negative net operating income over the first year of existence for absentee investors and turns slightly positive for the owner/operator and turns positive for both scenarios in Year 2. The owner/operator stands to make substantial money after the first year should business plan projections be accurate.

An additional van is required during the second year to meet market demands. When included in the expenses of the second and ongoing years, Kwik Chek can be expected to yield a net profit before tax of $41,208 for absentee owners and $89,808 for owner/operators.

Anyone who invests in a Kwik Chek franchise must be willing to risk between $70,000 and $100,000 in cash and wait between 2 and 4 years for a positive return on that investment.

Summary and Conclusion

It can be seen from the previous discussion that the investment potential of a Kwik Chek franchise is not a viable option for a person who treats it exclusively as an investment.

Exhibit XII shows what happens to the financials of the project if the owner is also the mechanic for the first van. This creates a saving on two counts: (1) The $5 incentive per inspection is not needed to motivate the mechanic because the mechanic is the owner, and (2) there is an $18,000 savings per year in the salary paid the mechanic.

It can be seen from Exhibit XII that there is still a substantial negative cumulative cash flow for the first year, but, for the investor scenario, the cash flow drain reverses direction in Month 11 as opposed to some time in Year 2. We see that the project becomes a positive cumulative cash flow project by the end of Year 2 and becomes a generator of substantial cumulative cash, $107,841, in Year 3.

It still requires $75,000 (plus living expenses) to ensure minimum cash reserves for the business. If the marketing penetration rampup is greater than expected, then the business will generate cash faster.

It is thus concluded that Kwik Chek is not a viable investment for someone who does not intend to operate the business himself, performing inspections in one of the vans. It does not generate a positive return on investment until Year 3 and requires over $100,000 in cash reserves to start. This time frame is simply too long for most investors.

If a person wants to invest his own time in the project and operate one of the vans, then there is substantial future revenue-earning potential from Year 3 onward. There is still over $75,000 in cash required to fund the business, but the long-term prospects for return are much improved over treating the project as only an investment.

Kwik Chek should be started in Austin by a mechanic who wants to start his or her own business. If it begins to show the returns expected, then the project should be set up for national franchising to mechanic/investor groups who want to provide the service. At that time, additional funding can be obtained based upon the company's successful track record.

Exhibits

Exhibit I: Scarborough Report on Automobile Purchases

From the Scarborough Report on Austin automobile purchases (1988)

Percent of adults planning to purchase a car:	31%
(This fact implies that people change cars every 3.2 years)	
Percent of adults planning a used car purchase:	14%
Total number of Austin SMSA adults:	569,355
Percent of women adults buying used cars:	69%
Total number of planned used car purchases:	81,190
Women planning to buy a used car:	56,021
Men planning to buy a used car:	25,169

Notes:
1) The median price range for women's purchases is $6,900
2) The median price range for men's purchases is $10,300
3) The bulk of those buying used cars have median incomes of $27,000
4) The total number of licensed drivers in the U.S.=   164,000,000
   There are   Number of male drivers=   85,000,000
                Number of female drivers=   79,000,000

Assuming the Austin ratios for adults purchasing used cars is valid for the
the entire U.S., then we can assume that the total number of used car purchases
in a year are:

Total number of drivers:	164,000,000
Percent buying used cars:	14%
Percent buying new cars:	16%
Total used car purchases:	23,386,400
Cars purchased by women:	16,136,616
Cars purchased by men:	7,249,784
Cars purchased from dealers:	7,607,172 [from Wards, p. 166]
Cars purchased on open market:	15,779,228

Exhibit II: Validation of Conservative Estimates

To determine whether Austin is representative of the U.S. in general, we
can compare the new car purchases nationally to those expected in Austin.
Austin is expecting new car percentage purchases of 15.5%.

New car information:

1988 new vehicle purchases:	15,245,843
Percent of licensed drivers:	9%

This information indicates that the national average of used car
purchases may actually be higher than that seen in Austin.

Total new car purchases:	15,245,843
Used car purchases:	23,386,400
Total annual purchases:	38,632,243
Total registered vehicles:	179,000,000
Percent purchases to registration:	22%
Average holding period:	5

The national average for holding a car is 3-4 years. These numbers
indicate that the numbers used for analysis are conservative and that
more used cars are probably sold annually than predicted.

Sources:
Motor Vehicles Manufacturers Association Facts and Figures (1988)
Wards Automotive Yearbook, 1989

Exhibit III: Price Demand Curve

Price ($)	Demand	Tot Rev ($)
0	100	0
20	70	1,400
40	50	2,000
50	38	1,875
60	25	1,500
110	0	0

Exhibit IV: Seasonality of Buyer Purchasing Habits (1987-1988)

Month	1987	% of total	Cumulative %	1988	% of total	Cumulative %
1	1,001,879	5.99%	5.99%	1,211,704	6.98%	6.98%
2	1,249,911	7.48%	13.47%	1,412,058	8.14%	15.12%
3	1,527,827	9.14%	22.62%	1,667,601	9.61%	24.73%
4	1,554,248	9.30%	31.92%	1,493,641	8.61%	33.34%
5	1,464,754	8.76%	40.68%	1,629,931	9.39%	42.74%
6	1,584,114	9.48%	50.16%	1,634,603	9.42%	52.16%
7	1,478,519	8.85%	59.01%	1,426,720	8.22%	60.38%
8	1,522,813	9.11%	68.12%	1,446,218	8.34%	68.72%
9	1,413,512	8.46%	76.58%	1,339,803	7.72%	76.44%
10	1,330,895	7.96%	84.54%	1,381,685	7.96%	84.40%
11	1,231,478	7.37%	91.91%	1,313,526	7.57%	91.97%
12	1,352,231	8.09%	100.00%	1,392,945	8.03%	100.00%
	16,712,181			17,350,435		

Exhibit V: National Potential Sales in Units and Dollars at 5, 10,& 20% Penetration

Month	1988 Percent	Used Car Sales (Units)	Total Kwik Chek Market @ $49.95 (Units)	Total Kwik Chek Revenues @ $49.95 (Dollars)	At a 5% Penetration of Total Market (Units)	At a 5% Penetration of Total Market (Dollars)	At a 10% Penetration of Total Market (Units)	At a 10% Penetration of Total Market (Dollars)	At a 20% Penetration of Total Market (Units)	At a 20% Penetration of Total Market (Dollars)
January	6.98%	1,633,238	612,464	$30,592,594	30,623	$1,529,630	61,246	$3,059,259	122,493	$6,118,519
February	8.14%	1,903,293	713,735	$35,651,048	35,687	$1,782,552	71,373	$3,565,105	142,747	$7,130,210
March	9.61%	2,247,735	842,901	$42,102,891	42,145	$2,105,145	84,290	$4,210,289	168,580	$8,420,578
April	8.61%	2,013,257	754,971	$37,710,821	37,749	$1,885,541	75,497	$3,771,082	150,994	$7,542,164
May	9.39%	2,196,960	823,860	$41,151,814	41,193	$2,057,591	82,386	$4,115,181	164,772	$8,230,363
June	9.42%	2,203,258	826,222	$41,269,771	41,311	$2,063,489	82,622	$4,126,977	165,244	$8,253,954
July	8.22%	1,923,055	721,146	$36,021,228	36,057	$1,801,061	72,115	$3,602,123	144,229	$7,204,246
August	8.34%	1,949,336	731,001	$36,513,505	36,550	$1,825,675	73,100	$3,651,351	146,200	$7,302,701
September	7.72%	1,805,901	677,213	$33,826,784	33,861	$1,691,339	67,721	$3,382,678	135,443	$6,765,357
October	7.96%	1,862,353	698,382	$34,884,203	34,919	$1,744,210	69,838	$3,488,420	139,676	$6,976,841
November	7.57%	1,770,483	663,931	$33,163,353	33,197	$1,658,168	66,393	$3,316,335	132,786	$6,632,671
December	8.03%	1,877,530	704,074	$35,168,491	35,204	$1,758,425	70,407	$3,516,849	140,815	$7,033,698
		23,386,400	8,769,900	$438,056,505	438,495	$21,902,825	876,990	$43,805,651	1,753,980	$87,611,301

Notes:

1) 1988 percentages taken from Exhibit IV: Seasonality of Buyer Purchasing Habits
2) Used car sales derived from data in Exhibit II for total national used car purchases
3) Total Kwik Chek market derived from Exhibit III. 37.5% demand expected at $50 pricing
4) 20% penetration is the maximum expected due to future entrants and other competition

Exhibit VI: Austin Potential Sales in Units and Dollars at 5, 10, & 20% Penetration

Month	1988 Percent	Used Car Sales (Units)	Total Kwik Chek Market @ $49.95 (Units)	Total Kwik Chek Revenues @ $49.95 (Dollars)	At a 5% Penetration of Total Market (Units)	At a 5% Penetration of Total Market (Dollars)	At a 10% Penetration of Total Market (Units)	At a 10% Penetration of Total Market (Dollars)	At a 20% Penetration of Total Market (Units)	At a 20% Penetration of Total Market (Dollars)
January	6.98%	5,670	2,126	$106,208	106	$5,310	213	$10,621	425	$21,242
February	8.14%	6,608	2,478	$123,769	124	$6,188	248	$12,377	496	$24,754
March	9.61%	7,803	2,926	$146,168	146	$7,308	293	$14,617	585	$29,234
April	8.61%	6,989	2,621	$130,920	131	$6,546	262	$13,092	524	$26,184
May	9.39%	7,627	2,860	$142,866	143	$7,143	286	$14,287	572	$28,573
June	9.42%	7,649	2,868	$143,275	143	$7,164	287	$14,328	574	$28,655
July	8.22%	6,676	2,504	$125,054	125	$6,253	250	$12,505	501	$25,011
August	8.34%	6,767	2,538	$126,763	127	$6,338	254	$12,676	508	$25,353
September	7.72%	6,270	2,351	$117,436	118	$5,872	235	$11,744	470	$23,487
October	7.96%	6,465	2,425	$121,107	121	$6,055	242	$12,111	485	$24,221
November	7.57%	6,147	2,305	$115,132	115	$5,757	230	$11,513	461	$23,026
December	8.03%	6,518	2,444	$122,094	122	$6,105	244	$12,209	489	$24,419
		81,190	30,446	$1,520,790	1,522	$76,040	3,045	$152,079	6,089	$304,158

Notes:
1) 1988 percentages taken from Exhibit IV: Seasonality of Buyer Purchasing Habits
2) Used car sales derived from data in Exhibit I for total Austin used car purchases
3) Total Kwik Chek market derived from Exhibit III. 37.5% demand expected at $50 pricing
4) 20% penetration is the maximum expected due to future entrants and other competition

Exhibit VII: National Dealer/Open Market Potential Sales in Units and Dollars at 10 & 20% Penetration

Dealer Percentage: 33%
Open Market Percentage: 67%

Month	1988 Percent	Used Car Sales (Units)	Total Kwik Chek Market @ 37.5% (Units)	Potential Dealer Sales @ 33% (Units)	Dealer Revenues @ 10% Penetrat. of Dealer Potential & $39 Price (Dollars)	Dealer Revenues @ 20% Penetrat. of Dealer Potential & $39 Price (Dollars)	Potential Open Market Sales @ 67% (Units)	Open Market Revenues @ 10% Penetrat. of Open Mrkt. Potential & $49 Price (Dollars)	Open Market Revenues @ 20% Penetrat. of Open Mrkt. Potential & $49 Price (Dollars)
January	8.14%	1,903,293	713,735	232,165	$905,443	$1,810,887	481,570	$2,405,441	$4,810,882
February	9.61%	2,247,735	842,901	274,180	$1,069,303	$2,138,607	568,720	$2,840,758	$5,681,517
March	8.61%	2,013,257	754,971	245,579	$957,756	$1,915,512	509,393	$2,544,417	$5,088,835
April	9.39%	2,196,960	823,860	267,987	$1,045,148	$2,090,297	555,873	$2,776,587	$5,553,175
May	9.42%	2,203,258	826,222	268,755	$1,048,144	$2,096,288	557,467	$2,784,546	$5,569,093
June	8.22%	1,923,055	721,146	234,576	$914,845	$1,829,690	486,570	$2,430,418	$4,860,835
July	8.34%	1,949,336	731,001	237,781	$927,348	$1,854,695	493,220	$2,463,632	$4,927,265
August	7.72%	1,805,901	677,213	220,285	$859,112	$1,718,224	456,928	$2,282,354	$4,564,709
September	7.96%	1,862,353	698,382	227,171	$885,967	$1,771,935	471,211	$2,353,700	$4,707,401
October	7.57%	1,770,483	663,931	215,965	$842,262	$1,684,525	447,966	$2,237,592	$4,475,183
November	8.03%	1,877,530	704,074	229,022	$893,188	$1,786,375	475,051	$2,372,882	$4,745,764
December		0	0	0	$0	$0	0	$0	$0
		23,386,400	8,157,436	2,653,466	$10,348,517	$20,697,034	5,503,970	$27,492,329	$54,984,657

Notes:
1) 1988 percentages taken from Exhibit IV: Seasonality of Buyer Purchasing Habits
2) Used car sales derived from data in Exhibit II for total national used car purchases
3) Total Kwik Chek market derived from Exhibit III. 37.5% demand expected at $50 pricing
4) 20% penetration is the maximum expected due to future entrants and other competition
5) It is assumed that dealers will want a 20% discount off of retail to use the service
6) The breakdown of dealer to open market sales percentages is taken from Exhibit I

Exhibit VIII: Austin Dealer/Open Market Potential Sales in Units and Dollars at 10 & 20% Penetration

Dealer Percentage: 33%
Open Market Percentage: 67%

Month	1988 Percent	Used Car Sales (Units)	Total Kwik Chek Market @ 37.5% (Units)	Potential Dealer Sales @ 33% (Units)	Dealer Revenues @ 10% Penetrat. of Dealer Potential & $39 Price (Dollars)	(Units)	Dealer Revenues @ 20% Penetrat. of Dealer Potential & $39 Price (Dollars)	(Units)	Potential Open Market Sales @ 67% (Units)	10% Penetrat. of Open Mrkt. Potential & $49 Price (Dollars)	(Units)	Open Market Revenues @ 20% Penetrat. of Open Mrkt. Potential & $49 Price (Dollars)	(Units)
January	6.98%	5,670	2,126	692	$2,697	69	$5,395	138	1,435	$7,166	143	$14,332	287
February	8.14%	6,608	2,478	806	$3,143	81	$6,287	161	1,672	$8,351	167	$16,702	334
March	9.61%	7,803	2,926	952	$3,712	95	$7,425	190	1,974	$9,862	197	$19,724	395
April	8.61%	6,989	2,621	853	$3,325	85	$6,650	171	1,768	$8,833	177	$17,667	354
May	9.39%	7,627	2,860	930	$3,628	93	$7,257	186	1,930	$9,639	193	$19,279	386
June	9.42%	7,649	2,868	933	$3,639	93	$7,278	187	1,935	$9,667	194	$19,334	387
July	8.22%	6,676	2,504	814	$3,176	81	$6,352	163	1,689	$8,438	169	$16,875	338
August	8.34%	6,767	2,538	825	$3,219	83	$6,439	165	1,712	$8,553	171	$17,106	342
September	7.72%	6,270	2,351	765	$2,983	76	$5,965	153	1,586	$7,924	159	$15,847	317
October	7.96%	6,465	2,425	789	$3,076	79	$6,152	158	1,636	$8,171	164	$16,343	327
November	7.57%	6,147	2,305	750	$2,924	75	$5,848	150	1,555	$7,768	156	$15,536	311
December	8.03%	6,518	2,444	795	$3,101	80	$6,202	159	1,649	$8,238	165	$16,476	330
		81,190	30,446	9,904	$38,624	990	$77,248	1,981	20,543	$102,610	2,054	$205,221	4,109

Notes:

1) 1988 percentages taken from Exhibit IV: Seasonality of Buyer Purchasing Habits
2) Used car sales derived from data in Exhibit II for total national used car purchases
3) Total Kwik Chek market derived from Exhibit III. 37.5% demand expected at $50 pricing
4) 20% penetration is the maximum expected due to future entrants and other competition
5) It is assumed that dealers will want a 20% discount off of retail to use the service
6) The breakdown of dealer to open market sales percentages is taken from Exhibit I

Exhibit IX: Operations Breakdown for Austin to Determine the Number of Vans Required

Dealer Price: $39.00
Open Market Price: $49.95

Number of inspection hours per day: 11
Number of days per week: 7

Inspection hours per week: 77
Inspection hours per year: 4,004
Average inspection hours per month: 334
Maximum inspections per van/month: 272
(Assuming 33%-67% dealer-open market split)

Inspect time (Hrs.): 1.50 (Open market inspection time including 30 minutes travel)
Inspect time (Hrs.): 0.67 (Dealer inspection time of 40 minutes)

Month	20% Penetrat. of Dealer Potential & $39 Price (Dollars)	(Units)	Inspection Hours Required	20% Penetrat. of Open Mrkt. Potential & $49 Price (Dollars)	(Units)	Inspection Hours Required	Total Num. Inspt.	Total Van Hours Needed	Total Vans Needed
January	$5,395	138	92	$14,332	287	430	425	523	1.6
February	$6,287	161	107	$16,702	334	502	496	609	1.8
March	$7,425	190	127	$19,724	395	592	585	719	2.2
April	$6,650	171	114	$17,667	354	531	524	644	1.9
May	$7,257	186	124	$19,279	386	579	572	703	2.1
June	$7,278	187	124	$19,334	387	581	574	705	2.1
July	$6,352	163	109	$16,875	338	507	501	615	1.8
August	$6,439	165	110	$17,106	342	514	508	624	1.9
September	$5,965	153	102	$15,847	317	476	470	578	1.7
October	$6,152	158	105	$16,343	327	491	485	596	1.8
November	$5,848	150	100	$15,536	311	467	461	567	1.7
December	$6,202	159	106	$16,476	330	495	489	601	1.8
	$77,248	1,981	1,320	$205,221	4,109	6,163	6,089	7,483	1.9

Exhibit X: Fixed and Variable Cost Breakdown per Van and Inspection

Van Equipment	Cost	
The van	$15,000	
Test equipment:	$290	
Compression	$50	
Calipers	$50	
Depth gauge	$50	
VOM	$125	
Hydrometer	$15	
Scope and analyzers	$3,500	
Portable personal computer	$3,000	
Other equipment:	$1,350	
Generator	$200	
Hydraulic jack	$200	
Jack stands	$150	
Scooter	$50	
Misc hand tools	$750	
Van Customization	$1,000	
Total Van Cost:	$24,140	

Van Fixed Costs:	$2,925	
Monthly payment	$779	(Finance over 3 years at 10%)
Technician wages	$1,800	($20k per year + benefits)
Paging service	$25	
Insurance	$220	
Maintenance (@ 5%)	$101	

General Overhead Costs:	$7,191	(Including 20% buffer for error)
Office rent	$450	
Postage	$150	
Marketing	$2,500	
Insurance/benefits	$500	
Franchise fee ($15K)	$417	(Divided over 36 months)
Telephone	$140	
Secretary/appointment	$1,500	(Includes appointment scheduling)
Office equipment:	$336	(Finance over 3 years at 10%)

Computer	$5,000	
FAX	$900	
Copier	$1,500	
Furniture	$1,500	
Telephone	$500	
Misc	$1,000	
Total	$10,400	

Fixed Cost per Van Assuming Two Vans Are in Operation: $6,520

Van fixed cost $2,925
Office overhead (pro-rated) $3,595

Fixed Cost per Van-Hour of Operation (The Scarce Item): $20

Pro-rated cost per dealer inspection $13
Pro-rated cost per open market inspection $29

Variable costs per Inspection: $11

Gasoline $1   (Assume 10 miles/call @ 10mpg & $1/gal.)
Misc consumables $5
Incentive to tech $5

Profit Margin Analysis for Dealer and Open Market Inspections

	Open Market	Dealer
Revenue	$49.95	$39.00
7% franchise fee	($3.50)	($2.73)
Variable cost	($11.00)	($10.00) (No gas for dealer insp.)
Contribution	$35.45	$26.27
Inspections per month:	342	165
Segment contribution:	$12,138	$4,336

Monthly expected total contribution: $16,475
              Less: total fixed cost   ($13,040)

Net total profit before tax: $3,435

Assuming a 33% Dealer/67% Open Market Breakdown in Inspections:

              Break-even monthly inspections quantity: 402
              Total 2-van fixed cost: $13,040
              Dealer inspections: 133
              Open market inspections: 269

Break-even Quantity for Justifying Another Van Purchase:

              Van break-even for 33%/67% split: 90
              Van incremental fixed cost: $2,925

Exhibit XI: Summary Financial Analysis for Kwik Chek in Austin

	Start	Mo. 1	Mo. 2	Mo. 3	Mo. 4	Mo. 5
Market share	0%	1%	2%	2%	3%	3%
Dealer inspections	0	8	17	17	25	25
Open market inspections	0	17	34	34	51	51
Total inspections	0	25	51	51	76	76
Number of vans needed	1	1	1	1	1	1
INCOME FROM PRODUCTION ACTIVITIES						
Dealer sales ($)	0	322	644	644	966	966
Open mkt sales ($)	0	855	1,710	1,710	2,565	2,565
Less: cost of good sold						
Variable costs	0	(271)	(542)	(542)	(813)	(813)
Franchise royalty	0	(82)	(165)	(165)	(247)	(247)
Gross margin	0	824	1,647	1,647	2,471	2,471
OPERATING EXPENSES						
General fixed costs	(7,191)	(7,191)	(7,191)	(7,191)	(7,191)	(7,191)
Van fixed costs	(2,925)	(2,925)	(2,925)	(2,925)	(2,925)	(2,925)
Net operating income	(10,116)	(9,292)	(8,469)	(8,469)	(7,645)	(7,645)
ADDITIONAL EXPENSES						
Promotion cost	(10,000)	[Initial advertising, public relations, etc.]				
Misc. startup cost	(5,000)					
Net profit before tax	(25,116)	(9,292)	(8,469)	(8,469)	(7,645)	(7,645)
CUMULATIVE CASH FLOW	(25,116)	(34,408)	(42,877)	(51,345)	(58,990)	(66,635)

Assumptions:
1) There is a 33%/67% quantity split between dealers and open market inspections
2) Dealer inspections cost $39.00 and open market inspections cost $49.95
3) The maximum number of inspections per van is 272 per month
4) Office fixed expenses can handle up to 4 vans without expansion
5) Demand will never exceed 37.5% of all used car purchases
6) Kwik Chek can achieve a 20% share of the demand within 2 years
7) More than 20% share may not be possible due to competition
8) Available market for dealers and open market inspections in units is:

    Dealers: 9,904 (From Exhibit VIII)
    Open Mkt: 20,543 (From Exhibit VIII)

	Mo. 6	Mo. 7	Mo. 8	Mo. 9	Mo. 10	Mo. 11	Mo. 12	Year 2	Year 3
	4%	4%	5%	6%	7%	8%	9%	20%	20%
	33	33	41	50	58	66	74	1,981	1,981
	68	68	86	103	120	137	154	4,109	4,109
	101	101	127	152	178	203	228	6,089	6,089
	1	1	1	1	1	1	1	2	2
	1,288	1,288	1,609	1,931	2,253	2,575	2,897	77,251	77,251
	3,420	3,420	4,276	5,131	5,986	6,841	7,696	205,225	205,225
	(1,083)	(1,083)	(1,354)	(1,625)	(1,896)	(2,167)	(2,438)	(65,003)	(65,003)
	(330)	(330)	(412)	(494)	(577)	(659)	(741)	(19,773)	(19,773)
	3,295	3,295	4,119	4,942	5,766	6,590	7,414	197,700	197,700
	(7,191)	(7,191)	(7,191)	(7,191)	(7,191)	(7,191)	(7,191)	(86,292)	(86,292)
	(2,925)	(2,925)	(2,925)	(2,925)	(2,925)	(2,925)	(2,925)	(70,200)	(70,200)
	(6,821)	(6,821)	(5,997)	(5,174)	(4,350)	(3,526)	(2,702)	41,208	41,208
	(6,821)	(6,821)	(5,997)	(5,174)	(4,350)	(3,526)	(2,702)	41,208	41,208
	(73,456)	(80,277)	(86,274)	(91,448)	(95,797)	(99,323)	(102,026)	(60,818)	(19,610)

Exhibit XII: Owner/Mechanic Summary Financial Analysis for Kwik Chek in Austin

	Start	Mo. 1	Mo. 2	Mo. 3	Mo. 4	Mo. 5
Market share	0%	1%	2%	2%	3%	3%
Dealer inspections	0	8	17	17	25	25
Open market inspections	0	17	34	34	51	51
Total inspections	0	25	51	51	76	76
Number of vans needed	1	1	1	1	1	1
INCOME FROM PRODUCTION ACTIVITIES						
Dealer sales ($)	0	322	644	644	966	966
Open mkt sales ($)	0	855	1,710	1,710	2,565	2,565
Less: cost of good sold						
Variable costs	0	(144)	(288)	(288)	(432)	(432)
Franchise royalty	0	(82)	(165)	(165)	(247)	(247)
Gross margin	0	951	1,901	1,901	2,852	2,852
OPERATING EXPENSES						
General fixed costs	(7,191)	(7,191)	(7,191)	(7,191)	(7,191)	(7,191)
Van fixed costs	(1,125)	(1,125)	(1,125)	(1,125)	(1,125)	(1,125)
Net operating income	(8,316)	(7,365)	(6,415)	(6,415)	(5,464)	(5,464)
ADDITIONAL EXPENSES						
Promotion cost	(10,000) [Initial advertising, public relations, etc.]					
Misc. startup cost	(5,000)					
Net profit before tax	(23,316)	(7,365)	(6,415)	(6,415)	(5,464)	(5,464)
CUMULATIVE CASH FLOW	(23,316)	(30,681)	(37,096)	(43,511)	(48,975)	(54,439)

Assumptions:
1) There is a 33%/67% quantity split between dealers and open market inspections
2) Dealer inspections cost $39.00 and open market inspections cost $49.95
3) The maximum number of inspections per van is 272 per month
4) Office fixed expenses can handle up to 4 vans without expansion
5) Demand will never exceed 37.5% of all used car purchases
6) Kwik Chek can achieve a 20% share of the demand within 2 years
7) More than 20% share may not be possible due to competition
8) Available market for dealers and open market inspections in units is:

Dealers:　9,904　(From Exhibit VIII)
Open Mkt:　20,543　(From Exhibit VIII)

Mo. 6	Mo. 7	Mo. 8	Mo. 9	Mo. 10	Mo. 11	Mo. 12	Year 2	Year 3
4%	4%	5%	6%	7%	8%	9%	20%	20%
33	33	41	50	58	66	74	1,981	1,981
68	68	86	103	120	137	154	4,109	4,109
101	101	127	152	178	203	228	6,089	6,089
1	1	1	1	1	1	1	2	2
1,288	1,288	1,609	1,931	2,253	2,575	2,897	77,251	77,251
3,420	3,420	4,276	5,131	5,986	6,841	7,696	205,225	205,225
(576)	(576)	(720)	(864)	(1,008)	(1,152)	(1,296)	(65,003)	(65,003)
(330)	(330)	(412)	(494)	(577)	(659)	(741)	(19,773)	(19,773)
3,802	3,802	4,753	5,704	6,654	7,605	8,556	197,700	197,700
(7,191)	(7,191)	(7,191)	(7,191)	(7,191)	(7,191)	(7,191)	(86,292)	(86,292)
(1,125)	(1,125)	(1,125)	(1,125)	(1,125)	(1,125)	(1,125)	(21,600)	(21,600)
(4,514)	(4,514)	(3,563)	(2,612)	(1,662)	(711)	240	89,808	89,808
(4,514)	(4,514)	(3,563)	(2,612)	(1,662)	(711)	240	89,808	89,808
(58,953)	(63,466)	(67,029)	(69,642)	(71,303)	(72,014)	(71,775)	18,033	107,841

Legal Considerations

The primary legal issues that should be considered in establishing Kwik Chek as a national franchise are (1) franchiser liability for franchisee actions, and (2) termination of franchise agreement by either the franchiser or the franchisee.

The principle way that the franchiser can be held liable for the actions of a franchisee is if the franchisee represents itself as an agent of the parent company. To avoid this agency issue, all collateral literature published by the franchiser should indicate that all Kwik Chek operations are independently owned and operated. In this way, there can be no mistake on the part of the customer that the local franchisee is working their own business and on their own behalf.

A clear definition of the agency relationship will protect the franchiser from liability related to injury or accidents resulting from improper inspection and also from any financial liabilities that the franchisee may incur.

To address the termination of franchise agreement issue, it should be clearly delineated in the franchise agreement what the required payment procedures and time frames should be from the franchisee to the franchiser. In addition, the level of support that the franchisee can reasonably expect from the franchiser should also be clearly defined. In this way, there is less likelihood of misunderstanding by either party, and the franchiser is protected from having a franchisee that is not performing up to expectations bring down the rest of the organization.

In addition, if the franchiser has agreed to supply credit to the franchisee to start the business, then the franchiser should protect the investment by having strict reporting procedures as to the actions being taken by the franchisee to meet the required revenue goals.

Franchising agreements are being treated more as "relational contracts" that extend over a longer period of time than as individual contracts that have a clearly defined duration and outcome. Many courts are treating franchise agreements as a sort of marriage, and many of the precedents established for divorce law in community property states are being incorporated into termination of franchise agreements. The relationship is treated as a type of partnership, and the parties involved are compensated for their "expected" returns from the venture should it be terminated.

In this way, it should be clearly understood by the franchisee that should the franchisee lose the right to operate under the Kwik Chek name, the business is returned to the franchiser. An equitable settlement for the return can be established at the time of transfer.

Resources

The following list offers you extra resources on a variety of business and entrepreneurial subjects. I included website addresses where possible.

Small Business–General

**American Chamber of
Commerce Executives**
4232 King Street
Alexandria, VA 22302
703-998-0072
www.acce.org

**The American Institute for
Small Business**
Educational Materials for Small
Business and Entrepreneurship
7515 Wayzata Boulevard
Minneapolis, MN 55426
1-800-328-2906
www.aisb.biz

American Success Institute
5 North Main Street
Natick, MA 01760
508-651-3303
www.success.org

Business Resource Center
www.morebusiness.com

**CCH Business Owner's
Toolkit**
www.toolkit.cch.com

**eWeb: Education for
Entrepreneurship**
eweb.slu.edu/Default.htm

Small Business Development Centers (SBDC)
www.sbaonline.sba.gov/SBDC

The National Association for the Self-Employed
PO Box 612067
DFW Airport
Dallas, TX 75261-2067
1-800-232-6273
www.nase.org

National Business Incubation Association
20 East Circle Drive, Suite 190
Athens, OH 45701-3571
740-593-4331
www.nbia.org

Service Core of Retired Executives (SCORE)
www.score.org

Small Business Development Center Research Network
www.smallbiz.suny.edu

U.S. Chamber of Commerce
1615 H Street, NW
Washington, DC 20062-2000
1-800-638-6582
www.uschamber.com

U.S. Department of Commerce
14th & Constitution Avenue NW, Room 5053
Washington, DC 20230
202-482-5061
www.mbda.gov

U.S. Small Business Administration (SBA)
409 3rd Street, SW
Washington, DC 20416
202-205-7701 or 1-888-324-1551
www.sba.gov

U.S. Business Advisor (Sponsored by the SBA)
www.business.gov

IRS Small Business/Self Employed Resource
www.irs.gov/businesses/small

SmartBiz.com General Business Information
www.smartbiz.com

Special Topics

The following are specialized resources that may be of use to you in your business.

Census Information

Here is an excellent place to obtain information regarding general population characteristics in your area of question.

U.S. Bureau of the Census
Washington, DC 20233
301-763-4636
www.census.gov

On the CD

A large number of additional websites are included on the CD as document AppB-01.

Financing

Here are several locations you can review for information on preparing for financing, or actually obtaining financing for your venture.

SBA Finance Website
www.sba.gov/financing

General and Comprehensive Business Loan Information Link Page
www.smallbusinesscenter.com

LendingTree.com Loan Center
www.lendingtree.com/stm/sblc/default.asp

National Financial Services Network
www.nfsn.com

Yahoo! Finance Info Page
dir.yahoo.com/Business_and_Economy/Finance_and_Investment

American Express Home Page
www.americanexpress.com

Haines General Financing Source Web Page
hainesbiz.org/financing.html

Franchises

Don't buy a franchise before talking to these people to determine as much as possible about the parent company of your possible franchise purchase.

American Association of Franchisees & Dealers
PO Box 81887
San Diego, CA 92138-1887
1-800-733-9858
www.aafd.org

International Franchise Association
1350 New York Avenue NW, Suite 900
Washington, DC 20005-4709
202-628-8000
www.franchise.org

Nettizen.com Franchise Resource
www.nettizen.com

Franchise Solutions
www.franchisesolutions.com/resource

Bison.com Franchise Opportunity Web Page
www.bison1.com

International Business

Business Network International
199 S. Monte Vista, Suite 6
San Dimas, CA 91773
www.bni.com

International Chamber of Commerce
156 Fifth Avenue, Suite 308
New York, NY 10010
212-206-1150
www.iccwbo.org/index.asp

International Small Business Consortium
3309 Windjammer Street
Norman, OK 73072
www.isbc.com

U.S. Agency for International Development (USAID)
Public Inquiries
320 21st Street NW
Washington, DC 20523-0016
www.usaid.gov

U.S. Council for International Business
1212 Avenue of the Americas
New York, NY 10036
212-354-4480
www.uscib.org

Michigan State University GlobalEdge.com Web Page
globaledge.msu.edu/ibrd/ibrd.asp

University of Kansas International Business Page
www.ibrc.bschool.ukans.edu

Import-Export Help General Links Web Page
www.importexporthelp.com

Marketing General

Marketing Resource Center
Concept Marketing Group, Inc.
115-B Mark Randy Place
Modesto, CA 95350
1-800-575-5369
www.marketingsource.com

Software Marketing General Resource Web Page
www.softwaremarketingresource.com/
software-marketing-resource.html

Market Research

Your public library may already subscribe.

InfoTrac General Business Information Source
www.infotrac.com

Specialized Market Research Reports
www.newsletters.com

The Wall Street Journal
www.wsj.com

General Internet Trends and Statistics
www.nua.ie/surveys

Minorities in Business

National Minority Business Council
25 West 45th Street, Suite 301
New York, NY 10036
212-997-4753
www.nmbc.org

National Minority Supplier Development Council
1040 Avenue of the Americas, 2nd Floor
New York, NY 10018
212-944-2430
www.nmsdcus.org

Hispanic Business Magazine Website
www.hispanicbusiness.com

Minority Business Entrepreneur Magazine Website
www.mbemag.com

General Entrepreneurship Information for the Black Community
www.einfonews.com

SBA Office of Minority Enterprise and Development
www.sba.gov/8abd

Patents

U.S. Patent and Trademark Office
PO Box 1450
Alexandria, VA 22313-1450
703-557-4636
www.uspto.gov

General Patent Information
From a Law Firm: Oppedahl & Larson LLP
www.patents.com

General Intellectual Property Information
From the Franklin Pierce Law School, New Hampshire
www.piercelaw.edu/tfield/ipbasics.htm

Women in Business

Interagency Committee on Women's Business Enterprise
National Economic Council
The White House
Washington, DC 20500
202-456-2174

National Association of Women Business Owners
8405 Greensboro Drive, Suite 800
McLean, VA 22102
703-506-3268
www.nawbo.org

Center for Women's Business Research
1411 K Street, NW, Suite 1350
Washington, DC 20005-3407 USA
202-638-3060
www.nfwbo.org

U.S. Small Business Administration Office of Women's Business Ownership
409 Third Street SW
Washington, DC 20416
202-205-6673
www.sbaonline.sba.gov/womeninbusiness

Women's Business Enterprise National Council
1120 Connecticut Ave. NW, Suite 950
Washington, DC 20036
202-872-5515
www.wbenc.org

Online Women's Business Center
Sponsored by the SBA
www.onlinewbc.gov

Business Buzzword Glossary

accounting period   A period of time used to correlate revenues and expenses, usually defined as a day, week, month, quarter, or year.

accrual basis of accounting   A method of accounting that relates revenues and expenses based on when the commitments are made as opposed to when the cash is spent or received.

action plans   The steps needed to achieve specific goals.

advisory board   A group of business associates who act as advisors to your company on an informal basis. You can set regular meeting dates and times for the group to come together to discuss business issues, but you do not compensate advisors for their advice. You may want to pay for dinner, however, so they know you appreciate their time.

analysis statement   A statement provided by your bank that details the various deposits and charges associated with your business account. It is used to detail the bank account service fee amounts.

angel investors   People, or groups of people, who invest in ventures that nobody else wants to touch.

articles of incorporation   A set of documents that are filed with the secretary of state's office that formally establish your corporation in that state.

assets   Those items of value the company owns, such as cash in the checking account, accounts receivable, equipment, and property.

authorized shares   The total number of shares of stock the corporation is permitted to issue. For instance, if 1,000 shares of stock are authorized at the start of the corporation, only a total of 1,000 shares can ever be sold to shareholders—no more than that unless the articles are amended to allow more authorized shares.

bad debt ratio   The amount of money you believe customers will never pay (also called uncollectible funds), divided by total sales and expressed as a percent.

balance sheet   One type of financial statement that you (or your accountant) create to show all the company's assets and all the liabilities and equity owned by investors. The value of your assets must equal the value of your liabilities and equity for the statement to balance, which is where the term came from.

banking day   The days of the week that banks are open for business. You must make deposits at the bank before a certain time of day, which is usually around 2:00 P.M., for the deposit to be credited on that same day. If you make the deposit after the 2:00 P.M. cutoff, the deposit is not credited to your account until the next banking day, which may be the next day. If you make a deposit near the end of the week, the next banking day may not be until Monday of the next week.

benefit   What the customer gains by using your product or service. For example, the benefit of a drill bit is that it makes holes.

board of accountancy   The group of accountants who make decisions regarding generally accepted accounting principles.

board of directors   A group of experienced business leaders who are asked or elected to serve as advisors to a company. In return for assuming responsibility for the long-term growth of the company, directors generally receive either cash compensation or shares of stock. In other cases, the largest shareholders may ask for or require a seat on the board of directors as a means of protecting their large stake in the company.

bookkeeping   A system for accurately tracking where your money is coming from and where it is going. You can hire a bookkeeper to manage your record-keeping or invest in a computer program to do much the same thing. Bookkeepers are not necessarily accountants, although they do help organize all your information for use by your accountant.

break-even analysis   An analysis technique used to determine the quantity of an item that must be produced or sold to cover the fixed expenses associated with the time period in question.

break-even point   The quantity point where the gross margin equals the fixed expenses for the period in question. Above the break-even point, the company makes money, and below the break-even point, the company loses money.

browser   A software program that runs on a computer and allows Internet HTML pages to be properly viewed.

business inertia   The inability of a company to change its thinking or ways of doing business. Generally, larger, more bureaucratic companies have more inertia than smaller, leaner businesses that can respond quickly to changes in the marketplace.

business judgment rule   A concept that protects members of corporate boards of directors from lawsuits filed by shareholders, customers, or others if the decision that caused the lawsuit was made in the best interests of the corporation.

business plan   A document that outlines your overall business objectives, their viability, and the steps you intend to take to achieve those objectives. Can be for internal use, external use, or both.

bylaws   The overall rules for operation of a corporation. Bylaws are an integral part of the corporation filing procedure.

C-corporation   The business structure used primarily by major corporations so they can sell shares of stock to the public. Other forms of a corporation have restrictions on the number of shareholders that can exist, but a C corporation does not.

calendar fiscal year   A financial year that starts on January 1 and ends on December 31.

card identification number (CIN)   A number printed on the face of an American Express card that is used to verify validity of credit cards presented for purchases.

card processing company   A company that processes the credit card transactions for the retailers by verifying the account validity, the credit amounts available, and the transfer of funds into your company checking account.

cash basis of accounting   A method of accounting where expenses and revenues are tracked based on when cash is received or actual checks are written.

cash flow analysis   A financial statement that shows how much money the company had at the beginning of the month, how much money came in through sales and payments, how much went out in the form of payments, and what was left at the end of the month. Successful entrepreneurs carefully watch the amount of money coming in and going out of a company (cash flow) so the business doesn't run out of cash.

chain style franchise   A franchise arrangement where the franchisee pays a fee for an established chain store outlet like Midas or McDonald's.

chargeback   When a credit card processing company charges a sale back against your account, usually because the customer denies having actually made that particular purchase. It is the merchant's responsibility to show that this purchase actually happened, or the merchant could have to take the loss on the transaction.

chart of accounts   A list of all the categories a business uses to organize its financial expenditures and sales.

class of stock   Corporations can issue different types of stock that each have different legal rights with regard to dividends, voting, and other rights. Each of these different stock categories is called a class of stock.

clipping services   Companies such as Bacon's and Luce Clipping Services that read thousands of newspapers and magazines on the lookout for articles about or references to specific companies. Many businesses hire clipping services to watch for articles about their company and the competition. Unless you have the time to read virtually every major business magazine and newspaper, you might want to hire some professionals to do it for you.

close   A request by the salesperson for a specific action on the customer's part. Asking for the order is the ultimate close, but there are smaller closes that occur at each stage of the selling process to gradually move the customer closer to the sale.

close corporation   A company where owners or shareholders are active in the daily management of the corporation, which has no public investors.

commodities   Products that have no distinguishing features or benefits, such as flour, salt, and pork bellies, so that there is little or no difference in pricing between competitive products.

company policy manual   A manual that outlines the overall company policies that apply to all employees.

consideration   Something of value, such as money or a right to do something, that is usually given at the signing of a contract.

content (website)   The information included in a website that is viewed by Internet visitors.

corporation   A legal entity that is created as an umbrella under which business operation can occur. Corporations are chartered with the state and come in various forms, such as the S-corporation and the Limited Liability Company (LLC).

cost of sales   The costs directly linked to the production or sale of a product or service, also called the Cost of Goods Sold (COGS). These generally include the cost of raw materials, the cost of labor to run the machine that produced the widget you sold, and other expenses that were required to sell the product or service.

cost-plus-profit pricing   Calculating your price using the cost to the company plus your desired profit markup. A widget that costs $1 to produce or purchase with a desired 50 percent markup would sell for $1 + ($1 \times 0.5) = 1.50.

credit card transaction processing company   An organization that processes the typical credit card transaction and handles the transfer of funds from a credit card account into yours.

cumulative cash flow   The total amount of cash needed to handle the sum of all month-to-month negative cash flow (loss) experienced until the company starts to make a monthly profit.

current assets   Company assets that are liquid or can be converted to cash in less than one year.

CVC2   A three- or four-digit value that is used by MasterCard to verify the value of the information embossed on a credit card. If the card embossed information does not match the CVC2 value, then the card may be a forgery. Similar to CVV2 for Visa.

CVV2   A three- or four-digit value that is used by Visa to verify the value of the information embossed on a credit card. If the card embossed information does not match the CVV2 value, then the card may be a forgery. Similar to CVC2 for MasterCard.

cyberspace   A term used to designate the networked computer world that continues to permeate business.

debt financing   A means of securing funding to start or expand your business by way of a loan of some sort. The business takes on debt, instead of investors, as a way of getting the money it needs immediately.

demographic profile   Usually refers to a specific set of demographic characteristics used by sales and marketing to target likely sales prospects. Sometimes called an ideal customer profile.

demographics   A set of objective characteristics that describes a group of people. Includes characteristics such as age, home ownership, number of children, marital status, residence location, job function, and other criteria.

depreciation   A tax-related accounting procedure that deducts a certain amount of an asset's worth for each year of its operation.

direct competitor   Anyone who can, and will, eat your lunch today if you let them. (These are companies that sell the same product or service your company does, going after the same customers.)

direct shareholder vote   A voting procedure where the shareholders personally cast their votes instead of voting by proxy.

discount rate   Refers to the amount (percent) that a credit card processing company charges a merchant for processing each transaction.

distribution channel   However your product or service gets from your facilities into the hands of customers. Different ways of distributing your product include direct sales, employees selling your offerings, retail stores, mail order, the Internet, and independent sales representatives or manufacturers' representatives.

distributor franchise   A franchise arrangement where the franchisee actually acts as a distributor for a major manufacturer's products, such as with a large auto dealership.

dividends   Money paid to shareholders out of the C-corporation's net income (after taxes are taken out). This is a form of compensation to the shareholders for having made the investment in the corporation by purchasing shares.

doing business as, or **d/b/a**   When you start a sole proprietorship that is named something other than your given name, you must complete some forms to officially use that name. The form you complete is a doing business as, or d/b/a, form. For instance, Jane Smith & Associates would need to file a d/b/a at the county clerk's office because the name is something other than just Jane Smith. Sometimes called a tradename.

domain name   A unique name used to define an Internet location.

double taxation   Where the business pays tax on its annual profits and then passes part of that income as a dividend to you, the majority shareholder, who again gets taxed at the personal level; thus, the same dollar is taxed twice.

earned income   Income attributed to business operations during a specific period of time.

electronic mail   A method of sending mail from one location to another using an electronic delivery medium such as the Internet.

employee manual   A document prepared by the company and issued to all employees, indicating the company's policies and procedures.

employer identification number (EIN)   A number issued by the IRS to any company with employees. May also be called FEIN or TIN.

entrepreneur   Someone who is willing to take personal and financial risks to create a business out of a perceived opportunity. A cool person who bought this book and wants to make more money than the rest by running the show.

equity financing   When someone gives you money in return for ownership of a portion of your company. You are giving up equity in the business in return for capital, which is equity financing. The other kind of financing is debt financing, which is when you get a loan that is paid back later. Equity financing does not get paid back. Investors get their money back by selling their shares to someone else.

exchange rate   The rate at which one form of currency is converted into another.

exchange rate liability   The uncertainty that comes from holding a purchase/sale agreement that is not in your home country's currency in an environment where exchange rates change.

factoring   The process of receiving money now for payments your customers are expected to make to you in the next few weeks. There is a cost to having that money now, which is paid in the form of a percentage fee to the factoring company or factor.

feature   The different characteristics of a product or service. For example, the features of a drill bit might include its size, length, and the type of material it is made of.

federal tax deposit coupon   Coupon issued by the IRS for collection of employee withholding taxes on a regular basis. Your employee identification number (EIN) and the amount due for the tax period are printed on the coupon. The coupon then accompanies your check made payable for the amount due.

fictitious name statement   See *doing business as*, or *d/b/a*.

firewall   A hardware or software device that is designed to keep those already on the Internet from entering your particular systems or network unless specifically authorized by you to do so.

fiscal year   The period of time over which you track your annual business accounting operations.

fixed expenses   Business expenses that do not vary each month based on the amount of sales, such as rent, equipment leases, and salaries. Payments for these expenses are essentially the same each month, whether you achieve $1 million or $1 in sales.

float   The time period during which you have to cover expenses that should have been paid out of money received from customers. During this time, you are essentially lending money to your customers.

forum   A site on a computer service in which people with similar interests can post and read messages.

franchiser   A company that has created a successful business operation and concept that offers to sell the rights to the operation and idea on a limited geographic or market basis. The buyer of the franchise rights is called the franchisee.

freelancer   An individual who works for several different companies at once, helping out on specific projects. Freelancers are like consultants; they are paid a set rate for their services and receive no benefits, no sick pay, and no vacation allowance. The advantage is that freelancers can usually set their own hours, earn a higher hourly rate than they would get from full-time employment, and work with more than one company at a time.

freight forwarder   A company that specializes in shipping, duties, customs, and other administrative complexities related to international commerce.

Gantt chart   A method of tracking project items so that their order of completion, time frame, and status are easily monitored.

gating item   The section of a process that limits the overall process speed. Increase the gating item's throughput, and you increase the overall process throughput.

gross profit   The amount of money left after you cover the cost of sales. Out of gross profit, you pay your operational expenses. Gross profit = revenue ÷ cost of sales.

Hypertext Markup Language (HTML)   The programming code embedded in a website's pages that is interpreted by a browser for display on the user's computer.

IBM clone   A personal computer that uses technology similar to that used for the IBM personal computers.

imprint   When a credit card transaction is recorded by running the customer's credit card and carbon paper through a special roller machine.

income   The amount of money left over after expenses are deducted from the sales revenue amount.

income statement   A type of financial statement that reflects all the income and expenses for a particular period of time, which is generally a year.

independent contractor   Another word that the IRS frequently uses for a free-lancer. It means that the company you're doing work for is not your employer. You have the freedom to decide when, where, and how you will get the work done that your client has given you. You pay your own taxes and benefits, but you can also deduct expenses associated with getting your work done, such as a business phone line, travel, and supplies.

industrial espionage   The practice of collecting information about competitors through devious methods. Using public information sources that everyone has access to isn't considered espionage, but rummaging through corporate waste paper baskets after hours would be.

inertia   Indisposition to motion, exertion, or change; resistance to change.

initial public offering (IPO)   A stock trading event where the stock for a corporation is offered to the general public for the first time.

interests   Things that you enjoy doing, including the parts of your current job that you like the most, as well as what you do for fun in your spare time.

Internet   An electronically connected network of computers that spans the globe. Once you are connected to it, the usage is typically provided at a flat fee for unlimited usage.

Internet service provider (ISP)   A company that provides access to the Internet for users with a computer, modem, and the proper software.

job description   A detailed listing of the duties to be performed by the person filling the job in question; a listing of the required skills, education, certification levels, and other criteria directly related to the job.

job shop operation   A company that has a process flow that creates unique items at lower production volumes for each of its customers, as opposed to producing a standardized product in high volumes.

letter of credit (L/C)   A financial note that is set up through international banks by buyers and sellers who reside in different countries. Establishes a third-party, bank-to-bank handshake to ensure that both sides of the transaction are executed properly.

liabilities   Amounts that you owe. Typical liabilities include loans, credit cards, taxes owed, and other people to whom you owe money. Short-term liabilities, which are paid back within 12 months, are also called accounts payable. Long-term liabilities include mortgages and equipment loans.

life cycle   The four general phases that a product or service goes through between being introduced to the market and being discontinued or taken off the market.

limited liability company (LLC)   A new type of business structure available in almost every state that has many of the advantages of a partnership or subchapter S-corporation but fewer of its disadvantages.

limited liability partnership (LLP)   A special type of partnership wherein the partners protect their personal assets from being taken if the partnership gets into financial trouble. It blends the benefits of a general partnership with the liability protection of a limited partnership.

limited partnership   A special form of partnership in which one partner acts as the general partner and is fully liable for the business and the other partners are limited partners and as such can limit their liability to what they invest in the partnership.

link   A technological tool used to connect one Internet site's pages with website pages either on the home site or on another. A simple click on a link takes the viewer to the next page location attached to the link.

liquid assets   Anything the company owns that can be quickly sold and turned into cash, such as accounts receivable, computer equipment, or stocks and bonds. Assets such as buildings or huge machinery would not be considered liquid because selling them would take a considerable amount of time.

local area network (LAN)   A network setup inside of a company that connects computers and peripheral devices such as printers so that all network components can be shared.

logistics   The set of activities that deal with making the daily routine effective. The daily grind of answering the phone, mailing letters, and dealing with customers takes time. You will probably need clerical help once you become successful to offload the daily routine paperwork so you can have time for other activities.

long-term goals   Goals that extend beyond the next 12 months.

maintenance temperament   Someone who enjoys keeping established systems running like a well-oiled machine.

managerial accountants   People who help you use your financial information to make business decisions. Generally, these accountants are on staff at a company and are responsible for record-keeping and reporting.

manipulation   When customers feel that they are not in control of the sales process—that they will be encouraged and persuaded to purchase something they don't really need. Underlying this activity is the sense that the salesperson really doesn't have the customer's needs and interests at heart.

manufacturing franchise   A franchise arrangement where the franchisees are licensed to manufacture a specific product, such as Coca-Cola.

manufacturing requirement package (MRP)   A software package that integrates production forecasts with purchasing volumes to ensure that component parts needed to assemble a final product are available to meet production schedules.

market maker   A company with the clout to create an entire market opportunity simply by its involvement. IBM and Microsoft are examples of market makers in the high technology area.

market niche   A segment of the market that has an existing need for a product or service that nobody currently offers.

market penetration   The percent of prospective users of your products or services who are already existing customers.

market positioning   Creating a positive image in the minds of potential and existing customers. The purpose of market positioning is to have potential customers perceive your product or service in a particular way that makes them more likely to want to buy from you.

market segmentation   Dividing the total available market (everyone who may ever buy) into smaller groups, or segments, by specific attributes such as age, sex, location, interests, industry, or other pertinent criteria.

market value   The value of a product or service as determined by what the market will pay for it. The market value of a used computer is much less than what a business probably paid for it because computer values decline quickly.

market-based pricing   Where offerings are priced at a level set by what everyone else is charging, rather than by costs. With this strategy, you can generally make more money, assuming your competition is charging reasonable rates and you can keep your costs down.

marketing   Selecting the right product, pricing strategy, promotional program, and distribution outlets for your particular audience or market.

marketing theme   The overall thought that pops into people's minds when they think of your company and its offerings. For example, Pepsi's theme is "youth." Its soda is the drink for people who feel, or really are, young—the "new" generation.

markup   The amount of money over and above the cost of producing a product or service that is added to pay for overhead expenses and profit.

mass producers   Companies that produce the same product(s) in very high volume as opposed to a large number of products with very small production runs.

merchant number   A number given to your company that is used to identify which account should be credited when a customer makes a credit card purchase. It also verifies that you're allowed to accept credit cards in payment.

mind share   The portion of a person's thinking processes that includes perceptions of your company's offerings. One hundred percent mind share means that any time a person needs your type of offering, he or she thinks of your company.

mission statement   A simple statement that clearly defines the overall goals, or mission, of the company.

momentum   Describes the direction in which things are naturally moving and implies the amount of work or energy that would be needed to change the natural course of the business as it is currently operating.

MO/TO   A credit card processing company acronym that refers to mail orders and telephone orders. Has also been extended to include Internet orders.

net income   Money left over after all company expenses have been paid out of revenues. Net income can be either positive or negative, depending on how good a year you had, but it can't stay negative for long or you'll be bankrupt.

noncompete clause   An agreement that employees or suppliers sign indicating they won't steal your ideas or business methods and go to work for a competitor or become competitors by starting their own firm. Generally, noncompete clauses are one section in a larger employment agreement.

nonsolicitation clause   A statement included in most noncompete agreements that restricts former employees from contacting prior customers with the intention of soliciting business from that customer for the employee's current employer.

nuisance   Someone who takes up a lot of your time but really poses no threat to your lunch plans. (A weak competitor who has no clue.)

objectives   Goals that define the overall direction of an organization, which can be divided into a number of shorter-range action items.

officers   Senior members of a management team or board of directors elected to serve as secretary, treasurer, president, and vice president of the corporation or board.

operational expenses   Those expenses associated with just running your business. No matter how much you sell this month, you will still have these expenses. These include your salary, your rent payment, the cost of the electricity in your office, and other similar costs of operating the company.

opportunity cost   The profit that would have been gained by pursuing another investment instead of the one currently in process. For example, if you go out on a date with one person, you lose the potentially good time you could have had with someone else. Sound familiar? That is opportunity cost.

outsourcing   Corporate-speak for hiring outside consultants, freelancers, or companies to provide services that in the past have been provided by employees.

overpromise   When you promise more to a customer than you actually deliver. It is never a good idea if you want to keep happy customers.

overdeliver   Delivering more to the customer than was agreed to, or more than the customer expected. It is usually a good idea if you can afford it.

owner's equity   What is left over when the liabilities are subtracted from the assets. Take what you have, subtract what you owe, and you are left with owner's equity. This is the number that you want to maximize because it reflects the value of your company. The initial value of your company stock and retained earnings are added together to calculate owner's equity.

partnership   When you and one or more people form a business marriage; your debts and assets are legally linked from the start. Any partner can make a commitment for the business, which also commits the other partners.

pending event   A future event with a specific date that forces business people to make decisions that they would otherwise put off until later.

perceived risk   The risk assessment as seen through the eyes of the investor. You always want to be working to minimize the level of perceived risk on the part of the investor.

perceived value   The overall value the customer places on a particular product or service. This includes much more than price and considers other features such as delivery lead time, quality of salesmanship, service, style, and other less tangible items than the price. Essentially, a perceived value pricing strategy means determining what people are willing to pay and charging that amount, assuming you can still cover all your costs.

percentage markup   The amount of money a business adds into a product's price, over and above the cost of the product, expressed as a percent. A piece of candy costing $.05 to produce that has a markup of $.10 (meaning that the price to the consumer is $.15) has a percentage markup of 200 percent. This is calculated by taking the original cost, dividing it into the amount of markup, and then multiplying the result times 100.

performance to plan   A measurement tool used by investors to determine how close an organization is to performing according to the initial business plan goals.

personal attributes   Things such as being patient, working with other people, taking initiative, and other intrinsic personality-related traits.

point of sale system (POS)   This is a system set up to automatically record a customer sale transaction. Often, these systems are tied into the accounting system so that the sale transaction is automatically added to the accounting system, keeping sales automatically current.

potential sale revenue   A measurement of the total amount of money that can be made from a specific customer or event.

pretax profit   The amount of money left over after all the business expenses and costs of goods sold are subtracted from total sales, but before taxes have been subtracted and paid.

price erosion   When competitive sales present enough alternative product selections to your customers that you must drop your price to keep their business. This erodes both price and profit margins.

price war   When all competitors compete based on price and keep undercutting their competitors to get sales. As each company lowers its own price, others drop their prices to compete, resulting in profit margins in the industry as a whole falling to critically low levels.

probationary period   A time frame within which an employee is evaluated by the company, and vice versa. At the end of the probationary period, the employee and company can part ways with no negative implications or connotations.

processing company   A credit card-related company that acts as an intermediary between your customer's credit card sale transaction and your bank account where the sale amount, less a processing fee, is deposited.

product positioning   A conscious attempt on the part of your company to differentiate between your offering and those of your competitors. You position your product in people's minds by creating a perception of your product or service so that potential customers think of your products or services when they have a need.

professional corporation   A type of corporation, such as the subchapter S and subchapter C, used by professionals such as attorneys and accountants. Such corporations have P.C. after the company name to indicate the company is a professional corporation.

pro-forma balance sheet   A balance sheet comprised of numbers that are calculated based on historical performance and known future events. Typically used to project future financial expectations.

prospectus   A formal legal document a company prepares before being able to sell shares of stock to the public. The prospectus details all the pros and cons of investing in that company, so the potential purchaser of the company's stock is fully informed of the potential risks up front.

proxy statement   A form distributed to shareholders who will not be attending the company's annual meeting so their votes regarding the election of the board of directors, or other issues, can be counted. If a shareholder cannot attend the company's annual meeting but wants to vote, he can submit a signed proxy statement turning over the right to vote a certain way to the board.

publicity   Working with the media to have your company covered by the professional media such as magazines, newspapers, TV, and radio.

pull and push marketing strategy   A pull strategy convinces your potential customers to request your offering through their suppliers. In essence, the end user pulls your offering through the distribution channel by putting pressure on suppliers to carry it in their inventory. A push strategy sells your product to distributors, who then promote it to their customers. A pull strategy is driven by customers. A push strategy is driven by distributors.

registered agent   The official contact point for all legal matters. The registered agent is located at the registered office, which is the official address for corporate business.

retained earnings   Earnings from the company that are reinvested in operating the business. An item usually found on a company's balance sheet.

revenue   Money you receive from customers as payment for your services or the sale of your product. Some people also call it sales.

reward   What an investor expects to receive for having made the investment in the first place. This is usually some form of payment to the investor within a specified time frame.

risk   The possibility that something, like an investment, will not turn out as well as expected. The higher the risk associated with an investment, the higher the expected return on investment.

routine tasks   Things you do that are pretty much the same as the last time you did them, except for minor variations. Printing out monthly invoices or counting inventory are two routine tasks that don't take much brain power but that have to be done.

S-corporation   A type of corporation that has a limited number of shareholders, and the profits are passed directly through to the owner.

sales   Begins where marketing leaves off and involves all the steps you take to get the customer to buy your product or service.

sales revenue targets   The sales goals you set that affect all the other financial figures.

scattergun marketing   A scattergun sends buckshot in a wide pattern in the hopes of hitting something. Scattergun marketing sends marketing information everywhere in the hopes that someone will hear it and buy—the opposite of target marketing.

scope of work   A highly recommended section of a proposal that defines the overall intent of the work to be performed. This can be detailed or simple, depending on the work to be performed.

search engine   Internet technology that allows a program to categorize website information in such a way that a search can be performed on the site based on specific key words.

secured line of credit   A line of credit that has some form of asset such as accounts receivable or equipment as collateral for the loan.

Securities and Exchange Commission (SEC)   A regulatory body that monitors and defines policy for the exchange of stock on the public markets.

shareholders   Any individual or organization that owns shares of stock in a company.

short-term goals   Goals that occur within a short period of time, typically less than 12 months, and ideally lead to the completion of a long-term goal.

short-term loan   A loan that is to be paid off within one year.

shrinkage   The loss of product due to any number of means including loss in shipment or theft.

skills   Acquired skills include typing, speaking a foreign language, playing golf, and so on. Natural skills are inherent and less quantifiable, such as speaking voice quality, physical appearance, running speed, and so on.

sole proprietorship   You transact business without the legal "safety net" associated with a corporation. You are personally responsible for all the business's obligations, such as debt.

startup temperament   Someone who thrives on new and exciting projects and challenges.

strategy   A careful plan or method; the art of devising or employing plans toward a goal.

suite   A term used in relation to software where a number of different application programs are sold under the same name, so that purchasing a single product actually provides a variety, or suite, of other software packages.

sunk cost   Money already spent that you cannot recover. Does not take into account opportunity cost or how else you could have spent the money.

superstore   An organization that provides a little, or a lot, of everything as opposed to specializing in a specific area.

swipe card   The action of running a credit card through a machine so that the magnetic strip on the back side is automatically read for transmission to the processing company.

tactics   Relating to small-scale actions serving a larger purpose, such as a strategy.

target marketing   A marketing approach involving focusing your marketing efforts on those groups—those potential customers—most likely to buy your products or services.

tasks   Things that need to be completed as part of working toward goals.

tax accounting   A type of accounting concerned solely with how much money you will have to pay in taxes. Tax accountants can help you take steps to minimize your tax bill.

underdeliver   Delivering less to the customer than you promised. Guaranteed to create a disappointed customer.

underpromise   Promising less to a customer than you actually plan to deliver.

underwriter   A company responsible for marketing and selling shares of stock in a company to outside investors.

unearned revenue   An accrual accounting term for payments made by a customer for work that has not yet been performed but still shows up as revenue on the financial statements. There will usually be a special account with this name.

unqualified prospect   An individual who says he or she needs your product or service but who has not yet confirmed that he or she is able to make the purchase decision.

unsecured line of credit   A line of credit such as a credit card that a company can turn to for cash and that is not backed by some form of collateral. Secured lines of credit are usually backed by some form of deposit, accounts receivable statement, or other company asset that the bank can use to pay off the debt if the company can't pay off the line of credit.

variable expenses   Those costs that vary according to how much of a product or service is produced. Just as things usually cost less when you buy them in bulk, producing a product in large quantities works the same way. The more you produce, generally the lower the cost per product. The cost of sales varies according to how much is produced.

wealth   Consistently having money left over after all your bills are paid.

World Wide Web (WWW)   The interconnection of many Internet locations, or sites. These sites consist of HTML-coded pages that are read by a user's browser. These sites also refer to each other through links so that users can easily move from one Internet site to another.

Index

C

X–Y–Z